7⁵⁰

D1068356

DARK PASSAGES

The Decadent Consciousness in Victorian Literature

For my parents

. . . many doors are set open—but all dark—
all leading to dark passages—
We see not the ballance of good and evil.

John Keats,
Letter to John Hamilton Reynolds,
3 May 1818.

Acknowledgments

This book was originally a thesis written under the direction of Professor Jerome Buckley, and I am happy to have the opportunity now of thanking him for all the help he gave me. I am grateful too to Professors Douglas Bush, W. J. Bate, Howard Mumford Jones, and Clark Emery for their encouragement and advice. Professor Denis Donoghue's suggestions aided me greatly in my revision of the manuscript—a revision made possible through a summer faculty fellowship from the University of California—and many other friends have made helpful suggestions: particularly Professors Edgar Bowers, Adele Emery, Albert Gelpi, Robert Kiely, Joel Porte, Jill Conway, and Dennis Chaldecott.

The librarians of Houghton Library and of the Widener Collection as well as those at the University of Miami, the University of California at Santa Barbara, and the William Andrews Clark library have all made my way easier. Indeed, given the book's theme, it seems ironic that while working on *Dark Passages* I have met with nothing but help and human kindness and at every step of my way have time and again had pleasant conversations about Decadence, self-centeredness, isolation, and despair.

B. C.

Santa Barbara, California
July, 1964

Contents

The heart should have fed
upon the truth, as insects on a leaf, till it be tinged
with the colour, and show its food
in every . . . minutest fibre.
S. T. *Coleridge*

Introduction

Perhaps the term "Decadence" is useful only to mark off bound-
aries: to delineate a period in English literary history between
approximately 1890 and 1900. For if it is used to describe the
characteristics of literature or of writers during that period the
word obscures thought. It carries the implication that the Romantic tradition came to a whimpering end in the nineties and
that modern poetry began in, say, 1910. Such a patterning of
literary history, given our awareness of the intellectual and
emotional involvement which such modern poets as Yeats, Pound,
Eliot, Stevens, and Frost had with the ideas and feelings of the
nineties, is naïve. The 1890's, like the 1790's, was a period of
change, and if part of that change was a gradual stiffening of old
forms and old ideas, part of it was also the growth of new ones.
The term, in other words, conveys only half, the less important
half, of the process. And yet, like the words "Gothic" and "Ro-

mantic," it has acquired a certain authority and grace through usage and thus communicates more than a newly coined word might.

Anecdotes about the colorful personalities of the nineties are often delightful, but beneath them, as beneath the lives of the people whom they describe, one has a sense of sadness and frustration. Graham Hough captures that sense when he describes the period as one of "an immense number of false starts and blind alleys, and not a few personal tragedies, all directed to finding some sort of accommodation between art and a bourgeois industrial society."[1] The problem for these artists might be described as one of self-definition in a society whose values they felt they could not accept.

G. H. Mead gives this explanation of the way in which a self is created: "The human self arises through its ability to take the attitude of the group to which he belongs—because he can talk to himself in terms of the community to which he belongs and lay upon himself the responsibilities that belong to the community; because he can recognize his own duties as over against others—that is what constitutes the self as such."[2] His definition of self offers a means of understanding the dilemma in which the artists of the late nineteenth century found themselves: they could not accept the religious, social, or economic attitudes of their society. In religion their choice, as they saw it, lay between an overly rational "muscular Christianity" and an anti-intellectual fundamentalist faith; in economics between the harshness of *laissez-faire* and the sentimentality of philanthropic works. And the society created by such economic attitudes and upheld by such religious beliefs was spiritually, emotionally, and intellectually confused. It offered no community to which they wished to belong and no responsibilities which they felt they should undertake.

It is not necessary, however, that a man approve of his society in order to create a self by taking its attitudes. Matthew Arnold is a case in point. Although painfully aware of the faults of his own age, he found a role in it by seeking to reform those faults. The same is true of Ruskin, Morris, Shaw, and other Victorian "reformers." In order to effect changes in society, these men were obliged to communicate with its members, and they could do so only by putting themselves in the place of those whose attitudes they wished to modify or correct. Through that dialogue with society each created a self.

But there were those who believed that such a dialogue was impossible. The most succinct and influential statement of their position is Walter Pater's "Conclusion" to *The Renaissance*. Its premise is that nothing outside the mind has any meaning save that given it by the mind. Everyone creates for himself a reality which is personal, incommunicable, and imprisoning. However, each individual has sensory experience as a means of escape to the world outside the mind. Such experience may be an illusory escape, but the question of its truth or falsehood simply does not apply, for the mind gives it reality.

Only one of the senses receives no mention in Pater's "Conclusion": hearing. For each individual is a "solitary prisoner," and there is no communication from cell to cell. Nevertheless, each can turn his attention to forms momentarily beautiful and discipline himself to catch them at precisely that moment of perfect beauty: "Every moment some form grows perfect in hand or face; some tone on the hills or the sea is choicer than the rest; some mood of passion or insight or intellectual excitement is irresistibly real and attractive to us,—for that moment only."[3]

It is possible, then—even if somewhat arbitrary—to divide Victorian society into three groups: the Philistines whose ideal was the attainment of wealth, power, and physical luxuries and whose selves were formed by the attainment of those things through social institutions; the Reformers whose ideal was the attainment of the good, the humane life and whose selves were formed in the attempt to apply that ideal within society; the Decadents whose ideal was the attainment of as many moments as possible of heightened sensory experience, enjoyed within the mind outside the society. Members of the first group, with its solid objectives, created solid selves—although in doing so they led their society into the First World War. In the end, then, they worked more harm to society than did the Decadents. But although the Decadents were correct when they believed the Philistine ideals to be false, their own alternative ideal was a destructive one which led them into personal disaster. In the "moment" they had not a proper basis upon which to form a self. The consequence of their attempt to put it to that purpose was the Decadent self, impermanent and insubstantial, a self dependent upon the moment, a series of selves, separate and distinct from one another, appearing and vanishing on the continuum of time.

This state closely resembles that which George Santayana describes as the condition of the sceptical solipsist:

He will see the masked actors (and he will invent a reason) rushing frantically out on one side and in at the other; but he knows that the moment they are out of sight the play is over for them; those outlying regions and those reported events which messengers narrate so impressively are pure fancy; and there is nothing for him but to sit in his seat and lend his mind to the tragic illusion.

The solipsist thus becomes an incredulous spectator of his own romance, thinks his own adventures fictions, and accepts a solipsism of the present moment.[4]

None of the figures who appear in this study is a consistent sceptical solipsist, but all subscribed at least in part and for a time to what Arthur Symons describes as the ideal of Decadence: "to fix the last fine shade, to fix it fleetingly; to be a disembodied voice, and yet the voice of a human soul."[5] They do not, of course, represent the whole company of those who shared the ideal; even such important figures as Ernest Dowson and Aubrey Beardsley are absent. My purpose, however, is not to consider every Decadent in the light of the ideal but to study the ideal as it affected some who lived by it.

Since my concern is primarily with the 1890's, it may seem quixotic to devote so much of the book to a discussion of D. G. Rossetti, A. C. Swinburne, and Walter Pater. None of these men belonged to the Decadent generation; Rossetti died in 1882, Pater in 1894, and Swinburne, although alive throughout the nineties, had only the slightest personal connection with any of the Decadents. It is not, however, the physical absence or presence of these three that is significant but rather their intellectual, moral, and emotional influence upon the men of "the tragic generation." The latter were so conscious of being disciples that any attempt to understand them must begin with a consideration of their masters.

DARK PASSAGES

The Decadent Consciousness in Victorian Literature

> It is bad enough when there
> is a gifted and powerful opposition to the teaching of the
> best minds in any period: but when the best
> minds themselves are on a false tack,
> who shall stem the tide?
> *D. G. Rossetti*

Chapter I

Dante Gabriel Rossetti

The first number of the Pre-Raphaelites' short-lived magazine *The Germ,* which appeared in January, 1850, contains a parable by D. G. Rossetti called "Hand and Soul." It is a story about Chiaro dell 'Erma, a young artist of extraordinary sensibility, who passionately loved the outward aspect of all natural things and in his love for them wanted to depict them worthily: "The extreme longing after a visible embodiment of his thoughts strengthened as the years increased . . . until he would feel faint in sunsets and at the sight of stately persons."[1] He was ambitious for worldly fame as well—and indeed he quickly achieved it—but in his work he tried always to offset his ambition by making his art a means by which to worship God. Even so, he came to feel that "much of the reverence which he had mistaken for faith had been no more than the worship of beauty." And he reacted by creating works of art which had moral instruction as their conscious aim.

3

These were large "public" paintings, allegorical depictions of virtue.

Then one day, as he looked out from the window of his room, Chiaro saw the large allegorical fresco of Peace which he had painted on a church wall spattered by the blood of townsmen fighting among themselves in the square. In despair he felt that religious belief and ambition and even morality had failed him. At that moment a beautiful woman appeared in the room. She called herself the image of his own soul and told him to distress himself no further over whether or not he was fulfilling God's will: "What He hath set in thy heart to do, that do thou, and even though thou do it without thought of Him, it shall be well done." It is, in other words, God's will that the artist work for art's sake. And she concluded: "Chiaro, servant of God, take now thine Art unto thee, and paint me thus, as I am, to know me . . . . Do this; so shall thy soul stand before thee always, and perplex thee no more" (*CW*, I, 394–95).

A strange story, one that creates more perplexities than it solves. Rossetti's conscious desire, one gathers, is to make a statement through it about the relationship between art and morality. That art which has a consciously moral intention will be bad because it imposes a pattern on life instead of discovering a pattern in life; in his depreciation of Chiaro's cold allegories, Rossetti is repeating the "organic" theories of Romantic criticism. His conception of good art, however, shows his own modification of those theories: such art is created by a man alone in his room who paints the picture of his own soul. But there are questions which his theory leaves unanswered: if a man's soul stands always before him, will it no longer perplex him? is a man's own soul all that he can ever know? can he, for that matter, know his soul? And so around again. Like the phrase "art for art's sake" the questions turn back upon themselves; they encircle and imprison the artist whom it was the story's conscious intention to set free.

To the Decadents Rossetti was himself a Chiaro dell 'Erma, type of the ideal artist. Their descriptions of him, then, are also further definitions of that ideal, and it is noteworthy that they put special stress upon his isolation from society. Wilde describes him as "a pillar of fire to the few who knew him, and a cloud to the many who knew him not."[2] Arthur Symons thinks of him as one who never cared to leave the dream world of his own imagination, but who lived, wrote, and painted in an interior world "like a perfectly contented prisoner to whom the sense of imprisonment is a joy." Symons mentions another characteristic by which Rossetti exemplifies the true artist: his desire to live, as much as possible, in a state of heightened awareness amounting to ecstasy. In his own interior world, conscious only of "the love of beauty, the love of love" he lived an imaginative life in which at every moment he might hope for some new revelation of love or of beauty.[3]

As it worked out in practice, Rossetti's conception of the artist's life is very close to that which Tennyson had symbolized in "The Lady of Shalott," one of the Pre-Raphaelites' favorite poems. Its central image is that of a lady who, though forbidden to look directly at the scenes of life, weaves into her "magic web" images of the world which she sees reflected in a mirror. Like her, the artist creates beautiful forms from those "magic sights" mirrored in his imagination. But if he has the gift which enables him to do this, he may not turn his gaze from the mirror to the world; he must live, like the Lady of Shalott, in a world of shadows, separated from the common life of men. "Here is a fine saying of Keats's in one of his letters," Rossetti wrote to his mother; " 'I value more the privilege of seeing great things in loneliness than the fame of a prophet.' "[4] Pater echoes his approval of solitude when he writes of the glimpses of landscape one catches in Rossetti's poems, "not indeed of broad open-air effects, but rather of a painter concentrated upon the picturesque effect of one or two selected objects at a time . . . as he sees it from one of the windows, or reflected in one of the mirrors of his 'house of life.' "[5] His identification of Rossetti with the Lady of Shalott is clear; so too is his intimation that in writing as he did Rossetti had accepted a thought which lesser souls might not be able to bear: that we are each of us enclosed in a room lined with mirrors.

There remains, however, the question: if the artist's gaze is necessarily fixed upon the mirror of his imagination, by what standard is he to judge the reality of what he sees? Behind that question lies the possibility of a loneliness in which the only "great things" before him are vast shadows of himself. Coleridge described it at the conclusion of "Constancy to an Ideal Object." Writing of his love for a woman, he wonders whether the woman as he thinks he knows her and the love he believes himself to feel for her are not both creations of his own imagination:

> And art thou nothing? Such thou art, as when
> The woodman winding westward up the glen
> At wintry dawn, where o'er the sheep track's maze
> The view-less snow-mist weaves a glistening haze,
> Sees full before him, gliding without tread,
> An image with a glory round its head;
> The enamoured rustic worships its fair hues
> Nor knows he makes the shadow he pursues![6]

Yeats brings together many of these ideas as he considers the tragic lives of Dowson and Johnson. He wonders whether the poetry of Coleridge and of Rossetti might not help to explain that tragedy. First he alludes to the conflict between art and morality by describing Lord Burghley's objection to Spenser's islands of Phaedria and Acrasia, and he continues, "In those islands certain qualities of beauty, certain forms of sensuous loveliness were separated from all the general purposes of life, as they had not been hitherto in European literature." Most poets, including Spenser, have had some means of sharing in the life of their time, "some propaganda or traditional doctrine to give companionship with their fellows":

But Coleridge of the *Ancient Mariner,* and *Kubla Khan,* and Rossetti in all his writing made what Arnold called that "morbid effort," that search for "perfection of thought and feeling, and to unite this to perfection of form," sought this new, pure beauty, and suffered in their lives because of it.[7]

The story of Rossetti's search is found in his sonnet sequence, *The House of Life.* It describes his purpose, his method, and the result of his quest.

Rossetti, as we have noted, wanted to live continuously in a state of heightened perception. Such a life is, of course, not feasible, and so he contented himself with striving for as many moments as possible in such a state. With a theory somewhat resembling Wordsworth's doctrine of "recollection in tranquillity," he made of the sonnet both a talisman by which the moment might be prolonged and a memorial in which its passing might be commemorated. "I hardly ever do produce a sonnet," he wrote to William Bell Scott, "except on the basis of special momentary emotion." [8] And the introductory sonnet of *The House of Life* stresses the occasional aspect of the work:

> A Sonnet is a moment's monument,—
> Memorial from the Soul's eternity
> To one dead deathless hour.

Had the moment not passed, there would be no need for the poem. Each sonnet of *The House of Life* recalls a "deathless hour," but each is a monument to a *dead,* deathless hour.

Rossetti begins, then, with a dignified admission of defeat, and the same proud submissiveness motivates his demand that the moment be described with all possible care and ceremony. Like Pater, he insists on a clear hard outline, not for the form's sake alone but for the better preservation of the moment:

> Look that it be
> Whether for lustral rite or dire portent
> Of its own arduous fulness reverent:
> Carve it in ivory or in ebony,
> As Day, or Night may rule; and let Time see
> Its flowering crest impearled and orient.
> (*CW*, I, 176)

Rossetti's emphasis upon the "moment" is related to his painting as well as his poetry. A sonnet written in very early Pre-Raphaelite days shows his belief in the revelatory power of the moment's insight; the painter's depiction of a particular scene caught at a specific time becomes, by a process resembling metonomy in language, a "tangible equivalent" (in Kenneth Burke's phrase) of a spiritual reality. Tracing the history of art, Rossetti makes its climax that period in which

> soon having wist
> How sky breadth and field-silence and this day
> Are symbols also in some deeper way,
> She looked through these to God and was God's priest.
> (*CW*, I, 214)

The step from this doctrine to the theories of Symbolism is a short one, and Arthur Symons, who was to make that step, took special note of the interest of the Pre-Raphaelites in life's critical moments.[9]

Prosper Mérimée criticized the Pre-Raphaelite brotherhood for failing to distinguish properly between poetry and painting. In his opinion they had not read Lessing's *Laocoön* with sufficient care; they attempted to record a conversation, when painting should confine itself to a single instant of time.[10] But Mérimée's criticism has only a reverse application to Rossetti's work. It is true that Rossetti makes little distinction between the temporal and spatial arts, but he confuses them not so much by attempting to make time a part of his canvas as by trying to describe in poetry that single instant which sculpture and painting are, but poetry is not, equipped to render.

In 1849 Rossetti visited the Louvre and wrote a sonnet about Giorgione's "Venetian Pastoral"; for half a century after that the picture was a symbol of the "exquisite moment":

> Water, for anguish of the solstice:—nay
> But dip the vessel slowly,—nay, but lean
> And hark how at its verge the wave sighs in
> Reluctant. Hush! beyond all depth away
> The heat lies silent at the brink of day:
> Now the hand trails upon the viol-string
> That sobs, and the brown faces cease to sing,
> Sad with the whole of pleasure. Whither stray
> Her eyes now, from whose mouth the slim pipes creep
> And leave it pouting, while the shadowed grass
> Is cool against her naked side? let be:—
> Say nothing now unto her lest she weep,
> Nor name this ever. Be it as it was,—
> Life touching lips with immortality.
>
> ("For a Venetian Pastoral, by Giorgione," *CW*, I, 345)

This revised version of the sonnet appeared in *Poems* of 1870; originally the last line had read, "Silence of heat and solemn poetry." William Rossetti expressed a preference for the earlier version, thinking the revised one too "ideal," but Rossetti disagreed, saying that his revision gave "the momentary contact

with the immortal which results from sensuous culmination, and
is always a half-conscious element of it."[11] The moment of most
intense sensuous perception is at the same time a moment of
spiritual insight, perhaps of vision.

Such was Rossetti's faith. His difficulty lay in the fact that it
was faith. What link could he posit between objects in experience
and a spiritual reality of which they are symbols save that of his
own imagination? As we shall see, the possibility that "God and
the Imagination are one" did occur to Rossetti—and later to
Symons—as it had to Coleridge, but in the face of such a thought
they had none of Stevens' calm.

Pater, who worked out the aesthetic theory of the moment far
more elaborately than did Rossetti, made Rossetti his exemplar of
one to whom "life is a crisis at every moment."[12] Symons expanded and intensified that thought in describing Rossetti's
central motivations, those which gave his life its pattern: "Here
[in Rossetti] all energy is concentrated on the one ecstasy, and
this exists for its own sake, and the desire of it is like a thirst,
which returns after every partial satisfaction. The desire of beauty,
the love of love, can be but a form of martyrdom when, as with
Rossetti, there is also the desire of possession."[13] His vision of
Rossetti's life has its justification in the poem "Soul's Beauty."
There Rossetti describes himself as a Romantic wanderer pur-
suing an ideal of love and beauty which constantly eludes him.
The pursuit is "a form of martyrdom," and there is no suggestion
that the wanderer will ever come to the end of his journey:

> This is that Lady Beauty in whose praise
> Thy hand and voice shake still—long known to thee
> By flying hair and fluttering hem—the beat
> Following her daily of thy heart and feet,
> How passionately and irretrievably,
> In what fond flight, how many ways and days!
>
> (*CW*, I, 215)

But in earlier sonnets of *The House of Life* there are moments
in which the quest seems to have gained its end. The beauty of
an earthly woman is incarnation, symbol, proof of ideal beauty:

Sometimes thou seemest not as thyself alone,
But as the meaning of all things that are;
A breathless wonder, shadowing forth afar
Some heavenly solstice, hushed and halcyon;
Whose unstirred lips are music's visible tone,
Whose eyes the sun-gates of the soul unbar,
Being of its furthest fires oracular;—
The evident heart of all life sown and mown.
                  ("Heart's Compass," *CW*, I, 190)

Just before "Heart's Compass" is a sonnet, "Mid-rapture," which describes the poet's worship of Beauty made manifest:

What word can answer to thy word—what gaze
To thine, which now absorbs within its sphere
My worshiping face, till I am mirrored there
Light-circled in a heaven of deep-drawn rays?
                  (*CW*, I, 189)

At first the beloved is described in terms usually applied to transcendent beauty; she is a beatific vision in which the poet loses all consciousness of self; then, in front of one's eyes, as it were, the sense of a human face disappears, to be replaced by a mirror reflecting upon the worshipper an idealized image of himself. Here, as in Coleridge's poem, is "an image with a glory round its head," a magnified shadow of the self, but the tone of "Mid-rapture" and of "Heart's Compass" following it does not suggest that Rossetti intended to give the image that meaning. His thought, rather, is that in the contemplation of love and beauty the self is at once lost and glorified. But the image he uses to express his idea is significant.

Such ecstatic moments are not the only ones which Rossetti finds meaningful and desires to commemorate in verse. Often he wishes to hold fast those times in which he is suddenly conscious of the warmth, safety, and comfort of love in a world ordinarily harsh and unfeeling. He writes in "The Monochord" of the love that "draws round me at last this wind-warm space" after "the lifted shifted steeps and all the way" (*CW*, I, 216). With the sudden harmony and sense of communion that it brings, the moment serves as might a small shelter in the lee of the wind to a mountain-climber.

Remembered afterward the moment is a sanctuary; while it is experienced it is a "sensuous culmination." A poem like "Silent Noon" shows how both aspects of the moment may create together a perfect instant of time, a heaven-haven. In "Silent Noon" the impersonal appreciation of Giorgione's "Venetian Pastoral" becomes personal description of an earthly Paradise:

> Your hands lie open in the long fresh grass,—
> The finger-points look through like rosy blooms:
> Your eyes smile peace. The pasture gleams and glooms
> 'Neath billowing skies that scatter and amass.
> All round our nest, far as the eye can pass,
> Are golden king-cup fields with silver edge
> Where the cow-parsley skirts the hawthorn hedge.
> 'Tis visible silence, still as the hour glass.
>
> Deep in the sun-searched depths the dragon-fly
> Hangs like a blue thread loosened from the sky:—
> So this wing'd hour is dropt to us from above.
> O! clasp we to our hearts, for deathless dower,
> This close-companioned inarticulate hour,
> When two-fold silence was the song of love.
>
> (*CW*, I, 186)

Though Rossetti evokes a scene of perfect silence, harmony, and peace and, as it were, fills the center of his mind and his emotions with these qualities, still time and change move menacingly around the outskirts; they show themselves in the "billowing skies that scatter and amass," in the hour-glass which, though motionless itself, is a symbol of mutability, and in the knowledge that this hour is "wing'd." And yet time and change may not be such dreadful enemies, for by the contrast they provide to its permanence and eternity within the mind they serve to deepen the intensity of the moment within the poem. This "sensuous culmination" has no violence in it; the passion is *there* in the poem, but it is mingled—as so often in Pater's work also—with a deeply inward, quiet melancholy. A similar melancholy characterizes Rossetti's comment on Blake's designs: "If they be for him, he will be joyful more and more the longer he looks, and will gain back in that time some things as he first knew them, not encumbered behind the days of his life; things too delicate for memory or years since forgotten; the momentary sense of spring in winter-sunshine, the long sunsets long ago, and falling fires on many distant hills" (*CW*, I, 448). Even the style of the passage fore-shadows the slightly weary cadences of Pater.

The idea implicit in "Silent Noon" is that the moment's perfection will act as shoring against the ruins of daily life. Other poems —"The Lovers' Walk," for instance, and "Youth's Spring Tribute"— carry the same thought, and "Lost Fire" makes it explicit:

> Many the days that Winter keeps in store,
> Sunless throughout, or whose brief sun-glimpses
> Scarce shed the heaped snow through the naked trees.
> This day at least was Summer's paramour,
> Sun-coloured to the imperishable core
> With sweet well-being of love and full heart's ease.
>
> (*CW*, I, 191)

But it is easy to see that, with only a slight darkening of his mood, Rossetti may become more aware of the moment's passing than he is of its permanence. In that state of mind, escape from his own consciousness, even for a short time, seems impossible, and the silence of perfect communion becomes the silence of utter isolation: "Two separate divided selves . . . . Such are we now," he writes in "Severed Selves." And he tries to comfort himself, as so often before, with the thought of a future time, even though it be only "one hour" when the sense of isolation will be lifted. He tries, but the comfort fails:

> One hour how slow to come, how quickly past,
> Which blooms and fades, and only leaves at last
> Faint as shed flowers, the attenuated dream.
>
> (*CW*, I, 196)

Worse than his consciousness of the moment's passing (which mars his happiness even as he feels it) is Rossetti's fear that he cannot really trust the validity of the moment. Those questions implied by the mirror image of "Mid-rapture" demand an answer when the ecstasy has passed. Perhaps such moments cannot serve as proof or even as sign of an ideal of love transcending the self; perhaps the sense of communion with another was an illusion created by that self which was one's only real companion all along. Thus the sonnet "Love and Hope" begins, typically enough, with images of mutability and isolation and, still typically, describes "one hour at last" when the lovers may escape into their private world. Then suddenly the very force of his desire to have that hour be the reflection of some permanence lessens his hope that it really is so:

> Cling heart to heart; nor of this hour demand
> Whether in very truth, when we are dead,
> Our hearts shall wake to know Love's golden head
> Sole sunshine of imperishable land;
> Or but discern, through night's unfeatured scope,
> Scorn-fired at length the illusive eyes of Hope.
> (*CW*, I, 198)

The final image, like that of "A Superscription"—"Sleepless with cold commemorative eyes" (*CW*, I, 225)—takes its forcefulness and horror from the sense it gives of a malevolent Watcher in the darkness, inescapable because he is oneself. "Lost Days" makes that horror explicit:

> I do not see them here; but after death
> God knows the murdered faces I shall see,
> Each one a murdered self, with low last breath;
> "I am thyself—what hast thou done to me?"
> "And I—and I—thyself," (lo! each one saith,)
> "And thou thyself to all eternity."
> (*CW*, I, 220)

Part of Rossetti's difficulty may be that the moments he treasures are those which serve as an escape from reality, not those which bring greater awareness of it. Both the dark, quiet moments of love, those experienced "Beneath her sheltering hair / In the warm silence near her breast" (*CW*, I, 97), when the sense of self is lost in one way, and the moments of blazing light like the one described in "Mid-rapture," in which that sense is lost in another, serve as escapes from the true self. A passage in Rossetti's poem "Dante in Verona" helps to define the escapist tendency of a Rossettian moment by the implicit contrast it gives with a Dantean moment.

In the poem Dante, lonely and misunderstood at the Court of

Verona, is comforted by the memory of Beatrice:

> For then the voice said in his heart,
> "Even I, even I am Beatrice";
> And his whole life would yearn to cease:
> Till having reached his room apart
> Beyond vast lengths of palace floor,
> He drew the arras round his door.
>
> At such times, Dante, thou hast set
> Thy forehead to the painted pane
> Full oft, I know; and if the rain
> Smote it outside, her fingers met
> Thy brow; and if the sun fell there
> Her breath was on thy face and hair.
>   (*CW*, I, 7)

The line "Even I, even I am Beatrice" is a translation of "Guarda-mi ben: ben son, ben son Beatrice" from the scene which one might consider the emotional center of *The Divine Comedy*. Having climbed the Mount of Purgatory, Dante at last meets Beatrice, but she appears to him veiled and stern, like Christ in judgment. Her words "Guardami ben . . ." are not a comfort, they are a stern reproach, and in telling Dante to look well upon her, she forces him also to see himself. With the "harsh pity" of genuine love she turns him from the self-involvement of remorse to the self-awareness of repentance, and in that revelation of self, Dante moves closer to beatitude:

> Gli occhi mi cadder giù nel chiaro fonte;
> ma, veggendomi in esso, i trassi all 'erba
> tanta vergogna mi gravò la fronte.[14]

The words which for Dante were a challenge, love's demand that the lover come to clarity of vision, become in Rossetti's poem an invitation to escape into temporary oblivion. Because the beloved is not for Rossetti a "presence" (in Gabriel Marcel's sense of the term), his fear that their moment of communion may have been factitious is perfectly reasonable. Or to put it another way: Rossetti attempted to transcend the consciousness by merging with the consciousness of another. Such a desire sounds altruistic, seems so indeed as one feels it, but the force which impels it is an egotism in which one must inevitably become more and more deeply entangled as one struggles.

So it was with Rossetti. His frustration lay in the fact that no moment, however intense, really gave the sense of escape from self that he desired. And at times, like Keats and like Poe, he brooded upon the thought that one moment at least might serve as escape, as illumination, as the end of all conflict: the moment of death. William Bell Scott describes an afternoon in 1869 when he and Rossetti visited a black pool called the Devil's Punch Bowl, deep in a ravine. As Rossetti gazed down upon it, he looked so fascinated that Scott believed him to be thinking, "One step forward, and I am free!" [15]

About that time Rossetti was working on a poem called "The Orchard Pit," for which he wrote a prose outline, though he finished only a few, fragmentary verses. The poem was to tell of a siren singing in an apple-tree which screens from view a pit filled with the bodies of dead men. She offers an apple which brings death to any man who tastes it. The story's narrator, although he is betrothed to a beautiful young girl, is drawn irresistibly to the siren, toward a meeting he has always feared and yet always desired. At first her song is "Come to Love," and next she sings "Come to Life." Then the narrator says, in words which echo the conclusion of Keats' sonnet "Bright Star": "But long before I reached her, she knew that all her will was mine: and then her voice rose softer than ever, and her words were, 'Come to Death;' and Death's name in her mouth was the very swoon of all sweetest things that be" (*CW*, I, 430).

If that were the end of the story as Rossetti planned it, one might suppose that he hoped for some revelation in death, but his outline concludes:

And one kiss I had of her mouth, as I took the apple from her hand. But while I bit it, my brain whirled, and my feet stumbled; and I felt my crashing fall through the tangled boughs beneath her feet, and saw the dead white faces that welcomed me in the pit. And so I woke cold in my bed; but it still seemed that I lay indeed at last among those who shall be my mates forever, and could feel the apple still in my hand (*CW*, I, 430).

The siren echoes his own desires—for life, for love, for death. As an emanation of his own consciousness, she gives him the promise of escape from self through those things which, when grasped, are seen to be illusions. He is still enclosed within the self; he has always been so.

Rossetti was a divided man. His emotions cried out for the existence of a transcendent realm while his reason questioned its existence. Yeats expresses the division by saying that "Coleridge, and Rossetti, though his dull brother did once persuade him that he was an agnostic, were devout Christians."[16] And it is true that the last sonnet of *The House of Life* expresses the thoughts of a Christian agnostic:

> When vain desire at last and vain regret
> Go hand in hand to death, and all is vain,
> What shall assuage the unforgotten pain
> And teach the unforgetful to forget?
> Shall Peace be still a sunk stream long unmet,—
> Or may the soul at once in a green plain
> Stoop through the spray of some sweet life-fountain
> And cull the dew-drenched flowering amulet?
>
> (*CW*, I, 227)

His vision is modelled upon Dante's earthly Paradise, a green plain in which the soul, after long imprisonment, breathes clear air. But the poem's questions and uncertainties, its conscious lack of rational foundation, change Dante's vision to day-dream.

Rossetti was also divided between his commitment on the one hand to introspection and self-discovery—to painting his soul as it was—and his belief on the other hand that the ideal of the self must not lie within the self. There must be an external ideal around which it can move in order and harmony. "Seek thine ideal anywhere except in thyself," he wrote in his notebook. "Once fix it there, and the ways of thy real self will matter nothing to thee, whose eyes can rest on an ideal already perfected" (*CW*, I, 152). Arnold, feeling the same need for an external standard, found one in the vision of a good society and turned his energies toward making a part of that potential good actual. His answer, however, was not really a synthesis between the self and the world outside the self. Feeling that he must choose and that no

synthesis was possible, he chose the latter, thinking it less dangerous. And he was right; it *was* less dangerous.

Rossetti was faced with a similar division, but the world of
social action had no interest for him. The world outside the self
to which he looked for a standard was a spiritual, eternal realm
of love and beauty. Through the concept of the moment he tried
to establish a link between that realm and the mind; his·thought
was that in a state of heightened perception the consciousness
recognizes in objects and persons the spiritual reality of which
they are a reflection. He never gave up his emotional commitment
to that reality, but he never succeeded in answering the question
Coleridge had raised: "And art thou nothing? . . ."

That doubt threw him back constantly upon himself and made
his effort an unhappy one. There was, moreover, a danger in-
herent in the effort itself. Writing of Edgar Allan Poe, D. H.
Lawrence makes a comment which might, word for word, be
applied to Rossetti—not surprisingly, since the two men have
much in common: "The root of all evil is that we all want this
spiritual gratification, this flow, this apparent heightening of life,
this knowledge, this valley of many-coloured grass, even grass
and light prismatically decomposed, giving ecstasy. We want all
this *without resistance*. We want it continually. And this is the
root of all evil in us."[17] It is "the root of all evil" because its
object so easily becomes a magnification of the self attained
while all consciousness of self seems lost. The moment takes
on more reality than the consciousness which experiences it, and
the real self becomes liable to disintegration.

In Swinburne's reaction to Rossetti's work one sees that process
beginning to take place. Swinburne describes the "angels and
virgins" of Rossetti's early canvases and the "strange visions" of
his later work: Venus, Helen, and Cassandra. He takes from
this change in Rossetti's subjects the thought that

any garden of paradise on earth or above earth is but a little of a
great world, as every fancy of man's faith is a segment of the truth
of his nature, a splintered fragment of universal life and spirit and
thought everlasting; since what can he conceive or believe but it
must have this truth in it, that it is a veritable product of his own
brain, and outcome for the time of his actual being, with a place

and a reason for its own root and support to it through its due periods of life and change and death?[18]

The paradisal moment has become a "segment," a "splintered fragment," given temporary validity by a consciousness which is itself splintered and fragmented. What had been to Coleridge and to Rossetti an awful possibility was to Swinburne a simple matter of fact: the "Lady Beauty" whose "fluttering hem and flying feet" Rossetti had pursued, was a shape within his own imagination, subject, like his imagination, to "life and change and death." Thus interpreted, Rossetti's moment became the Decadent moment.

The wasted and weary beauty
of the one, the faultless and fruitful beauty of the other,
bear alike the stamp of sorrow; of perplexities
unsolved and desires unsatisfied.

A. C. Swinburne

Chapter II

Algernon Charles Swinburne

"It was blue summer then, and always morning, and the air sweet
and full of bells."[1] That is the way Edward Burne-Jones describes
the months from August to December, 1857, when D. G. Rossetti
and his disciples came down to Oxford to fresco the walls of the
Union debating hall. In October young Algernon Swinburne
came up for the fall term of his second year at Oxford, and on
November 1 he met Rossetti, Burne-Jones, and Morris in the
rooms of a friend. A few days later he went to the debating hall
to watch the work.

There are so many accounts of those days in the Union that it
is easy to imagine the scene into which Swinburne entered.[2] High
up on a scaffolding, a paint-spattered Morris was drawing
medieval animals all over the ceiling. Burne-Jones was frescoing
the ceiling too—with pictures of fat little William Morrises.
Models in medieval armor or flowing draperies were posing for

the fourteen-foot frescoes of Val Prinsep and John Pollen amid
a litter of overturned paint buckets, soda water bottles, and odd
bits of scaffolding. Beside Rossetti himself, as model for Guinevere, stood the darkly beautiful Jane Burden, soon to marry
William Morris. Her face was to haunt Rossetti all the rest of his
life. The fresco on which Rossetti was working depicts Sir
Launcelot asleep before the chapel of the Holy Grail. Between
him and the shrine there rises the dream-image of Guinevere,
barring his entrance; her arms are extended in the branches of an
apple tree, and in one hand she holds an apple.[3]

A dark subject, prefiguring the still darker theme of "The
Orchard Pit"—but the atmosphere in the Union was anything
but gloomy. Swinburne was swept away by the delight of it all:
the boyish comradeship, the laughter, the romantic medievalism.
He was brought into that company immediately and dubbed
"Little Carrots," and since he could not paint even so much as
a medieval animal, he set himself to the writing of Arthurian
romances and border ballads.

Those poems are apprentice work and are not in themselves
significant, but they served as preparation for the poems which
Swinburne wrote "for art's sake." In the latter, as a disciple
of Rossetti, he followed the master's injunction to look inward
for the sources of poetic inspiration. The "studies of passion and
sensation" which resulted (for it is thus that Swinburne described
Poems and Ballads[4]) are fantasies which express the conflicting
ideas and emotions of his consciousness.

During the time in which he was concerned with the portrayal
of these inner states, Swinburne was drawn to the work of
Charles Baudelaire, who had the same purpose and whose poetry
described internal divisions closely resembling those which
Swinburne felt. In an article on Baudelaire which introduced that
poet's work into England, Swinburne wrote:

His perfect workmanship makes every subject admirable and re-
spectable. Throughout the chief part of this book he has chosen to
dwell mainly upon sad and strange things—the weariness of pain and
the bitterness of pleasure—the perverse happiness and wayward sorrows of exceptional people. It has the languid and lurid beauty of
close and threatening weather—a heavy, heated temperature with

dangerous hot-house scents in it; thick shadow of cloud about it, and the fire of molten light.[5]

This paragraph gives Swinburne's version of the doctrine of art for art's sake. The only demand one may make of a poet is that of "perfect workmanship." His subject matter is his own concern—in two senses of that phrase: he may write whatever he chooses, and what he chooses will be to depict the divisions he finds within himself. Baudelaire's purpose was serious, and so—even in the midst of all the boyish skylarking of his younger days—was Rossetti's. Swinburne, although he could describe its results enthusiastically, never really understood the purpose of this introspection, and as a result he was always of two minds about the worth of his own erotic poetry.

Of course, he was easily swayed by the opinions of those whom he admired, and comments like the following from John Ruskin may have given him pause:

For the matter of it [*Poems and Ballads*] I consent to much—I regret much—I blame, or reject nothing. I should as soon think of finding fault with a thundercloud or a night-shade blossom. . . . There is assuredly something wrong with you—awful in proportion to the great power it affects, and renders (nationally) useless. So it was with Turner, so with Byron. It seems to me to be the peculiar judgment-curse of modern days that all their greatest men should be plague-struck. But the truth and majesty which is in their greatest, causes the plague which is underneath, in the hearts of meaner people, smooth outwardly, to be in turn visible outside while there is purity within. The rest are like graves which appear not—and you are rose graftings set in dung.[6]

Any comfort Swinburne might take from knowing that he was not a whited sepulchre was effectively cancelled by the image of himself as a rose grafted in dung beside the sepulchre. And so, one gathers, he often wanted to get out of the graveyard altogether.

He wrote this little quatrain of self-mockery:

> Some sinners delighting in curses,
> Though sinful, have splendidly sinned;
> But my would-be maleficent verses
> Are nothing but wind.[7]

The ironic tone of the quatrain makes it possible, of course, for him to enjoy describing his verses in this way without really taking the description seriously himself or expecting his reader to do so. Yet time and again, even before his "reformation" in 1879, he writes that *Songs before Sunrise,* a volume given over mainly to philosophic or political poems—and very heavy-handed ones at that—is the best expression of his true self and of his most genuinely poetic mode.[8]

At the same time, Swinburne took a very personal pleasure, a schoolboy's delight, in shocking people. One sees it in this ingenuous sentence to Charles Howell: "I have added yet four more jets of boiling and gushing infamy to the perennial and poisonous fountain of Dolores" (*Letters,* I, 122). Then too, he insisted on the publication of *Poems and Ballads* (in the face of advice to tone down the work from Ruskin, Rossetti, William Bell Scott and many others who so often worried over "What to do about Algernon") and did courageous battle with reviewers because the cause of "art for art's sake" was identified in his mind with his own integrity. William Bell Scott wrote to Lady Trevelyan when Swinburne was about to publish *Chasterlard:*

You will perhaps see certain things there—the total severance of the passion of love from the moral delight of loving or being loved, so to speak, and the insaneness of the impulses of Chasterlard—for example, which may give you a text for writing to him. With all his boasting of himself and all his belongings he is very sensitive about society, and I certainly think you will do him the very kindest of actions if you can touch his sensibility on his vanity—a little sharply (*Letters,* I, 135–36).

Scott was shrewd but—for his purposes—not shrewd enough. Swinburne's very vanity made it a matter of personal honor to him to publish his work; moreover, the fact that he knew he would be victimized for doing so acted as a stimulus rather than as a deterrent to his masochistic nature.

So much for his motives in insisting upon free expression for his imagination. The important thing about the poems themselves is that when Swinburne allowed his imagination such freedom he came to more truth than he knew. In writing this kind of poetry he was facile, and that facility could be dangerous; nevertheless, the poems that resulted were much more genuine than those "nationally useful" poems in which he consciously set himself to the expression of high thoughts. Paradoxically, he found the latter sort of poem very difficult to write and complained of the problem in a letter to William Rossetti:

If I do finish this poem ["A Song of Italy"] at all to my satisfaction, there will be a bit of enthusiasm in verse for once—rather. After all, in spite of jokes and perversities . . . it is nice to have something to love and believe in as I do in Italy. It was only Gabriel and his followers in art (l'art pour l'art) who for a time frightened me from speaking out . . . . Only, just as one hears that intense desire has made men impotent at the right (or wrong) minute, my passionate wish to express myself in part, for a little about this matter [of Italian nationalism] has twice or thrice left me exhausted and incompetent: unable to write, or to decide if what has been written is or is not good. I never felt this about my poems on other subjects (*Letters*, I, 195–96).

The passage is full of the most astonishing paradoxes. Swinburne feels that his temporary belief in "art for art's sake" frightened him from "speaking out"; it was at that time that he wrote the "jokes and perversities" which the Victorians found so shocking. Now he intends to pluck up his courage and thunder out republican sentiments which, as it turns out, will interest very few, alarm even fewer. Swinburne should have been warned by his difficulties in writing those nationalistic poems. They were almost unwritable; they are now unreadable. But the poems which were simply "self-expression," written for their own sake—the poems about whose sentiments one might say he scarcely *thought* at all have, in spite of all their very obvious faults, something significant to say about human experience.

What Swinburne had to say in these poems will be made clearer by stopping to consider another work which he wrote purely for its own sake, his unfinished novel *Lesbia Brandon*. The fragments of *Lesbia Brandon* are really more a series of fantasies than a coherent story, but Swinburne has written enough to show the plot that he had in mind. It is very close to the plot of the first half of *Wuthering Heights*, one of Swinburne's favorite novels: "It may be true," he wrote, "that not many will ever take it [*Wuthering Heights*] into their hearts; it is certain that those who do like it will like nothing very much better in the whole world of poetry or prose" (*Works*, XIV, 54), and when attempting his own novel he paid *Wuthering Heights* the compliment of imitation.

The real heroine of *Lesbia Brandon*, as Swinburne's letters show[9] (for not he but Thomas Wise or Sir Edmund Gosse gave it that title), is Lady Margaret Wariston. She and her brother, Herbert Seyton—an idealized Swinburne—are the book's central figures. And Lady Wariston is placed in a position precisely analogous to Catherine Earnshaw's. She is married to a man who gives her affection, kindness, material comfort—but not passionate love: "Her husband did not embitter and did not enliven her life. . . . He had for her a little love, and she had much liking for him. He could fill up his life with little satisfactions, but she could find no single expression of her wants and powers. In those years, a maiden at heart, she had a vague and violent thirst after action and passion. . . . Of one thing only she never thought: of love."[10] Breaks in the manuscript make it necessary to piece her later history together: she falls passionately in love, we gather, with a man named Denham, her brother's tutor, who we know has been in love with her for years. Denham discovers, however, that he is in reality her half-brother; the only fragment relating to the love affair is a scene in which Margaret Wariston and Denham decide that they must part. Shortly afterward he is brought back to the house, shot through the heart in what is reported to be an accident.

Herbert Seyton (Lady Wariston's brother), meanwhile, has fallen in love with Lesbia, who dies in a bizarre and "decadent" manner from an overdose of opium and eau-de-cologne. And the end of it all—like the end of Swinburne's other novel, *Love's Cross-Currents*—is emotional deadlock. Lady Wariston and Herbert Seyton both become people to whom nothing will ever happen: "As for him [Seyton] I cannot say what he has done or will do, but I should think, nothing. This may certainly be affirmed of his sister, whose husband, one of our happiest countrymen, is content to farm, to shoot, to vote in the House where he never speaks, and to adore his family" (p. 353).

Lady Wariston, one might say, is as much an ancestress of

Lady Chatterley as a descendant of Catherine Earnshaw. There is, however, an interesting point of difference between *Lesbia Brandon's* theme and that of a typical novel by Lawrence. Lawrence's heroines must always learn to rejoice in their separateness from the men they love: it is only by an understanding of *that* division that they may achieve harmony within themselves and peace with their men. In order to escape self-division, Lawrence preaches again and again, one must conquer the narcissism which would use another simply as a means for loving oneself. His vehemence shows that he thinks it no small temptation; the important point here, though, is that he is consciously concerned with it as a temptation. *Lesbia Brandon* might serve as an exemplum for a Lawrentian sermon. The passionate feelings of all the principal characters are narcissistic, and their result is barrenness and sterility.

The central pair of divided lovers in *Lesbia Brandon* are Lady Wariston and her brother Herbert. The book opens with an elaborate description of both which repeatedly stresses their resemblance to one another, while emphasizing at the same time their difference in sex. And the most harmoniously sensual passage in the book describes an evening in Herbert's boyhood when Margaret kissed him, pleased with his courage in saving a young neighbor from drowning. It is a scene with scarcely a hint of the torment and violence which characterize the other love affairs of the book:

"I say, let your hair go," said Herbert, pressing his arms under hers: she loosened the fastenings, and it rushed downwards, a tempest and torrent of sudden tresses, heavy and tawny and riotous and radiant, over shoulders and arms and bosom; and under cover of the massive and luminous locks she drew up his face against her own and kissed him time after time with all her strength (p. 265).

When he discusses *Wuthering Heights* and *Jane Eyre*, Swinburne picks out for special comment the passage in which Catherine Earnshaw says: "I *am* Heathcliff," and that in which Jane Eyre answers Rochester's question "whether she feels in him the absolute sense of fitness and correspondence to herself which he feels to himself in her, with the words which close and crown the history of their twin-born spirits—'To the finest fibre of my nature, sir'" (*Works*, XIV, 9). Swinburne's choice of those particular incidents in other novels when placed beside the incidents of his own novel shows what he believed to be passion's driving impulse: the desire to unify the self through love. But Swinburne begins with the knowledge that such a desire can meet only with frustration and self-division, and these are the "passions and sensations" he chooses most often to describe.

One of the poems in which he does so very movingly is "Laus Veneris," Swinburne's version of the Tannhäuser legend. He begins his poem at what is usually the story's conclusion, after Tannhäuser's return to the Hörselberg; the reason he gives for doing so is interesting: "The immortal agony of a man lost after all repentance—cast down from a fearful hope into fearless despair—believing in Christ and bound to Venus—desirous of penitential pain, and damned to joyless pleasure—this in my eyes was the kernel and nucleus of the myth . . . . The tragic touch of the story is this: the knight who has renounced Christ believes in him; the lover who has embraced Venus disbelieves in her" (*Works*, XIV, 353).[11] The poem has no logical development; nor has it really any emotional development. One simply joins the knight in spirit as he moves through the conflicting emotions which obsess him. There is no escape from them and no hope of bringing them into unity. From stanza to stanza—sometimes from line to line—the speaker's mood changes, and the only real constant is that change. The very pattern of a stanza like the following shows all these fluctuations obviously enough:

> Alas, Lord, surely thou art great and fair.
> But lo her wonderfully woven hair!
> And thou didst heal us with thy piteous kiss;
> But see now, Lord; her mouth is lovelier.
>   (*Works*, I, 147)

That stanza shows that even Swinburne's analysis was an over-simplification. The knight still desires Venus, still clings to her, although at times he thinks her fearful. With one hysterical image of torture and imprisonment after another he describes her torments: "Her little chambers drip with flower-like red . . . ," but suddenly his mood changes:

> Yea, all she slayeth; yea, every man save me;
> Me, love, thy lover that must cleave to thee
> Till the ending of the days and ways of earth,
> The shaking of the sources of the sea.
>
> (*Works*, I, 151)

The change is obvious not only in the sudden shift of tone to gentle melancholy but also in the change from indirect description of a terrifying Venus to direct address of a pathetic one. Nor does the knight always desire the heaven he has lost:

> Ah love, there is no better life than this;
> To have known love, how bitter a thing it is,
> And afterward be cast out of God's sight;
> Yea, these that know not, shall they have such bliss
>
> High up in barren heaven before his face
> As we twain in the heavy-hearted place,
> Remembering love and all the dead delight,
> And all that time was sweet with for a space?
>
> (*Works*, I, 161)

The knight's only harmonious, whole-hearted desire is for total oblivion:

> Ah yet would God this flesh of mine might be
> Where air might wash and long leaves cover me,
> Where tides of grass break into foam of flowers,
> Or where the wind's feet shine along the sea.
>
> (*Works*, I, 148)

The last line of the stanza refers specifically to the sea, but the images of the two preceding lines describe the earth as if it were a sea. For to Swinburne death's symbol is not the earth, which reminds man of his duality by its identification with the body, but the sea, which is at once the origin of all life and an element alien to human life.

"Anactoria," another dramatic monologue, has an emotional pattern which closely resembles that of "Laus Veneris." Sappho is the speaker. Through her imprisoned consciousness circle the obsessive thoughts and desires created by her love for Anactoria. Neither this poem nor "Laus Veneris" has the character of a Browning monologue; they do not catch the speaker at a partic-

ular spatial and temporal moment but—as in Tennyson's "Titho-
nus"—in what seems to be an eternal moment. "Anactoria" is a
more violent poem than "Laus Veneris"—the division it describes
is more bitter—but it is clearer too. The mingled love and the
hatred which Sappho feels for Anactoria are not emotions which
really relate to any object outside herself. She is caught by the
dualities of self-love and self-hatred:

> Yea, though thou diest, I say I shall not die,
> For these shall give me of their souls, shall give
> Life, and the days and loves wherewith I live,
> Shall quicken me with loving, fill with breath,
> Save me and serve me, strive for me with death.
>
> (*Works,* I, 198)

So it seems as if her thoughts will drift off, but with a sudden
revulsion she abandons the desire for any sort of immortality in
her longing for oblivion:

> Alas, that neither moon nor snow nor dew
> Nor all cold things can purge me wholly through,
> Assuage me nor allay me nor appease,
> Till supreme sleep shall bring me bloodless ease;
> Till time wax faint in all his periods;
> Till fate undo the bondage of the gods,
> And lay, to slake and satiate me all through,
> Lotus and Lethe on my lips like dew
> And shed around and over and under me
> Thick darkness and the insuperable sea.
>
> (*Works,* I, 198–99)

As "Anactoria" shows, one of the moments which Swinburne
wishes to capture in verse is that of desire just before it reaches
its limit to become pain and frustration in the consciousness of
limit. The difference between this moment and a similar Rossettian moment is clearest in Swinburne's description of Rossetti's
"Venetian Pastoral": "In the verse as on the canvas there is the
breathless breath of over-much delight, the passion of overrun-
ning pleasure which quivers and aches on the very verge of
heavenly tears—tears of perfect moan for excess of unfathomable
pleasure and burden of inexpressible things only to be borne by
Gods above" (*Works,* XV, 31). Rossetti's moment passes as he

becomes aware once more of time and of self: its passage leaves a deep but very quiet melancholy, as quiet as the moment itself. But there is violence even in the pleasure of Swinburne's moment, and the violence increases as the frustration implicit in Rossetti's description becomes explicit in Swinburne's.

As frustration at the "otherness" of the beloved increases, the moment of love and near-communion becomes one of consuming hatred—of the beloved, of oneself, of life and its limitations. Thus in "Anactoria," Sappho's desire for total possession of Anactoria changes into the desire to kill her and afterward to kill herself; at least by destruction of all consciousness she can come to a negative communion:

> O that I
> Durst crush thee out of life with love, and die,
> Die of thy pain, and my delight, and be
> Mixed with thy blood and molten into thee!
> (*Works*, I, 194)

The limitations of love become identified with all human limitation, so that it is with an analogous feeling that Sappho turns upon God:

> Him would I reach, him smite, him desecrate
> Pierce the cold lips of God with human breath,
> And mix his immortality with death!
> (*Works*, I, 195)

In such a moment God and Man would be mixed, God would become mortal, Man God-like, and both would be destroyed—as if in one instant *both* Jupiter and Semele were shattered. This is love's desired consummation, and so it is that in Swinburne's mind love and death are not opposites: they are identical.

In his quasi-autobiographical poem "Thalassius," Swinburne describes an innocent boy, child of the sun and the sea, who on an April day meets the God of Love. The god's form is child-like, and he wanders helpless and blind; in pity Thalassius guides him, thinking himself the stronger of the two. But as they travel the god becomes huge and terrifying. He turns on Thalassius suddenly and mocks him: "O fool, my name is sorrow; / Thou fool, my name is death" (*Works*, III, 297). With those words he vanishes.

From the bitter hopelessness of love Thalassius turns to a life of violent pleasure, the life described in "Dolores." In his "Notes on Poems and Reviews" Swinburne describes the same change of feeling: "I have striven here [in "Dolores"] to express that transient state of spirit through which a man may be supposed to pass, foiled in love and weary of loving, but not yet in sight of rest; seeking refuge in those 'violent delights' which have 'violent ends,' in fierce and frank sensualities which at least profess to be no more than they are" (*Works*, XVI, 360). Swinburne also writes that the placing of "Dolores" within *Poems and Ballads* is significant: "Dolores," "The Garden of Proserpine," and "Hesperia" should be considered as a trilogy—an arrangement which reflects the self-division and longing for death that one finds in the book's individual poems. For "Hesperia" and "Dolores" are expressions of opposite states of mind, the one dominated by a Diana-like goddess that redeems, the other by an Astarte that consumes. Hesperia is "a bride rather than a mistress, a sister rather than a bride" (*Works*, XVI, 362) to whom the speaker flees. He is one who "has loved overmuch" in his life and turned from the pain of love to the respite which lust at first seemed to offer:

Was it myrtle or poppy thy garland was woven with, O my Dolores?
Was it pallor of slumber, or blush as of blood, that I found in thee fair?
For desire is a respite from love, and the flesh not the heart is her fuel.

(*Works*, I, 306)

Nevertheless, Dolores has cruelties of her own, and the speaker has fled from her, Our Lady of Pain, to seek refuge with Hesperia:

Let her lips not again lay hold on my soul, nor her poisonous kisses
To consume it alive and divide from thy bosom,
Our Lady of Sleep.
Ah daughter of sunset and slumber, if now it return into prison,
Who shall redeem it anew? . . .

(*Works*, I, 307)

The speaker's address to Hesperia as "Our Lady of Sleep" and his identification of her with sunset suggest that Hesperia is Death. If she is, does Swinburne's analysis of the poem make sense? It does if one thinks of Hesperia as that lost innocence which, emotionally if not intellectually, it seems possible to regain—but only by death. For the poem concludes with a fantasy in which the speaker and Hesperia ride across the landscape which resembles the Northumbria of Swinburne's boyhood: they ride furiously, pursued by "the goddess that consumes":

And our spirits too burn as we bound, thine holy but mine heavy-laden
As we burn with the fire of our flight; ah love, shall we win at the last?
(Works, I, 308)

Between "Dolores" and "Hesperia" comes "The Garden of Proserpine," which describes that state in which the spirit "without fear or hope of good things or evil hungers and thirsts only after perfect sleep" (*Works*, XVI, 362). In the poem's final image that sleep of death is identified with the sea; there the human spirit is promised a blessed release from consciousness and an end of all dualities.

In "The Triumph of Time" the sea also grants unity of spirit but of a slightly different kind: it returns the poet to that innocence which was destroyed by the divisions of love. Nevertheless the sea's singleness and freedom are unattainable except in death; the sea's gift is one of her "pure cold populous graves" (*Works*, I, 177). When he wrote "Thalassius" in 1879–1880, however, Swinburne described a return to innocence and unity of spirit which is attained without suffering death. Thalassius simply leaves his revelling companions and returns to the sea, his mother:

> The tidal throb of all tides keep rhyme
> And charm him from his own soul's separate sense
> With infinite and invasive influence.
(Works, III, 302)

Herbert Seyton, like Thalassius, is brought up beside the sea and finds in it the deepest pleasure he will ever have. There he can keep his identity without all the conflict of love and at the same time can merge his identity in an overpowering force. Swinburne describes the boy after he has been swimming as "wet and rough, blown out of shape and beaten into colour, his ears full of music and his eyes of dreams: all the sounds of the sea

rang through him, all its airs and lights breathed and shone upon
him."[12] The echo of "and the glory of the Lord shone round about
them" (Luke 2:9) emphasizes the visionary quality of the experience. Swinburne uses a similar vocabulary in a letter to his sister:
"The whole sea was literally golden as well as green—it was liquid
and living sunlight in which one lived and moved and had one's
being. And to feel that in deep water is to feel—as long as one is
swimming out if only a minute or two—as if one was in another
world of life, and one far more glorious than even Dante ever
dreamed of in his Paradise" (*Letters*, V, 275).

The moments in which the sea gives him a sense of infinite
expansion are those which Swinburne most prizes, but, like
Rossetti's moments of supreme peace in love, they can bring no
genuine revelation. Using Blake's terms, one might say that
Swinburne rejects Experience and returns to the state of Innocence. He does not come into the state of imaginative maturity
which makes it possible to understand and therefore to accept
Experience, the state which Yeats described in "A Dialogue of
Self and Soul" when he wrote:

> I am content to follow to its source
> Every event in action or in thought;
> Measure the lot; forgive myself the lot![13]

Instead Swinburne retreats into fantasy, withdrawing from all that
is not the self, expanding the self into infinity. The sea is his
Paradise because as he swims in it, he can enjoy the illusion of
solitary existence, and as he identifies with it, he can make that
existence seem infinite.

Swinburne's legacy to younger poets was, first of all, his career
itself, already legend even as he lived it, and secondly *Poems and
Ballads* which captivated generation after generation of adolescents—Oscar Wilde, Ernest Dowson, and Arthur Symons among
them. Its images, surrounded by a haze of undefined but powerful
emotion and described in language whose effect was virtually
hypnotic, created for its readers a separate world—a realm of
fantasy "separated from the general purposes of life." T. S. Eliot
was thinking of the book in this way when he wrote that in

Poems and Ballads "the object has ceased to exist . . . because language, uprooted, has adapted itself to an independent life of atmospheric nourishment."[14] His words recall Yeats' thought that "these images grow in beauty as they grow in sterility." That is to say, *Poems and Ballads* provided no link between the fantasies of the mind and a reality outside the mind, and because it was, therefore, at least potentially imprisoning, it was a dangerous book for those adolescents who best appreciated its effects.

At least as important as his influence upon the adolescents of his time is Swinburne's effect upon a contemporary, Walter Pater. The two men seem to have stood off from one another; they were acquaintances, not friends. But Pater was quick and gracious in admitting a debt to Swinburne when the latter complimented him on his first essays in the *Fortnightly*. "He replied," Swinburne writes, "that he considered them as owing their inspiration entirely to the example of my own work in the same line" (*Letters*, II, 241). Perhaps it was as well that Pater was so courteous, for Swinburne and Rossetti had, in fact, remarked between themselves on certain likenesses. "I liked Pater's article on Leonardo very much," Swinburne wrote to Rossetti. "I confess I did fancy there was a little spice of my style as you say, but much good stuff of his own, and much of interest" (*Letters*, II, 58). Although the tone of his comment is slightly patronizing—and one gets the impression that neither Rossetti nor Swinburne *liked* Pater—its truth is unquestionable. Indeed, there are similarities of material as well as of style between Swinburne's "Notes and Designs of the Old Masters at Florence" and Pater's "Leonardo da Vinci." This, for instance, is Swinburne's description of a study by Michelangelo: "But in one separate head there is more tragic attraction than in these: a woman's three times studied, with divine and subtle care; sketched and re-sketched in youth and age, beautiful always beyond desire and cruel beyond words; . . . In one drawing she wears a head-dress of eastern fashion rather than western" (*Works*, XV, 159–60). The mixture of beauty and cruelty in the subject, the emphasis upon care in its portrayal, and even the hint of connections with the East all appear in Pater's description of the Mona Lisa.

But Pater's dependence on Swinburne's previous criticism for

such details is not as important as the similarity of critical attitude which one finds in the two men. In "Notes on Some Pictures
of 1868" Swinburne described several works by Rossetti: pictures
of Lilith, of Proserpine, and of Beatrice. He has of each a different
impression; Lilith's "sleepy splendour" as she contemplates herself
in a mirror gives him pleasure, as do Proserpine's "sacred eyes and
pure calm lips" and "the symbolic and ideal head" of Beatrice.
Each of these works, however different, shows the artist's "love of
beauty for the very beauty's sake, the faith and trust in it as in a
god indeed." The critic's function is to worship this beauty "trans-
formed and incarnate in shapes without end" (*Works*, XV, 215–
16). But the manner of Swinburne's worship shows that he is not
loving those works of art for their own sake; he uses the art work
as material for fantasy. His descriptions are not so much of the
paintings themselves as of the different fantasies and resultant
moods which they evoke in his consciousness.

Pater's method, as he describes it in the preface to *The Renaissance*, sounds more scientific; the aesthetic critic's function is "to
distinguish, to analyse, and separate" the particular qualities of
a work of art. But the questions upon which that analysis is based
are these: "What is this song or picture, this engaging personality
presented in life or in a book, to *me*? What effect does it really
produce on me? Does it give me pleasure? and if so, what sort or
degree of pleasure? How is my nature modified by its presence or
under its influence?"[15] Such a method of criticism is, like Swinburne's, solipsistic in that it makes no clear separation between
the observer and the art work. All objects outside the self, whether
in art or in immediate experience, are, in one sense, equally removed from the self: their meaning is that which the self imposes.
All are, in another sense, part of the self, since they have meaning
only as they contribute to its fantasies. And yet, ironically, the
criticism of both Swinburne and Pater sets consciousness itself
adrift in the flux of experience; before each new object—Beatrice,
Lilith, or Proserpine—the observer is a different man. The end
result is that the enjoyment of an object takes on more reality
than either the object itself or the observing consciousness. Pater
was to come to such a point in the "Conclusion" to *The Renaissance* when he described the enjoyment of "strange dyes, strange

colours, and curious odours, or the work of an artist's hands," as a way of grasping at life "while all melts under our feet."

Of the two men Pater was the better critic in that he gave intelligent expression to concepts that remain darkly implicit in Swinburne's work, and it is doubtful that Swinburne himself could have done so. He had the incapacity for ideas of a genuine Barbarian. But he had as well the Barbarian charm and high spirit. Causes not ideas interested him, and if the cause were his own or a friend's, he was thereby convinced of its justice and impatient for battle. Thus, for the ten years from 1857 to 1867 he was proud to think of D. G. Rossetti as, so to speak, his general and of himself as a captain, leading a charge of young recruits to battle against the Philistines. Had the combat been in fact so physical, he would have acquitted himself bravely, for he had a gallant heart. But in that "mental fight" he was a confused and therefore a dangerous leader.

The central interest of his own
youth—of his profoundly impressible youth—as happens
always with natures of real capacity, gives
law and pattern to all that succeeds it.
Walter Pater

Chapter III

Walter Pater

In the late spring of 1884, close to the publication date of *Marius
the Epicurean,* William Sharp came to Oxford to visit Walter
Pater. There, as they walked in the spring sunshine, the talk
turned to William Blake, and Pater said, "I never repeat to myself
without a strange and almost terrifying sensation of isolation and
long weariness, that couplet of his:

> "Ah, sunflower, weary of time,
> Who countest the steps of the sun."[1]

Pater's singling out of that particular couplet as well as his reaction to it is a clue to what he himself might call his "formula,"
his principal preoccupation, perhaps one could even say his obsession: the consciousness always with him that time—with all the
events, friendships, and sense impressions contained within it—
was moving past him, and, worse still, the knowledge that he too

was caught up in the movement so that he could not take even himself as a point of rest. Yet neither could he float simply in the consciousness that "everything flows," for—to continue the metaphor—in such turbulent water he might well not float but drown. Pater believed that there must be an answer, a possibility of order, and though he changed his ideas of what that ordering principle might be, it always had its foundation in a moment of insight, a moment in which the flux was formed into a pattern within the consciousness of the observer. In Pater's changing attitudes towards the "moment" one finds a key to an understanding of his thought, and the changes are clearest in *Marius the Epicurean*. There Pater summed up and commented upon his earlier opinions and showed the direction of all his later thought.

A year after his visit, Sharp reviewed *Marius* in *The Athenaeum*. It was the enthusiastic review of a fervent disciple, but some of its sentences show that he had missed his master's point: "There are . . . some pages here and there in these two volumes which unmistakably present the personal opinions of the author, and these conjointly with portions of Mr. Pater's other published writings, constitute sufficient basis for the assumption that he does, indeed, recognize the teaching of Epicurus as—in its quintessential doctrine—not unworthy . . . of serious consideration as a practical philosophy of life."[2] Rather inconsistently he went on to say that if Pater had intended to show the Epicurean philosophy as futile and Christianity alone as "really responsive to man's deepest needs" he had hardly been successful. John Pick has pointed out that of all Pater's disciples only Lionel Johnson followed or seemed even to understand the changes that took place in their master's thought;[3] Sharp is clearly among those who stuck with the Pater of *The Renaissance*. In order to do so he had to disregard facts that would be clear even in a quick reading: first that Marius is a Roman mask for Pater himself and second that Pater recognized his earlier Epicurean philosophy as inadequate and, while still working from its basic principles, made it more spiritual without really making it Christian.

Heraclitus' philosophy was always important to Pater; he used a line from Heraclitus as an epigraph for the "Conclusion" of *The Renaissance*, and, much later in his life, he began his lectures on

Plato and Platonism with a discussion of the phrase Πάντα ῥεῖ, all things are in flux.[4] The same philosophy serves as a point of departure in *Marius the Epicurean.* When Marius, shocked by the death of his friend Flavian, begins to consider the meaning of that experience and of his whole life, he turns first to the philosophy of Heraclitus—or, more precisely, to that of Protagoras, since Marius accepts Heraclitus' description of the problem without following him when his intellectual ladder "seemed to pass into the clouds."[5] Pater himself had shown much the same attitude as a young man when he objected to Coleridge's attempt to escape the phenomenal world into a world of pure being, an absolute world beyond change. In an early essay entitled "Coleridge's Writings," he pointed out that any metaphysical hypothesis remains only and always hypothesis; it is a sad expense of spirit, therefore, to turn away from physical experience in order to walk in the grey world of the abstract. The case of a potentially great artist like Coleridge is especially sad, because the artist, with his extraordinary sensitivity to real objects and emotions, will find a better answer to life's meaning through them than the philosopher ever can: "The true illustration of the speculative temper is not the Hindoo, lost to sense, understanding, individuality; but such a one as Goethe, to whom every moment of life brought its share of experimental, individual knowledge, by whom no touch of the world of form, colour, and passion was disregarded."[6] Pater could scarcely even understand the tension between metaphysics and art that Coleridge felt and that Yeats was later to feel. The lectures on *Plato and Platonism* allow for the necessity and even the virtue of abstraction but not for metaphysical speculation—and even abstraction or generalization has as its final end only the illumination of the particular. "Converse with the general," as Pater understands it, is worthwhile for the sudden vision it can bring, when once mastered, of the concrete: "By a kind of short-hand now, and as if in a single moment of vision, all that which only a long experience moving patiently from part to part, could exhaust, its manifold alliance with the entire world of nature, is legible upon it, as it lies there in one's hand."[7]

Pater believed that Coleridge failed as an artist because he turned metaphysician, whereas Plato was the best of philosophers because he was actually an artist, not lost in the light of the invisible but turning that light upon the visible in order to fuse the material and the spiritual into unity. "While in that fire and heat, what is spiritual attains the definite visibility of a crystal, what is material on the other hand, will lose its earthiness and impurity."[8] And so, interestingly enough, Pater finally adopted the same principles as those of the abstract Coleridge and even used the same image in explaining them: the beautiful image of crystal. Coleridge had written: "Something there must be to realize the form, something in and by which the *forma informans* reveals itself: . . . An illustrative hint may be taken from a pure crystal . . . . The crystal is lost in the light which yet it contains, embodies, and gives a shape to."[9] Yet it is unfair to quote a man against himself, and the Pater of *Plato and Platonism* was in many ways very different from the Pater who wrote "Coleridge's Writings." The latter, like the young Marius, clearly balked at an attempt to fuse material and spiritual because, though exquisitely conscious of the material world, he questioned the existence of a spiritual one.

Marius disliked an attempt at metaphysical ordering of the universe for yet another reason, the one given by Pater in the preface to *The Renaissance.* There, as we have noted, counting metaphysical ponderings on the abstract nature of beauty as worthless, he makes the critic's first question: "What is this song or picture, this engaging personality presented in life or in a book, to *me*?"[10] Ruth Child has interpreted this to mean that the critic must first define himself to himself—must, in a word, find his own "formula."[11] Certainly that seems true; yet we should remember as well that Pater wrote those words with a consciousness of every man's imprisonment within himself. He explains that Marius stopped at the threshold of philosophy because he saw that every system attempting to reflect "reality" could use but the mirror of the human mind and personality creating it, and that "the little knots and waves" of that mirror's surface would destroy the truth of the reflected image.[12] Moreover, there is not only the problem of a perfect reception of reality; there is also the problem of its communication. Since each man's vision of the

world is hopelessly personal, he cannot really find common terms
with which to express his feelings about it to others or by which
he can be sure to understand theirs.

Implicit too in the awareness of isolation which the preface
to *The Renaissance* expresses is an idea which was to have as
great an impact on Oscar Wilde's thought as the "gem-like flame"
passage of the "Conclusion." It is, if you will, a secular Calvinism
which encloses every individual in the cocoon of his own heredity
and his personal history, yet does not allow for that grace through
which God releases the elect. In the "Conclusion" the idea forces
its way into expression in a terrifying image: "Experience, already
reduced to a group of impressions, is ringed round for each one
of us by that thick wall of personality through which no real
voice has ever pierced on its way to us, or from us to that which
we can only conjecture to be without. Every one of those impressions is the impression of the individual in his isolation, each
mind keeping as a solitary prisoner its own dream of a world."[13]
Pater, as Ernest Tuveson has shown,[14] was carrying one of John
Locke's ideas to a perfectly logical conclusion; Tuveson compares Pater's image of the mind as a prison with a passage in
which Locke compares the mind to a dark room: "for methinks
the understanding is not much unlike a closet wholly shut from
light, with only some little opening left, to let in external visible
resemblances, or ideas of things without."[15]

Those "ideas of things" were much more fleeting, more evanes-
cent to Pater than they were to Locke; nevertheless, when the
young Marius had thought himself down and down into the
prison of himself he (like the young Pater) found in them a
secret spring which promised release: "But our own impressions!
—The light and heat of that blue veil over our heads, the heavens
spread out, perhaps *not* like a curtain over anything!— How re-
assuring, after so long a debate about the rival criteria of truth,
to fall back upon direct sensation . . . how natural the determination to rely exclusively upon the phenomena of the senses, which
certainly never deceive us about themselves, about which alone
we can never deceive ourselves."[16]

With this as his answer, Marius put aside all abstract speculation and found himself happy in the doctrine of Aristippus of

Cyrene, an "anti-metaphysical metaphysic," which taught that
one must live "a full or complete life," a life of various yet select
sensation "whose direct and effective auxiliary must be, in a
word, Insight." Through a moment's insight he might shape the
flux into meaning and so give order and peace to his soul. In order
to do so, he must refine and develop his sensations and his intui-
tions; he must make them into so many sensitive media for reception, trained upon the vision—"the 'beatific vision' if one cared to
make it such," writes Pater in a significant aside—of his experience.[17]

The sensations and ideas of Marius at this point in his life are
those of Pater when he wrote *The Renaissance*. And, though, as
we have seen, Coleridge was to Pater an example and a warning
of the wrong way in which to think, Coleridge's theory of art
and that of the German philosophers on whose work it was
based gave Pater the answer to the question, How to live? The
Romantic theory of art also began with an aching consciousness
of mutability which must somehow be soothed. More than that,
it refused any abstract system which would impose a form by
cutting in, somehow, anyhow, to make a pattern through separation. It insisted that the answer lay not in analysis but in vision.
Schelling had written: "If, as the excellent man of discernment
remarked, every natural growth has only one moment of true
and consummate existence, we may say that it also has only one
moment of complete existence. At this moment it is what it is for
all eternity: beyond this its lot is merely a becoming and a passing
away. Art, by depicting the creature at this moment, raises it up
out of time and presents it in its pure being, in the eternity of its
life."[18] A sentence like the following by Hegel also had its comfort: "Art liberates the real import of appearances from the
semblance and deception of this bad and fleeting world, and
imparts to phenomenal semblances a higher reality, born of
mind."[19]

Pater simply expanded this so that it made every thinking man,
every truly conscious spirit—and it was only "choice spirits" to
whom he addressed himself—an artist, or perhaps one should say
an "aesthetic critic." In Pater's opinion the artist and the aesthetic
critic may be equated because the fundamental quality in both

is an ability to recognize and catch a perfect moment, a moment which, using the vocabulary of this organic criticism, Pater says has *grown* perfect.[20] Objects in the external world gradually come to their momentary perfection, and the mind gradually acquires the capacity for recognizing that perfection. The sudden meeting of mind and object creates the moment. Simply to recognize it is to endow it with the permanence "born of mind." Thus when he speaks of "life as the end of life" or "the love of art for its own sake," he is saying the same thing: the perfect work of art is the perfection of a moment in life, and the recognition of the beauty in both is the whole of what we may expect in human happiness.

It is easy to understand, then, why Pater shares Rossetti's desire for definition of form and outline in a work of art and why he makes clarity of memory one of the chief characteristics of any artist. Marius, he writes, gave up his youthful attempts to write poetry (as Pater himself did[21]) and labored instead to perfect his prose. Nevertheless, he had always "the poetic temper: by which I mean, among other things, that quite independently of the general habit of that pensive age, he lived much, and, as it were by system, in memory."[22] Pater has come to the same idea which Eliot was later to express in "Burnt Norton":

> Time past and time future
> Allow but a little consciousness.
> To be conscious is not to be in time.
> But only in time can the moment in the rose garden,
> The moment in the arbour where the rain beat,
> The moment in the draughty church at smokefall
> Be remembered: involved with past and future,
> Only through time time is conquered.[23]

Like Eliot he makes it the poet's function to hold the moment "out of time" in his memory so that gradually its significance may become as clear as the experience once was.

So it is that in his writing Pater almost makes physical objects of his memories, twisting them this way and that so that a moment caught in the mind may in a new light or a different place reveal something of itself that was hidden before. He writes of his childhood over and over again, setting it in different countries perhaps, and at different historical periods, yet remembering always the clean white house, the sunlight, his own religious devotion: in *Marius the Epicurean* itself, in "The Child in the House," *Gaston de Latour,* and "Emerald Uthwart."[24]

Of all these the most appropriate for this discussion is "The Child in the House," first published in 1878, because it is not so much a story as an attempt to recall certain moments of childhood. "Memory" is perhaps too simple a word for the process by which this is done; the heightened recollection takes on an almost visionary light, not supernatural perhaps, but preternatural. Pater writes of "the finer sort of memory" which brings its object to mind with great clarity, "yet, as sometimes happens in dreams, raised a little above itself, above ordinary retrospect."[25]

Florian, the little boy who serves in this story as a persona for Pater's childhood self, found the garden gate open one evening. He walked through it with a sense of excitement, for ordinarily the gate was closed, and saw before him a beautiful red hawthorn in full flower:

> Was it some periodic expansion of soul within him, or mere trick of heat in the heavily-laden summer air? But the beauty of the thing struck home to him feverishly, and in dreams, all night, he loitered along a magic roadway of crimson flowers which seemed to open ruddily in thick, fresh masses about his feet, and fill softly all the little hollows in the banks on either side. Always afterwards, summer by summer, as the flowers came on, the blossom of the red hawthorn seemed absolutely the reddest of all things; and the goodly crimson, still alive in the works of old Venetian masters, or old Flemish tapestries, called out always from afar, the recollection of the flame in those little petals, as it pulsed gradually out of them kept long in the drawers of an old cabinet.[26]

To attempt to hold the vision by keeping the petals in a drawer is hopeless, as Pater the man knew—and Marcel Proust after him —though Pater the child had still to learn it. Only the memory can hold the color fixed. And looking ahead for a moment to the death of Marius, we find memory again as the finest hope, the best, perhaps the only comfort. After all his questioning of how to live Marius finds as he is dying that he can rest his mind only by gazing inwardly at the remembered faces of those whom he has loved, "like a child, thinking over the toys it loves, one after another."[27]

All this is some comfort perhaps, but come at it how one will, it is not much, as Pater knew. Of course—though this is by the way—the recognition of what one feels to be a grim truth and the consciousness of bearing it bravely can give a self-satisfaction which almost makes up for the mental bleakness that goes with it. And Pater will comfort himself this way often enough.[28] Nevertheless, though in his consciousness of the moment's passing he relied on memory to "hold Beauty back," he knew, like Hopkins, that the attempt was unrealistic, and there comes even into his earlier, more agnostic work a longing to believe that moments of perfection might be kept safe for us in a drawer where they will not fade. In the original version of the essay on Giorgione, Pater writes:

Who, in some such perfect moment, when the harmony of things inward and outward beat itself out so truly, and with a sense of receptivity, with entire inaction on our part, some messenger from the real sound of things must be on his way to one, has not felt the desire to perpetuate all that, just so, to suspend it in every particular circumstance, with the portrait of just that one spray of leaves lifted just so high against the sky, above the well, forever? A desire how bewildering with the question of whether there be indeed any place wherein those desirable moments take permanent refuge. Well! in the school of Giorgione you drink water, perfume, music, lie in receptive humour thus for ever, and the satisfying moment is assured.[29]

And he has Marius think to himself: "Could he but arrest, for others also, certain clauses of experience, as the imaginative memory presented them to himself! In those grand, hot summers he would have imprisoned the very perfume of the flowers."[30] At this time in his life Pater, like the young Marius, believed that the work of art, by reincarnating the moment held in the memory, offered sufficient permanence, or at least as much as one might demand. It was for this reason that the clear form and the definite outline were so important. The object of memory must be brought into that clear, preternatural light and held there, whole.

That quality of Marius' prose which Pater singles out as primary is "a certain firmness of outline, that touch of the worker in metal amid its richness."[31] The phrase brings to mind the central image in an "Imaginary Portrait" called "An English Poet." The sensitive boy described there, who lives in the rough Cumberland country in surroundings he cannot see as beautiful, finds one object which at once excites and satisfies his imagination: in a church there is a wrought-iron grille worked in a honeysuckle pattern. In time he becomes a poet, and his verse is noted for "a peculiar character, as of flowers in metal," the strength and elasticity of his language blended with a subtlety that can follow "a tender, delicate feeling as the metal followed the curvature of the flower."[32] There was such a grille on the door of Pater's room in Brasenose College; one can see that Pater took pleasure in it as an image of his aesthetic theory because it brings together the ideas of form as organic, growing by necessity from within the thing it expresses, and of form as that which makes permanent, capturing beauty laboriously by chiselling and rubbing until the form within reveals itself. Like the French Parnassians and like Rossetti, Pater believed that the moment must be carved "in ivory or in ebony."

This paradox of the way form is achieved is almost impossible to express except through symbol; nevertheless one feels that the symbols used do express a real process. Certainly Pater understood the symbol and the process which it revealed—understood it so well that he could manipulate it at will and apply it to the creation of a work of art or of a view of life. For instance, in this passage from *Plato and Platonism* one sees an early expression of what Hulme and Pound were to say in a few years about "the form within the stone":

Κόσμος; order; reasonable, delightful order, is a word that became very dear, as we know, to the Greek soul, to what was perhaps most essentially Greek in it, to the Dorian element there. Apollo, the Dorian god, was but its visible consecration. It was what, under his blessing, art superinduced upon the rough stone, the yielding clay, the jarring metallic strings, the common speech of every day. Philosophy, in its turn with enlarging purpose, would project a similar light of intelligence upon the at first sight somewhat unmeaning world we find around us;—project it, or rather discover it, as being really preexistent there, if one were happy enough to get one's self to the right point of view. To certain fortunate minds the efficacious moment of insight would come, when, with the delightful adaptation of means to ends, of the parts to the whole, the entire scene about one, bewildering, unsympathetic, unreasonable, on a superficial view, would put on, for them at least, κοσμιότης, that so welcome expression of fitness, which it is the business of the fine arts to convey into material things, of the art of discipline to enforce upon the lives of men.[33]

The passage brings together all the points we have discussed so far: the whirl of impressions seen and ordered differently by each individual; the moments of insight which give at least a temporary escape; the process through which those moments are caught and held in art work where they may offer the consolation of their coherence in an incoherent world.

Marius sets off for Rome, rather serious and severe in his ways considering his age, but possessed in his soul of something like cheerfulness once he has thought his way through to the "new Cyrenaicism"—a philosophy we have noted to be close to that of Pater when he wrote the "Conclusion" to *The Renaissance*. Yet as the years pass Marius discovers that he has not found an answer that will do once and for all; the moments of intensity for which he had found it sufficient to live, these remain, but they are changed into sudden, vivid realizations of pain until "his 'observation of life,'" says Pater, "had come to be like the constant telling of a sorrowful rosary, day after day."[34] It is difficult to understand how, having read that, William Sharp could suggest that Pater was putting Epicureanism forward as a "practical philosophy of life." On the contrary, three-quarters of the book is taken up with demonstrating that the philosophy of Epicurus is insufficient for the human happiness which it makes its end.

Pater does not denounce his earlier philosophy as evil—perhaps that was how the misunderstanding arose in the minds of his disciples. He simply counts it as a partial truth, one for which the young have a special affinity, "based on a vivid, because limited, apprehension of the truth of one aspect of experience—in this case, the beauty of the world and the brevity of man's life in it."[35] Pater has every sympathy with the young who continue to come to this answer, but if they fail to grow out of it by realizing its limitations, they will themselves remain limited.

The reason for the failure of Cyrenaicism lies in the very principle on which it is based: that the individual has no knowledge beyond his own experience, and no sense of an external order, either metaphysical or moral, save that of which he himself is aware in his happiest and best moments. Now from the moment he makes the Cyrenaic philosophy his own, Marius understands that the desire for a life full of every kind of experience might lead to acts which, if not sinful according to this relativist philosophy, could still be harmful to oneself and painful to others. He has no real answer to this save his own early conditioning at "White Nights," the "first early, boyish ideal of priesthood" which made him desire always "hieratic beauty and order in the conduct of life."[36] For stability Marius really needs the precepts of a religion in which he no longer believes. Or rather, as B. A. Inman has pointed out, Marius takes from Cyrenaicism only those precepts which are congenial to his "temperament,"[37] and that temperament was formed in part by the religion in which he was raised:

> He hardly knew how strong that old religious sense of responsibility, the conscience, still was within him—a body of inward impressions, as real as those so highly valued outward ones—to offend against which, brought with it a strange feeling of disloyalty, as to a person. And the determination, adhered to with no misgiving, to add nothing, not so much as a transient sigh, to the great total of man's unhappiness, in his way through the world:—that too was something to rest on, in the drift of mere "appearances."[38]

What, though, of those who had not that "sense of responsibility"? Pater never answered that question;[39] or perhaps it is truer to say that his criticism of Cyrenaicism is based on a moral concern at once subtler and broader than that of simply doing good and avoiding evil. His concept of morality, like that of Matthew Arnold and of Henry James, centers upon the individual's development of all his finest human attributes. Marius feels that his nature is becoming cramped, narrowed, one-sided—and sees suddenly that this is true of the Cyrenaic philosophers too:

If they did realize the μονόχρονος ἡδονή, as it was called—the pleasure of the "Ideal Now"—if certain moments of their lives were high-pitched, passionately coloured, intent with sensation, and a kind of knowledge which, in its vivid clearness, was like sensation—if, now and then, they apprehended the world in its fullness, and had a vision, almost "beatific," of ideal personality in life and art, yet those moments were a very costly matter: they paid a great price for them in the sacrifice of a thousand possible sympathies, of things only to be enjoyed through sympathy, from which they detached themselves, in intellectual pride, in loyalty to a mere theory that would take nothing for granted, and assent to no approximate or hypothetical truths. In their unfriendly and repellent attitude towards the Greek religion and the old Greek morality, surely, they had been faulty economists.[40]

So Marius, conscious of his spiritual barrenness, casts off the Cyrenaic ordering of the world and sets himself again, as he had after Flavian's death, to the task of making his experience meaningful. But the "formula" has not changed: he is still conscious only of the flux of events, unable to believe in an absolute order *there* objectively within it, and still aware that his world vision must always be entirely personal.

The danger of holding such a position, the danger to which Marius is particularly liable, is that of falling into the state of Decadence. Nor is it just the wisdom of hindsight which says so, for Pater himself was perfectly aware of the possibility. In his essay on Prosper Mérimée he described the effects of the philosophy which would make all speculation about the unseen world nonsense; the state of consciousness which results is the Decadent one:

The désillusionné, who had found in Kant's negations the last word concerning an unseen world . . . will demand, from what is to interest him at all, something in the way of an artificial stimulus. He has lost that sense of large proportion in things, that all embracing prospect of life as a whole (from end to end of time and space, it had seemed), the utmost expanse of which was afforded from a cathedral tower of the Middle Age . . . . Deprived of that exhilarating yet pacific outlook, imprisoned now in the narrow cell of his own subjective experience, the action of a powerful nature will be intense, yet exclusive and peculiar. It will come to art, or science, to the experience of life itself, not as portions of nature's daily food, but as something that must be, by the circumstances of the case, exceptional; almost as men turn in despair to gambling or narcotics, and in a little while the narcotic, the game of chance or skill is valued for its own sake. The vocation of the artist, of the student of life or books will be realised with something—say! of fanaticism, as an end in itself, unrelated, unassociated.[41]

And yet Pater himself had expressed the point of view of the "désillusionné" in the "Conclusion" to *The Renaissance*. This passage, by describing so grimly the dangers of his own earlier philosophy, is as strong a retraction of that philosophy as one finds anywhere in Pater's writing. It also disproves Arthur Symons' theory that Pater was "quite content that his mind should 'keep as a solitary prisoner its own dream of the world.' "[42] Perhaps Symons confused Pater's withdrawn and distant personality with his philosophy of life, or perhaps he read the "Conclusion" but did not take sufficient notice of this passage about Mérimée or of another which describes Gaston de Latour climbing the tower of Jean de Beauce at Chartres. Gaston enjoys as he does so the "exhilarating yet pacific outlook" which Pater praises in the essay on Mérimée: "At each ascending storey, as the flight of birds, the scent of the fields swept past him, till he stood lost amid the unimpeded light and air of the watch-tower above the great bells, some coil of perplexity, of unassimilable thought or fact, fell away from him."[43] Gaston may still be isolated, but he is not confined in the narrow prison of the self; he stands in a watch-tower from which he can see and share in all human life. "And with that vision he can guess the secret of some older, deeper, more permanent ground of fact" (p. 52).

Marius has a similar moment of insight while he enjoys the quiet of the Sabine hills. There the answer, so far as there is an answer, comes to Marius in a moment of clearer understanding than he is ever to have again and on a day in which he seemed, like Shelley's ideal poet, in "possession of his own best and happiest self."[44] On this day Marius was considering a sentence from Marcus Aurelius: " 'Tis in thy power to think as thou wilt," which leads him to wonder whether a bold willingness to accept "the hypothesis of an eternal friend to man, just hidden behind the veil of a mechanical and material order," might not lead the intellect eventually into certitude of that being's existence. It is the philosophy of a divided man—emotions, will, and intellect each operating in him separately—but of a man who desires internal unity and coherence. And indeed for a moment at least the very possibility of such an internal harmony mirroring a universal coherence frees Marius: "The purely material world, that close, impassible prison-wall, seemed just then the unreal thing, to be dissolving away all around him."[45] With the thought that the world of material things may be only a reflection of the divine mind—this making it not less but much more permanent— Marius feels comforted: no longer solitary but companioned by the divine assistant, no longer aware of time passing so much as of the moment made permanent:

How often had the thought of their brevity spoiled for him the most natural pleasures of life, confusing even his present sense of them by the suggestion of disease, of death, of a coming end, in everything! How had he longed, sometimes, that there were indeed one to whose boundless power of memory he could commit his own most fortunate moments, his admiration, his love, Ay! the very sorrows of which he could not bear quite to lose the sense: . . . And he had apprehended to-day, in the special clearness of one privileged hour, that in which the experiences he most valued might as it were take refuge.[46]

The speculation which leads Marius into his moment of vision reminds one of the philosophy of William James—and, looking to the end of the story, one might even think of Marius as a pragmatic martyr, for though he cannot assent completely to the truths of Christianity, he acts *as if* they were true. Given a crucial choice, he goes to the side of the believers.

By generously taking for granted the hypothesis that there is a transcendent reality, Marius saves himself from the Decadent's vision in which all activity is "unrelated, unassociated." With it he finds a way to enjoy and even to preserve the perfect moment without a sense of desperation as he does so. It is true that his answer, like the conclusion of the novel, is still tenuous and even melancholy—Marius would not be one to shout "alleluia" even if he were suddenly convinced of salvation. As it is, his attitude is more a provisional assent to a hypothesis than an active assertion of belief. But it is sufficient to give him an "outlook," an escape from the prison of the self.

Thinking of the book only in relation to *The Renaissance* one might say that Pater had a negative and a positive purpose in writing *Marius the Epicurean:* on the one hand, he wanted to show the insufficiency and even the danger of the point of view he had expressed in the "Conclusion" to *The Renaissance;* and on the other, the positive side, he wished to offer a possible escape from the ultimate dissolution of the self which was the threat of a skeptical impressionism. The book, though an achievement in other ways, did not fulfill either of these practical purposes; of all the young writers who looked to Pater for guidance, only Lionel Johnson heeded the warning in *Marius the Epicurean.* Of course, simple chronology can explain the fact that *Marius* had very little effect upon Oscar Wilde. He came to Oxford the year after *The Renaissance* was published, read the book while he was there, and was strongly influenced by it. But by the time *Marius the Epicurean* was published Wilde was no longer a docile student, ready to change opinions as Pater changed his.

What, though, of someone like Arthur Symons? He was still a very young man when Pater first wrote to him in 1886, a year after the publication of *Marius.* Why was he also influenced by *The Renaissance* and not by *Marius the Epicurean?* The reason may lie in the fact that Pater's first discussion of the problem, his description of modern man's situation, was masterful, unforgettable, but his later solution of it was tentative and vague. The sentences of the "Conclusion," with their clear images and urgent tone, are forceful even now when their ideas and their phrases are perfectly familiar: "Not to discriminate every moment some passionate attitude in those about us, and in the very brilliancy of their gifts some tragic dividing of forces on their ways, is, on this short day of frost and sun, to sleep before evening."[47] We need only compare that sentence, or any sentence from the "Conclusion," with this passage from the essay on Mérimée: "Fundamental belief gone, in almost all of us, at least some relics of it remain—queries, reactions, after-thoughts; and they help to make an atmosphere, hazy perhaps, yet with many secrets of soothing light and shade, associating more definite objects to each other by a perspective pleasant to the inward eye against a hope-fully receding background of remoter and even remoter possi-bilities."[48] This is Pater's answer, the same answer as that of *Marius the Epicurean,* but in writing it Pater manipulates his prose almost with cunning, as if he wished to cover the tracks of his thought. When the sentence finally drifts to an end, "we are in a Mist." Thus the answer that Pater offered, though it seems to have been useful to him personally, could not guide others through the labyrinth, and Pater's disciples were left where Pater himself had begun, "ringed round . . . by that thick wall of personality."

Man is least himself
when he talks in his own person. Give him a mask,
and he will tell you the truth.
Oscar Wilde

Chapter IV

Oscar Wilde

In *A Vision* Yeats used Oscar Wilde as one of his examples of
those who live in the nineteenth phase of the lunar cycle, the
phase which marks the beginning of "the artificial, the abstract,
the fragmentary, and the dramatic." The man of this phase is
forced "to live in a fragment of himself and to dramatise that
fragment."[1] Others have had the same sense of Wilde's fragmentation. Arthur Symons describes him as one who made for himself
many souls "of intricate pattern and elaborate colour, webbed
into infinite tiny cells."[2] Then he modifies the image: Wilde is not
only a craftsman but also a skilled juggler who amuses people by
whirling his separate "souls" before them. Later he uses yet another metaphor, clearing the theatre and making Wilde the only
spectator of his own performance: "One sees that to him everything was drama, all the rest of the world and himself as well;
himself indeed always at once the protagonist and the lonely

king watching the play in the theatre emptied for his pleasure."[3]

On the basis of a somewhat similar theory about Wilde, Arthur Nethercot made a study of *The Picture of Dorian Gray* and of Wilde's plays in which he suggested that "he [Wilde] split himself into two parts, into two types of self-representative."[4] The later discovery of a letter from Wilde to an otherwise unknown admirer, Ralph Payne, helped to prove that both his theory and Symons' were correct: that is to say, that Wilde, even more consciously than most writers, split himself into various characters and saw in all of them some portion of his actual or potential self: "I am so glad you like that strange many coloured book of mine [*The Picture of Dorian Gray*]: it contains much of me in it. Basil Hallward is what I think I am: Lord Henry, what the world thinks me: Dorian what I would like to be—in other ages, perhaps."[5] This letter suggests the way in which it might best be possible to understand Oscar Wilde: by separating him, as he separated himself, into several selves (each, however, watching the other selves and offering comments upon or even engaging in dialogues with the self at stage-center), remembering always that the man and his work are inextricable, though the work too is a mask.

1 *The Mask of Dorian Gray*

In the opening scene of *The Picture of Dorian Gray* Basil Hallward and Lord Henry Wotton discuss Dorian Gray's physical beauty and his innocence: these are his given characteristics, but when he himself appears, the qualities in him that seem more striking are his quickness and docility—he is a good student. When Lord Henry "with that graceful wave of the hand that was always so characteristic of him" (and of Wilde) tells him that "the aim of life is self-development," Dorian understands immediately, just as a good student in the humanities might, the relevance of the doctrine to actual experience. And Oscar Wilde, like Dorian Gray, was also in this sense a good student. In his first term at Oxford in 1874, Wilde attended Ruskin's lectures on the "Aesthetic and Mathematic Schools of Art in Florence"; he became such an enthusiastic follower of Ruskin's teaching that he was one of the group which helped to build—or attempted to build—a road between Upper and Lower Hinksey. "Art and the Handicraftsman," one of Wilde's American lectures, gives his version of the story; in it he becomes one of the students with whom Ruskin first discussed the project. And, after all, he made it a good story, although the road-work had already begun when Wilde arrived in Oxford. Wilde's telling of it is only a slight elaboration, nothing to compare to the splendid lie with which he begins his account: "Well, let me tell you how it first came to me at all to create an artistic movement in England, a movement to show the rich what beautiful things they might enjoy and the poor what beautiful things they might create."[6]

While he was still a student Wilde wrote an essay on the Grosvenor Gallery exhibition of 1877 that showed a truer sense of intellectual history. There he mentioned "that revival of culture and love of beauty which in great part owes its birth to Mr. Ruskin, and which Mr. Swinburne, and Mr. Pater, and Mr. Symonds, and Mr. Morris, and many others, are fostering and keeping alive, each in his own particular fashion."[7] The review itself is written wholly under the influence of Ruskin: Wilde praises all the pictures done in the Pre-Raphaelite manner and gives Whistler only a slighting mention; moreover, his criticism itself tends, like Ruskin's, to be anecdotal. For instance, Wilde praises a painting called "Afterglow in Egypt" for its coloring, but, he says, "It is difficult to feel a human interest in this Egyptian peasant."[8]

It was partly as a result of this essay that Wilde began to move from the orbit of Ruskin towards that of Walter Pater: Wilde sent Pater a copy of his essay and received a cordial reply in which Pater suggested that they meet to discuss certain points about which they were not in agreement, "though," he continued, "on the whole I think your criticisms very just, and they are certainly very pleasantly expressed" (*Letters*, p. 47).

In *De Profundis* Wilde says that it was in his first term at Oxford, the term in which he trundled stones for Ruskin's road, that he read Pater's *The Renaissance*, "that book which was to have such strange influence over my life"[9] (*Letters*, p. 471). Of course, it may be an oversimplification—more than that, an affectation—to say that the course of one's life has been changed by a book; nevertheless, it is possible that, like many of Wilde's dramatic simplicities, this "explanation" is true in essentials.[10] A single book could change the whole course of a man's life if it expressed all the things that he was already prepared to believe. And Pater's uncanny ability to catch and hold the drift of intellectual experience in his time gave his work extraordinary power. Arthur Symons, for instance, also writes about *The Renaissance* as a book which "opened a new world to me, or rather, gave me the secret of the world in which I was living," and with a single detail he gives his comment the ring of truth: he says that he read *The Renaissance* in its first edition on ribbed paper—"I have the feel of it still in my fingers."[11]

In the world of art, in any event, such things are possible, and Lord Henry Wotton changes Dorian Gray's life within the space of an afternoon by preaching a sermon based on the "Conclusion" to *The Renaissance*, beginning with the horror of time's passing, the loss of youth, the short time in which strong sensation is possible, and ending with the exhortation: "Live! Live the wonderful life that is in you! Let nothing be lost upon you. Be always searching for new sensations."[12] As he preaches, Lord Henry notices the strong effect of his words, and his memories make it clear that he is not meant to represent Pater; he is the older Wilde remembering what he himself had once learned: "He [Lord Henry] was amazed at the sudden impression that his words had produced, and, remembering a book that he had read when he was sixteen, a book that had revealed to him much that he had not known before, he wondered whether Dorian was passing through a similar experience" (p. 23). The point is an important one because of the changes which Lord Henry makes in the message of *The Renaissance;* the words he uses may almost paraphrase Pater's, but the doctrine is Wilde's.

A scene from *The Ambassadors* shows the difference. The situation is very like that in *The Picture of Dorian Gray:* an older man, Lambert Strether, is giving a younger one, Little Bilham, the philosophy taught him by his own experience. The very words echo Lord Wotton's: "Live all you can; it's a mistake not to. It doesn't matter what you do in particular, so long as you have your life."[13] But the difference between Lord Wotton and Lambert Strether lies in Strether's belief that he must desire nothing, save his impressions, for himself. In his selflessness he is a Paterean saint, while Lord Wotton, whose search is not for "impressions" but for "sensations," is among the damned. Strether finds his pleasure in his vision of others; Lord Wotton is interested in the effects of external stimuli upon his own consciousness. His gaze is fixed upon himself. Pater had written, "We may well grasp at any exquisite passion, or contribution to knowledge that seems by a lifted horizon to set the spirit free for a moment."[14] The moment of great intensity, whether sensual, emotional, or intellectual, serves as an escape from imprisoning self-consciousness. Dorian Gray, under the tutelage of Lord Wotton, takes pleasure not so much in enjoyment of the moment as in watching the effect of the moment upon himself.

Gray makes another important modification of Pater's doctrine when he uses evil acts as a means of achieving "sensations." His hope as he does so is to come to ever deeper self-knowledge, ever wider self-expression. And so it fascinates him to think that he can watch the gradual process of his own corruption in the portrait: "He would be able to follow his mind into its most secret places. This portrait would be to him the most magical of mirrors. As it revealed to him his own body, so it would reveal his own soul" (p. 128).

But the portrait really gives only a partial revelation; it presents no vision of the "best self," and by taking its partial revelation for the whole truth, Dorian Gray narrows his consciousness. Pater in his review of the book makes that point and protests at the same time against the interpretation put upon his theory—if so strong a word as "protest" may be used for his blandly remote comment: "A true Epicureanism aims at a complete though harmonious development of man's entire organism. To lose the moral sense, therefore, for instance, the sense of sin and righteousness, as Mr. Wilde's hero—his heroes seem bent on doing as speedily, as completely as they can, is to lose, or lower, organization, to become less complex, to pass from a higher to a lower degree of development."[15] And indeed, although his first letter to Wilde was flatteringly cordial, Pater came in time to find his young student just as distressing as he later found the fictitious Dorian Gray.[16]

André Gide's account of one of the stories Wilde often told (though from behind the Lord Henry mask) makes Pater's distrust understandable. Wilde had noticed that Gide listened with intensity to all that was said: "You listen with your eyes," Wilde commented, and he went on to tell of the flowers which had asked the river for water that they might weep for Narcissus, who had just died. The river refused, saying that all the drops of water it contained were not enough for his own tears, so much had he loved Narcissus:

" 'Oh!' replied the flowers of the field, 'how could you not have loved Narcissus? He was beautiful.' 'Was he beautiful?' said the river. 'And who could know better than you? Each day, leaning over your banks, he beheld his beauty in your water . . .' "

Wilde paused for a moment . . .

" 'If I loved him,' replied the river, 'it was because, when he leaned over my water, I saw the reflection of my waters in his eyes.' "

Then Wilde, swelling up with a strange burst of laughter, added, "That's called *The Disciple*."[17]

This, however, is the attitude of a different Oscar Wilde; his youthful change from following Ruskin to following Pater was much less conscious and not at all cynical. By the time he wrote another criticism of a Grosvenor Gallery exhibition, that of 1879, he showed a difference in his views by the praise he gave to Whistler;[18] in "L'Envoi," written in 1882 while he was in America, Wilde formally avowed his withdrawal from Ruskin's sphere of influence and made his presence in Pater's apparent by his generous (though unacknowledged) quotation from the master.

Although Wilde says that "we of the younger school have made a departure from the teaching of Ruskin,—a departure definite, and different and decisive," he realizes at least partially the effect Ruskin's teaching had had upon Oxford. Wilde's opinion of the nature of his achievement is interesting in that, with some justice, it relates Ruskin's work more closely to Pater's than either man might have liked; he writes that Ruskin "taught us at Oxford that enthusiasm for beauty which is the secret of Hellenism." But Ruskin cannot be an acceptable master, "for the keystone of his aesthetic system is ethical always."[19]

Wilde posed in "L'Envoi" as the acknowledged leader of his

generation. Indeed, his high-handedness offended Rennell Rodd, the author of *Rose Leaf and Apple Leaf* for which this essay served as preface, because Wilde, as self-appointed editor, cut out of the book two poems Rodd had intended to publish and then wrote himself a fulsome dedication in Rodd's name.[20] But Wilde's lofty tone and loftier actions show that he would have liked to be what later he attempted to make of Dorian Gray: "Indeed there were many . . . who saw, or fancied that they saw, in Dorian Gray the true realization of a type of which they had often dreamed in Eton or Oxford days—a type that was to combine something of the real culture of the scholar with all the grace and distinction and perfect manner of a citizen of the world (pp. 155–56). It may have been Wilde's desire to be the man of this new Renaissance—a Renaissance patterned by Pater—that moved him in 1881 to issue his *Poems*. It is hard otherwise to explain how a man who wrote so fine a critical essay as "The Critic as Artist" would not recognize his own poems as bad art.

A good many of the *Poems* are simply schoolboy exercises in which Wilde wrote patriotic, hortatory sonnets in the manner of Milton and Wordsworth; wistful, Catholic sonnets in the manner of Rossetti; lush, pagan effusions in the manner of Swinburne.[21] Nevertheless, the general pattern of the book parallels Wilde's account of Dorian Gray's "search for sensations." In the section of *Dorian Gray* modelled mainly upon Huysmans' *A Rebours* Wilde says that Dorian, desiring experience "that would be at once new and delightful, and possess that element of strangeness so essential to romance . . . would often adopt certain modes of thought that he knew to be really alien to his nature" (p. 159). He was, for instance, attracted for a while to the Roman Catholic ritual, as well as to mysticism ("and the subtle antinomianism that seems to accompany it") and to the materialism of the *Darwinismus* movement in Germany. "Yet as has been said before, no theory of life seemed to him to be of any importance compared with life itself" (p. 160).

Now as it happened there seemed also the possibility around the year 1877 that Wilde might become a Catholic,[22] and several of the earlier poems in the book describe the Church's fascination for him: "Rome Unvisited," "Urbs Sacra Æterna," and "Sonnet on hearing the Dies Irae sung in the Sistine Chapel." Following the section of the book which contains these poems comes "The Burden of Itys," which rejects Catholicism and celebrates the return of a splendid new Hellenism:

> Poor Fra Giovanni bawling at the mass
> Were out of tune now, for a small brown bird
> Sings overhead, and through the long cool grass
> I see that throbbing throat which once I heard
> On starlit hills of flower-starred Arcady.[23]

A later poem, "Panthea," takes the position that human happiness lies in the recognition that we shall "through all æons mix and mingle with the Kosmic Soul!" (*Poems*, p. 191)—while further on "Humanitad" asserts that "That which is purely human, that is Godlike, that is God" (*Poems*, p. 228). Of course, it is possible to argue that Dryden's *Collected Works* would show just as many changes of opinion: the opinion itself is poetically not of importance so much as the truth of its expression, its truth, so to speak, to itself. But this is precisely where Wilde fails: he is not true even to his changing opinions; he is much more conscious of himself as Wilde the Catholic, Wilde the pagan, Wilde the humanist, than he is of the Catholicism, paganism, or humanism he professes. Knowing that such an objection is possible, he gives this justification for the "insincerity" of Dorian Gray:

Is insincerity such a terrible thing? I think not. It is merely a method by which we can multiply our personalities.

Such at any rate was Dorian Gray's opinion. He used to wonder at the shallow psychology of those who conceive the Ego in man as a thing simple, permanent, reliable, and of one essence. To him, man was a being with myriad lives and myriad sensations, a complex multiform creature that bore within himself strange legacies of thought and passion, and whose very flesh was tainted with the monstrous maladies of the dead (pp. 171–72).

As the passage continues, it becomes obvious that the adoption of a new idea or belief serves only as the opportunity for acting a different role, for Wilde moves from a discussion of Dorian Gray's changing opinions to a description of his imaginative identification with different personalities, first those of his historical

ancestors and then those of his "ancestors in literature." It is
worth noting that he is drawn only to depravity, but what is
really more important is that his imagination shows a reverse,
a Decadent "negative capability." Instead of losing himself in
other people or ideas, he brings them into himself until indeed
only his own ego exists: "There were times when it appeared to
Dorian Gray that the whole of history was merely the record of
his own life, not as he had lived it in act and circumstance, but
as his imagination had created it for him, as it had been in his
brain and in his passions" (pp. 173–74).

Wilde's poem "The Sphinx" and the play *Salomé* are both
marred by qualities which resemble those of Dorian Gray's
reveries. Both are sexual fantasies which dwell on the morbid and
even the depraved, but although the subject matter itself can
partially account for the atmosphere of decay which pervades
them, it is its manner of presentation which throws around these
works an even more lurid, phosphorescent light. The meditations
on the strange half-bestial lovers of the Sphinx or on Salomé's
passion for John the Baptist are auto-eroticism, not negative
capability. There is no question of Wilde thinking himself into
the soul of Salomé, understanding her motivation, suffering her
passion; he is simply using Salomé imaginatively in order to experience a new *frisson*. And, when Herod turns at the end of the
play and gives orders, "Tuez cette femme,"[24] the act itself means
nothing save that the reverie is over: Salomé has fulfilled her
function.

When Dorian Gray, frightened by the near success of Jim
Vane's vengeful attempt to kill him, decides that he will reform
his life, his first act of virtue is to spare the honor of a country
maiden—an act which shows Gray's lack of originality in virtue as
well as in sin. But Lord Henry Wotton makes him realize that
even goodness is now only another form of self-consciousness for
him, still another *frisson* for one to whom every sort of vice has
now become monotonous. Dorian begins to wonder: "Had it
been merely vanity that had made him do his one good deed? Or
the desire of a new sensation, as Lord Henry had hinted with his
mocking laugh? Or that passion to act a part that sometimes
makes us do things finer than we are ourselves? Or perhaps all of

these?" (p. 269). At last he concludes that it was, indeed, all of these, and utterly trapped, he stabs the portrait and kills himself.

One of the reasons that *De Profundis* makes such painful reading is that Wilde there shows himself equally trapped within the mask of Dorian Gray. Though he may wish and intend repentance, he cannot keep himself from dramatizing the wish at the same time, so that it becomes unreal, perhaps even to himself. Repentance itself becomes a new and different kind of "moment":

I remember that as I was sitting in the dock on the occasion of my last trial listening to Lockwood's appalling denunciation of me . . . and being sickened with horror at what I heard, suddenly it occurred to me, *How splendid it would be, if I was saying all this about myself.* I saw then at once that what is said of a man is nothing. The point is, who says it. A man's very highest moment is, I have no doubt at all, when he kneels in the dust, and beats his breast, and tells all the sins of his life (*Letters*, p. 502).

But Lord Henry Wotton, watching such a performance, would have given his mocking laugh.

ii *The Mask of Lord Henry Wotton*

Throughout the trials, but especially in the first, Wilde retained the mask by which he was at the time best known: that of the dandy—calm, intellectually acute, remote and almost cynical (for even outright cynicism would imply too much emotion) —in the tradition described by Barbey d'Aurévilly. He was the aphorist, the creator of paradoxes which, however light-hearted and even light-minded they might seem, showed the ability to detect and expose affectation in a moment. Moreover, he could expose evil or weakness without professing to be either good or strong—only indifferent. This was the mask of Lord Henry Wotton, which Wilde said was "what the world thinks me."

Wilde put on the mask of Lord Henry very early; at least it is possible to catch glimpses of him wearing it even on his trip to America, when his part was more often that of a young man living for the sake of intense experience, a Dorian Gray. Lord Henry's attitude toward experience, though it possesses similarities, is really quite different: " 'I have known everything,' said Lord Henry, with a tired look in his eyes, 'but I am always ready

for a new emotion. I am afraid, however, that, for me at any
rate there is no such thing' " (p. 95). George Woodberry, who
met Wilde in Lincoln, Nebraska, wrote a long letter to Charles
Eliot Norton describing him; in it he mentions a very similar pose
of world-weary remoteness from vital experience, a self-conscious
abstention from life instead of a self-conscious desire to enjoy it:
"He [Wilde] told every[thing] of his early life to show that he
had developed, and he may keep on; but I am sorry for the man
who loves Ruskin and says that 'like Christ he bears the sins of
the world,' and who straightway speaks of himself as 'always, like
Pilate, washing his hands of all responsibility.' The contrast is
unfortunate."[25]

It is possible to think of all the essays in *Intentions,* including
"The Soul of Man under Socialism," as spoken through the mask
of Lord Henry Wotton, not so much for the ideas expressed in
them as for the way in which they are expressed: the pose of the
writer, or of the main speaker in the dialogues, is in all of them
that of the detached ironist, the aristocratic observer. The necessary separation between art and nature is the first premise of
Wilde's mature criticism: it was an old doctrine, but it had been
given a new interpretation, its truth revealed in a new way by
Baudelaire when he insisted that "la première affaire d'un artiste
est de substituer l'homme à la nature et de protester contre elle"[26]
and that "Tout ce qui est beau et noble est le résultat de la raison
et du calcul."[27] Even as early as 1882, Wilde with his enormous
capacity for the fruitful combination of ideas, if not for their
creation, had brought this theory into harmony with the doctrine
of Rossetti and Pater on art's capturing of the "moment":

For him [the poet] there is but one time, the artistic moment; but one
law, the law of form; but one land, the land of Beauty—a land removed
indeed from the real world yet more sensuous because more enduring;
calm, yet with that calm which dwells in the faces of Greek statues,
the calm which comes not from the rejection but the absorption of
passion.[28]

Wilde wrote whimsically in "The Decay of Lying" and "The
Critic as Artist," but his theory is the same: out of the flux of
experience art must create form, for raw experience is meaning-

less—the only pattern possible is that made within the human mind. Wilde also takes the next logical step to a position which superficially resembles Arnold's on the poet's role as "myth-maker" in the society of the future[29] but actually stands Arnold on his head—Arnold intended that poetry serve as a bridge between man and the world surrounding him; Wilde makes it a defense, a drawbridge: "I am certain that, as civilization progresses and we become more highly organized, the elect spirits of each age, the critical and cultured spirits, will grow less and less interested in actual life, and will seek to gain their impressions almost entirely from what Art has touched. For Life is terribly deficient in form."[30]

One of Wilde's most interesting paradoxes allows for a relationship between art and nature but reverses their usual order of precedence, saying that, if the truth of the matter is properly understood, it is obvious that nature does her fumbling best to imitate art. The Impressionists created "those wonderful brown fogs that come creeping down our streets"; Rossetti and Swinburne have made "the long throat, the strange square-cut jaw, the loosened shadowy hair" common attributes in women;[31] that is to say, the artist by making us aware of objects, brings them into existence for us. Along with this rather simple psychological point, however, goes a more mysterious interpretation of art's function:

The Greeks, with their quick artistic instinct, understood this [art's influence on life], and set in the bride's chamber the statue of Hermes or Apollo, that she might bear children as lovely as the work of art she looked at in her rapture or her pain. They knew that Life gains from Art not merely spirituality, depth of thought and feeling, soul-turmoil or soul-peace, but that she can form herself on the very lines and colours of art, and can reproduce the dignity of Pheidias as well as the grace of Praxiteles.[32]

Yeats read that sentence while "The Decay of Lying" was still on galley sheets,[33] and although he may also have found the doctrine elsewhere, especially in the work of the Symbolists, it is interesting to see it appear, relatively unchanged, even in his very late poems. In "The Statues" he refers to it—and mentions Phidias—in the lines:

when Phidias
Gave women dreams and dreams their looking-glass.[34]

His final poem, "Under Ben Bulben," has this stanza:

> Poet and sculptor, do the work,
> Nor let the modish painter shirk
> What his great forefathers did,
> Bring the soul of man to God.
> Make him fill the cradles right.[35]

Wilde, at least in his character of Lord Henry, would not have liked to see the matter put so strongly. He always insisted on art's inutility; and yet his interest in art as the mirror of the creator's personality led him to give much less importance to form and style than, say, Gautier would have given, even when he seems to be repeating Gautier's ideas. For instance, in a review of George Sand's letters Wilde writes that "art for art's sake is not meant to express the final causes of art but is merely a formula of creation." The review continues: "She [George Sand] thought Flaubert too much preoccupied with the sense of form and makes these excellent observations to him—perhaps her best piece of literary criticism. 'You consider the form as the aim, whereas it is but the effect. Happy expressions are only the outcome of emotion and emotion itself proceeds from a conviction.' "[36] George Woodberry even questioned the real strength of Wilde's feeling for form: "He speaks of form; it seems to me he has more sense of color. He spoke of prose style, but he cared for its iridescence, as in Pater."[37] And it is true that Wilde's interpretation of "art for art's sake" carries none of the overtones of an almost grim dedication to the careful chiselling of a line, the arduous polishing of a phrase. Wilde's doctrine is really "art for the artist's sake": "*A work of art is the unique result of a unique temperament. Its beauty comes from the fact that the author is what he is. It has nothing to do with the fact that other people want what they want.*"[38]

As early as 1882 Wilde's eclectic talent had established a relationship between the ideas of "art for art's sake" and of "self-realization":

For it is not enough that a work of art should conform to the aesthetic demands of its age: there must be also about it, if it is to affect us with any permanent delight, the impress of a distinct individuality, an individuality remote from that of ordinary men.

La personalité, said one of the greatest of modern French critics, voilà ce qui nous sauvera.[39]

Admittedly, Baudelaire had already done much of Wilde's work for him when he established two principles: first that the thought of the artist dominates his model, and second that an artist must work with enormous fidelity to his craft.[40] However, Wilde makes an extremely important change in the theory by linking it with his own interpretation of Pater's impressionism. When Baudelaire writes of an artist's "naïveté"—his ability to express his essential nature—he makes that nature a constant, perhaps the only constant in the artist's work. Wilde, however, like Anthony Beavis in Aldous Huxley's *Eyeless in Gaza*, thought the permanence of personality "a very subtle metaphysical problem";[41] the "chameleon poet" thus has his counterpart in a Wildean "chameleon critic," but just as Wilde reversed the direction of negative capability, bringing all outside experience into himself, so he makes the process of appreciation "the record of one's own soul" and criticism "the only civilized form of autobiography," one which deals with "the spiritual moods and imaginative passions of the mind."[42]

Nevertheless, any change Wilde makes in Baudelaire's theory is the result of a difference in emphasis and not in theory—the outcome of Wilde's tendency to link critic and artist more closely than Baudelaire would have done, for Wilde's impressionism is very closely related to Baudelaire's belief that "la meilleure critique est celle qui est amusante et poétique . . . un beau tableau étant la nature réfléchie par un artiste,—celle qui sera ce tableau réfléchi par un esprit intelligent et sensible. Ainsi, le meilleur compte rendu d'un tableau pourra être un sonnet ou une élégie."[43] Wilde entirely agreed—as had his aesthetic masters Pater, Rossetti, and Swinburne—though when he himself attempted such critical set pieces (as he did, for instance, when describing *A Rebours* in *The Picture of Dorian Gray*), he was not really successful at all: his very self-consciousness, his desire to do a piece of "fine writing" came between the art work and his "esprit intelligent et sensible." When he reached for less, as he did in the essays of *Intentions,* he achieved more real insight, and if he was not poetic, he was very amusing. Moreover, he was, willy-nilly, instructive; his two sentences on Wordsworth are the equal of several paragraphs on the "egotistical sublime": "Wordsworth went to the lakes but he was never a lake poet. He found in stones the sermons he had already hidden there."[44]

Of the names which have appeared so far as influences upon Wilde, only one might cause a slight start of surprise—Matthew Arnold—and yet he is, one might say, the guest of honor in Wilde's criticism. In "The Critic as Artist" Wilde (or rather, Gilbert, the Wildean character in the dialogue) speaks of Arnold as one "whose gracious memory we all revere" but adds that Arnold's definition of the aim of criticism—"to see the object as in itself it really is"—is "a very serious error, and takes no cognizance of Criticism's most perfect form, which is in its essence purely subjective, and seeks to reveal its own secret and not the secret of another."[45] But although Wilde and Arnold may begin by describing their ideal critic in opposite terms, their concepts of his role within society are surprisingly similar. Wilde's individualist critic, like Arnold's man of culture, is not active but contemplative. He is devoted to the principle of beauty, just as the Arnoldian perfect man is devoted to "sweetness and light," and as a result of his disciplined devotion he has a similar order, harmony, and breadth of mind: "The true critic will, indeed, always be sincere in his devotion to the principle of beauty, but he will seek for beauty in every age and in each school, and will never suffer himself to be limited to any settled custom of thought, or stereotyped mode of looking at things."[46] Wilde, like Arnold, must defend the contemplative vision of the individualist's "good life" from those who would charge that in remaining aloof from all philanthropic and humanitarian activity, in refusing to be socially useful, the critic is not only unsocial but anti-social. He makes a very telling point: philanthropic activity, if carried on unthinkingly, only serves to increase social injustice because it glosses over and sentimentalizes but does not eradicate social evil:

The proper aim is to try to reconstruct society on such a basis that poverty will be impossible. And the altruistic virtues have really prevented the carrying out of this aim. Just as the worst slave-owners were those who were kind to their slaves, and so prevented the horror of the system being realized by those who suffered from it, and understood by those who contemplated it, so, in the present state of things in England, the people who do most harm are the people who try to do most good.[47]

Summing up the world in a phrase, Wilde concludes: "There is also this to be said: It is immoral to use private property in order to alleviate the horrible evils that result from the institution of private property. It is both immoral and unfair." Philanthropic endeavor is individually as well as socially harmful in Wilde's opinion: its necessary activity and emotion have the bad effect of beclouding what might otherwise have been a clear mind: "The sure way of knowing nothing about life is to try to make oneself useful."[48]

Gilbert says, "But perhaps you think that in beholding for the mere joy of beholding, and contemplating for the sake of contemplation, there is something that is egotistic. If you think so, do not say so."[49] And Wilde's analysis, through Gilbert, has been so intelligent that the reader, like Ernest, is silent—but is he convinced? The difficulty is that Wilde, when he writes of the good life for the individual and for society, is writing in the spirit of Lord Henry Wotton: that is to say, his intellectual understanding of society's problems carries with it no desire "to make reason and the will of God prevail." Sometimes one senses even in the Arnold of *Culture and Anarchy* a latent wish to remove himself from society, a latent fear of Victorian society's violent growth and change: Wilde makes both the wish and the fear overt by transforming the Arnoldian man of culture into a Baudelairean dandy: "Calm and self-centered and complete, the aesthetic critic contemplates life, and no arrow drawn at a venture can pierce between the joints of his harness. He at least is safe, he has discovered how to live."[50] The dark side of that statement finds its expression in Lord Henry's comment: "I can sympathize with everything except suffering . . . . It is too ugly, too horrible, too distressing. There is something terribly morbid in the modern sympathy with pain" (pp. 47–48).

To the Romantics' sense of isolation from society and Arnold's distrust of "the masses," Wilde added the contempt of Gautier and of Baudelaire for "la marée montante de la démocratie" which is one of the most important elements in both *Dandyisme* and Parnassianism.[51] Or, it would be more truthful to say, Wilde seems at times to have wished that he could be capable of a dandy's lofty contempt. Time and again, however, his desire to win approval, his extraordinary dependence on the good opinion of the whole society, shows through the mask of Lord Henry. When he writes privately, as in this note to Lord Alfred Douglas, it is obvious: "Please *always* let me see *anything* that appears about myself in the Paris papers—good or bad, but especially the *bad*. It is a matter of vital import to me to know the attitude of the community" (*Letters*, p. 591).

Although Wilde's desire for others' good opinion may seem a "happy fault," no matter how ridiculous it might occasionally make him appear, it is necessary to remember that, in part of his nature at least, he himself regarded it as a terrible weakness; though he could not always preserve the mask of Lord Henry, he would have liked to do so, as he confessed to André Gide: "It is not through excessive individualism that I have sinned. My great mistake, the error I cannot forgive myself, is having, one day, ceased to believe in it in order to listen to others, ceased to believe that I was right to live as I did, doubted myself."[52] Nevertheless a part of Wilde's nature always doubted the "self" of Lord Henry; the spokesman for that part is Basil Hallward.

III *Basil Hallward*

Basil Hallward is, on the surface at least, a much less interesting character than either Lord Henry or Dorian Gray. Yet it is of him that the flamboyant Wilde writes, "Basil Hallward is what I think I am." His comment adds greatly to the significance of Basil's murder, which otherwise has the air of a plot device that is both awkward and ineffective, and it also gives yet another possible explanation for Wilde's decision to remain in England and face trial for homosexuality. It is now almost a tradition for those who write on Wilde to offer an explanation for his refusal to flee the country when flight was still possible: Frank Harris says that Wilde's cowardice made it impossible for him to face a decision, so that, in a lethargy of fear, he stayed; Yeats believes that Wilde showed his greatest courage in remaining and makes his doing so a proof of the theory that Wilde really was a man of action; Hesketh Pearson thinks Wilde's resolution the result of his incurable love of self-dramatization, itself caused by his emotional immaturity; Robert Sherard believes that Wilde was caught in the grip of megalomania.[53] What is interesting about every one of these theories is that each is a reflection of the particular biographer's ordering vision of Wilde's character. And although every one of them might be partially true in the case of a personality as fragmented as Wilde's, none offers the explanation hidden in the character of Basil Hallward: that there was in Wilde an "ordinary man" who felt terrible guilt for the sins of that part of him represented by Dorian Gray and who could never really be convinced, as Lord Henry Wotton was convinced, that sin is merely another form of self-realization.

Conversations between Lord Henry, Basil Hallward, and Dorian Gray become very interesting, then, if one thinks of them as an internal dialogue.[54] First Dorian Gray, the student, the one given over to influences, asks:

> "What do you mean by good, Harry?"
> "To be good is to be in harmony with oneself," he replied, touching the thin stem of his glass with his pale, fine pointed fingers. "Discord is to be forced to be in harmony with others" (p. 93).

Lord Henry continues with an exposition of the philosophy of individualism, and in the course of it makes a telling point: the dandy, by making himself the center of his morality, is at least without illusions. He is not acting from a pretended belief in a code no longer in existence: "Modern morality consists in accepting the standards of one's age. I consider that for any man of culture to accept the standard of his age is a form of the grossest immorality." Lord Henry had adjusted to a world without absolute values by making himself his own absolute. But Basil Hallward still believes in objective absolutes of right and wrong and even gives society the right to punish those who transgress them, not because society really understands either the sin or the sinner but because society's vengeance is the sinner's purification:

> "But surely, if one lives merely for one's self, Harry, one pays a terrible price for doing so?" suggested the painter.
>
> "Yes, we are overcharged for everything nowadays . . . Beautiful sins, like beautiful things, are the privilege of the rich."
>
> "One has to pay in other ways but money."
>
> "What sort of ways, Basil?"
>
> "Oh! I should fancy in remorse, in suffering, in . . . well, in the consciousness of degradation" (p. 94).

There is another conversation which gives the impression of interior dialogue: it is held between Basil Hallward and Dorian Gray not long before Basil's murder: " 'I owe a great deal to Harry, Basil,' he [Dorian Gray] said at last—'More than I owe to you. You only taught me to be vain.' 'Well, I am punished for that Dorian—or shall be some day'" (p. 131). And later Dorian says: "I am changed, but you must always be my friend. Of course, I am very fond of Harry. But I know you are better than he is. You are not stronger—you are too much afraid of life—but you are better" (p. 133). Basil seems weaker than Lord Henry only because his conscience makes him vulnerable as Lord Henry is not.

Still another point is illuminated by thinking of Hallward as a reflection of Wilde. The sins with which Dorian Gray experiments are left vague, though the suggestion that homosexuality is the chief of them is clear enough, and Lord Henry talks much about self-realization through sin but never seems to commit any (with the single, but terrible, exception of Hawthorne's unforgivable sin[55]): as the book was originally written, however, it is Basil who openly confesses to homosexuality and regards it as a sin that he must expiate. At the suggestion of Walter Pater, the whole passage was much toned down in the book's final version, with the result that Basil's central explanation falls a little flat; he explains only the obvious. In the earlier version, this was not so; Basil there says to Dorian Gray:

> It is quite true that I have worshipped you with far more romance of feeling than a man usually gives to a friend. Somehow, I have never

loved a woman. I suppose I never had time. Perhaps, as Harry says, a really "grande passion" is the privilege of those who have nothing to do, and that is the use of the idle classes in a country. Well, from the moment I met you, your personality had the most extraordinary influence over me. I quite admit that I adored you madly, extravagantly, absurdly. I was jealous of every man to whom you spoke. I wanted to have you all to myself. I was only happy when I was with you. When I was away from you, you were still present in my art. It was all very wrong and foolish. It is all wrong and foolish still.[56]

André Gide is of the opinion that, although Wilde always "insisted on the mask" in his work, yet "always he managed in such a way that the informed reader could raise the mask and glimpse, under it, the true visage (which Wilde had such good reasons to hide)."[57] His description of a reading of Wilde's work is unfortunate, however, if not unfair; it creates such an ugly picture of the knowing, rather prurient reader who, with an insinuating leer, can enjoy a special peep show of the soul—whereas in actuality, Wilde is like an elegant Ancient Mariner who fixes his readers with a glittering eye and demands that they hear his confession over and over again.

Gide's interpretation of the reasons behind Wilde's use of the mask is also open to question. In his opinion "this artistic hypocrisy was imposed on him by respect, which was very keen in him, for the proprieties, and by the need of self-protection."[58] Gide does not take into account the possibility that Wilde's respect for propriety may have had its basis in a respect for morality. Wilde can repeat as much as he pleases that "the artistic critic, like the mystic, is an antinomian always";[59] he remained in his heart a Manichean, nonetheless. His Manicheanism sometimes turns up unexpectedly, in fact, to contradict points he has carefully made about the complete separation between aesthetics and ethics; for example, it does so in his letter to the *St. James Gazette* about *Dorian Gray*. In defending his book he describes the sin committed by each of the main characters and the inevitable punishment it brings. He concludes: "Yes, there is a terrible moral in *Dorian Gray*—a moral which the prurient will not be able to find in it, but it will be revealed to all those whose minds are healthy." Then, catching himself up in the realization that all this talk of morality is beneath his dignity as an artist, he adds: "Is this an artistic error? I fear it is. It is the only error in the book."[60]

The stories told in *The House of Pomegranates* offer further evidence that Wilde was disturbed by a sense of guilt which he attempted to soothe by this partial, hidden confession. Each one of the stories, except "The Birthday of the Infanta," tells of a sin and a resulting fragmentation of personality, of repentance and ultimate healing—though sometimes the last is won only by death. The only mask Wilde uses in telling these stories is that of the style itself: it is a mingling of the ornate "jewelled" style (a mixture of Swinburne, perhaps, and Gautier) which he often uses in *Dorian Gray* and the carefully simple phrasing of Rossetti's *Hand and Soul*, heavily seasoned with the Bible and the *Arabian Nights*.[61] The result is exotic but not really unpalatable, perhaps because, in spite of their artifice, the stories have the quality of parables and carry a genuine human emotion.

"The Young King" describes the dreams by which a young "lover of the beautiful" is made aware of the human suffering necessary to provide him with beautiful robes and jewels; "The Star Child" concerns the long repentance of a beautiful child who in his pride repudiated his mother. But the most interesting of these tales is "The Fisherman and his Soul," which tells of a young fisherman's love for a mermaid. She promises to carry him with her to the caverns of the sea if he first will separate himself from his soul. The fisherman goes to the priest for help in sending his soul away and explains the reason, concluding:

"And as for my soul, what doth my soul profit me, if it stand between me and the thing I love?"

"The love of the body is vile," cried the Priest, knitting his brows, "and vile and evil are the pagan things God suffers to wander through His world. Accursed be the Fauns of the woodland, and accursed be the singers of the sea!"[62]

The fisherman finally gets his wish in spite of the priest, though he must use the powers of black magic to do it. He cuts off his soul and sends it away, refusing it the heart it pleads for; then he dives into the sea. Each year the soul attempts to lure him away from his mermaid, once with the promise of wisdom, next with the promise of wealth; each time the fisherman refuses, saying that love is stronger than either, but at the last temptation, which is really only that of physical desire—the promise that he shall see the white feet of a dancer nearby—the fisherman leaves the sea. Then he discovers not only that he cannot return but that his soul, which is heartless, leads him into acts of evil: violence, robbery, and finally murder.

Repentant and horrified, the fisherman binds himself so that his soul may not influence him further and returns to the shore (though always dogged by his soul) to search for the mermaid. Only after her death does he find her; at the sight of her body his heart breaks, and his soul, now purified, can again be united with him. The story has a coda: the priest's vision of the world is changed by the discovery of flowers growing from the grave in which the mermaid and the fisherman are buried:

And in the morning, while it was still dawn, he went forth with the monks and the musicians, and the candle-bearers and the swingers of censers, and a great company, and came to the shore of the sea, and blessed the sea, and all the wild things that are in it. The Fauns also he blessed, and the little things that dance in the woodland, and the bright-eyed things that peer through the leaves. All the things in God's world he blessed, and the people were filled with joy and wonder.[63]

Both Basil Hallward and Lord Henry Wotton have as their ideal the union of heart, soul, and body that "The Fisherman and his Soul" describes. Lord Henry believes that he has found the secret in his new hedonism: "to cure the soul by means of the senses, and the senses by means of the soul" (p. 25), but Basil, while he too says, "The harmony of soul and body—how much that is!" (p. 12) does not feel that such a harmony can be achieved by going against conscience. It is on the question of conscience that he and Lord Henry disagree: " 'Conscience and cowardice are really the same thing, Basil. Conscience is the trade-name of the firm. That is all.' 'I don't believe that, Harry, and I don't believe you do either' " (p. 8). The conflict in Basil between his conscience and his love for Dorian Gray is not resolved intellectually at all, though it finds an emotional resolution in his death. Through the more complex character of Sir Robert Chiltern, however, Wilde continues the discussion, the weighing and considering of the validity of conscience.

Sir Robert is the protagonist of Wilde's play, *An Ideal Husband*.[64] When the play opens Sir Robert is presented as a wealthy and very successful, highly respected undersecretary for foreign affairs. The mask he attempts to wear—and until the opening of the play he has been successful—is nothing less than perfection: he appears to be an incorruptible servant of the state, a supremely happily married man, an omniscient financier. However impossible it is to relate the mask to reality (and one of Wilde's points is that it is indeed impossible), the wearing of it proves how conventional Sir Robert is, how much he is bound by the code of society. Very early in the play Mrs. Chevely, an intelligent woman even though the villainess, points out society's hypocrisy:

In old days nobody pretended to be a bit better than his neighbours. In fact to be a bit better than one's neighbour was considered excessively vulgar and middle class. Nowadays, with our modern mania for morality, every one has to pose as a paragon of purity, incorruptibility, and all the other seven deadly virtues—and what is the result? You all go over like ninepins. . . . Not a year passes in England without somebody disappearing. Scandals used to lend charm, or at least interest, to a man—now they crush him.[65]

The whole play turns on Sir Robert's fear of unmasking, his imaginative picturing of "the loathsome joy" with which the newspapers would describe his fall and of the hypocritical dismay which would be expressed by his colleagues who "every day do something of the kind themselves. Men who, each one of them have worse secrets in their own lives" (p. 76). The secret of Sir Robert's life is that at the beginning of his career he had given state information to a Baron Arnheim about the British Government's intention to buy Suez Canal shares; on the strength of that knowledge the Baron had brought into the company when its stock was still very low and had made a fortune; in "gratitude" he gave Sir Robert £110,000.

Sir Robert is described in the stage directions as a man whose very features suggest "an almost complete separation of passion and intellect, as though thought and emotion were each isolated in its own sphere through some violence of will-power" (p. 11). The division becomes clear in his attitude toward the swindle: one side of his nature thinks it perfectly justifiable—more than that, courageous. He describes Baron Arnheim, who rather resembles Lord Henry Wotton and has "a strange smile on his pale, curved lips,"[66] as a man of splendid intellect, and he holds, with the Baron, that to wield power is the one pleasure of which one never tires. When his friend Lord Goring says that he was weak in yielding to Baron Arnheim's temptation, Sir Robert is almost indignant: "Weak? Do you really think, Arthur, that it is weakness that yields to temptation? I tell you that there are terrible temptations that it requires strength, strength and courage to yield to. To stake all one's life on a single moment, to risk everything on one throw, whether the stake be power or pleasure, I care not—there is no weakness in that. There is a horrible, a terrible courage" (pp. 82–83). When Lord Goring only answers that he is sorry for him, Sir Robert says immediately, "I don't say that I suffered any remorse. I didn't. Not remorse in the ordinary, rather silly sense of the word." Nevertheless, the remorse he goes on to describe bears all the characteristics of the ordinary variety, including the uselessness—silliness, one might say—of remorse without repentance: "But I have paid conscience money many times. I had a wild hope that I might disarm destiny. The sum Baron Arnheim gave me I have distributed twice over in public charities since then." (Lord Goring, speaking as one part of Wilde to another, cannot let that pass: "In public charities? Dear me, what a lot of harm you must have done, Robert!" [p. 85].) And later the purely emotional side of Sir Robert cries out, "I would to God that I had been able to tell the truth . . . to live the truth. Ah! that is the great thing in life, to live the truth" (p. 96).

Through the good offices of Lord Goring, who, like the Scarlet Pimpernel, is a dandy with a heart, Sir Robert is finally able to tell the truth, at least to his wife, and to win forgiveness; at the same time he preserves and even increases his position in the world. All this is done, though, in such a whirl of attempted blackmail, intercepted letters, and mutual misunderstandings and reassurances that the central conflict in the principal character is left unresolved—or rather, its resolution is practical, not psychological. Lord Goring is able to convince the puritanical Lady Chiltern that "life cannot be understood without much charity" (p. 101), and he says of Sir Robert: "What you know about him is not his real character. It is an act of folly done in his youth, dishonourable, I admit, shameful, I admit, unworthy of him, I admit, and therefore . . . not his real character" (p. 177). Even granted that this is so, there is nothing in the play to suggest that Sir Robert himself comes to know his own "real character," or that there is any final union between his intellectual amorality and his emotional sense of sin. By the end of the play the relation of the mask to the reality is as great a mystery as ever.

Indeed, *The Importance of Being Earnest* is the only one of Wilde's successful plays in which mask and reality prove to be one; it is possible to think of it (as it is of Mark Twain's *The Adventures of Huckleberry Finn*) as the author's evocation of a never-never land in which the individual, though part of society, is in his essence free of its rule.[67] In their self-centeredness Jack Worthing and Algernon Moncrieff have mastered life; they live remote from any real evil, any scarring emotion, any intellectual problem. But they can only do so in a world specially patterned for them and by them: one in which a broken engagement or a buttered muffin is of equal moment because all the members of it know both engagement and muffin to be at once all-important and unimportant. This knowledge gives all the freedom that life on the Mississippi gave to Huck.

The Importance of Being Earnest has one sort of sincerity; "The Ballad of Reading Gaol" has another. Certainly the poem has any number of artistic faults: it is repetitive, has abrupt and unnecessary changes of style and imagery, and moves equally abruptly from realism to melodrama. Yet in spite of all this the poem works because the emotion behind it is a genuine, not a constructed one, and because in the writing of it Wilde seems more conscious of the situation than of himself describing the situation. The letters Wilde sent to Robert Ross while he was writing the "Ballad" make a delightful collection, because in them too Wilde seems almost self-forgetful. Moreover, his tone is that of a genuine artist-critic: he gives his achievement its proper value. Once he writes whimsically, "I think bits of the poem very good now—but I will never again out-Kipling Henley" (*Letters,* p. 649). He is amusing again when he insists on putting in a few melodramatic stanzas in the style he enjoyed:

I have just sent Smithers four more stanzas for insertion—one of them very good, in the romantic vein you don't quite approve of; but on the whole it will, I think, make a balance in the poem. I can't be always "banging the tins." Here it is:

> It is sweet to dance to violins
> When Life and Love are fair:
> To dance to flutes, to dance to lutes,
> Is delicate and rare:
> But it is not sweet with nimble feet
> To dance upon the air.

On the whole, I like the poem now, except the second and third stanzas of Part III. I can't get that part right (*Letters,* pp. 652–53).[68]

"The Ballad of Reading Gaol" also has a significance beyond itself as the last communication, so to speak, between Wilde and the world outside him, before he became completely enclosed in the prison of himself. While he was still in Reading, Wilde wrote to Robert Ross: "Of course from one point of view I know that I shall be merely passing from one prison to another, and there are times when the whole world seems to me no larger than my cell and as full of terrors for me. Still I believe that at the beginning God made a world for each separate man, and in that world which is within us we should seek to live" (*Letters,* p. 512). When he was released from one prison and found himself indeed in another, he struggled for escape and failed. Then he fell back without hope, resigned to living in "that world which is within us," the world of Walter Pater's "Conclusion" to *The Renaissance,* which now, however, bore a great resemblance to Reading Gaol, where there are "crowds of people, walking round in a ring": "I must reconsider my position as I cannot go on living here as I am doing, though I know there is no such thing as changing one's life—one merely wanders round and round within the circle of one's own personality" *(Letters,* p. 671).

Wilde took the name "Sebastian Melmoth" when he left prison, the first name after the martyred Saint Sebastian, whom Wilde had once identified with Keats: "Fair as Sebastian, and as early slain,"[69] and the second after Melmoth, the outcast of Maturin's novel, doomed to wander eternally through the world. Thus the name itself is a sort of analogue for the title of Yeats' story, "The Crucifixion of the Outcast"; at their last meeting, just before his downfall, Wilde told Yeats that the story was "sublime, wonderful, wonderful."[70] Wilde took a family pride in the fact that Charles Maturin was his great-great-uncle[71]—and indeed the terrible, living portrait of Melmoth may have been in Wilde's mind when he wrote *Dorian Gray*—but in his choice of the name Melmoth he was undoubtedly influenced as well by Baudelaire's comments on "la grande création satanique du reverend Maturin": "Il [Melmoth's laughter] est, qu'on me comprenne bien, la résultante nécessaire de sa double nature contradictoire, qui est infiniment grande relativement à l'homme, infiniment vile et basse relativement au Vrai et au Juste absolus. Melmoth est une contradiction vivante."[72] And although it suited Wilde's melodramatic nature to wrap himself in the great cloak of such a name, playing the part of a "last Romantic," still there is this justice in his using it: his too was a nature of contradictions from which he could find no escape, and in which he finally walked solitary, utterly isolated.

With the intelligence to understand all the conflicts of his age, yet without the ability or the will to resolve them, Wilde was finally broken by them. Arnold had made Empedocles complain because the mirror of his soul caught only glimpses of reality, but at least the mirror itself was whole; in Wilde it was as if the glass were shattered and he set dancing and posturing before its pieces like the dwarf in his own story, "The Birthday of the Infanta"—seeing himself as an aesthete, a member of the Oxford Movement, an artist like Balzac wrapped in a white gown, a disciple of Renan, an aristocratic dandy. All these were, he believed, ways of expressing himself, of multiplying his personality, and all the time his real personality remained as much a puzzle to

him as it was to those who described him. The bewilderment that
one senses beneath all the posing, and the strange quality that
could only be called sincerity—or at least the desire to be sincere,
could he only find a basis for sincerity—these and his very real
humor give Wilde charm almost in spite of himself. Even George
Woodberry, who saw through all the poses, said of him: "I have
seen no one whose charm stole on me so secretly, so rapidly, and
with such entire sweetness. His poems are better than his theories,
and he better than his poems."[73] His charm would not have to be
very impressive to be better than his poems, it is true; however,
Woodberry's statement might be made broad enough to include
all of Wilde's works. His writings, like the costume of a court
jester, were a fantastic patchwork of other men's ideas in which
he walked proudly as a king, thinking himself splendidly attired.
And, like a court jester, he made it his business to amuse his age
—by his wit, if possible; by his antics, if necessary. But it may
well be that at times he caught sight of himself in his own shattered mirror and stopped short.

Vicisti et vivimus—conquered
yet alive—is our motto—from an old legend of the
Scottish border where we were a clan of
Johnstones—I like it, for it means
so much in different ways.
Lionel Johnson

Chapter V

Lionel Johnson

During Wilde's first trial, Lionel Johnson wrote Yeats a letter in which he denounced Wilde for his "cold scientific intellect" and for the triumphant pleasure he took "at every dinner-table he dominated, from the knowledge that he was guilty of that sin which, more than any other possible to man, would turn all those people against him if they but knew."[1] Yeats was saddened to find that Johnson had "changed with the rest," and yet, given the differences between his temperament and Wilde's, Johnson's lack of sympathy is hardly surprising. Wilde became so intent on the images of himself presented to the world that he lost the sense of his "true self"—and it is interesting that Johnson places him imaginatively thus, putting on a performance evening after evening. Johnson, on the other hand, cut himself off so effectively from all contact with society that by the end of his short life he was completely alone. Wilde's personality seems best described

by one of his favorite words, "many coloured"; the world in which
Johnson lived, spiritually and physically, was gray, relieved only
by gold, the color he associated with fantasy. In a room which
had curtains of gray corduroy hung over the doors, the windows,
and the bookcases, Johnson slept all day and read during the
night. Yeats asked him whether his schedule did not separate
him from men and women; he replied, "In my library I have all
the knowledge of the world I need."[2]

His answer was confident enough to silence Yeats, but a short
story by Johnson called "Incurable" shows that he himself had
doubts about his relationship with society. On the surface the
sketch pokes fun at aestheticism by describing a young poet who
feels that life holds no more for him. He decides to commit
suicide, regretting only that the river most convenient for his
purpose is waterlily-less. But even without waterlilies he finds it
possible to imagine himself floating down, like a male Lady
of Shalott (in Elizabethan costume), to a heartless and unthinking
London. In the midst of this reverie he falls absent-mindedly into
the river, comes to himself, and swims strongly for shore.

Underneath its satire, the story has a personal quality, a note
of both self-mockery and self-pity. In one passage, for instance,
the poet thinks of his present state: "I am just thirty [Johnson's
age at time of publication] . . . and quite useless. I have a good
education and a little money. I must do something and poetry is
what I want to do. I have published three volumes, and they are
entirely futile. They are not even bad enough to be interesting."
He riffles impatiently through his verses and comes back to the
problem: "And why can't I write better? I know what imagination
is and poetry, and all the rest of it. I go on contemplating my own
emotions, or inventing them; and nothing comes of it but this.
And yet I'm not a perfect fool." Yet no matter how frustrated he
is by his self-enclosure, the poet cannot free himself by taking
part in the concerns of the busy commercial empire which under-
lay Victorian society—he turns away from that: "He would be of
no use: if he went out to the colonies, or upon the stock exchange, he would continue to write quantities of average and
uninteresting verse."[3] Does it not seem possible that this internal
conversation was familiar to Johnson because he had been

speaker and listener in many similar ones?

He was himself from a typical Victorian family, one involved with the fortunes of England, whose men traditionally became officers in the army. Johnson's father was a retired captain; his three brothers were officers who served faithfully in the colonies. But even as a schoolboy Johnson was detached, cut off from any family bonds. The letters he wrote in his last years at Winchester— 1883–1885—invariably refer to his family as "Philistine," and when Lord Francis Russell planned to visit him at home, Johnson wrote to J. H. Badley: "A. [Francis Russell] comes to us on the second for a few days: which will be a break in the monotony of spiritual solitude."[4] Later he described the visit to Charles Sayle: "A. [Russell] is with us tasting the quality of Philistia: he rather seems to endure it, and reproaches me with intentional cruelty towards my people—a strange side of the matter."[5] Remarks like these are not at all extraordinary in the correspondence of an adolescent, especially of a very consciously "intellectual" one; as Johnson became less consciously and more truly intellectual, one would expect him in the ordinary course of things to accept his family and his place within it, just because he could accept the many inevitable separations between its ideas and his own. But that was not the pattern of Johnson's development. He may, very occasionally, make a reference that shows some family pride: when reviewing *Barrack-Room Ballads* he writes a little scornfully of those critics who complain of difficulty in reading technical army phrases—"Such criticism is of a piece with the prevailing apathy and ignorance concerning the army"[6]—but with time he turned more and more completely away from his family. By the end of his life, he was living on a pension given him by his mother, but he had no personal connection with his family whatever.

Connected with Johnson's withdrawal from his family's worldly concerns was his rejection of the family form of worship; with his parents' devout, "middle" Anglicanism he had very little patience and wrote to Russell after the latter's visit: "As you see faith in my family is a large element of belief: my father with his 'omnipotent,' my mother with her Churchism—see what faith is. I feel rather bitter in temper, as though selfishness was really more strong than love: it never is. But I seem lonely."[7] The *Winchester Letters* begin with a correspondence between Russell and Johnson in which they both consider Buddhism as a possible substitute for the more Philistine religions; after they read Sinnett's *Esoteric Buddhism,* Johnson publicly announced his conversion. His father replied by forbidding him to write to Russell or to read Buddhist literature,[8] a reaction that seems, indeed, a little pompous as well as unwise, but without doubt it was unthinkable to his parents that Johnson should not follow perfectly naturally in the faith of his fathers. At any rate, Johnson moved very quickly from Buddhism into Shelleyan Platonism, Emersonian Transcendentalism, Whitmanesque Humanism—what you will. Yet the confusion is not as great as it might seem, for all the masters Johnson acknowledges are those whose mental set is towards the transcendental. Just as Yeats would listen respectfully to any doctrine which might help in the overthrow of "Carolus Duran, Bastien-Lepage, Huxley and Tyndall,"[9] so Johnson writes: "Eschew altogether the miserable affectations of Schopenhauer, Hartmann, Comte; hate all systems of that nature: but love the great idealists, Kant, Schelling, Fichte, Emerson."[10]

Johnson's reading was enormously important to him not only as a schoolboy but throughout his life because, having turned away from his family and the social order it embodied and having, therefore, refused the identity which any role in society might offer, he worked at the creation of a self through identification with those authors who attracted him. He searched his library for fragments to shore against his ruin. For Johnson would have been one of those agreeing with Yeats when the latter wrote in 1897: "In our time we are agreed that we 'make our souls' out of some of the great poets of ancient times, or out of Shelley, or Wordsworth, or Goethe, or Balzac, or Count Tolstoy . . . or out of Mr. Whistler's pictures."[11]

When Santayana first visited Johnson in the latter's room at Oxford, he noticed—indeed he could scarcely help noticing—a secular shrine on a center table. A jug of Glengarry whiskey stood between two open books: *Les Fleurs du Mal* and *Leaves of Grass;* looking down upon them were portraits of Cardinal Newman and Cardinal Wiseman.[12] These arrangements have the quality of a still life, an exquisitely careful and conscious patterning of elements with a perhaps unconscious desire behind it to show that the life might disintegrate were the pattern to be disturbed. The element of conscious affectation, however, is not nearly so important as the fact that the two books have an air of holiness, as if two Massbooks were open at once upon an altar. Johnson chooses his influences, one might say, excluding all thinkers of the materialistic sort, and, having done so he thinks of the poets, essayists, or philosophers whom he admires as possible guides to his life. The feeling behind his reading of them often resembles the one he described in his cousin when he wrote to Badley: "Can you tell me where I can get a portrait of him [Shelley], not unworthy of his name. I have hunted all London, and can't light upon what I want. It is for a cousin who almost literally prays to Shelley, having lost all her other gods." [13]

The *Winchester Letters* begin with a series in which, along with their common study of Buddhism, Johnson is encouraging and directing Russell in the latter's "first plunge into the turbid waters of Browning." [14] Browning had the great admiration of all the members of the aesthetic movement, beginning with Rossetti. His introspectiveness and his fascination with the macabre were among the qualities which most appealed to Rossetti, [15] but Johnson revered Browning as a philosopher-poet: "Do read Browning; I feel much more cheerful about things in general when I read him. Read in the volume you are reading, 'Saul,' 'The Guardian Angel,' 'Two in the Campagna,' 'Old Pictures in Florence,' and, above all, 'Evelyn Hope.' " [16] Browning's influence had less effect on Johnson's thought as the latter grew older; there are not the references to him in Johnson's poetry or criticism which would give him a place equal to those men who most formed his mind: Newman, Arnold, and Pater. Nevertheless, in a review of Stevenson's *The Wrecker*, Johnson quotes from Browning, giving the impression as he does so that Browning has captured half the human experience. Comparing Stevenson and Pater, Johnson says:

The one [Pater] is more meditative, more learned, more gentle than the other; but both are men who feel the pathos, the heroism, the living significance of things—Virgil's "sense of tears in mortal things" and Browning's:

> "How good is man's life, the mere living!
> how fit to employ
> All the heart and the soul and the senses
> forever in joy!"[17]

The coupling of these quotations from Virgil and Browning is illumined by a further sentence: "The world [to Stevenson] is a pageant of vices and of virtues, to be endured by all means, to be enjoyed if may be." Thus in the end both the tears and the joy become only "literature," both seen from a distance, both meaningless save as they form a pattern in the mind of the beholder.

This is a vision of life very much like Pater's, and indeed Pater was one of the strongest influences on Johnson's thought. The high praise that Johnson gives Pater, higher than that given to Stevenson, is echoed time and again elsewhere in Johnson's criticism: it is Johnson's opinion that Pater's scholarship, taste, and prose style made him the final authority and arbiter of critical taste for his time. Even before he went to Oxford Johnson had read Pater's work; he read *Marius the Epicurean* in 1885 and wrote to Russell praising it ecstatically as "a book to love and worship." At that time he obviously read it, as so many others did, as if it were a repetition, not a development, of the ideas in *The Renaissance,* for his letter to Russell continues in *The Renaissance* manner:

I simply hate the days flying past so speedily. When the endless region of faith and doubt is once entered, life becomes weary of itself: and to remain without that land, contented with the colours of a rainbow and a curtain, the sound of a storm and a sonata, appears the higher, more dignified way. But life is very difficult always and every-way. And this philosophy or want of it is catholic: it allows me to delight in the irreverent cleverness of Orange and the boisterous in-difference of—my brother.[18]

Certainly it is true that Johnson consciously changed his opinion on the higher dignity of watching all life with great but uncommitted interest. In *The Art of Thomas Hardy* he writes of the danger in "vague and dreamy thought" to the man of wide culture, deep knowledge, broad reading. For this man there arises the possibility of thinking that "nothing, not truth itself is at stay"; he may become fascinated by "'the flowing philosophers,' to whom life is a drifting and a change; the votaries of aesthetics to whom it is a pageant."[19] His tone is disapproving, but his recognition of the danger and his description of the particular kind of man for whom the danger exists might be taken as signs that he had himself experienced the temptation to view life this way—had perhaps succumbed to the temptation. Yeats, after all, said of Johnson that "it often seemed as if he played at life, as if it were an elaborate ritual that would soon be over."[20] Granted the validity, then, of John Pick's argument that Johnson was a much truer disciple of Pater than Wilde was, is it not still possible that Johnson shared Pater's fear that life might indeed be meaningless—though the human mind, to preserve itself, must give life meaning, surrounding it with "elaborate ritual"? And given this interpretation, is it not also possible that Pater's insistence upon *ascesis* may be more melancholy than Pick suggests, not an ordering which is directed to a goal outside itself, but a rigorous care about and insistence upon the details of life so that one may somehow get through the days without madness?

Yet it was Newman's thought, not Pater's, that Johnson really wanted to share, Newman's pattern that he wished to impose upon experience. His effort could only be superficially successful, for in Newman's faith the pattern of the universe is not imposed but revealed; its reality is objective, its order directed toward a definite goal. But Johnson tried at least to make his mind and heart one with Newman's, saying that he knew the thirty-six volumes of Newman's writings better than any other works in literature; more than that, he held Newman's work to be a refuge from modern philosophies of doubt, the sense of futility which they give to life, the "sick and morbid" beauty which they cause in literature. To an age suffering from these ills, Newman "sets forth a solution and a cure."[21]

When Johnson wrote about Matthew Arnold, the third of his major influences, he described an attitude, a quality in him which he found common to all three and took from all three in "making his soul":

Paradoxical as it may sound, there is something very hieratic about Arnold: his apprehension of the beauty of holiness, his love for what is clear and lofty in the pleasures of thought, his constant service of meditation. . . . The false worship of words, the conventional acceptance of phrases, all the spurious wisdom in the world he fought against, and conquered much of it; and there is no one left to take his place in the struggle against vulgarity and imposture: no voice like his to sing as he sang of calm and peace among the turbulent sounds of modern life.[22]

This description of Arnold closely resembles Johnson's lines on Walter Pater:

> Patient beneath his Oxford trees and towers
> He still is gently ours:
> Hierarch of the spirit, pure and strong.[23]

Arnold went out from his books into the midst of the "vulgarity and imposture" against which he struggled. But Johnson found in his work a very different attitude: a lofty, almost contemptuous retreat before a vulgarity that had, in Johnson's opinion, already conquered. *Vicisti et vivimus* was the motto of his family, one that Johnson thought peculiarly appropriate to himself,[24] and so it was, for among the essential qualities in his character were a sense of defeated aristocracy and a contempt far more genuine than Wilde's for the world around him. It was this aristocratic remoteness, this dandyism, in Johnson that most deeply impressed Yeats; it is also the characteristic which Yeats most often associates with all "the tragic generation" who liked to murmur, "as for living—our servants will do that for us."

Johnson's sense of aristocracy was based not on family but on learning, an aristocracy of culture. On the very simplest level his attitude reveals itself in what Katherine Tynan calls "a little haughtiness towards the men who lacked Latin and Greek."[25] Now Yeats was among those with that unfortunate deficiency, and one has the impression that Johnson's aloof manner at times made Yeats feel gauche and uncomfortable; for instance, Yeats' tendency to seize impetuously upon ideas and work them out, his desire to talk to other Rhymers about the world "as a bundle of fragments," met only with Johnson's freezing silence.[26] For what, in Johnson's mind, was the use of noisy opinions, of ideas which were to be put into action? Ignoring that part of Arnold's theory of culture which reflected a hope for social melioration, Johnson envisioned the man of culture as one who stood aside completely from a world intent on its own destruction, a world not worth saving.

Thus, when he writes of Erasmus, Johnson compares him to Arnold but says as well:

Erasmus was an aristocrat of letters, loving their finer spirit, feeling an impatient irritation at the thought and in the presence of those who had not drunk their wisdom and undergone their discipline. In all matters, scholarly or ecclesiastical, his attitude toward the multitude was: "Lord, what fools these mortals be!" . . . He felt that it was easy to be vehement and intense, so hard to be gracious and urbane.[27]

In a paragraph about Pascal Johnson shows by his quotation of Newman's motto—"cor ad cor loquitur"—that he associates Newman as well as Arnold and Pater with a tradition of aristocratic temper, almost of hauteur:

A lover of superiorities, he [Pascal] has pity for their opposites, but mere contempt for the meagre and the middling . . . . France has no writer, certainly no lay writer who resembles him in his superb austerity: *"on mourra seul,"* he said, and in truth he both was and is a man of isolation, dwelling apart. . . . He is one of the voices which at rare intervals come from the heart of a man, and go to the hearts of men: *cor ad cor loquitur,* and deep answers deep.[28]

A similar hauteur may have been one of the elements which turned Johnson toward Roman Catholicism. For, as Newman pointed out in "The Second Spring," Catholicism in England was associated with two groups: Irish immigrants, "coming and going at harvest time, or a colony of them lodged in a miserable quarter of the vast metropolis," and a few members of the very good old families, "an elderly person, seen walking in the streets, grave and solitary, and strange, though noble in bearing, and said to be of good family and a 'Roman Catholic.' "[29] Both of these groups were free in Johnson's mind from any connection with Philistia—and indeed, his discovery of Irish ancestry was, in Santayana's opinion, another of Johnson's ways of rejecting the Philistine world.[30]

But besides its connections with aristocrat and peasant and its remoteness from the middle classes, Roman Catholicism may well have had a link in Johnson's mind with intellectual superiority and wideness of culture; at least one sees it allied to both in works as widely different as "Bishop Blougram's Apology" and Harold Frederic's *The Damnation of Theron Ware*. If Johnson read the latter work, he would have found a reflection of his own feelings in its presentation of the Irish priest, Father Forbes, and the Irish (and aristocratic) girl, Celia Madden, as the two people of greatest polish and intellectual culture in an otherwise narrowly provincial, deeply Philistine small town.[31]

While he approves of its cultured flexibility on the one hand, Johnson is also proud of a deliberately outmoded dignity in Catholicism; in fact, a modern Catholic might almost be alarmed by his pleasure in connecting the Church with the old, the out-worn, the cast-off, as it appears in his poem "The Church of a Dream." The poem was written in 1890, only a year before Johnson's conversion to Catholicism, so that its intention, one gathers, was to praise:

> Sadly the dead leaves rustle in the whistling wind,
> Around the weather-worn, gray church, low down the vale:
> The Saints in golden vesture shake before the gale;
>
> .   .   .   .
>
> Still in their golden vesture the old saints prevail;
> Alone with Christ, desolate else, left by mankind.
> Only one ancient Priest offers the Sacrifice,
> Murmuring holy Latin immemorial.[32]

Thus Johnson's acceptance of the Catholic faith, however genuine it may have been, did not really serve as a bond between him and the rest of the world; on the contrary, he made his religion into yet another protective wall. Nevertheless, the very care that Johnson took in using his religion, his culture, even the daily routine of his life, to separate himself from the world argues for the possibility that in his heart he wished for acceptance. His frailty, his short stature, his bookishness, may have set him apart in a family whose men were all expected to be good soldiers, strong believers, and good sports; he, in return, rejected all his

family's values; yet did so with a hidden emotion which suggests
that secretly the values must still have meant a good deal to him.

Lionel Johnson was not a man to take even his closest friends
into his confidence; it must, therefore, be mainly his reading of
Johnson's poetry that makes Yeats say, "much falling he / Brooded
upon sanctity."[33] Yet even those lines, though beautifully succinct
and delicate, especially in their echo of Johnson's "Go from me:
I am one of those, who fall"[34]—the line that Yeats intuitively knows
as the best expression of Johnson's spirit—do not, save for that
echo, state the truth of the matter in all its negation: Johnson
brooded not on sanctity but on sin. His poetry is much more concerned with damnation than with beatitude:

> That hate, and that, and that again,
> Easy and simple are to bear:
> My hatred of myself is pain
> Beyond my tolerable share.
>
> .   .   .   .
>
> Darker than death, fiercer than fire,
> Hatefuller than the heart of Hell:
> I know thee, O mine own desire!
> I know not mine own self so well.[35]

Very often, God seems remote to Johnson, or if He be near, He
comes in vengeance not in love:

> I can die. To quit the light,
> Hide my misery in gloom,
> Well indeed! But in that night,
> At his voice, to meet my doom!
> And Death's Angels, who may fight?[36]

"The Dark Angel" tries to reach a better and more hopeful solution; yet again most of the poem is taken up with terrible internal
conflict of which the resolution is simply imposed by a change
from Manichean to Neoplatonic theology:

> Dark Angel, with thine aching lust!
> Of two defeats, of two despairs:
> Less dread, a change to drifting dust,
> Than thine eternity of cares.

> Do what thou wilt, thou shalt not so,
> Dark Angel! triumph over me:
> *Lonely, unto the Lone I go;*
> *Divine, to the Divinity.*[37]

Johnson does not believe that he will change to drifting dust, although he wishes perhaps that he did, for a complete materialism would offer him escape; he accepts instead the complete spiritualism of Neoplatonic thought because, paradoxically, it offers a similar escape from all personality and with it all sense of sin.

What all these, his central poems, show is that Johnson, who had of his own will turned away from society, found himself separated as well from a sustaining belief in the presence of God. His attitude to life removed him from society, his conscience and his fear of death made him feel very far from God. As a result, he was left in that state of mind which Eliot describes in "The Waste Land." After the Thunder's word "Dhayadhvam" —sympathize—Eliot describes the fate of the man who has not done so:

> I have heard the key
> Turn in the door once and turn once only
> We think of the key, each in his prison
> Thinking of the key, each confirms a prison.[38]

As it happens, Johnson once used that very image in one of his letters to Russell: "You must forgive my silence, if speech pleases better in this hollow prison vault of a world, where we fumble and grope in the dark to find the keys."[39]

From this loneliness, alcohol served as one escape; his books served as another. For although they could not really help him to "find" himself, Johnson discovered that he could lose himself in books. In his library he could forget the society of his own time, forget frustration, bad conscience, failed hopes, forget loneliness— his books made for him "the good place." Indeed Wilde's prophecy that certain elect spirits would in time seek their impressions not from actual life but from art had its fulfillment in Johnson almost as soon as it was made.[40] For Johnson's "moments" were different from those described by Pater, in that they did not arise from immediate, strong sensory impressions: they were moments of sensuous, emotional, and spiritual culmination lived vicariously, at one remove from the experience itself. Other men's moments swept Johnson out of himself: "Take me with you in spirit, Ancients of Art, the crowned, the sceptred, whose voices this night chaunt a *gloria in excelsis,* flooding the soul with a passion of joy and awe."[41]

Books carried Johnson to the past, especially the past of England in the eighteenth century, "the enchanted, the golden, the incomparable age."[42] It is true that he then brought the past back with him into the details of his actual life, modelling his punctuation and even his calligraphy on eighteenth-century style, often modelling his phrasing on that of Samuel Johnson. But all these mannerisms served only as props to continue the dream as long as possible. Johnson did not read of the past in order to achieve a better understanding of the present; he did so to escape the present. In "Oxford Nights," after describing his pleasure in works of the eighteenth century—books read at night while all the rest of Oxford sleeps—Johnson continues:

> Dream, who love dreams! forget all grief:
> Find, in sleep's nothingness, relief:
> Better my dreams! Dear, human books,
> What kindly voices, winning looks!
> Enchaunt me with your spells of art,
> And draw me homeward to your heart:
> Till weariness and things unkind
> Seem but a vain and passing wind.[43]

Even the Rhymers' Club served Johnson as an elaborate daydream. Arthur Symons thought of the Club's meetings as pale and ineffectual imitations of Bohemian gatherings in the Latin Quarter,[44] but to Johnson they were re-enactments of the Friday meetings of Samuel Johnson's Club. If they were subdued and gray re-enactments, so much the better; the mind might then be freer to envisage the past and to enjoy its melancholy difference from the present. Thus in a poem—or rather, in some doggerel verses—on a modern meeting of the Johnson Club, Johnson imagines the pleasure of the evening if Samuel Johnson were present, and then sighs:

> If only it might be! . . . But, long as we may,
> We shall ne'er hear that laughter, *Gargantuan* and gay,
> Go pealing down *Fleet Street* and rolling away.
> In silence we drink to the silent, who rests
> In the warmth of the love of his true lovers' breasts.[45]

Perhaps Johnson's tendency to give the world of his books a greater reality than the world around him is one explanation (though admittedly a surface one, resting upon depths too dark and salt for greater exploration) of Johnson's "imaginary conversations." According to Yeats, Johnson would tell anecdotes of meetings with Newman, Gladstone, or Arnold, always with perfect truth to detail, always consistent with an earlier telling, so that Yeats for a long time believed them to have been actual.[46] And though, in fact, these meetings had not taken place, it is possible that Johnson fell so completely a victim to the "dangerous prevalence of imagination" that he himself also believed them real—just as he came to think of himself as Irish. Fantasy changed into delusion.

Related to Johnson's flight to the literary past is his constant returning to his own youth, not the childhood spent with his family—not even were he to simplify it by dreams would he be part of that world—but his youth at Winchester:

> A place of friends! a place of books!
> A place of good things olden!
> With these delights, the years were golden;
>   And life wore sunny looks.
>   They fled at last:
>   But to the past
>   Am I in all beholden.[47]

The mourning of youth and its recollection as a period without struggle, without consciousness of self within or responsibility without, is a major theme in Johnson's poems:

> Pity thyself! youth flies, youth flies.
> Thou comest to the desert plain
> Where no dreams follow in thy train:
> They leave thee at the pleasaunce close;
> Lonely the haggard pathway goes.
> Thou wilt look back and see them, deep

In the fair glades where thou dost keep
Thy summer court, thy summer sleep:
But thou wilt never see them more.
Till death the golden dreams restore.[48]

And yet, according to the pattern set by Rossetti's artistic isolation and by Pater's cultured retirement in Oxford, a total rejection of life could appear almost noble. Thus when Johnson
describes J. C. Mangan's life as one of "dreams and misery, and
madness, yet of a self-pity which does not disgust us, and of a
weakness which is innocent," when he says that Mangan's was "the
haunted enchanted life of one drifting through his days in other
days and other worlds, golden and immortal,"[49] he intends a high
compliment—the compliment of identification, and the recognition as well that Mangan is living by the code: in artistic terms
he has kept himself unspotted from the world. And Johnson's air
of high lineage may well have come from his interior sense that
he too was doing so: Newman's gentleman, Arnold's man of
culture, Rossetti's true artist, Pater's scholar, Wilde's individualist,
each represents a very different vision of the good life; nevertheless, out of each of them it is possible to extract a single common
element: an isolated pursuit of and pleasure in a beauty which
the mass of men cannot enjoy or even understand, a beauty
caught momentarily in one's own fantasies. Johnson extracted
that element and lived by it to his great unhappiness.

Lord Francis Russell, describing Johnson's influence upon him,
writes: "He taught me a lesson I have never forgotten, and that is
that all the supposedly real things of life, that is to say the
external things, the physical things, the humours, the happenings,
disgraces, successes, failures are in themselves the merest phan-
toms and illusions, and that the only realities are within one's
own mind and spirit."[50] Finding nothing in society which he
could "love or believe in," Johnson turned his gaze upon himself, but that created "a torment of perpetual self-consciousness"
from which he had to escape if he were not to end in "an un-
natural state of mind."[51] His escape was fantasy, and so, paradoxically, the "realities of his own mind and spirit" became
illusions, daydreams which eventually destroyed what had been
a clear mind, a disciplined intelligence.

It was himself, really,
that he had been seeking all the time, conscious at least
of that in all the deviations of the way;
himself, the ultimate of his curiosities.
Arthur Symons

Chapter VI

Arthur Symons

When Arthur Symons came up to London in 1889 he was almost
unknown, though he had put in an apprenticeship by writing
An Introduction to the Study of Robert Browning; he had no
advantage of family name nor even the distinction of being an
"Oxford man," and, unlike Yeats, he was not a genius. Nevertheless, he corresponded with Walter Pater, became a member of
the Rhymers' Club, moved into Fountain Court, where he became
George Moore's "boon companion" and Yeats' friend, and was
what Ernest Dowson called a "standing dish" with *The Academy*.[1]
More than that, he was very busy in Paris as well as in London:
he attended Mallarmé's "Tuesdays," visited Edmond de Goncourt
at his small, exquisitely furnished villa, and waited patiently to
catch Paul Verlaine at the latter's favorite café. It was Symons
who made most of the arrangements for Verlaine's trips to London in 1893 and 1894 and Symons with whom Verlaine stayed

each time.[2] And it was Symons who translated Mallarmé's *Hérodiade* and the poetry of Verlaine for Yeats,[3] Symons who gave Yeats private tutoring in the French tradition, just as it was Symons whose book *The Symbolist Movement in Literature* later became, one might say, a public lecture on the same subject.

A delightful note from Symons to William Rothenstein gives a notion of his itinerary on what appears to have been an ordinary evening. It is written on the back of a printed card which announces Verlaine's intended visit to London and his lecture on "Contemporary French Poetry":

My dear Rothenstein
It is MOST important that I should see you at once, about the Verlaine affair. I shall be dining at Galti's about 7; then I go to the New Gallery, to hear Image's "Arts and Crafts" Lecture, at 8:30; then I shall go to the Alhambra, to see an adorable lady in a new part; finally I shall go to the Crown. Now I depend absolutely on your meeting me at one or all of these places.

Yours
Arthur Symons[4]

He went everywhere and he seemed to know everyone. Thus, when Leonard Smithers planned *The Savoy* to take *The Yellow Book*'s place as an avant-garde quarterly—for *The Yellow Book* had lost its right to that position by taking alarm and dismissing Aubrey Beardsley after Oscar Wilde's downfall—he asked Symons to be editor of the magazine.

Wilde once wrote Vincent O'Sullivan that he knew Symons to be not a man but the trade name of a literary corporation: "I have written to my solicitor to inquire about shares in Symons Ltd. Naturally in mass production of that kind you can never be certain of the quality. But I think one might risk some share in Symons."[5] Symons' career as editor of *The Savoy* had shown Wilde's humorous exaggeration to be very close to the truth, for when *The Savoy* became too poor to pay any contributors, Symons and Aubrey Beardsley put out an entire issue by themselves. Beardsley contributed all the drawings and Symons wrote (1) a poetic sequence on cruel and despairing love, (2) an analysis of the work of Walter Pater, (3) a short story, (4) a translation of

Mallarmé's *Hérodiade,* (5) a travelpiece on the Aran Islands, and (6) an editorial comment.[6]

Because he turns up in so many places and has his head so full of projects, one tends to think of Symons in the half-ironic, half-patronizing way that is reflected in Wilde's comment; he seems a cheerful, bustling Decadent who could talk the prattle of the nineties without really understanding its significance: the casino of Dieppe has some "amusing chandeliers," and a fair held in the town was horrid, but "I managed to snatch a few amusing sensations out of even this discomfort"[7]—that sort of thing. Yet this picture of Symons fades out and must be readjusted, refocussed, as soon as one learns the central fact of his life: in 1908 he went mad. Two years later he recovered his reason, and he even returned to his writing. But his later work is almost painful to read, so much is it dependent on his early writing—old sentences and old phrases reappear in contexts to which they are scarcely applicable, and his essays wander constantly from the point.

His breakdown may have been the effect, at least in part, of an inherited strain of insanity and of the worries caused him by financial difficulties,[8] but his writings show also that he lost his reason because he could not find a "mask" which would adequately define his intense self-consciousness. He was a man who thought much about masks—what friend of Yeats would not?—and his ideas on their significance often have greater lucidity than the rather dark and cryptic oracles of Yeats. For instance, in his "Conclusion" to *Studies in Prose and Verse,* Symons almost seems to be thinking the problem out aloud. He begins by mentioning Barbey D'Aurévilly's famous comment after reading *A Rebours,* that Huysmans had left himself the choice of the end of a gun or the foot of the Cross. In questioning its truth Symons brings together those ideas around which he tried to center his life: "Yet perhaps the choice is not quite so narrow as Barbey D'Aurévilly thought; perhaps it is a choice between actualising this dream or actualising that dream. In his escape from the world, one man chooses religion and seems to find himself; another, choosing love, may also seem to find himself; and may not another, coming to art as to a religion and as to a woman, seem to find himself no less effectually?"[9] That part of the meditation drifts off with a question, a possibility but not a statement of belief. Then Symons turns to think of art, curiously blending the ideas of Rossetti, Pater, and Wilde:

Art begins when a man wishes to immortalize the most vivid moment he has ever lived. Life has already, to one not an artist, become art in that moment. And the making of one's life into art is after all the first duty and privilege of every man. It is to escape from material reality into whatever form of ecstasy is our own form of spiritual existence. There is the choice; and our happiness, our "success in life," will depend on our choosing rightly, each for himself, among the forms in which that choice will come to us (pp. 290–91).

Symons understood perfectly how vital the choice was; he knew that the mask is not separate from personality but a partial reflection of it and realized too that, once habitual, it influences personality. This was the insight that he had into Wilde's nature when he described Wilde making himself many souls;[10] with a truly beautiful clarity and intelligence (for these were new and complex ideas with scarcely a vocabulary fitted to explain them) he expressed a similar thought when he wrote about Mérimée: "Does he realise, unable to change the temperament which he has partly made for himself, that just there has been his own failure?"[11] Later in the essay on Mérimée, Symons describes the process by which the mask becomes inescapable:

Indifference in him [Mérimée], as in the man of the world, is partly an attitude, adopted for its form, and influencing the temperament just so much as gesture always influences emotion. The man who forces himself to appear calm under excitement teaches his nerves to follow instinctively the way he has shown them. In time he will not merely seem calm but will be calm, at the moment when he learns that a great disaster has befallen him. But, in Mérimée was the indifference even as external as it must always be when there is restraint, when, therefore, there is something to restrain? Was there not in him a certain drying up of the sources of emotion?[12]

Yet Symons also knew that the modern consciousness cannot attempt to throw off the mask altogther—even if that were socially possible—and be "natural." So well did he understand Wilde's paradox that "being natural is simply a pose, and the most irri-

tating pose I know,"[13] that he could only listen with amazement
when Walter Pater said he believed *Imaginary Portraits* to be his
best book because it was the most natural. Symons says won-
deringly, "I think he was even beginning to forget that it was
not natural to him to be natural." Pater's life and his art were
both so consciously, so ceremoniously ordered that "it became a
last sophistication to aim at an effect in style which should bring
the touch of unpremeditation, which we seem to find in nature,
into a faultlessly combined arrangement of art."[14] And in *The
Symbolist Movement* he generalizes about any modern writer:
"I affirm that it is not natural to be what is called 'natural' any
longer."[15]

Symons' history, then, is that of his conscious attempt to find
himself by identifying with an ideal or a person outside himself;
he tried to do so through religious faith, through love, through the
search for sensations, in the "perfect moment," and in the doctrines of Symbolism: every attempt failed, and finally, completely
self-imprisoned, he went mad.

Very early in his life he turned away violently from the
possibility of self-realization through religious belief. Although
Symons himself never mentions it, his father was a Wesleyan
Methodist minister.[16] Between 1865 and 1885 he was in charge
of nine different circuits, and therefore the family moved often.
But even though he does not discuss its cause, Symons attaches
enormous importance to this lack of stability, making it the primary reason for his own restlessness and inability to find a center.
He mentions it in two autobiographical pieces, *Confessions* and
"A Prelude to Life," one of the stories in *Spiritual Adventures;* in
the latter he writes: "If I have been a vagabond, and have never
been able to root myself in any one place in the world, it is because I have no early memories of any one sky or soil. It has
freed me from many prejudices in giving me its own unresting
kind of freedom; but it has cut me off from whatever is stable,
of long growth in the world."[17]

If we may trust the account he gives in "A Prelude to Life,"
Symons was even more completely cut off from his family than
was Lionel Johnson. He describes his father as a sombre, dryly

intellectual man, something of a valetudinarian, "unimaginative, cautious in his affairs, a great reader of the newspapers" (p. 21)— the last perhaps the most cutting point he could make, since Symons thought of newspapers as fit reading only for the very average man.[18] He says that he did not dislike his father, regarding him rather with indifference, but adds, almost as an afterthought, "perhaps a little more than indifference, for if he came into a room, and I did not happen to be absorbed in reading, I usually went out of it" (p. 20).

Symons' description of his mother is very different; as he depicts her, she would have fulfilled Pater's ideal of sanctity, for she had the capacity to appreciate beauty in all its aspects, and Symons even echoes Pater's vocabulary in describing her: "She had the joy of life, she was sensitive to every aspect of the world; she felt the sunshine before it came, and knew from what quarter the wind was blowing when she woke in the morning. I think she was never indifferent to any moment that ever passed her by; I think no moment ever passed her by without being seized in all the eagerness of acceptance" (p. 22).

Even as a boy Symons would willingly have rejected his father's religious beliefs and met his father's solemn attempts to talk to him about his soul only with sullen resentment: "If to be good was to be like him, I did not wish to be good." But his mother too was deeply religious, with a strong and very simple faith which the boy could not but share: "Her certainty helped to make me more afraid." For though she might give him her belief in another world, she could not give him her quiet hope for salvation, and Symons says that as a child he was always convinced that he himself would be damned: "And so the thought of hell was often in my mind, for the most part very much in the background, but always ready to come forward at any external suggestion. Once or twice it came to me with such vividness that I rolled over on the ground in a paroxysm of agony, trying to pray to God that I might not be sent to hell, but unable to fix my mind on the words of the prayer" (p. 19). And with the fear of hell went a terrible fear of death that was always to afflict him.

As he came to adolescence Symons resisted his parents' religious beliefs more and more strongly, and he mentions a revival meeting in which he sat rigid, teeth clenched, refusing to confess his wickedness or to repent as those around him were doing. In "Seaward Lackland," another of the stories in *Spiritual Adventures,* he describes a similar meeting; Seaward, the son of devout Methodists, has been dedicated to the Lord at his birth, but he too refuses in the meeting to succumb to the emotion felt by those around him:

As Seaward saw the preacher coming near him, he felt a horrible fear, he did not know of what; and he rose quietly and stepped out into the night. But there, as he stood listening to some exultant voices which he still heard crying, "Hallelujah!" and as he felt the comfort of the cool air about him, and he looked up at the stars and the thin white clouds which were rushing across the moon, a sense of quiet and well-being came over him, and he felt as if some bitter thing had been taken out of his soul, and he were free to love God and life at the same time, and not, as he had done till then, with alternate pangs of regret. "If God so loved the world," he found himself repeating, and the whole mercy of the text enveloped him. He walked home along the cliff like one in a dream: he only hoped not to awaken out of that happiness (pp. 212–13).

Yet Seaward's tenuous moment of balance between love of God and of the world is very brief, and as the story continues he becomes obsessed with the idea that he has unwittingly committed the unforgivable sin. Symons too would have wished that he could be "free to love God and the world at the same time," but in "A Prelude to Life," he describes no moment at which that ever seemed possible, and given the necessity of choice between his father's God and the world beyond his father's authority, Symons chose the world and risked damnation.

Although the family life that he describes sounds gloomy, even if brightened by his mother's nature, Symons himself must have done very little to add any cheerfulness. He was, if we may trust his account, thoroughly spoiled, completely self-involved, resentful of his parents' poverty and of the fact that they were "surrounded by commonplace, middle-class people, and I hated commonplace and the middle class." It seems almost certain that he exaggerates his egoism, for he makes it very nearly monstrous;

nevertheless, his account of it is interesting for the emphasis it places on his self-enclosure, his inability to go out to others:

From as early a time as I can remember, I had no very close consciousness of anything external to myself; I never realised that others had the right to expect from me any return for the kindness they might show me or refuse me, at their choice. I existed, others also existed; but between us there was an impassible gulf, and I had rarely any desire to cross it. I was very fond of my mother, but I felt no affection toward anyone else, nor any desire for the affection of others. To be let alone, and to live my own life for ever, that was what I wanted, and I raged because I could never escape from the contact of people who bored me and things which depressed me (pp. 28–29).

When Symons' father suggested that the time had come for him to have a job, he flatly refused, choosing, he said, rather to starve than to soil his hands with business; he would become an "aristocrat of letters."[19] So he withdrew to his study and not only read but wrote: "I wanted to write books for the sake of writing books; it was food for my ambition, and it gave me something to do when I was alone, apart from other people. It helped to raise another barrier between me and other people" (p. 47).

"A Prelude to Life" concludes with Symons' arrival in London where "alone, and in the midst of a crowd, I began to be astonishingly happy" (p. 49). The whole piece so lacks detail and is so personal in feeling that one could only call it quasi-autobiography, but the emotion with which it is written shows how much an alien Symons felt himself to be in the world, how rootless and drifting, and shows as well why religious belief was of no use to him in his search for something with which he might identify. His early religious belief left him with a permanent fear of death and, perhaps, an unrecognized but continuing belief in life after death—a life in which he found damnation imaginatively much more vivid than salvation. All this was put in the back of his mind, however, as Symons enjoyed his new freedom in London.

He now began to move so rapidly back and forth among several ideals in his search for himself that any attempt to order them must base itself upon logic, not upon biographical fact. It was this tendency in Symons to move quickly from one emotional or intellectual point of view to another that Frank Harris particularly noted; at their first meeting he and Symons struck up a conversation about the London music halls, then just becoming popular, which Symons admired enormously: "In the middle of the animated discussion I reminded him that Plato had called music the divinest of the arts, and forthwith, to my astonishment, Symons changed front in a jiffy and took up this new position."[20] Harris is a notoriously unreliable witness,[21] but here his account is given validity by the fact that Yeats also noted Symons' ability "to slip . . . into the mind of another";[22] the difference between the two analyses is that Harris saw as shilly-shallying what Yeats felt to be an ability to understand "all sides of the question."

Like one of his characters, Christian Trevalga,[23] Symons tried "to find himself, to become real by falling in love."[24] His early poems about women, however, scarcely seem to describe realities: for instance, Rossetti's Lilith, Pater's Mona Lisa, and Swinburne's Lady of Pain come together to form "A Woman":

> They [her eyes] without labour, bought and sold
> Heart's faith, a precious merchandise,
> With tears for silver, blood for gold
> And bargaining of costly sighs
> For the rich treasuries of those eyes.
>
> Dowered with all beauty bodily
> Her soul she meshed in her own snare;
> Beyond herself she might not see
> Infantine—idly unaware
> Of any end but being fair.[25]

Rossetti's ideal woman, his "Soul's Beauty," is also Symons': "Mournful, beautiful, calm with that vague unrest,"[26] she broods "mysteriously alone / And infinitely far away,"[27] or if she be near the poet begs, "Shake out your hair about me."[28] And if she be won, it is with Rossettian passion:

> Spirit to spirit was fused in living flame, and neither knew,
> In that transfiguring ardency of perfect fire,
> Body from body, spirit from spirit, life from death.[29]

Yet the fact that many of Symons' love poems sound like Rossetti processed, put, as it were, through an IBM machine, does not mean that Symons' attitude toward women resembles Rossetti's.

Rossetti idealized women, Symons feared them. Although he found women physically attractive, he used sexual desire as a means of keeping them at a distance and began each love affair by making it already a memory, something passing:

> And every woman with beseeching eyes,
> Or with enticing eyes, or amorous,
> Offers herself, a rose, and craves of us
> A rose's place among our memories.[30]

And when he cannot take love in this way, lightly, as a sensual pleasure without any deeper meaning, then he can think of it only as something painful, an obsession, a disease, in which resentment at his bondage makes his passion as much hate as it is love:

> I have not loved love, nor sought happiness,
> I have loved every passionate distress,
> And the adoration of sharp fear, and hate
> For love's sake, and what agonies await
> The unassuaged fulfilment of desire
> Not eased in the having.[31]

The same poem, "An Epilogue to Love," has a phrase which catches precisely Symons' attitude: "Passionate and untender," and he finally cries out:

> I have not loved love; let me be; O give
> Not love, but life: I would not love but live![32]

All this is not just posing; Symons used the symbols and even the vocabulary of Rossetti and Swinburne because he had not sufficient poetic genius to create symbols of his own, but the emotions behind his borrowed images are perfectly genuine. Yet why did the thought of falling in love cause Symons to suffer such violent conflict? The poems themselves scarcely give an answer: they can only state the emotions, not their cause. In his prose, however, Symons analyzed his difficulty and gave its reason, though he could not find its solution.

It is the stories in *Spiritual Adventures*, especially "Christian Trevalga," "An Autumn City," and "The Journal of Henry Luxulyan," which best explain Symons' fear of the feminine principle: these are not told as autobiography, it is true, but their tone is personal enough to justify our interpreting them as Symons himself interpreted Pater's *Imaginary Portraits:* "Each, with perhaps one exception ["Denys l' Auxerrois"], is the study of a soul, or rather of a consciousness; such a study as might be made by simply looking within, and projecting now this now that side of oneself on an exterior plane."[33] Similarly, Christian Trevalga, Daniel Roserra in "An Autumn City," and Henry Luxulyan are all characters through whom Symons was perfectly consciously describing a part of himself. Of these perhaps the most interesting is Christian Trevalga, the man who had tried to find himself by falling in love. He is a brilliant musician, and at music school he meets Rana Vaughan, who admires him and shares his delight in music. In describing her Symons creates a personality very like that of his mother:

She cared intensely for the one thing he cared for [his music], and not less intensely (and here was the wonder to him) for all the other things that existed outside his interests. For her, life was everything, and everything was part of life. . . . She made no selections in life, beyond picking out all the beautiful and pleasant things, whatever they might be. Trevalga studied her with amazement; he felt withered, shrivelled up, in body and soul, beside her magnificent acceptance of the world; she vitalised him, drew him away from himself; and he feared her. He feared women (p. 99).

The clause "and he feared her" comes as a very deliberate shock; up to that point in the paragraph Rana Vaughan has been presented as a possible salvation, a way of breaking out of the circle of self-consciousness, but suddenly her very presence makes Trevalga only the more aware of being imprisoned: "To live with a woman, thought Christian, in the same house, the same room with her, is as if the keeper were condemned to live by day and sleep by night in the wild beast's cage" (p. 99). To him it is the worst, "the no longer solitary imprisonment." So Christian allows Rana to drift away from him, and the rest of the story describes his gradual descent into madness.

"An Autumn City" is the story of Daniel Roserra, an aesthete, a sensualist, who always said that woman disturbed the even tenor of the aesthetic life and that, like a liqueur, she is "a delightful luxury, to be taken with discretion" (p. 178). At forty,

however, he suddenly fell in love and married; a few months
after the wedding, he took his bride to Arles, a city that Symons
himself particularly liked, that she might appreciate its autumn
beauty, the beauty of decay. When she took no pleasure in the
city's sad, gray peace and begged that they might return to vulgar
Marseilles, Roserra agreed, but in his mind everything about their
marriage had changed. Now for him his wife was a creature from
whom he would take what physical pleasure he could, feeling
even so that he had made a very poor bargain:

A nausea, a suffocating nausea, rose up within him as he felt the heat
and glare of this vulgar, exuberant paradise of snobs and   tourists
[Marseilles]. He sickened with revolt before this over-fed nature,
sweating the fat of life. He looked at Livia; she stood there, perfectly
cool under her sunshade . . . . She was once more in her element, she
was quite happy; she had plunged back into the warmth of life out
of that penitential chilliness of Arles, and it was with real friendliness
that she turned to Roserra, as she saw his eyes fixed upon her (p. 197).

Roserra had been right, at least about himself; for him woman
was a very dangerous luxury. When his contact with her was only
ephemeral and essentially meaningless, he might be utterly self-
centered, but he was not unhappy, nor did he make others unhappy. His attempt to enjoy a relationship with woman that was
meaningful did not simply fail, returning him to his old self-
enclosure; it stirred up in him a resentment and a violence which
had been passive before and left his last state much worse than
his first.

   The final "case," Henry Luxulyan, is on the verge of a nervous
breakdown after an unhappy love affair when the story opens.
He is prey to horrible fears, the fear of death and of annihilation,[34]
which he relates somehow to his fear of women:

I realise, on thinking it over in a perfectly calm mood, without any
sort of nervous excitement, that I have always been afraid of women;
and that is one reason, the chief perhaps, why I have always been so
lonely, both when Clare was with me, and before it and after it. Just
as I cannot get it out of my head that there is some concealed con-
spiracy against me, in earthly things, so there seems to be, in the other
sex, a kind of hidden anger or treachery which makes me uneasy. I

was never really happy when a woman sat on the other side of the table, at the corner of the fireplace.[35]

Again one gets the sense of a man trapped, like Christian Trevalga, in a wild beast's cage. Moreover, although that image is only implicit in this passage, it appears explicitly within a few pages of it: Luxulyan has a moment's respite one afternoon as he sits quietly in Regent's Park, until he realizes that the strange, mournful cry of which he had been vaguely aware was "the crying of the wild beasts, over yonder, inside their bars" (p. 261). That shatters his peace, and he leaves the park.

Luxulyan has been befriended by the Baroness Eckenstein, a woman whom he finds physically repulsive, because one side of her face is badly scarred, but who catches his interest and his pity; little by little his friendship for her draws him out of himself, away from the danger of emotional breakdown. At least, the Baroness helps him until she falls in love with him; partly out of pity, partly out of fascination with physical ugliness, Luxulyan takes her as his mistress. By the time the journal ends he has lost his reason.

Like Roserra's aesthetic detachment, Luxulyan's uneasiness with women was a safeguard as well as a barrier. It is also a state of mind which Symons says he himself never quite escaped. Uneasiness, he writes, "creeps over me stealthily, perfidiously, insidiously, when I am most unaware of its existence: even in the presence of those I am passionately fond of." Then, continuing his self-analysis, he gives the reason: "I except from this category neither my mother nor my mistress—whose names were identical—Lydia[36]—for, in spite of my fondness for the one, and the intolerable vehemence and violence of my passion for the other, the most consuming, the most animal passion I ever had, there were times when my uneasiness, either in their presence or their absence, became exasperating."[37] One might say that every woman Symons loved or tried to love had his mother's name. And just as his repudiation of his father made it impossible for him to find an ideal outside himself in religious faith, so his emotional dependence upon his mother—an imprisoning emotion which he could not escape but which he bitterly resented—destroyed the hope of release from himself through love of a woman. He thought women mysterious and terrible because his own emotions toward them were confused and terrifying; he believed all sexuality essentially cruel because he used it cruelly, as a way of expressing the resentment he could not conquer. And, like the religion in which he could not believe, the love which he could not feel convinced him nevertheless of his own damnation:

> Annihilation awaits me, or some more infamous peril,
> Shot from a mad girl's eyes, as if some one behind me
> Stood in the midnight to stab me, and I was forsaken
> Even of myself, lost in caresses, lost in sedition,
> Saved in no sense, but hurled halfway down to Perdition.[38]

"Interludes of wholesome air, as through open doors, upon those hot, impassioned scenes": with this image Pater describes those passages in *Days and Nights* which make art alone the changeless, the enduring ideal in an otherwise meaningless world —"though," Pater adds, "on what grounds we hardly see, except his own deep, unaffected sense of it."[39] Symons, who had told his father he would not soil his hands with trade and had set himself to become an aristocrat of letters, described his ideal of the artist in his first book: Aprile in *Paracelsus* is, he says, the supreme artistic type, "the lover of beauty and beauty alone," so much a type indeed that he is scarcely a "realisable human being,"[40] yet an ideal, nonetheless, and one to which the young Symons clearly aspired as a way of salvation. In choosing this ideal Symons seems never to have questioned the necessity of separation between artist and society nor to have hoped that each might be of use to the other. He takes it as given that the artist is isolated and that he should be so, for society can never understand his work. Even further, if society does understand and accept his art, either his art is bad, or society has accepted it for the wrong reasons. There are those who may compromise, but any compromise is dangerous, for artist and society are always at war.[41]

There is no real need to linger over these doctrines or even over their application in the praise of Mallarmé's deliberate attempt to bewilder any bourgeois readers who might stumble upon his

works, or of Villiers de l'Isle-Adam's haughty disdain for the
world in which he unfortunately found himself; they are by now
very familiar, are, in fact, clichés whose validity is perhaps once
again a question—we have circled back to the point where the
role of the artist in society might be debated in a new "Palace
of Art." In Symons' time, however, although these ideas had been
in the air for years, there was still something a little brazen and
daring about this manifesto: "It is for their faults that any really
artistic productions become popular: art cannot appeal to the
multitude. It is wise when it does not attempt to; when it goes
contentedly along a narrow path, knowing, and caring only to
know, in what direction it is moving."[42]

Supported by the violently anti-bourgeois tradition of the
French, Symons separates the artist as completely from society
as a monk is separated from domestic life: his is to be a different
world. So he states in his essay on Verlaine, and there he gives
as well the duty of the artist, the narrow path along which he is
to walk, holding up Verlaine as his example of one who lived the
perfect artistic life. Verlaine, Symons says, was a great poet because "he got out of every moment all that that moment had to
give him," and his whole art was "a delicate waiting upon
moods."[43] His ideal poet lives by the doctrines of Pater's *The
Renaissance*.

For in Symons' early years in London his ideas on "the perfect
moment" all showed the influence of Pater's *The Renaissance*.
Symons describes himself as one who devoutly practiced "the
religion of the eyes," looking into every omnibus, watching faces
in the crowds which passed him in Piccadilly lest he miss a sudden, gracious gesture, a beautiful face;[44] he found in his eyes a
way of turning himself from "that strict tedious world within."[45]
This was also the pleasure that the music halls gave him: backstage especially he enjoyed, like Dégas, the vision of a world in
flux—moving shapes and shadows; sudden, unreal glimpses of the
dancers on stage; profiles of the spectators. And if he watched
carefully, the flux might momentarily resolve itself into an arrangement. He describes such a moment, one in which he suddenly caught a glimpse of the ballet at the Alhambra as he was
passing on the street outside: "In the moment's interval before

the doors closed again, I saw in that odd, unexpected way, over the heads of the audience, far off in a sort of blue mist, the whole stage . . . . It stamped itself on my brain, an impression caught just at the perfect moment, by some rare felicity of chance."[46] On that occasion the doors closed, ending the impression at the moment it was realized, but had they not done so, Symons would have turned quickly away: "When I have seen a face, an aspect of the sky, pass for a moment into a sort of crisis, in which it attained the perfect expression of itself, I have always turned away rapidly, closing my eyes on the picture which I dread to see fade or blur before me. I would obtain from things, as from people, only their best."[47]

Put this way, his philosophy sounds almost altruistic, though in fact (as Symons often realized himself) to take from things and people "only their best," to find that anything but that best is tedious or disgusting, reflects the coldest possible egoism. And Symons' concept of the artistic vision often has a certain coldness; since the artist is isolated from the world around him, he tends to be more interested in people's gestures than in their personalities; he resembles the actress Esther Kahn in one of Symons' stories: "At night, after supper, the others [her family] used to sit around the table, talking eagerly. Esther would get up and draw her chair into the corner by the door, and for a time she would watch them, as if she were looking on at something, something with which she had no concern, but which interested her for its outline and movement."[48] Pushed to its extreme, the habit of watching life from the outside can so reduce life's emotional content and its significance that one may come to the point of saying, as Symons says, "I have always been apt to look on the world as a puppet show . . . ."[49]

Yet there is no need to preach at Symons about the dangers of his "impressionist" philosophy; he knew them well enough himself, recognized them, one feels, from the very beginning, for his religious background had made it impossible for him ever really to be amoral. When he writes, for instance, of Gabriele D'Annunzio, praising him as a man who is an "artist in life itself," because he can feel more passionately than others "the heat of sunlight, the juicy softness of a ripe fruit, the texture of

women's hair," Symons suddenly turns just in the midst of his
praise to point out that all D'Annunzio's books are tragedies
which end in gross, material horror: "And they are tragedies because no man has yet found out a remedy against the satiety of
pleasure, except the remedies hidden away somewhere in the
soul. Youth passes, desire fades, attainment squeezes the world
into a narrow circuit; there is nothing left over, except dreams
that turn into nightmares, or else a great weariness."[50] To attempt
to free oneself from the circle of the inner world by enjoying
every possible sensation of the physical world will end, paradoxically, only by making the circle of the trap narrower. Pater
was not the only one who found that the life of sensation, the
life spent grasping at exquisite passions, beautiful sights, delicious
odors which might serve "to set the spirit free for a moment," was
bound to end in failure. At the end of Symons' "A Prelude to Life,"
the sadness and frustration underlying Pater's "Conclusion" rise to
the surface and the murmur of Heraclitus' stream becomes a roar
in which all other sounds are lost. After he has described his
"religion of the eyes," Symons continues:

This search without an aim grew to be almost a torture to me; my
eyes ached with the effort, but I could not control them. At every
moment, I knew, some spectacle awaited them; I grasped at all those
sights with the same futile energy as a dog that I once saw standing
in an Irish stream, and snapping at the bubbles that ran continually
past him on the water. Life ran past me continually, and I tried to
make all its bubbles my own (p. 50).

To realize that the search is aimless and that the moments enjoyed during it are meaningless is fearful; and Symons' vision of
the horror may have been the quality in him which deepened
Yeats' desire for a "sacred book" that would bring the supernatural
back into the world. Yeats says that Symons had this effect upon
him "without ever being false to his own impressionist view of art
and life," and yet his next sentence makes it seem likely that it
was Symons who turned to Yeats for help and that together they
hoped to find in Symbolism a way in which the "perfect moment"
might be considered something more than a photograph kept in
the album of the mind. Yeats writes: "It seems to me, looking

backward, that we always discussed life at its most intense moment, and that moment which gives a common sacredness to the Song of Songs, and to the Sermon on the Mount, and in which one discovers something supernatural, a stirring at the roots of the hair."[51] If the moment were a symbol pointing toward some divine reality, or, coming at it from the other direction, if it were a breakthrough of divine energy into the material world, then its appreciation need not make one aware always of its passing; rather the moment "in time and out of time" would serve as a reflection of the permanence behind it, and in identification with that permanence, discovered through the moment, might lie the possibility of finding the true self.

In the letter with which he dedicates *The Symbolist Movement in Literature* to Yeats, Symons mentions the talks that he and Yeats had together, and says, like Yeats, that they were not arguments, nor was one teaching the other, but both were engaged in a common exploration of the doctrines of Symbolism. Yeats, nevertheless, was the leading spirit, for, says Symons, "You have seen me gradually finding my way, uncertainly but inevitably, in that direction which has always been to you your natural direction." In fact, Symons appears a little self-conscious and shamefaced over the fact that he has changed from his old, "impressionist" position: "I speak often in this book of Mysticism, and that I, of all people, should venture to speak, not quite as an outsider, of such things, will probably be a surprise to many."[52]

Indeed the book which Symons had intended in 1896 to call *The Decadent Movement in Literature* would probably have had a very different focus from the book which appeared in 1899 as *The Symbolist Movement*. Certainly in 1893, when Symons wrote an article called "The Decadent Movement in Literature," his emphasis was on appreciation of the moment for its own sake: "To fix the last fine shade, to fix it fleetingly; to be a disembodied voice, and yet the voice of a human soul; that is the ideal of Decadence."[53] By 1899 Symons dismissed even the term "Decadence" as descriptive only of an "interlude, half a mock-interlude" held before the scenes while preparations were being made backstage for the dramatic appearance of Symbolism; if the term "Decadence" meant anything at all, it might be applied only to style, to "ingenious deformation of language."[54]

But when Symons, having set Decadence to one side, attempts to define the meaning and purpose of Symbolism, his writing loses some of the clarity, the precision of thought, that so often makes it a joy to read. Clearest, perhaps, is his discussion of the negative value of Symbolism—as a weapon against materialism—and that may have been the area in which Symons felt on his surest footing. He ends his "Introduction" to *The Symbolist Movement* with a ringing—and very Yeatsian—denunciation of "exteriority," "rhetoric," and the "materialistic tradition." And he adds that in its capacity to create symbols imaginative literature becomes "a kind of religion, with all the duties and responsibilities of the sacred ritual" (pp. 8–9). The conclusion of his essay on Mallarmé further explains the religious function of Symbolism; Symons has been describing the imprisoning self-consciousness of modern times and the impossibility of escaping it through a false—a necessarily false—attempt to be "natural." Yet there is an escape: "Symbolism, implicit in all literature from the beginning, as it is implicit in the very words we use, comes to us now, at last quite conscious of itself, offering us the only escape from our many imprisonments. We find a new, an older sense in the so worn out forms of things; the world, which we can no longer believe in as the satisfying material object it was to our grandparents, becomes transfigured with a new light" (p. 134).

This passage echoes the positive definition of Symbolism which appears at the beginning of Symons' book. There he makes the artist's creation of symbol analogous to God's creation of the world, both kinds of creation being forms of expression "for an unseen reality apprehended by the consciousness" (pp. 1–2). Later, when discussing Gérard de Nerval, Symons links this theory with the doctrine of "correspondences": since the visible world is the symbolic expression of the divine imagination, then every part of it is filled with divine energy and is divinely significant—all is bathed in a "light overflowing from beyond the world" (p. 30). It is this doctrine which makes it possible for Symbolism to offer an "escape from our many imprisonments"; the summarizing paragraph on the work of Mallarmé concludes: "And it is on the lines of that spiritualising of the word, that perfecting of form in its capacity for allusion and suggestion, that confidence in the eternal correspondences between the visible and the invisible universe . . . that literature must now move, if it is in any sense to move forward" (pp. 134–35).

These attempts at definition are inadequate, being themselves necessarily symbolic, but even Yeats' very beautiful definition of symbol, formulated in the years when he and Symons were discussing these things, is given only in an image: "A symbol is indeed the only possible expression of some invisible essence, a transparent lamp about a spiritual flame."[55] And Symons' words do give a feeling, an emotion more than an idea, of freedom and clear light for the soul in the vision of a world suddenly made significant because it reflects pure being. There remains, however, a question: is the unseen reality mirrored by symbols a reality discovered or one imposed? In *The Symbolist Movement* Symons does not come to any decision, but he was, of course, aware of both possibilities: one of the book's essays is on Villiers de l'Isle-Adam, who said: "Know once for all that there is for thee no other universe than that conception thereof which is reflected at the bottom of thy thought," and "Thou art but what thou thinkest: therefore think thyself eternal." On the page in which he quotes these lines from Villiers' *Axël*, Symons adds a note: " 'I am very far from sure,' wrote Verlaine, 'that the philosophy of Villiers will not one day become the formula of our century' " (pp. 41–42).

The philosophy was one that fascinated Symons—as, indeed, it fascinated Yeats—for it was something of which he had long been aware. Even as early as 1886, when he wrote of Browning's dramatic monologue, Symons notes of the speakers that "life exists for each as completely and as separately as if he were the only inhabitant of our planet."[56] Symons noted too that Meredith "carries the world behind his eyes, seeing, wherever he goes, only his own world,"[57] and he made Wilde's psychological theory that nature copies art into a mystical doctrine: "It is one of the privileges of art to create nature, as according to a certain mystical doctrine, you can actualise, by sheer fixity of contemplation, your mental image of a thing into the thing itself."[58]

The theory that the human imagination creates its own world and is its own eternity is very ancient, but its age does not make it any less dangerous if it strike forcefully upon a mind not properly balanced. When Symons wrote about Gérard de Nerval, his own mind, one can see, was reeling from the force of thoughts like these:

Who has not often meditated, above all what artist, on the slightness, after all, of the link which holds our faculties together in that sober health of the brain which we call reason? Are there not moments when that link seems to be worn down to so fine a tenuity that the wing of a passing dream might suffice to snap it? The consciousness seems, as it were, to expand and contract at once, into something too wide for the universe, and too narrow for the thought of self to find room within it. Is it that the sense of identity is about to evaporate, annihilating all, or is it that a more profound identity, the identity of the whole sentient universe, has at last been realised? (pp. 23–24).

The doctrine which began by making each individual a reality entirely to himself can leave him ultimately unsure of any identity whatsoever. Worse still, the symbols of man's imagination become terrifying and menacing as he loses control over them and as they begin to reflect his own fear of himself.[59] All this Symons saw and described in his essay on Gérard de Nerval; later, when he tells of his own period of insanity, it is this essay to which he most often alludes. He writes almost as if he were appalled that, having understood so well, he could still have gone mad. Quoting sentence after sentence from the essay, he keeps saying, "It was I who had done all this, I in that madhouse": "I . . who had quoted from *La Rêve et la Vie*—a madman's narrative—such sentences as these. 'First of all I imagined that the persons collected in the garden of the madhouse all had some influence on the stars, and that the one who always walked round and round in a circle regulated the course of the sun.'"[60]

Symons and Yeats, as they discussed and put into practice the doctrines of Symbolism, may well typify the two kinds of artists whom Symons describes in "Gérard de Nerval." Yeats was one of those who could look fearlessly into the darkness of the self and see, for "with him, imagination is vision," while Symons suffered the fate of "the vague dreamer, the insecure artist, and the un-certain mystic" who, when he gazes, sees only shadows, terrifying reflections of his own imagination (p. 25).

Always, however, Symons had at hand two possible escapes from self, which, though he knew them to be purposeless, were nevertheless very useful in holding off the darkness that pressed in upon him: walking alone through crowds and travelling in foreign countries. To take country walks would not help him, for Symons says that he could walk for hours without hearing or seeing anything at all, with no sensation save the physical delight of walking.[61] In "Christian Trevalga" he describes this withdrawal into self in a very dramatic image: "And outward things, too, as well as people, meant very little to him, and meant less and less as time went on. What he saw, when he went for long walks with his father, had vanished from his memory before he returned to the house; it was as if he had been walking through underground passages, with only a faint light on the roadway in front of his feet."[62] But in a crowd the noise, the confusion and movement, demanded attention: Symons tells of seeing Coventry Fair in his late teens, his first plunge into "the bath of the multitude," which "seemed, for the first time in my life, to carry me outside myself."[63] During his first years in London, there was never an evening in which he did not go out, sometimes just to walk among the crowds in the Strand or in Piccadilly, and in his *Confessions* he identifies his feelings about the crowd with those of Gérard de Nerval: "The real world seeming to be always so far from him, and a sort of terror of the gulfs holding him, in spite of himself, to its flying skirts, he found something at all events realisable, concrete, in those drinkers of Les Halles."[64] Christian Trevalga also walks in Piccadilly "that he might take hold of something real," but as he succumbs to madness his doing so only adds to his sensations of unreality; the disorder and noise of the crowd bewilder and horrify him, having become the reflection of his own confused consciousness, and at the same time they rob him of any remaining sense of his individual existence: " 'I can see no reason,' he said to himself, 'why I am here rather than there, why these atoms which know one another so little, or have lost some recognition of themselves, should coalesce in this particular body, standing still where all is movement.' "[65] For the sense of reality which a crowd can give is a tenuous one at best, and Symons' pleasure in walking through crowds was a dubious therapy.

Symons' other escape lay in travelling for its own sake. Just as the crowd at once heightens and dissolves the sense of individuality, so a winding white road both symbolizes and negates all sense of time and space. In "The Wanderers" Symons writes:

> . . . life, a long white road,
> Winds ever from the dark into the dark,
> And they [the wanderers], as days, return not.[66]

The vision of the road whose whiteness shines out in a surrounding darkness resembles the tunnel in which Trevalga walked, so little thought is there of the scenes past which the road may wind. Defiantly, too, Symons takes pleasure in the very fact that on the road time's passage has no more meaning than the spatial surroundings have. The road is its own world, caught between past and future, yet without present:

> Because life holds not anything so good
> As to be free of yesterday, and bound
> Towards a new tomorrow; and they wend
> Into a world of unknown faces, where
> It may be there are faces waiting them,
> Faces of friendly strangers, not the long
> Intolerable monotony of friends.[67]

It was while he was travelling in Italy that Symons went insane; he says that on his way there, he was curiously unaware "that past and future are continually with us; only the present flies continually from under our feet."[68] Perhaps at that time he was unaware of it, had lost the sense of it, but ordinarily the consciousness of the present flying continually from under his feet was always with him. The desperation with which he tried to hold the present moment, like the feverish activity with which he attempted to make himself believe in his own reality, only made matters worse; finally, like Henry Luxulyan, Symons could say: "The world, ideas, sensations, are all fluid, and I flow through them, like a gondola carried along by the current: no, like a weed adrift on it."[69]

Confessions, Symons' account of his madness, begins in Venice, moves to Bologna, and then to Ferrara, where his breakdown became complete. It is a strange book, made up as it is of long quotations from Symons' earlier works, of sudden images which came to him in his madness, and of descriptions which have an almost preternatural lucidity. Images of imprisonment dominate the book. Symons quotes, for instance, from an article he wrote while in Venice on the music of that city; it begins by describing the harsh sounds, the cries and songs heard on the Venetian canals, but soon becomes a fascinated meditation on the dungeons under the Bridge of Sighs: "They are dark cells, a torture-room, rusty chains and bolts and bars, chains just long enough to enclose an ankle or two wrists, chains long enough to enclose the body in permanent inaction against the wall."[70] When he came to Ferrara, already close to insanity, Symons was suddenly terrified by the sight of the grim Castello Vecchio, black in the moonlight, its moat glittering around it, and by the thought again of the dungeons lying beneath its battlements (p. 18).

He was discovered a few days later wandering helplessly outside Ferrara, and he was thrown into one of the prisons of the Castello where he was chained and cruelly beaten by the guards: "Fettered on both ankles and both wrists I dragged myself with painful steps round and round the stone walls of my cell, gazing hopelessly at the barred window that let in but a little light, and at the Judas, which was continually opened and shut, showing me the grimacing faces of those inhuman beasts" (p. 25). Rescued at last by the English consul, he was brought back to England and placed in an asylum, where, two years later, he recovered.

That scene in the Castello Vecchio lies at the end of the mind's darkest passages. The prison of the self, which was an image to Rossetti and a philosophical abstraction to Pater, became a terrifying reality in the mind of Symons. He tried to escape it in every way which was open to him—religious belief, the love of woman, the artistic and ordering imagination—but each of these passages, for him at least, led only the more directly down into the prison at the very center of his mind.

Whether the dream now purposed to rehearse
Be Poet's or Fanatic's will be known
When this warm scribe, my hand, is in the grave.
John Keats

Chapter VII

The Decadent Consciousness

Pater's "Conclusion" to *The Renaissance* is answered by two
sentences in *I and Thou*. Martin Buber writes: "We only need to
fill each moment with experiencing and using, and it ceases to
burn. And in all the seriousness of truth hear this: without *It* man
cannot live. But he who lives with *It* alone is not a man."[1] The
man who lives with It alone is the man subscribing to the "Conclusion"'s central doctrine: that each consciousness is totally
isolated and that all contacts with the world are experiences within that consciousness and nothing more. Every man, according to
this theory, dreams his life.

Marius the Epicurean describes Pater's eventually successful
struggle to escape the theory and its effects. When Marius finds
it possible to believe that he is, in fact, not alone but is in the
presence of "an eternal friend to man,"[2] he comes to know the
world of relation as well as the world of experience. But such a

faith never came to the men of "the Tragic Generation," partly perhaps because the interpretation they gave to the lives of such models as Rossetti and Swinburne made total isolation a tenet of their artistic faith.

Keats' account of a dream at the beginning of *The Fall of Hyperion* prophesies the outcome of that creed. He writes of finding himself in a beautiful garden before the remnants of a feast. Even those remnants are delicious, and the poet eats them gratefully but becomes thirsty as he does so. Then he sees a "vessel of transparent juice" and pledging "all the mortals of the world,"[3] he drinks from it. In that moment he undergoes the experience of all mortals: Paradise is taken from him. After a period of unconsciousness, he comes to himself in a great temple, an awe-inspiring human construction set up to the east of Eden.

At the temple's west end stands an image, flanked by steps, toward which the poet walks. When he reaches the steps, he is warned suddenly by a voice from the shrine that unless he can mount them he will die. At that moment a coldness grips his limbs and then his body so that only with pain and difficulty does he struggle to the lowest step and safety. Then the goddess explains:

> "None can usurp this height, . . .
> But those to whom the miseries of the world
> Are misery, and will not let them rest.
> All else who find a haven in the world,
> Where they may thoughtless sleep away their days,
> If by a chance into this fane they come,
> Rot on the pavement where thou rotted'st half."
>
> (ll. 147–153)

There are, however, many who are conscious of the world's misery yet are not present before the goddess. These are, so to speak, the "once-born," those whose awareness of life's sufferings impels them immediately to work at alleviating as much misery as they can; their way of salvation is clear. But Keats' concern in the parable is with those who, in Henry James' phrase, are burdened with "the oddity of a double consciousness," those men of imagination caught between their awareness of life's actualities, their dream of life's potential:

"Every sole man hath days of joy and pain,
Whether his labours be sublime or low—
The pain alone; the joy alone; distinct:
Only the dreamer venoms all his days,
Bearing more woe than all his sins deserve.
Therefore, that happiness be somewhat shar'd,
Such things as thou art are admitted oft
Into like gardens thou didst pass erewhile,
And suffered in these temples."

(ll. 172–80)

The imagination, source of his suffering, is also the dreamer's only means of salvation. Through his imagination he must come to the vision of reality.

Every poet, every person of imagination from Keats' time to the present, stands at some point in his life before Moneta's steps. And the poets of the nineties perished there, not because they "found a haven in the world" but because in the specious haven of their own imaginations they slept away their days. They desired moments of heightened consciousness, of imaginative insight, "simply," as Pater advised in the "Conclusion," "for those moments' sake." By doing so, they robbed such moments of all significance, narrowed them into the circle of the individual consciousness, and, destroying the possibility of vision, brought them wholly into the realm of dream.

At the same time, to speak practically, they left themselves without a subject for poetry. There is very little to be said about a moment when it is treated purely as experience, and what is said can be saved from banality only by tricks of style. The revelatory moment, the moment of meeting, on the other hand, offers a fruitful subject—as the works of Henry James attest. Nevertheless, it is in the area of subject rather than of form that a consistent poetic tradition exists from Keats through Rossetti and Pater, Symons and Johnson, to Yeats, Pound, Eliot, and Wallace Stevens. All are centrally concerned with the moment of heightened consciousness, but there is a crucial difference between the attitudes of the modern poets cited and those of the Decadents: either, as in the work of Yeats and Eliot, the poet has found a belief which will give significance to the moment, or, as in the work of Stevens

and Pound, the poet's subject is his very search for that belief—
the series of orderings, abandonments, and re-orderings with
which he strives to make his imagination "adhere to reality."[4]

The Decadents failed in their lives and in their art. But our
recognition of that failure and its accompanying bewilderment,
loneliness, and frustration should evoke not pity, that patronizing
emotion, but rather compassion: since the problems that the
Decadents faced have still no generally accepted solution, and
since every man must still make his own way, hoping only that
his inevitable mistakes may at least be remediable ones, then each
of the Decadents is in very truth one of us.

Notes

Introduction

1 Graham Hough, *The Last Romantics* (London, 1961), p. xix.
2 George H. Mead, *Movements of Thought in the Nineteenth Century* (Chicago, 1938), p. 375.
3 Walter Pater, *Studies in the History of the Renaissance* (London, 1873), p. 197.
4 George Santayana, *Scepticism and Animal Faith* (New York, 1955), p. 15.
5 Arthur Symons, "The Decadent Movement in Literature," *Harper's New Monthly Magazine*, LXXXVII (November, 1893), 862.

I *Dante Gabriel Rossetti*

1 D. G. Rossetti, *Collected Works*, ed. W. M. Rossetti (2 vols.; London, 1897), I, 384. Hereafter the *Collected Works* will be cited within the text as *CW*.

2 Oscar Wilde, "A Cheap Edition of a Great Man," *Reviews*, Vol. XII of Robert Ross's edition of Wilde's collected works (14 vols.; Boston, [1910]), p. 151.

3 Arthur Symons, "Dante Gabriel Rossetti," *Figures of Several Centuries* (London, 1917), p. 203.

4 William M. Rossetti, ed., *Dante Gabriel Rossetti: His Family Letters* (2 vols.; Boston, 1895), II, 328.

5 Walter Pater, "Dante Gabriel Rossetti," *Appreciations: With an Essay on Style* (London, 1889), p. 234.

6 S. T. Coleridge, *The Complete Poetical Works of Samuel Taylor Coleridge*, ed. Ernest Hartley Coleridge (2 vols.; Oxford, 1912), I, 456.

7 W. B. Yeats, *The Autobiography of William Butler Yeats* (New York, Macmillan, 1938), p. 267.

8 Rossetti, *Family Letters*, I, 418.

9 It was, according to Symons, from Madox Brown that the Pre-Raphaelites learned to focus their attention upon capturing the moment on their canvases.—Arthur Symons, *Dante Gabriel Rossetti: L'Art et le Beau*, Quatrième année, II (Paris, n.d.), 10.

10 Prosper Mérimée, "Les Beaux-Arts en Angleterre," *Revue des Deux Mondes*, II, Seconde Période (15 October 1857), 869.

11 Rossetti, *Family Letters*, II, 212.

12 Pater, *Appreciations*, p. 235.

13 Symons, *Figures of Several Centuries*, p. 204.

14 *Purgatorio*, XXX, ll. 76–78.

15 William Bell Scott, *Autobiographical Notes* (2 vols.; London, 1892), II, 112.

16 Yeats, *Autobiography*, p. 267.

17 D. H. Lawrence, *Studies in Classic American Literature* (New York, 1953), p. 86.

18 A. C. Swinburne, "D. G. Rossetti," *Essays and Studies* (London, 1875), p. 100.

ii *Algernon Charles Swinburne*

1 Cited by Georges Lafourcade in *La Jeunesse de Swinburne* (2 vols.; Paris, 1928), I, 137.

2 This source material is admirably gathered and used in Oswald Doughty's account, "The Jovial Campaign," *Dante Gabriel Rossetti: A Victorian Romantic* (New Haven, 1949), pp. 226–42.

3 Reproduced in *Memorials of Edward Burne Jones* by G[eorgiana]

B[urne]-J[ones] (London, 1906), p. 164.

4 A. C. Swinburne, "Dedicatory Epistle," *The Poems of Algernon Charles Swinburne* (6 vols.; New York, 1904), I, vii.

5 A. C. Swinburne, "Charles Baudelaire," *The Complete Works of Algernon Charles Swinburne,* ed. Sir Edmund Gosse and Thomas James Wise (The Bonchurch edition, 20 vols.; London, 1926), XIII, 419. Future references to this edition will be incorporated within the text under the title *Works*.

6 Letter by John Ruskin printed in A. C. Swinburne, *The Swinburne Letters,* ed. Cecil Y. Lang (New Haven, Yale University Press, 1959), I, 182. Future references to the letters will be incorporated within the text under the title *Letters*.

7 Georges Lafourcade, *Swinburne: A Literary Biography* (London, 1932), p. 228.

8 Swinburne wrote to Paul Hamilton Hayne on June 22, 1875: "Mr. Stedman's comparative depreciation of my Songs before Sunrise—at least his preference of my other books to this one— could not but somewhat disappoint me. For my other books are books; but that one is myself."—*Letters,* III, 35.

9 Proof, as C. Y. Lang points out, lies in Swinburne's letter to Watts on February 7, 1878: "Please don't on any account send any part of the MS [*Lesbia Brandon*] hither; but if you have by you the proofs of the chapter where the heroine (waiting to hear of her lover's death) sings songs (French and North-English) to her children, please send them at once."—*Letters,* IV, 40.

10 A. C. Swinburne, *The Novels of A. C. Swinburne: Love's Cross-Currents: Lesbia Brandon* (New York, 1963), p. 269.

11 The sincerity of this and other passages from *Notes on Poems and Reviews* has been questioned by critics, but Clyde Kenneth Hyder proves in *Swinburne's Literary Career and Fame* (New York, 1963), pp. 57–60, that one must take the *Notes* seriously.

12 Swinburne, *Lesbia Brandon,* pp. 202–3.

13 W. B. Yeats, "A Dialogue of Self and Soul," *The Collected Poems of W. B. Yeats* (New York, Macmillan, 1956), p. 232.

14 T. S. Eliot, *Selected Essays* (New York, 1950), p. 285.

15 Walter Pater, *Studies in the History of the Renaissance* (London, 1873), p. viii.

iii *Walter Pater*

1 William Sharp, "Personal Reminiscences of Walter Pater," *The Atlantic Monthly,* LXXIV (December, 1894), 810.

2 William Sharp, "*Marius the Epicurean: His Sensations and Ideas,*" *The Athenaeum,* No. 2992 (February, 1885), p. 273.

3 John Pick in "Divergent Disciples of Walter Pater," *Thought,* XXIII (March, 1948), 114–28.

4 Walter Pater, *Studies in the History of the Renaissance* (London, 1873), p. 205, and *Plato and Platonism: A Series of Lectures* [London, 1901], pp. 5–6—hereafter cited as *Plato.*

5 Walter Pater, *Marius the Epicurean: His Sensations and Ideas* (2 vols.; London, 1885), I, 143.

6 Walter Pater, "Coleridge's Writings," *Westminster Review,* n.s., XXIX (January, 1866), 108.

7 Pater, "The Doctrine of Plato," *Plato,* p. 158.

8 Pater, "The Genius of Plato," *Plato,* p. 135. These lectures on Plato are a fine summary of Pater's thought, though they may well leave the student rather bewildered about Plato's. The little jingle "Whatever Miss T. eats / Turns into Miss T." applies delightfully to Pater's treatment. Any Platonic theories which do not fit into Pater's world scheme are explained as unworthy of him, and like bits of gristle, left on the plate: "Generalisation, whatever Platonists, or Plato himself may have to say about it, is a method, not of obliterating the concrete phenomenon, but of enriching it, with the joint perspective, the significance, the expressiveness of all other things beside."—"The Doctrine of Plato," *Plato,* p. 157.

9 S. T. Coleridge, "On the Principles of Genial Criticism concerning the Fine Arts," *Criticism: The Major Texts,* ed. W. J. Bate (New York, 1952), p. 373.

10 Pater, "Preface," *The Renaissance,* p. viii.

11 Ruth Child, *The Aesthetic of Walter Pater* (New York, 1940), p. 111.

12 Pater, *Marius,* I, 149.

13 Pater, *The Renaissance,* p. 196.

14 Ernest Lee Tuveson, *The Imagination as a Means of Grace* (Berkeley, 1960), p. 88.

15 John Locke, *Essay Concerning Human Understanding,* Bk. II, Ch. xi, Section 17.

16 Pater, *Marius,* I, 149–50.

17 *Ibid.,* I, 154.

18 Friedrich Wilhelm von Schelling, "Concerning the Relation of the Plastic Arts to Nature," 1807, tr. Michael Bullock in Herbert Read's *True Voice of Feeling* (London, n.d.), pp. 333–34.

19 Bernard Bosanquet, tr., *The Introduction to Hegel's Philosophy of Fine Art* (London, 1886), p. 15.

20 Pater, *The Renaissance,* p. 196.

21 Pater thought the change a wise one for others as well. Oscar Wilde in his review of *Plato and Platonism* says that Pater suggested to him that he too should write in prose rather than verse (*Reviews,* p. 544). And Arthur Symons quotes a letter written to him by Pater in 1888 in which, after praising Symons' poetry, Pater tactfully makes his point: "You know I give a high place to the literature of prose as a fine art, and therefore hope you won't think me brutal in saying that the admirable qualities of your verse are those also of imaginative prose. . . . I should say, make prose your principal *métier,* as a man of letters, and publish your verse as a more intimate gift for those who already value you for your pedestrian work in literature."—Arthur Symons, "Walter Pater," *Figures of Several Centuries* (London, 1917), p. 327.

22 Pater, *Marius,* I, 165.

23 T. S. Eliot, "Burnt Norton," *Four Quartets* (New York, Harcourt, Brace, 1943), p. 5. Jean Sudrann in "Victorian Compromise and Modern Revolution" also recognizes a likeness between *Four Quartets* and *Marius,* comparing the latter's "fresh starts" to Eliot's spiritual journey.—*ELH,* XXVI (September, 1959), 443.

24 Thomas Wright has already noted closely the reflections of Pater's early years in his work (*Life of Walter Pater* [2 vols.; New York, 1907], I, 19–30). He points out, however, that "The houses in 'Emerald Uthwart' and 'The Child in the House' are less the Paters' house at Enfield than what, in Pater's opinion, that house ought to have been. And this is the key to all the quasi-autobiographical elements in his works."—*Ibid.,* I, 19–20.

25 Walter Pater, "The Child in the House," *Miscellaneous Studies: A Series of Essays* (London, 1895), p. 147. The story appeared originally in *Macmillan's Magazine,* XXXVIII (August, 1878), 313–21.

26 Pater, "The Child in the House," *Miscellaneous Studies,* p. 159.

27 Pater, *Marius,* II, 244.

28 *Ibid.,* I, 154.

29 Quoted in Arthur Symons, *A Study of Walter Pater* (London, 1932), p. 29.

30 Pater, *Marius,* I, 166.

31 *Ibid.,* I, 168.

32 Walter Pater, "Imaginary Portraits 2. An English Poet," ed. May Ottely, *Fortnightly Review,* n.s., CXXXV (April, 1931), 446.

33 Pater, *Plato,* pp. 36–37.

34 Pater, *Marius*, II, 145.

35 *Ibid.*, II, 16.

36 Wright says that Pater's favorite amusement as a child was playing at being a clergyman and that "he preached regularly and with unction to his mother, grandmother, and his admiring Aunt Bessie."—*Life of Walter Pater*, I, 21.

37 B. A. Inman, "Organic Structure of *Marius the Epicurean*," *Philological Quarterly*, XLI (April, 1962), 491.

38 Pater, *Marius*, I, 167–68.

39 One might consider his withdrawal of the "Conclusion" in the second edition a kind of answer, if only a negative one. Pater writes, "This brief Conclusion was omitted in the second edition of this book, as I conceived it might possibly mislead some of the young men into whose hands it might fall." However, Jerome Buckley's supposition that the actual motivation for the withdrawal was probably provided by the description of Mr. Rose in Mallock's *New Republic* is a shrewd one.—"Pater and the Suppressed Conclusion," *MLN*, LXV (April, 1950), 247–49.

40 Pater, *Marius*, II, 24–25.

41 Walter Pater, "Prosper Mérimée," *Fortnightly Review*, LIV (December, 1890), 852–53.

42 Symons, "Walter Pater," *Figures of Several Centuries*, p. 335.

43 Walter Pater, *Gaston de Latour* (London, 1896), p. 51.

44 Pater, *Marius*, II, 72.

45 *Ibid.*, II, 70.

46 *Ibid.*, II, 81–82.

47 Pater, "Conclusion," *The Renaissance*, p. 211.

48 Pater, "Prosper Mérimée," pp. 853–54.

iv *Oscar Wilde*

1 W. B. Yeats, *A Vision* (New York, 1938), p. 148.

2 Arthur Symons, *A Study of Oscar Wilde* (London, 1930), p. 50.

3 *Ibid.*, pp. 84–85.

4 Arthur Nethercot, "Oscar Wilde and the Devil's Advocate," *PMLA*, LIX (September, 1944), 843.

5 Oscar Wilde, *The Letters of Oscar Wilde*, ed. Rupert Hart-Davis (New York, Harcourt, Brace, 1962), p. 352. Future references to this work will be cited in the text under the title *Letters*.

6 Oscar Wilde, "Art and the Handicraftsman," *Miscellanies*, Vol.

XIV of Robert Ross's edition of Wilde's collected works (14 vols.; Boston, [1910]), p. 307. This edition of Wilde's works will be referred to hereafter as *Collected Works.*

7 Oscar Wilde, "The Grovesnor Gallery," *Miscellanies* (*Collected Works,* Vol. XIV), p. 23.

8 *Ibid.,* p. 11.

9 Yeats remembers hearing Wilde say of *The Renaissance:* "It is my golden book; I never travel anywhere without it; but it is the very flower of decadence: the last trumpet should have sounded the moment it was written."—W. B. Yeats, *The Autobiography of William Butler Yeats* (New York, 1938), p. 114.

10 Robert Sherard, discussing the statement, "For years Dorian Gray could not free himself from the influence of this book [*A Rebours*]," says sharply, "This is, of course, silliness. Yet Oscar Wilde used to make the same silly self-deceiving statements about himself, and attributed to some 'poisonous book' which he had once read [*The Renaissance?*] many of the abnormalities of his conduct." —Sherard, *The Life of Oscar Wilde* (New York, 1928), p. 66.

11 Arthur Symons, "Introduction," *The Renaissance* (Modern Library Edition, New York, [1919]), p. xv.

12 Wilde, *Dorian Gray* (*Collected Works,* Vol. IV), p. 27.

13 Henry James, *The Ambassadors* (2 vols.; New York, 1909), I, 217.

14 Walter Pater, "Conclusion," *Studies in the History of the Renaissance* (London, 1873), p. 211.

15 Walter Pater, "A Novel by Mr. Oscar Wilde," *Uncollected Essays* (Portland, Maine, 1903), p. 127.

16 In the Introduction to his edition of Wilde's reviews Robert Ross comments: "The great men of the previous generation, Wilde's intellectual peers, with whom he was in artistic sympathy, looked on him askance. Ruskin was disappointed with his former pupil, and Pater did not hesitate to express disapprobation to private friends; while he accepted incense from a disciple, he distrusted the thurifer."—*Reviews* (*Collected Works,* Vol. XII), p. xii. Ross is not reliable in his interpretation or even his presentation of facts—it seems unlikely, for instance, that Ruskin thought about Wilde one way or another—but here he may be giving at least a partial truth.

17 André Gide, *Oscar Wilde,* tr. Bernard Frechtman (New York, 1949), pp. 3–4.

18 Wilde, *Miscellanies* (*Collected Works,* Vol. XIV), p. 27.

19 Oscar Wilde, "L'Envoi, an Introduction to *Rose Leaf and Apple*

Leaf," *Miscellanies* (*Collected Works,* Vol. XIV), pp. 31–32. In the Widener Collection there is a copy of *The Happy Prince and Other Tales* (London, 1888) which bears the autograph inscription: "To John Ruskin in all love and loyalty from Oscar Wilde. June '88."

20 A manuscript letter in Houghton Library from Walter E. Ledger to Thomas B. Mosher, written from Wimbledon, England, on February 12, 1906, says that "Sir Rennell Rodd quarrelled with Wilde when the latter published Rose Leaf and Apple Leaf, for it was without Rodd's permission. The original title of the work was 'Songs in the South' and it was dedicated to Rodd's father. Two of the poems in it were omitted in the American edition."

21 *The Athenaeum* reviewed the poem, listing the imitations from Shakespeare, Milton, Tennyson, and Swinburne, and concluding that "there is scarcely a poet of high mark in this century whose influence is not perceptible."—*The Athenaeum,* No. 2804 (July 23, 1881), p. 103.

22 A letter from Wilde to Reginald Harding, sent from Merrion Square, Dublin, in July, 1877, shows that Wilde's "Romish leanings" moved a wealthy cousin virtually to strike him from his will.—Vyvyan Holland, *Son of Oscar Wilde* (London, 1954), p. 243.

23 Oscar Wilde, "The Burden of Itys," *Poems* (*Collected Works,* Vol. I), p. 83. Future references will be made in the text under the title *Poems.*

24 Oscar Wilde, *Salomé* (*Collected Works,* Vol. VI), p. 67. Sometimes Wilde's inability to efface himself in a poetic reverie has very amusing consequences. In "The Burden of Itys," for instance, he adopts Baudelaire's lines on Michelangelo's "Night":

> Ou bien toi, grande Nuit, fille de Michel-Ange,
> Qui tords paisiblement dans une pose étrange
> Tes appas façonnés aux bouches des Titans!

(Charles Baudelaire, "L'Idéal," *Les Fleurs du Mal*)
and makes them:

> "O . . . that I could charm
> The Dawn at Florence from its dumb despair
> Mix with those mighty limbs and make that giant breast my lair!"
> (*Poems,* p. 92.)

25 Manuscript letter from George E. Woodberry to Charles Eliot Norton, written from Lincoln, Nebraska, April 25, 1882. Charles

Eliot Norton Collection, Houghton Library, Harvard University.

26 Charles Baudelaire, "De L'Eclectisme et du Doute: Salon de 1846," *Curiosités Esthétiques (Oeuvres Complètes de Charles Baudelaire* [Paris, 1868–73], Vol. II), p. 165.

27 Charles Baudelaire, "Éloge du Maquillage: Le Peintre de la Vie Moderne," *L'Art Romantique (Oeuvres Complètes*, Vol. III), p. 100.

28 Oscar Wilde, "The English Renaissance," *Miscellanies (Collected Works*, Vol. XIV), p. 258.

29 Matthew Arnold, "The Study of Poetry," *Essays in Criticism*, Second Series (London, 1898), p. 1.

30 Wilde, "Critic as Artist," *Intentions and The Soul of Man (Collected Works*, Vol. III), pp. 164–65.

31 Wilde, "Decay of Lying," *Intentions (Collected Works*, Vol. III), p. 33.

32 *Ibid.*, p. 34.

33 This was at the first meeting of Yeats and Wilde, just after the latter had written a review praising *The Wanderings of Usheen.* —Yeats, *Autobiography*, p. 118.

34 W. B. Yeats, *The Collected Poems of W. B. Yeats* (New York, Macmillan, 1956), p. 322.

35 *Ibid.*, p. 342. Yeats also echoed Wilde's idea in his prose when he wrote in 1937: "Somebody saw a woman of exuberant beauty coming from a public-house with a pot of beer and commended her to Rossetti; twenty years later Mrs. Langtry called upon Watts and delighted him with her simplicity. . . . Two painters created their public; two types of beauty decided what strains of blood would most prevail."—W. B. Yeats, "Introduction," *Essays and Introductions* (New York, 1961), p. xi.

36 Oscar Wilde, "The Letters of a Great Woman," *Reviews (Collected Works*, Vol. XII), pp. 49–50.

37 The discussion between Wilde and Woodberry on form touched upon the Grand Canyon: "He spoke of Colorado Canyons; 'but are they beautiful in form,' I said, and he said 'Oh yes!' and gave a description to convince me, that was pure color without one line in it."—Woodberry, manuscript letter to C. E. Norton, Charles Eliot Norton Collection, Houghton Library, Harvard University.

38 Wilde, "The Soul of Man," *Intentions (Collected Works*, Vol. III), p. 300.

39 Wilde, "The English Renaissance," *Miscellanies (Collected Works*, Vol. XIV), p. 251.

40 Charles Baudelaire, "Eugène Delacroix: Salon de 1846," *Curiosités Esthétiques (Oeuvres Complètes,* Vol. II), p. 102.

41 Wilde, "Pen, Pencil, and Poison," *Intentions (Collected Works,* Vol. III), pp. 88–89.

42 Wilde, "The Critic as Artist," *Intentions, (Collected Works,* Vol. III), p. 144.

43 Charles Baudelaire, "A Quoi Bon la Critique?: Salon de 1846," *Curiosités Esthétiques (Oeuvres Complètes,* Vol. II), p. 82.

44 Wilde, "Decay of Lying," *Intentions (Collected Works,* Vol. III), p. 21.

45 Wilde, "The Critic as Artist," *Intentions (Collected Works,* Vol. III), p. 145.

46 *Ibid.,* p. 197.

47 Wilde, "The Soul of Man," *Intentions (Collected Works,* Vol. III), pp. 274–75.

48 Wilde, "The Critic as Artist," *Intentions (Collected Works,* Vol. III), p. 184.

49 *Ibid.,* p. 185.

50 *Ibid.,* p. 183.

51 Baudelaire's dandy is the last representative of an old aristocratic order: "Le dandysme est un soleil couchant; comme l'astre qui décline, il est superbe, sans chaleur et plein de mélancolie. Mais, hélas! la marée montante de la démocratie, qui envahit tout et qui nivelle tout, noie jour à jour ses derniers représentants de l'orgueil humain et verse des flots d'oubli sur les traces de ces prodigieux mirmidons."—"Le Dandy: Le Peintre de la Vie Moderne," *L'Art Romantique (Oeuvres Complètes,* Vol. III), p. 95.

The link between aristocracy and dedication to poetic form had been made by Alexis de Tocqueville: "Prise dans son ensemble, la littérature des siècles démocratiques ne saurait présenter, ainsi que dans les temps d'aristocratie, l'image de l'ordre, de la régularité, de la science et de l'art: la forme s'y trouvera, d'ordinaire, négligée et parfois méprisée."—*De la Démocratie en Amérique* (2 Vols.; Paris, 1951), II, 83.

In De Tocqueville's opinion, however, there was to be a gain as well as a loss. The Parnassians saw only the loss and set themselves to proving De Tocqueville false. The fear of democracy that they felt in doing so is obvious in the violence with which Théophile Gautier "explains" his principles: "Non, imbéciles, non, crétins et goîtreux que vous êtes, un livre ne fait pas de la soupe à la gélatine."—"Preface," *Mademoiselle de Maupin* (Paris, 1873), p. 18.

52 André Gide, *The Journals of André Gide,* tr. Justin O'Brien (4 vols.; New York, 1947–51), II, 400.

53 Frank Harris, *Oscar Wilde: His Life and Confessions* (2 vols.; New York, 1918), I, 299; Yeats, *Autobiography,* p. 245; Hesketh Pearson, *Oscar Wilde: His Life and Wit* (New York, 1946), p. 271; Sherard, *Life of Oscar Wilde,* pp. 354–57.

54 Arthur Nethercot's study "Oscar Wilde and the Devil's Advocate" uses a similar method in analysing *The Picture of Dorian Gray* and Wilde's plays, though he insists too much perhaps on the truth of the "moral" Wilde, saying, "He [Wilde] knew that the truth about the man Oscar Wilde was preserved in his writings" (p. 850). Is it really clear, however, that Wilde ever came to so good an understanding of himself?

55 When describing Lord Henry, Wilde writes: "And so he had begun by vivisecting himself as he had ended by vivisecting others" (p. 68); this is the sin of Roger Chillingworth and of Ethan Brand. Julian Hawthorne reviewed *The Picture of Dorian Gray* for *Lippincott's Magazine;* there he compares it with Balzac's story "La Peau de Chagrin" and with Stevenson's *Dr. Jekyll and Mr. Hyde,* but, disappointingly, he makes no parallels between his father's stories and *Dorian Gray;* yet there are enough similarities in thought and even in method to make such a comparison very interesting.—Julian Hawthorne, "The Romance of the Impossible," *Lippincott's Magazine,* XLVI (September, 1890), 412–15.

   Vincent O'Sullivan says that Wilde did not take American literature seriously except for the works of Poe, Whitman, and Hawthorne, "not really liking any of them, I think, but Hawthorne—the Hawthorne of *The Scarlet Letter."—Aspects of Wilde* (New York, 1936), p. 133.

56 H. Montgomery Hyde, ed., *The Trials of Oscar Wilde* (London, 1948) p. 128. This is also the version printed in *Lippincott's Magazine,* XLVI (July, 1890), 1–100, but its repetition at the trial is cited here because in the course of the questioning the point was made that through Pater's influence this passage was changed.

57 Gide, *The Journals of André Gide,* II, 409.

58 *Ibid.,* pp. 409–10.

59 Wilde, "The Critic as Artist," *Intentions* (*Collected Works,* Vol. III), p. 221.

60 Wilde, *Miscellanies* (*Collected Works,* Vol. XIV), pp. 139–40.

61 Aubrey Beardsley drew a delightful cartoon which serves as frontispiece for Stuart Mason's *Bibliography of Oscar Wilde* (Lon-

don, 1914). The picture is entitled "Oscar Wilde at Work '(Il ne faut pas le regarder)' "; it shows Wilde at his desk surrounded by those works on which he is particularly dependent: books by Gautier, Flaubert and Swinburne, a copy of *French Verbs at a Glance,* and, largest of all, a well-thumbed family Bible.

62 Oscar Wilde, *A House of Pomegranates* (*Collected Works,* Vol. II), p. 74.

63 *Ibid.,* pp. 128–29.

64 Frank Harris gave Wilde the central idea for the plot when he told him of an event in the life of Benjamin Disraeli that had been described to him while he was in Cairo: there a Mr. Cope White-house told Harris that Disraeli had made money by entrusting the Rothschilds with the purchase of Suez Canal shares. The story is substantially true, though Frank Harris was not himself con-vinced. "It seemed to me strange that this statement, if true, had never been set forth authoritatively; but the story was peculiarly modern and had possibilities in it. Oscar admitted afterwards that he had taken the idea and used it in 'An Ideal Husband.' "—*Oscar Wilde: His Life and Confessions,* I, 182.

65 Oscar Wilde, *An Ideal Husband* (*Collected Works,* Vol. IX), p. 46.

66 André Gide recalls Wilde's saying to him: "I don't like your lips; they're straight, like those of someone who has never lied. I want to teach you to lie, so that your lips may become beautiful and twisted like those of an antique mask."—*Oscar Wilde,* p. 6.

67 "Never speak disrespectfully of Society, Algernon," says Lady Bracknell. "Only people who can't get into it do that."—Oscar Wilde, *The Importance of Being Earnest* (*Collected Works,* Vol. VII), p. 163.

68 In another letter Wilde also has a very sensible technical discus-sion on the difficulty there is in describing a prison within the objective, impersonal ballad form: "With regard to the adjectives, I admit there are far too many 'dreadfuls' and 'fearfuls'; the diffi-culty is that the objects in prison have no shape or form. To take an example: the shed in which people are hanged is a little shed with a glass roof, like a photographer's studio on the sands at Margate: for eighteen months I thought it *was* a studio for photographing prisoners. There is no adjective to describe it. I call it 'hideous' because it became so to me after I knew its use. In itself it is a wooden, oblong, narrow shed with a glass roof.

"A cell may be described psychologically with reference to its effect on the soul: in itself it can only be described as 'whitewashed' or 'dimly lit.' It has no shape, no contents; it does not exist from the point of view of form or colour.

"In point of fact, describing a prison is as difficult artistically as describing a water-closet would be. If one had to describe the latter in literature, prose or verse, one could say merely that it was well or badly papered; or clean or the reverse. The horror of prison is that everything is so simple and commonplace in itself, and so degrading and hideous and revolting in its effect" (*Letters*, pp. 654–55).

69 Oscar Wilde, "The Grave of Keats," *Poems*, p. 157.

70 Yeats, *Autobiography*, p. 244.

71 Sherard, *Life of Oscar Wilde*, p. 40.

72 Charles Baudelaire, "De L'Essence du Rire," *Curiosités Esthétiques* (*Oeuvres Complètes*, Vol. II), p. 369.

73 George Woodberry, manuscript letter to C. E. Norton, Charles Eliot Norton Collection, Houghton Library, Harvard University.

v *Lionel Johnson*

1 W. B. Yeats, *The Autobiography of William Butler Yeats* (New York, 1938), p. 242.

2 *Ibid.*, p. 259.

3 Lionel Johnson, "Incurable," *The Pageant*, I (1896), 131–33.

4 Letter from Rhual, December 29, 1884, in *Some Winchester Letters of Lionel Johnson* (London, 1919), p. 168. Russell himself edited the letters and published them anonymously.—George Santayana, *The Middle Span* (New York, 1945), p. 57.

5 Rhual, January, 1885, *Winchester Letters*, p. 170. According to Arthur Patrick it was allusions like these to the Johnson family that caused the edition to be withdrawn from circulation.—Arthur Patrick, *Lionel Johnson, Poète et Critique* (Paris, 1939), p. 9.

6 Lionel Johnson, "Barrack-Room Ballads and Other Verses by Rudyard Kipling," *The Academy*, XLI (May 28, 1892), 509.

7 *Winchester Letters*, p. 176.

8 *Ibid.*, p. 50 and p. 53. On July 19, 1884, Captain Johnson wrote to Russell permitting the resumption of the correspondence and explaining that he had stopped it "having been warned that it might tend to the unsettling of his [Lionel's] mind on religious matters" (p. 124).

9 Yeats, *Autobiography*, p. 165.

10 *Winchester Letters,* p. 105.

11 W. B. Yeats, "William Blake and the Imagination," *Essays and Introductions* (New York, 1961), p. 111. In "The Tower" Yeats wrote:

> Now shall I make my soul,
> Compelling it to study
> In a learned school.
> —W. B. Yeats, *The Collected Poems of W. B. Yeats* (New York, Macmillan, 1956), p. 197.

12 Santayana, *The Middle Span,* p. 55.

13 *Winchester Letters,* p. 111.

14 *Ibid.,* p. 15.

15 William Rossetti writes that Browning delighted Rossetti because in his poems were "passion, observation, aspiration, mediaevalism, the dramatic perception of character, act, and incident."—*Dante Gabriel Rossetti: His Family Letters* (2 vols.; Boston, 1895), I, 102. Largely through Rossetti's influence Browning became very popular at Oxford and by Johnson's time a devotion to him was part of the aesthetic tradition.—M. B. Cramer, "Browning's Literary Reputation at Oxford," *PMLA,* LVII (March, 1942), 232–40.

16 *Winchester Letters,* p. 20.

17 Lionel Johnson, *The Academy,* XLII (August 6, 1892), 103.

18 *Winchester Letters,* pp. 182–83.

19 Lionel Johnson, *The Art of Thomas Hardy* (London, 1894), p. 162.

20 W. B. Yeats and Lionel Johnson, *Poetry and Ireland* (Churchtown, Dundrum, 1908), p. 19.

21 Lionel Johnson, "Cardinal Newman," *Post Liminium: Essays and Critical Papers,* ed. Thomas Whittemore (London, 1911), p. 301.

22 *Ibid.,* pp. 297–98.

23 Lionel Johnson, "Walter Pater," *The Complete Poems of Lionel Johnson,* ed. Iain Fletcher (London, 1953), p. 269.

24 *Winchester Letters,* p. 165.

25 Katherine Tynan, *Memories* (London, 1924), p. 113.

26 Yeats, *Autobiography,* p. 165. Yeats' amusing pretense of bewilderment over Johnson's methods of punctuation (which he describes, nonetheless, with perfect accuracy) shows that he had his own methods of counter-attack: "He [Johnson] punctuated after the manner of the seventeenth century and was always ready to spend an hour discussing the exact use of a colon. 'One should use a colon where other people use a semi-colon, a semi-colon where other people use a comma,' was, I think, but a condescension to my ignorance, for the matter was plainly beset with many subtleties."

—*Ibid.*, p. 262.

27 Johnson, *Post Liminium*, p. 165.

28 *Ibid.*, p. 160.

29 John Henry, Cardinal Newman, "The Second Spring," *Sermons Preached on Various Occasions* (London, 1891), pp. 171–72.

30 Santayana, *The Middle Span*, pp. 61–62.

31 Harold Frederic, *The Damnation of Theron Ware* (New York, 1896).

32 Johnson, "The Church of a Dream," *Complete Poems*, pp. 82–83. A poem written in 1891, the very year of Johnson's conversion, and dedicated to Ernest Dowson, shows a very similar feeling:

> Leave we awhile without the turmoil of the town;
> Leave we the sullen gloom, the faces full of care:
> Stay we awhile and dream, within this place of prayer,
> Stay we, and pray, and dream: till in our hearts die down
> Thoughts of the world, unkind and weary.
> —"Our Lady of France," *ibid.*, p. 15.

33 Yeats, "In Memory of Major Robert Gregory," *Collected Poems*, p. 130.

34 Johnson, "Mystic and Cavalier," *Complete Poems*, p. 29.

35 Johnson, "To Passions," *ibid.*, pp. 174–75.

36 Johnson, "A Dream," *ibid.*, p. 143.

37 Johnson, "The Dark Angel," *ibid.*, p. 67.

38 T. S. Eliot, "The Waste Land," *Collected Poems, 1909–1935* (New York, Harcourt, Brace, 1936), p. 89.

39 *Winchester Letters*, p. 147.

40 Wilde, "Critic as Artist," *Intentions and The Soul of Man*, Vol. III of Robert Ross's edition of Wilde's collected works (14 vols.; Boston, [1910]), pp. 164–65.

41 Johnson, *Post Liminium*, pp. 217–18.

42 Lionel Johnson, "*Eighteenth Century Vignettes* by Austen Dobson," *The Academy*, XLII (December 19, 1892), 531.

43 Johnson, *Complete Poems*, p. 85.

44 Arthur Symons, ed., *The Poems of Ernest Dowson* (London, 1915), p. viii.

45 Johnson, "At the Cheshire Cheese," *Complete Poems*, p. 259.

46 Yeats, *Autobiography*, p. 260.

47 Johnson, "Winchester," *Complete Poems*, p. 227.

48 Johnson, "Lines to a Lady upon her Third Birthday, 1889," *ibid.*, p. 45. "At Eton" (pp. 201–2) and "A Dream of Youth" (pp. 53–57), both also written in 1889, have similar themes. A nostalgia for childhood is not, of course, peculiar to Johnson; so widely were

his feelings shared by others of his generation that England seems almost to have become one of the "nurseries of Heaven."

49 Johnson, *Post Liminium*, p. 218.
50 Lord Francis Russell, *My Life and Adventures* (London, 1923), pp. 90–91.
51 Johnson, *Post Liminium*, p. 247.

vi *Arthur Symons*

1 An unpublished letter to Arthur Moore from Dowson in the Morgan Library gives the latter's first impression of Symons: "I met Arthur Symons last night: do you know him? He is a standing dish with the 'Academy' and knows his Paris well; but on the whole I was not greatly impressed."—Quoted by Thomas J. Garbaty, "The Savoy, 1896: A Re-edition of Representative Prose and Verse" (unpublished Ph.D. thesis, University of Pennsylvania, 1957), p. 201.

2 Paul Verlaine, "My Visit to London (November 1893)," tr. Arthur Symons, *The Savoy*, No. 2 (April, 1896), pp. 119–35.

3 W. B. Yeats, *The Autobiography of William Butler Yeats* (New York, 1938), p. 272.

4 Unpublished letter from Arthur Symons to William Rothenstein [1893–1894], in the Rothenstein Collection, Houghton Library.

5 Vincent O'Sullivan, *Aspects of Wilde,* (New York, 1936), p. 77.

6 Arthur Symons, ed., *The Savoy*, No. 8 and last (December, 1896).
    1) "Mundi Victima," pp. 13–27.
    2) "Walter Pater," pp. 33–41.
    3) "The Childhood of Lucy Newcome," pp. 51–61.
    4) "Hérodiade," pp. 67–68.
    5) "The Isles of Aran," pp. 73–92.
    6) "A Literary Causerie: By Way of Epilogue," pp. 91–92.

7 Arthur Symons, "Dieppe: 1895," *The Savoy*, No. 1 (January, 1896), p. 85 and p. 93.

8 On the first page of *Confessions: A Study in Pathology* (New York, 1930), Symons mentions the strain of insanity in his family. Roger Lhombreaud, although he emphasizes Symons' battle against debt, mentions reports of witnesses which suggest that during the last years of her life Symons' mother was not completely sane.— *Arthur Symons: A Critical Biography* (London, 1963).

9 Arthur Symons, "Conclusion," *Studies in Prose and Verse* (London, [1904]), p. 290.

10 Arthur Symons, *A Study of Oscar Wilde* (London, 1930), p. 50.

11 Symons, "Prosper Mérimée," *Studies in Prose and Verse*, p. 32.

12 *Ibid.*, pp. 37–38.

13 Wilde, *Dorian Gray*, p. 5.

14 Symons, "Walter Pater," *Studies in Prose and Verse*, p. 76.

15 Arthur Symons, *The Symbolist Movement in Literature* (New York, 1908), p. 134.

16 Lhombreaud, *Arthur Symons*, p. 5.

17 Arthur Symons, "A Prelude to Life," *Spiritual Adventures* (London, 1905), p. 4.

18 Symons, "Fact in Literature," *Studies in Prose and Verse*, p. 3.

19 Symons does not use this phrase in "A Prelude to Life" but gives himself the title in *Confessions*, p. 48.

20 Frank Harris, *Contemporary Portraits*, Third Series (New York, 1920), p. 73.

21 Typical of Harris' slap-dash reporting is his account of Symons' attack of insanity, as garbled a piece of gossip as the story of H. C. E.'s crime in *Finnegans Wake*. Harris tells the story given him by a friend: "He [Symons] was walking with his wife one day in Genoa, I think it was, when he suddenly lost control of himself and began to break shop windows, muttering wildly all the while, 'Lost! Lost!' Lost, indeed, I'm afraid, down and out."—Harris, *Contemporary Portraits*, Third Series, p. 82.

   According to Symons' own account he was alone in Ferrara. He does not mention the shop windows.—*Confessions*, pp. 18–23.

22 Yeats, *Autobiography*, p. 272.

23 In *Confessions* Symons makes an explicit comparison between himself and this character described in *Spiritual Adventures*. See *Confessions*, p. 1.

24 Symons, "Christian Trevalga," *Spiritual Adventures*, p. 96.

25 Arthur Symons, "A Woman," *Days and Nights* (London, 1889), p. 143. Late in his life Symons put Rossetti's "The Orchard Pit" into verse, using the latter's outline and, at times, his phrasing, in a poem called "The Pit of Hell."—Arthur Symons, *Jezebel Mort and Other Poems* (London, 1931), pp. 9–34.

26 Arthur Symons, "Renée," *London Nights* (London, 1895), p. 6.

27 Arthur Symons, "In the Oratory," *Silhouettes* (London, 1896), p. 19.

28 Symons, "Perfume," *Silhouettes*, p. 41.

29 Arthur Symons, "New Year's Eve," *The Savoy,* No. 2 (April, 1896), p. 25. Lionel Johnson has a parody of this sort of Symons' poem, which he calls "an attempt at the sensuous love-lyric":

> Sometimes in very joy of shame,
> Our flesh becomes one living flame:
> And she and I
> Are no more separate but the same.
> —Johnson, "Incurable," *The Pageant,* I (1896), 131.

The parody is so close to many genuine poems that Symons must have winced.

30 Symons, "Paris," *London Nights,* p. 87.

31 Arthur Symons, "An Epilogue to Love, VI," *The Fool of the World* (London, 1906), p. 102.

32 *Ibid.,* p. 103.

33 Symons, "Walter Pater," *Studies in Prose and Verse,* p. 67.

34 Luxulyan's sudden moments of terror are described so vividly that they may also have been Symons'. Luxulyan describes a cab-ride home from a concert; when the cab turns out of narrow streets into a broad road, the fear of death suddenly possesses him: "One enters into it as into a long dimly lighted alley, and at the end of the road is the sky, with one star hung like a lantern upon the darkness; and it seems as if the sky is at the end of the road, that if one drove right on one would plunge over the edge of the world. All that is solid on the earth seems to melt about one; it is as if one's eyes had been suddenly opened, and one saw for the first time."—Symons, "Extracts from the Journal of Henry Luxulyan," *Spiritual Adventures,* pp. 254–55. In "A Prelude to Life," p. 17, Symons uses the last sentence to apply to his own fear of death.

At another time, Luxulyan wakes suddenly in great terror: "I had the sensation of a world in which the daylight had been blotted out, and men stumbled in a perpetual night, which the lamps did not make visible."—*Ibid.,* p. 262.

35 Symons, "Henry Luxulyan," *Spiritual Adventures,* p. 251.

36 The bride's name in "An Autumn City" is worth remembering; it is Livia.

37 Symons, "Unspiritual Adventures in Paris," *Wanderings* (London, [1931]), p. 103.

38 Arthur Symons, "For Des Esseintes. VI, Perdition, " *Love's Cruelty* (London, 1923), p. 31.

39 Walter Pater, "A Poet with Something to Say," *Uncollected Essays* (Portland, Maine, 1903), pp. 83–84.

40 Arthur Symons, *An Introduction to the Study of Browning* (London, 1886), p. 35.

41 Symons, "Paul Verlaine," *Symbolist Movement*, p. 81.

42 Symons, "A Literary Causerie," *The Savoy*, No. 8 (December, 1896), p. 92.

43 Symons, "Paul Verlaine," *Symbolist Movement*, p. 76 and p. 80.

44 Symons, "Prelude to Life," *Spiritual Adventures*, pp. 49–50. In *London*, he adds a few very interesting details: "I am able to remember how I used to turn out of the Temple and walk slowly towards Charing Cross, elbowing my way meditatively, making up sonnets in my head while I missed no attractive face on the pavement or on the top of an omnibus, pleasantly conscious of the shops yet undistracted by them, happy because I was in the midst of people, and happier still because they were all unknown to me." —Arthur Symons, *London: A Book of Aspects* (Minneapolis, 1909. Printed privately for Edmund D. Brooks and his friends), p. 22. The circumstances under which they were written may help to explain the casual organization of many of Symons' poems.

45 Symons, "Songs of the Poltescoe Valley," *Fool of the World*, p. 29.

46 Arthur Symons, "At the Alhambra: Impressions and Sensations," *The Savoy*, No. 5 (September, 1896), p. 75.

47 Symons, "The Magic of Auxerre," *Wanderings*, p. 178.

48 Symons, "Esther Kahn," *Spiritual Adventures*, p. 55. Symons noted Hawthorne's similar tendency to "watch life from a corner, as he watched the experimental life at Brook Farm."—Symons, "Nathaniel Hawthorne," *Studies in Prose and Verse*, p. 55.

49 Symons, *London*, p. 28.

50 Symons, "Gabriele D'Annunzio," *Studies in Prose and Verse*, p. 140.

51 Yeats, *Autobiography*, p. 273.

52 Symons, *Symbolist Movement*, p. vi.

53 Arthur Symons, "The Decadent Movement in Literature," *Harper's New Monthly Magazine*, LXXXVII (November, 1893), 862.

54 Symons, "Introduction," *Symbolist Movement*, p. 6.

55 Yeats, "William Blake and his Illustrations to the *Divine Comedy*," *Essays and Introductions* (New York, 1961), p. 116. This essay first appeared in *The Savoy*, No. 3 (July, 1896), pp. 41–57.

In his description of the trip he took with Yeats to the Aran Islands, Symons writes: "We talked of Parnell, of the county families, of mysticism, the analogy of that old Biblical distinction of body, soul, and spirit with the symbolical realities of the lamp, the wick, and the flame."—Arthur Symons, "The Isles of Aran," *The Savoy*, No. 8 (December, 1896), p. 73.

56 Symons, *Introduction to Browning*, p. 5.

57 Symons, "A Note on George Meredith," *Studies in Prose and Verse*, p. 143.

58 Symons, "Prosper Mérimée," *Studies in Prose and Verse*, p. 33. The doctrine appears in *Axël:* "For in your own pure will you hold the essence of all things and are the god you have it in your power to become. Such is the dogma and prime secret of true knowledge." —Auguste, Comte de Villiers de l'Isle-Adam, *Axël*, tr. H. P. Finberg (London, 1925), p. 214.

59 His understanding of the power of the imagination gave Symons this splendid insight into the later paintings of D. G. Rossetti: "Yet, as his intentions overpower him [Rossetti], as he becomes the slave and no longer the master of his dreams, his pictures become no longer symbolic. They become idols. Venus, growing more and more Asiatic as the moon's crescent begins to glitter above her head, and her name changes from Aphrodite to Astarte, loses all the freshness of the waves from which she was born, and her sorcery hardens into a wooden image painted to be the object of savage worship. Dreams are no longer content to be turned into waking realities, taking the color of daylight, that they may remain visible to our eyes, but they remain lunar, spectral, a dark and unintelligible menace."—Symons, "The Rossettis," *Dramatis Personae* (Indianapolis, 1923), pp. 130–31.

60 Symons, *Confessions*, pp. 86–87.

61 Symons, "Prelude to Life," *Spiritual Adventures*, p. 16.

62 Symons, "Christian Trevalga," *Spiritual Adventures*, p. 91.

63 Symons, "Prelude to Life," *Spiritual Adventures*, p. 42.

64 Symons, *Confessions*, p. 86, and "Gérard de Nerval," *Symbolist Movement*, p. 18.

65 Symons, Christian Trevalga," *Spiritual Adventures*, p. 107.

66 Symons, "The Wanderers," *Amoris Victima* (London, 1897), p. 34.

67 *Ibid.*

68 Symons, *Confessions*, pp. 10–11.

69 Symons, "Henry Luxulyan," *Spiritual Adventures*, p. 311.

70 Symons, *Confessions*, p. 8.

VII *The Decadent Consciousness*

1 Martin Buber, *I and Thou* (New York, 1958), p. 34.
2 Walter Pater, *Marius the Epicurean: His Sensations and Ideas* (2 vols.; London, 1885), II, 74.
3 John Keats, *The Poetical Works of John Keats,* ed. H. W. Garrod (Oxford University Press, 1956), p. 408, ll. 40–45.
4 Wallace Stevens uses the phrase when discussing the necessity and the difficulty of bringing together imagination and reality in "The Noble Rider and the Sound of Words," *The Necessary Angel* (New York, 1951), pp. 1–36.

Index

Alighieri, Dante. *See* Dante Alighieri

Aristippus of Cyrene, 40–41, 46–48

Arnold, Matthew: social thought of, xiv, 6, 16, 68, 69, 95; influence on Wilde of, 67, 68; influence on Johnson of, 85, 87–88, 89, 94; mentioned, 47, 64, 79

Art for art's sake: Rossetti's interpretation, 4; Swinburne's interpretation, 21–23; Pater's interpretation, 42; Wilde's interpretation, 65

Artist, isolation of: accepted by Decadents, xiv, 33, 95, 109–10, exemplified by Rossetti, 4–6, 9, 17; symbolized by Lady of Shalott, 5, 82; attitude of Pater toward, 49

Badley, J. H., 83, 85

Balzac, Honoré de, 79, 84

Barbey d'Aurévilly, Jules, 62, 98

Bastien–Lepage, Jules, 84

Baudelaire, Charles, 20–21, 63, 66, 68, 69, 79, 84, 134*n24*, 136*nn40,51*

Beardsley, Aubrey, xvi, 97, 137–38*n61*

Blake, William, 11, 32, 36

Brown, Madox, 128*n9*

149

3000 800027 22572

St. Louis Community College

W9-DIM-976

WITHDRAWN

FV

 St. Louis Community College

Forest Park
Florissant Valley
Meramec

Instructional Resources
St. Louis, Missouri

GAYLORD

▲ The American
Diabetes Association®

The American
Dietetic Association

FAMILY
COOKBOOK

Volume II

Revised Edition

The American Diabetes Association is the nation's leading voluntary health agency in the field of diabetes, with 55 state affiliates and more than 800 chapters across the country.

The American Dietetic Association is the nation's largest group of nutrition professionals, with more than 50,000 members.

Other books by the authors:

The American Diabetes Association
The American Dietetic Association
     Family Cookbook, Volume I (Rev. Ed.)

The American Diabetes Association
The American Dietetic Association
     Family Cookbook, Volume III
     With Microwave Adaptations

American Diabetes Association
     Holiday Cookbook
Betty Wedman, M.S., R.D.

▲.The American
Diabetes Association®

The American
Dietetic Association

FAMILY
COOKBOOK
Volume II

Revised Edition

Illustrated by Lauren Rosen

SIMON & SCHUSTER
NEW YORK LONDON TORONTO SYDNEY TOKYO SINGAPORE

Simon & Schuster

Rockefeller Center
1230 Avenue of the Americas
New York, New York 10020

Copyright © 1987 by The American Diabetes Association and
The American Dietetic Association

All rights reserved, including the right of reproduction in whole
or in part in any form.

Published in 1987 by Prentice Hall Press

SIMON & SCHUSTER is a trademark of Simon & Schuster Inc.

Originally published in 1984 by Prentice-Hall, Inc.

Manufactured in the United States of America

10 9 8 7 6

LC No. 87-42674

ISBN 0-671-76131-5

ACKNOWLEDGMENTS

The American Diabetes Association and The American Dietetic Association gratefully acknowledge the contributions made by:

Cookbook Advisory Committee

Marion Franz, R.D.
Georgia Kimmel, R.D.
Joy Kirkpatrick, R.D.
Madelyn Wheeler, R.D.
Judith Wylie-Rosett, Ed.D., R.D. (Chair)

Cookbook Computer Services

Indiana University Computing Facilities
Patricia S. Ours, R.D.
Lawrence A. Wheeler, Ph.D., M.D.

Contributors

Nutritional Needs Through Life's Stages

Margaret Bogle, R.D.
Sue Brady, R.D.
Judith Ernst, R.D.
Karyl Rickard, Ph.D., R.D.

On Fighting Fat II: Keeping Primed

>Marjan Schneider, M.S.W., A.C.S.W.

Exercise: Nutrition's Important Partner

>Peter J. Spiers, M.S. (Exercise Physiologist)

Introducing Tofu and Recipe for Scrambled Tofu

>Naoko Owaki Robinson, founder, House of Kenko, Center for Optimal Health and Oriental Studies

Chapters adapted from *Diabetes Forecast* magazine

>Nirmala Auerbach, R.D.
>Barbara Burgess, R.D.
>Marion Franz, R.D.
>Kathy McFarland
>Beth Naylor, R.D.
>F. Xavier Pi-Sunyer, M.D.
>Dorothea Sims
>Janice M. Whitfield, R.D.
>Judy Wylie-Rosett, Ed.D., R.D.

Recipe Development

>Alice Bachrach, R.D.
>Peggy Brown
>Alice Knight
>Frances H. Lee, R.D., Coordinator
>Lavoyce McCurdy
>Ruth Strickland, R.D.
>All the friends of the Associations, including *Diabetes Forecast* subscribers, who contributed recipes

Several recipes in this collection are reprinted or adapted from the Indiana University School of Medicine's Collection of Recipes, Department of Nutrition and Dietetics, Bloomington, printing, 1983; and from *Cooking to Stay in Shape*, by Marion Franz, Betsy Kerr Hedding,and Gayle Leitch.

In addition to the recipes submitted by individuals for testing and use in this collection, several were reprinted directly or adapted from the following sources:

Collection of Recipes of the Department of Nutrition and Dietetics, Indiana University School of Medicine, H. Bernice Boucher, M.S., R.D., editor, Indianapolis, IN, scheduled for publication in 1984.

Cooking to Stay in Shape, *by Marion Franz, Betsy Kerr Hedding and Gayle Leitch, SHAPE, Inc., Minnetonka, MN, 1983.*

An Apple a Day, *Volume 2, Loma Linda University School of Medicine Women's Auxiliary to the Alumni Association, Typecraft, Inc., Pasadena, CA, 1983.*

Nutritious and Delicious, *the Greater Cincinnati Dietetic Association and the Greater Cincinnati Nutrition Council, Joerger-Vetter Printing, Cincinnati, OH, 1982.*

Manuscript Production

> Mary M. Astarita
> Barbara Burgess, R.D., Coordinator
> Robert P. Lundy
> Ricki Rusting, Coordinator
> Caroline Stevens

□ CONTENTS

☐ FOREWORD

Volume II of the *Family Cookbook* was prepared to complement the first *Family Cookbook*, which was extremely well received. This book, like the first, is directed to anyone with diabetes as well as to others who care about their health.

In addition to giving you more than 200 new recipes, Volume II includes a nutrition guide that elaborates on many of the topics in the first volume and responds to reader requests for added information. For instance, chapters in Volume II deal with fiber, emotional aspects of dieting, and the various nutritional needs through life's stages. Moreover, up-to-the-minute information on diabetes is included, such as a discussion of the glycemic index (a new concept in meal planning), as well as a review of current dietary strategies for managing type I (insulin-dependent) and type II (non-insulin-dependent) diabetes.

We are proud of this new volume of the *Family Cookbook* and sincerely hope it will assist you to live more comfortably with diabetes until a cure or prevention can be found.

Karl E. Sussman, M.D.
President, American
Diabetes Association

The American Dietetic Association is again pleased to collaborate with the American Diabetes Association in the preparation of the second volume of the *Family Cookbook*. Recipes in this collection were developed consistent with the nutritional guidelines formulated by nutrition experts and health and government agencies for decreasing dietary risk factors associated with diabetes and other chronic diseases.

Health-conscious persons will not only find delightful, nutritious, and economical recipes but information on fitness and food management needed by individuals taking more responsibility for their own health. This volume expands on information in Volume I and offers new features, including a chapter on exercise, a walking program, a chapter on emotional considerations of weight control, information on tofu and its use in meal planning, an update on fiber, and advice on how to decrease sugar, calories, and fat in family meal preparation. As with Volume I of the *Family Cookbook*, families with a diabetic member, as well as individuals and families in pursuit of a healthier lifestyle, will find this to be an indispensable book, one that dietitians and physicians will happily recommend.

The American Dietetic Association enthusiastically presents this second volume of the *Family Cookbook* and acknowledges the contribution of the Advisory Committee of Registered Dietitians, The American Dietetic Association Publications Committee, and the many Registered Dietitians who assisted in preparation of the manuscript and reviewed the material for publication.

Kathleen Zolber, Ph.D., R.D.,
President,
The American Dietetic Association

☐ LOCATING THE ASSOCIATIONS

NATIONAL OFFICES

American Diabetes Association
1660 Duke Street
Alexandria, Virginia 22314
(703) 549-1500

The American Dietetic Association
430 North Michigan Avenue
Chicago, Illinois 60611
(312) 280-5000

AFFILIATE ASSOCIATIONS
OF THE AMERICAN DIABETES ASSOCIATION

Alabama Affiliate, Inc.
904 Bob Wallace Avenue
Suite 222
Huntsville, AL 35801
(205) 533-5775 or (205) 533-5776

Alaska Affiliate, Inc.
201 E. Third Avenue
Suite 301
Anchorage, AK 99501
(907) 276-3607

Arizona Affiliate, Inc.
7337 North Nineteenth Avenue
Room 404
Phoenix, AZ 85021
(602) 995-1515

Arkansas Affiliate, Inc.
Tanglewood Shopping Center
7509 Cantrell Road
Suite 227
Little Rock, AR 72207
(501) 666-6345

Northern California Affiliate, Inc.
2550 Ninth Street
Suite 114
Berkeley, CA 94710
(415) 644-0920

Southern California Affiliate, Inc.
3460 Wilshire Boulevard
Suite 900
Los Angeles, CA 90010
(213) 381-3689

Colorado Affiliate, Inc.
2450 South Downing Street
Denver, CO 80210
(303) 778-7556

Connecticut Affiliate, Inc.
40 South St.
P.O. Box 10160
Elmwood, CT 06110
(203) 249-9942 or 1 (800) 842-6323

Delaware Affiliate, Inc.
2713 Lancaster Avenue
Wilmington, DE 19805
(302) 656-0030

Washington, D.C Area
   Affiliate, Inc.
1819 H Street, N.W.
Suite 1200
Washington, DC 20006
(202) 331-8303

Florida Affiliate, Inc.
P.O. Box 19745 (mailing address)
Orlando, FL 32814
3101 Maguire Blvd.
   (street address)
Suite 288
Orlando, FL 32803
(305) 894-6664

Georgia Affiliate, Inc.
3783 Presidential Parkway
Suite 102
Atlanta, GA 30340
(404) 454-8401

Hawaii Affiliate, Inc.
510 South Beretania Street
Honolulu, HI 96813
(808) 521-5677

Idaho Affiliate, Inc.
1528 Vista
Boise, ID 83705
(208) 342-2774

Downstate Illinois Affiliate, Inc.
965 North Water Street
Decatur, IL 62523
(217) 422-8228

Northern Illinois Affiliate, Inc.
6 North Michigan Avenue
Suite 1202
Chicago, IL 60602
(312) 346-1805

Indiana Affiliate, Inc.
222 South Downey Avenue
Suite 320
Indianapolis, IN 46219
(317) 352-9226

Iowa Affiliate, Inc.
888 Tenth Street
Marion, IA 52302
(319) 373-0530

Kansas Affiliate, Inc.
3210 E. Douglas
Wichita, KS 67208
(316) 681-6091

Kentucky Affiliate, Inc.
P.O. Box 345 (mailing address)
Frankfort, KY 40602
306 West Main (street address)
Suite #513
Frankfort, KY 40602
(502) 223-2971

Louisiana Affiliate, Inc.
9420 Lindale Avenue
Suite B
Baton Rouge, LA 70815
(504) 927-7732

Maine Affiliate, Inc.
59 Northport Avenue
Belfast, ME 04915
(207) 338-5132

Maryland Affiliate, Inc.
3701 Old Court Road
Suite 19
Baltimore, MD 21208
(301) 486-5516

Massachusetts Affiliate, Inc.
190 North Main Street
Natick, MA 01760
(617) 655-6900

Michigan Affiliate, Inc.
The Clausen Bldg. North Unit
23100 Providence Drive
Suite 475
Southfield, MI 48075
(313) 552-0480

Minnesota Affiliate, Inc.
3005 Ottawa Avenue, South
Minneapolis, MN 55416
(612) 920-6796

Mississippi Affiliate, Inc.
10 Lakeland Circle
Jackson, MS 39216
(601) 981-9511

Greater St. Louis Affiliate, Inc.
1790 South Brentwood Boulevard
St. Louis, MO 63144
(314) 968-3196

Heart of America Affiliate, Inc.
9201 Ward Parkway
Suite 300
Kansas City, MO 64114
(816) 361-3361

Missouri Regional Affiliate, Inc.
P.O. Box 11 (mailing address)
811 Cherry (street address)
Suite 304
Columbia, MO 65201
(314) 443-8611

Montana Affiliate, Inc.
Box 2411 (mailing address)
Great Falls, MT 59403
600 Central Plaza (street address)
Suite 304
Great Falls, MT 59401
(406) 761-0908

Nebraska Affiliate, Inc.
7377 Pacific
Suite 216A
Omaha, NE 68114
(402) 391-1251

Nevada Affiliate, Inc.
4550 East Charleston Boulevard
Las Vegas, NV 89104
(702) 459-7099

New Hampshire Affiliate, Inc.
P.O. Box 595 (mailing address)
Manchester, NH 03105
104 Middle Street
  (mailing address)
Manchester, NH 03101
(603) 627-9579

New Jersey Affiliate, Inc.
P.O. Box 6423 (mailing address)
312 North Adamsville Rd.
  (street address)
Bridgewater, NJ 08807
(201) 725-7878

New Mexico Affiliate, Inc.
525 San Pedro, N.E.
Suite 101
Albuquerque, NM 87108
(505) 266-5716

New York Diabetes Affiliate, Inc.
505 Eighth Avenue
New York, NY 10018
(212) 947-9707

New York State Affiliate, Inc.
P.O. Box 1037 (mailing address)
Syracuse, NY 13201
113 East Willow Street
  (street address)
Syracuse, NY 13202
(315) 472-9111

North Carolina Affiliate, Inc.
2315-A Sunset Avenue
Rocky Mount, NC 27801
(919) 937-4121

North Dakota Affiliate, Inc.
P.O. Box 234 (mailing address)
Grand Forks, ND 58206-0234
101 North Third Street
  (street address)
Suite 502
Grand Forks, ND 58201
(701) 746-4427

Ohio Affiliate, Inc.
1855 Fountain Square Court
Suite 310
Columbus, OH 43224-1360
(614) 263-2330

Oklahoma Affiliate, Inc.
Warren Professional Building
6465 South Yale Avenue
Suite 423
Tulsa, OK 74136
(918) 492-3839 or 1 (800) 722-5448

Oregon Affiliate, Inc.
3607 S.W. Corbett Street
Portland, OR 97201
(503) 228-0849

Greater Philadelphia Affiliate,
Inc.
21 South Fifth Street
The Bourse
Suite 570
Philadelphia, PA 19106
(215) 627-7718

Western Pennsylvania Affiliate,
Inc.
4617 Winthrop Street
Pittsburgh, PA 15213
(412) 682-3392

Mid-Pennsylvania Affiliate, Inc.
2045 Westgate Drive
Suite B-1
Bethlehem, PA 18017
(215) 867-6660

Rhode Island Affiliate, Inc.
4 Fallon Avenue
Providence, RI 02908
(401) 331-0099

South Carolina Affiliate, Inc.
2838 Devine Street
Columbia, SC 29205
(803) 799-4246

South Dakota Affiliate, Inc.
P.O. Box 659
Sioux Falls, SD 57101
(605) 335-7670

Tennessee Affiliate, Inc.
1701 Twenty-first Avenue, South
Room 403
Nashville, TN 37212
(615) 298-9919

Texas Affiliate, Inc.
8140 North Mopac
Building 1
Suite 130
Austin, TX 78759
(512) 343-6981

Utah Affiliate, Inc.
564 East 300 South
Salt Lake City, UT 84102
(801) 363-3024

Vermont Affiliate, Inc.
217 Church Street
Burlington, VT 05401
(802) 862-3882

Virginia Affiliate, Inc.
404 Eighth Street, N.E.
Suite C
Charlottesville, VA 22901
(804) 293-4953

Washington Affiliate, Inc.
3201 Fremont Avenue North
Seattle, WA 98103
(206) 632-4576

West Virginia Affiliate, Inc.
Professional Building
1036 Quarrier Street
Room 404
Charleston, WV 25301
(304) 346-6418 or 1 (800) 642-3055

Wisconsin Affiliate, Inc.
10721 West Capitol Drive
Milwaukee, WI 53222
(414) 464-9395

Wyoming Affiliate, Inc.
2908 Kelly Drive
Cheyenne, WY 82001
(307) 638-3578

AFFILIATE ASSOCIATIONS
OF THE AMERICAN DIETETIC ASSOCIATION

The American Dietetic Association has state associations in each state and district associations in many areas. Your local American Diabetes Association can provide you with the address of the Dietetic Association nearest you. Or you can get the address through the national office of the The American Dietetic Association.

□ INTRODUCTION

If you want everyone in your family to enjoy the same menu at meals . . . if you want to make delicious yet healthy dishes with ease . . . if you want to learn more about eating to promote health and prevent diet-related diseases . . . if you want to learn more about the dietary side of diabetes care . . . this book is for you.

Volume II of the American Diabetes Association/The American Dietetic Association *Family Cookbook* builds on Volume I, yet can also stand alone. The content of Volume II is entirely new. It does the following:

□ Adds more than 200 delicious, economical, and nutritious recipes formulated according to healthful criteria and taste tests.

□ Addresses the special dietary dilemmas of people who take insulin.

□ Offers in-depth advice on weight control for the many individuals (diabetic or not) who are overweight, taking into account the *emotional* as well as behavioral side of the fight against fat.

□ Encourages you to exercise and gives you tips for doing it safely.

□ Includes great ideas for meal planning, with advice on how to add zest to your creations while reducing calories.

□ Suggests practical ways to cut kitchen costs.

□ Gives you an update on fiber and the "glycemic index" and includes the fiber content in one serving of each recipe as well as an array of high-fiber recipes.

□ Helps you to handle such special activities as wildernesss camping, canoeing, and hiking.

□ Adds ethnic recipes and "exchanges."

In addition, the elements that made Volume I so popular are here. Like the first cookbook, this one is meant for the whole family, so the recipes usually yield four to six servings. However, many also include directions for making two servings. Moreover, along with fiber content, all receipes are once again accompanied by a listing of the grams of protein, fat, and carbohydrate, the calories, and the milligrams of sodium, potassium, and cholesterol in a single serving. The exchange values are also listed for those of you who plan your meals on the basis of The American Diabetes Association/The American Dietetic Association's *Exchange Lists for Meal Planning*. In general, the recipes are in keeping with the national dietary guidelines aimed at helping all Americans reduce their risk of chronic disease. These guidelines are very similar to those of the American Diabetes Association and other health agencies and suggest reducing the total amount of fat eaten, particularly saturated fat and cholesterol, decreasing the amount of sugar and salt consumed, and increasing the amount of unrefined carbohydrates eaten (especially those with fiber), as well as controlling calories. The majority of the recipes, therefore, are limited in fat, saturated fat, and cholesterol, and are low in sugar and salt.

Volume I is an excellent introduction to the principles of good nutrition. It describes the basic food groups and explains the logic behind meal planning for the general population and for people who have diabetes. Volume II reviews that information briefly and emphasizes the practical side of living with diabetes without giving up good food. We want you to be happy with your meals because if you are, chances are good that you'll eat right and be a lot healthier, too.

FAMILY
COOKBOOK
Volume II

1 □ NUTRITION AND GOOD HEALTH

Good nutrition is essential to good health whether one has diabetes or not. But what exactly is meant by good nutrition? Simply put, it means maintaining an adequate supply of the materials the body needs for growth, tissue repair, and normal life functioning. These vital materials, or nutrients, may be classified as follows:

Proteins
Carbohydrates
Fats
Vitamins
Minerals
Water

The foods we eat provide us with these nutrients in a wide variety of forms. Through the processes of digestion, absorption, and metabolism, the foods are broken down chemically, and nutrients are taken into the bloodstream and moved from the blood into cells for storage or for immediate use as energy. Whatever the body cannot use is excreted as waste.

Some foods are better suppliers of certain nutrients than are others. Fish, for example, is relatively high in protein, whereas whole grain breads are a good source of carbohydrates, and nuts contain a large percentage of fat. To achieve the goal of good nutrition, therefore, you need to select a wide variety of foods. With a well-balanced diet, you can ensure that you get the right amount and variety of the essential nutrients. (For more information, see Volume I, Chapter 1, "The Basics of Good Nutrition.")

DIET AND DISEASE PREVENTION

Good nutrition is one of the most valuable forms of preventive medicine. Many aspects of our health are beyond our control. For example, our genetic makeup may leave us susceptible to certain chronic diseases. But diet and exercise are two crucial areas in which we can directly and positively influence our long-term well-being.

The consequence of failing to eat a balanced diet may be serious health problems, particularly if too much of the wrong kind of food is eaten over a long period of time and if poor diet is combined with inactivity. Overeating of foods high in calories, fat, salt, and sugar, for instance, may contribute in varying measures to heart disease, high blood pressure, obesity, stroke, diabetes, and, possibly, some forms of cancer. Prolonged alcohol abuse has been definitely linked to cirrhosis of the liver and to other health-threatening disorders. These and other food-related problems often start in youth. They may be difficult to cure once they are under way, so it is important to recognize them and, when possible, prevent them early.

Furthermore, the foods we eat affect more than our general physical health and risk of developing certain diseases. Current research suggests that mood, sleep patterns, appetite, and a host of other psychological and emotional functions may be influenced, at least in part, by dietary factors. This is because the nutrients obtained from food make up the chemical substances that control these processes in the brain.

Good nutrition is vital to the development of learning and motor skills in very young children; nutritional imbalances can contribute to behavior problems and poor concentration in school-age youngsters. Healthy eating also becomes especially important for maintaining brain power in older people. Often, the apparent symptoms of senility in the elderly are actually the cumulative results of malnutrition. Fortunately, in cases where physical damage to the brain has not occurred, many of these symptoms are reversible.

BALANCE IS THE KEY

The "balanced" diet you want for yourself and your family should:

- ☐ Furnish sufficient amounts of the various essential nutrients.
- ☐ Avoid excesses of certain nutrients that increase the risk of diet-related diseases.
- ☐ Provide sources of calories, or energy, needed to maintain an appropriate weight and activity level.

To plan well-balanced meals, be sure to select foods from each of the four major food groups:

- ☐ *Fruits and Vegetables.* These provide: vitamin A (deep yellow or dark green vegetables), vitamin C (citrus, berries, tomatoes), potassium, B vitamins, iron, calcium, carbohydrates, and fiber.
- ☐ *Whole Grain Cereals and Breads.* For: B vitamins, iron, vitamin E, carbohydrates, and fiber.
- ☐ *Dairy Products.* For: calcium, protein, riboflavin, vitamins A and D (if fortified), and vitamin B_{12}.
- ☐ *Meats, Fish, Poultry, Eggs, Dried Beans, Peas, and Nuts.* For: protein, B vitamins, iron, and zinc.

If you follow the exchange-type meal plan recommended by the American Diabetes Association, you will notice that you are told to choose foods from six, rather than four, food groups. In actuality, you are choosing foods from similar groups; the Exchange Lists simply divide the groups into like foods for more specificity.

The lists are titled: Starch/Bread, Meat, Vegetable, Fruit, Milk, and Fat.

HOW THE GROUPS COMPARE

BASIC 4	EXCHANGE LISTS
1. Fruits and Vegetables	Fruit
	Vegetable
	Starch/Bread
2. Breads	Starch/Bread
3. Dairy Products	Milk
4. Meats	Meat (subdivided by fat content; also includes fish, poultry, cheese, eggs, and peanut butter)
	Fat (derived from Meat and Milk groups; also includes such fatty items as nuts, oils, and salad dressings)

Work out the specific amounts you need from each food group with your doctor, dietitian, or diet counselor. Individual nutritional needs may vary according to age and activity level, among other factors. (Chapter 3 provides a description of some of these considerations at different stages of life.) However, the basic principle of a balanced diet for good health is a sound one and applies to everyone.

Finally, you should be able to have a well-balanced meal plan and meet all your nutritional requirements with ordinary food. Special supplements of food products, vitamins, and minerals are rarely needed. (Menstruating women who lose a lot of blood each month, however, may need additional iron to make up for the iron losses in the blood.) No scientific evidence shows that such supplements offer any significant improvement on a regular, well-balanced food plan. In some instances, very large quantities of certain vitamin supplements may have harmful side effects or may interfere with the absorption of other vital nutrients.

NUTRITIONAL GUIDELINES

The following seven basic nutritional guidelines were designed by nutrition experts for the federal government to promote healthful eating and to reduce the risk of food-related diseases in the general population. They are also consistent with the current recommended principles for the nutritional management of diabetes. They are appropriate for the whole family—small children and adolescents, as well as adults.

1. EAT A VARIETY OF FOODS. Variety is the spice of life, it is said; but when it comes to good nutrition, variety is essential. There are up to fifty known nutrients that the body needs to stay healthy, and no single food contains them all. The wider the variety of foods in your diet, the less likely you are to develop either a deficiency or an excess of any single nutrient. Variety also reduces the likelihood of exposure to large amounts of contaminants in any single food.

Choosing foods from each of the four major groups will help insure variety in your daily diet. However, people often forget that variety *within* the food groups is also important. If you reach for the green beans every night for vegetables, you are denying yourself and your family the nutrients present in butternut squash or corn. If orange juice and grapefruit are your only source of fruit, you are missing out on the nutritional advantages in tomato juice, grapes, and mangos. Naturally, season, location, and cost will determine the availability of some foods. Nevertheless, in this country you almost always have a range of choices wide enough to please any palate and meet all nutritional needs. Don't shortchange yourself.

Choosing a variety of food sources is crucial with respect to protein, in particular. Proteins are made of amino acids, which are important to growth in children and to tissue building and repair in everyone. Animal protein sources have different amino-acid patterns than plant-protein sources. Animal sources provide "complete" proteins (all the needed amino-acid combinations), while plant proteins do not. When choosing animal sources, emphasize *lean* items. Also, learn how to combine vegetables and starches so that you get the right pairings of amino acids even when you don't eat meat. (See Chapter 15.)

2. ADJUST CALORIE INTAKE AND EXERCISE FOR PROPER WEIGHT. Calories* are the basic units of measurement of energy taken in and used up by the body. When calories "in" exceed calories "out," the body stores the excess for future use. In other words, when the food you eat provides more calories than your body needs, unused calories are converted to fat—the body's main storage depot for energy—and you gain weight.

To lose one pound of body fat, you must cut back 3,500 calories from your food intake. Exercise of any kind will also help to use up these calories. And it may be beneficial to reduce your intake of fat. The body gets its energy (calories) from four sources: protein, carbohydrate, fat, and alcohol. Measure for measure, fat contains about twice as many calories as carbohydrate or protein. This is why fat has to be monitored even more carefully than the other calorie-suppliers when losing weight. (For more specifics on weight control, see Chapters 5, 6, 7, and 8 in this volume.)

3. LIMIT FATS AND CONSUMPTION OF HIGH-FAT FOODS. Fatty foods are more than just a weight-control problem. Excess fat—particularly saturated fats and cholesterol—may contribute to heart disease. And certain kinds of cancer may also be linked to fat intake. The average American gets 40 to 50 percent of his or her total calories from foods high in fat. Most dietitians recommend that this be reduced to 30 to 35 percent, except for infants, who need more. (Check with your pediatrician.)

Reducing fat consumption may be difficult because much of the fat content of many foods is hidden. The following list classifies selected common foods by fat content:

---

*The word *calorie,* as used here, is actually a shortened version of the term kilocalorie, which is used in science to describe the amount of energy in foods. Technically, however, a calorie (small "c") is 1,000 times smaller than a kilocalorie.

FAT CALORIES IN RELATION TO TOTAL CALORIES

More than 90% fat	Bacon, mayonnaise, butter, margarine, salad and cooking oils, lard, cream, baking chocolate, vegetable shortening, olives.
80–90%	Sausages, most salad dressings, corned beef, cream cheese, unsweetened coconut, walnuts, pecans, sesame seeds, avocados.
65–80%	Potato chips, dry-roasted peanuts, ham, frankfurters, American cheese, Swiss cheese, Cheddar cheese, sunflower seeds, cashews, peanut butter.
50–65%	Broiled beef, loin steak, roasted leg of lamb.
35–50%	Most cookies, crackers, cakes, donuts, round steak, lean ground beef, whole milk.
20–35%	2 percent milk, low-fat yogurt.
10–20%	Roasted chicken (without skin), broiled fish.
Negligible amount	Skim milk, dry cereal, dry cottage cheese, beans, baked or broiled potatoes, most breads, rice, pasta, fruits, vegetables (except avocados and olives).

Source: *Basic Nutrition Facts*, Michigan Department of Public Health, Lansing, Michigan, 1980.

Fat consumption can be reduced by making informed food choices, eating smaller portions, trimming fat before cooking, cooking with low-fat methods, and eating more dried peas and beans, grain products, fruits, vegetables, low-fat dairy products, and low-fat meats. (See Volume I of the *Family Cookbook* for discussion of fat subclasses and cholesterol, and their relationship to atherosclerosis.)

4. INCREASE INTAKE OF UNREFINED CARBOHYDRATES AND LIMIT INTAKE OF REFINED CARBOHYDRATES. Gram for gram, all carbohydrates contain the same number of calories, but different sources of carbohydrates will vary in overall nutritional value. Biochemically, carbohydrates are subdivided into three groups: the term "sugar" or "simple" carbohydrate is usually applied to "monosaccharides" (which have one sugar group per molecule) and "disaccharides" (which have two sugars per molecule). The term "complex" carbohydrates usually refers to "polysaccharides" (which have many sugar groups per molecule).

Complex carbohydrates are found primarily in legumes (beans and peas), grain products, and vegetables, while simple carbohydrates are found naturally in fruit and milk. Complex carbohydrates and foods with naturally occurring simple carbohydrates are each important sources of many essential nutrients, such as vitamins, minerals, and fiber. When carbohydrates are processed or "refined" into commercial sugar and other sweeteners, however, they are left with calories but very little else in the way of nutritional value. This is why the calories in refined carbohydrates are often called "empty" or "naked."

5. INCREASE CONSUMPTION OF FIBER-RICH FOODS. Fiber, or roughage, as our grandparents called it, is the portion of plants that the human body cannot readily digest. Rich sources of fiber include complex or unrefined carbohydrates such as fresh vegetables and fruits, whole grains, beans, peas, and nuts. Fiber comes in several forms and there is some evidence that different fibers may have different effects in the body. (See Chapter 10 called "Fiber: What's In It for You?")

6. REDUCE INTAKE OF SODIUM. Sodium, like saturated fat, may be associated with health problems, notably high blood pressure. The primary source of sodium in the American diet is table salt, which is about 40 percent sodium. (One teaspoon of

salt weighs 5 grams and has about 2,000 milligrams of sodium.) Relatively large amounts of sodium also enter our diet through convenience foods of all kinds. Foods that are salty to the taste— bacon or pickles, for example—may well contain high levels of sodium, but taste alone is not always an accurate indicator. Commercial soups, peanut butters, and salad dressings are a few of the many common foods that frequently have substantial amounts of sodium.

It takes a little effort at first to adjust to a reduced-salt diet, but it can be done. In fact, many people find that they don't enjoy very salty foods after they get used to cutting back.

Because of public concern about salt consumption, food manufacturers commonly print the sodium content of their products on the package label. In addition, several food companies have developed tasty new low-sodium lines. However, many canned goods still contain high sodium levels, so, it is a good idea to rinse these foods under tap water for a full minute before cooking or serving.

7. USE ALCOHOL SPARINGLY, IF AT ALL. Alcohol is high in calories and has almost no nutritional value. Therefore, if weight reduction is an issue, even light drinkers should consider cutting back on those empty calories. The general rule is: If you do drink, do so in moderation at all times. One or two drinks daily appears to cause no harm in most adults. Pregnant women, however, should avoid alcohol to be on the safe side. People with diabetes should consult their physicians about alcohol use; they may have to observe special restrictions concerning times for drinking and amounts consumed. (See Volume I, Chapter 11: "Alcohol and Diabetes.")

2 □ NUTRITION AND DIABETES

Role of Diet in Treatment . . .
Goals of Diet Therapy . . .
The "Glycemic Index"

The dietary recommendations of the American Diabetes Association are very similar to the general nutrition guidelines outlined in Chapter 1, but they take into account the special concerns of people who have diabetes. To understand the Association's recommendations, you may first need to review the definition and causes of diabetes.

"Diabetes" is a disorder characterized by the body's failure to properly convert the fuel derived from food into energy for the body's cells. This processing difficulty causes high blood-glucose levels. Untreated, diabetes can cause such immediate problems as fatigue and excessive hunger, thirst, and urination. Over the long term, it also damages nerves and blood vessels, sometimes leading to such serious health problems as blindness, kidney failure, gangrene (with possible foot and leg amputations), and heart disease.

Broadly speaking, diabetes develops when a person has too little insulin for the body's needs. Insulin, a hormone produced in the pancreas, has many roles, but one of its major ones is to help body cells use blood glucose (sugar). Glucose, which is formed when food (especially carbohydrate) is digested, is a fuel for the body much as gasoline is a fuel for cars. If the fuel is in the tank but can't feed the engine properly, the car won't run very smoothly. Similarly, if the body doesn't have enough insulin or can't use it efficiently, the glucose stays in the blood and the starved body cells won't run very smoothly, either.

TYPE I
(INSULIN-DEPENDENT)
DIABETES

People with insulin-dependent diabetes mellitus (also known as IDDM or type I) produce essentially no insulin. As a result, they need daily injections of insulin to survive. Insulin lowers blood-glucose levels and would cause *low* blood glucose if the user did not eat enough food. Therefore, people with type I diabetes have to eat enough food to avoid low blood glucose, but not so much food as to overcome the insulin and send blood glucose soaring. This is quite a balancing act, because food and insulin are not the only factors that affect blood-glucose levels; exercise, for instance, generally lowers blood glucose, and stress (either emotional or physical) can raise it. This kind of diabetes used to be called juvenile-onset diabetes because it typically develops during childhood or adolescence, although it can occur later, too. About 10 percent of all people with diabetes have type I.

TYPE II
(NON-INSULIN-DEPENDENT)
DIABETES

People who have non-insulin-dependent diabetes mellitus (also known as NIDDM or type II) produce insulin. In fact, they may have a normal amount or even higher-than-normal amounts, but the insulin is not as effective as it should be, a problem referred to as *insulin resistance*. (That is, cells don't respond as they should to insulin's messages. As a researcher once put it, "The cells are like children who are busy playing. Their mom can yell at them all she likes, but they aren't listening.") Insulin resistance is largely due to excess body fat, which is common in people with type II diabetes. This form of diabetes, formerly called maturity-onset diabetes, usually develops after age 40.

About 90 percent of people with diabetes have type II, and 80 percent of them are overweight at the time of diagnosis. Being too fat seems to make people resistant to insulin whether or not they have diabetes, and losing weight often causes a remarkable improvement. Therefore, weight loss and maintenance of ideal weight is the major goal of therapy in type II diabetes in the overweight. Exercise also helps the body to use its insulin and to lower blood-glucose levels, so most doctors recommend a combination of caloric limitation and regular exercise. Some people with type II diabetes take insulin or pills for controlling blood glucose when their weight-loss and exercise program does not control blood glucose acceptably. People who are treated with insulin, and some people who are treated with pills, need to eat food at prescribed times. But those whose diabetes is managed by diet and exercise alone are not prone to low blood glucose. Therefore, it is not as important for them to eat on a rigid schedule.

A small number of people with type II diabetes are of normal or near-normal weight when they develop this condition. These people, too, can often benefit from losing a few pounds, especially if they are pushing the high end of normal. However, not everyone needs to reduce. Some of these people also need insulin therapy.

If you are relatively thin and have type II diabetes, you may find that frequent small feedings are better than three big meals a day. Smaller meals allow the body to use its insulin most efficiently because they do not make heavy demands on the pancreas for insulin. Fiber-rich and whole foods as well as regular exercise are also recommended to help reduce blood-glucose fluctuation.

YOUR GOALS

No matter what kind of diabetes you have, the following are the goals of diet therapy:

□ Improve overall health through optimal nutrition.

□ Provide for normal growth in children.

□ Achieve and/or maintain a body weight appropriate for height.

□ Maintain blood glucose at as close to normal levels as possible.

□ Prevent or delay heart, kidney, eye, nerve, and other complications associated with diabetes. (Much research suggests that keeping blood-glucose levels at or near the normal range may prevent or delay long-term complications.)

To achieve these goals, the American Diabetes Association recommends the following guidelines in addition to the ones outlined in Chapter 1:

□ Pay particular attention to caloric intake—excess calories cause high blood-glucose levels and obesity.

□ Increase your intake of fiber-rich complex carbohydrates. Limit your intake of highly refined carbohydrates and sugars. In addition to being low in vitamins and other nutrients, these sugary foods cause a rapid and high rise in blood glucose.

□ Follow an individualized meal plan that suits your lifestyle. Work with a dietitian familiar with diabetes to develop the plan. (See Chapter 15 for advice on finding a dietitian.) Generally, dietitians will suggest a meal plan in which about 55 to 60 percent of calories come from carbohydrate, mostly unrefined carbohydrates (dried beans and peas, whole-grain cereals and breads, vegetables, fruit); 12 to 20 percent from protein; and less than 30 percent from fat, mainly vegetable fat. A mimeographed meal plan given to you without discussion is *not* adequate. Many dietitians also recommend that you follow a meal plan based on the *Exchange Lists for Meal Planning,* a joint publication of the American Diabetes Association and The American Dietetic Association. (See Appendix 1, page 412.)

MEAL PLANNING OF TOMORROW:
A GLYCEMIC INDEX?

In the future, meal planning may be more precise than it is today. It has long been believed that simple carbohydrates (sugars) cause the greatest rise in blood-glucose levels, while complex carbohydrates (which also often contain fiber) cause a less dramatic blood-glucose rise. However, some complex carbohydrates don't seem to fit the mold. They act more like sugars—at least in some studies.

Because of such findings, nutritional researchers are continuing to evaluate the need for a "glycemic index" for diabetic meal planning. Such an index could, theoretically, rate individual foods on their effects on blood-glucose levels, and you could then choose your foods based on their rating.

However, research is still conflicting. More studies are needed to see if a standardized index could be used by people with diabetes. After all, the effect of a given food depends not only on the food itself, but on how it is prepared, when it is eaten, what else is eaten with it, when the last meal was eaten and what it contained, and finally, who is eating it, since people can respond differently to the same foods. Particularly in people with type I diabetes, the amount of insulin in the body makes a big difference in how high the blood glucose rises after eating.

Until questions raised by this research are answered, continue to favor foods high in complex carbohydrate and low in sugar and follow the other recommendations of your dietitian and in Volumes I and II of the *Family Cookbook*. (Also, you can see how *your* body responds to different foods by testing your blood after eating them.)

Of course, knowing what you should do to eat properly and doing it are two different things. After describing the ways that nutritional needs are influenced by age, the next several chapters will give you practical advice on how to cope with diet dilemmas of insulin use and, for the overweight, on how to lose weight . . . and keep it off.

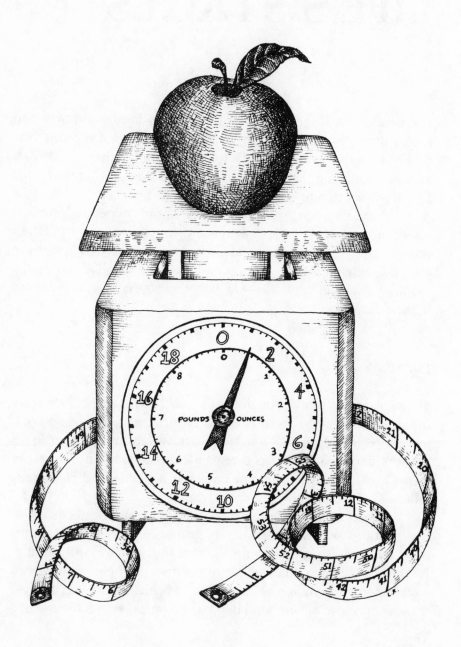

3 □ NUTRITION NEEDS THROUGH LIFE'S STAGES

The general nutrition principles outlined so far are important to follow throughout life. But there is no denying that the amounts of foods needed and the obstacles to getting nutrient needs met vary as people move through different life stages. Therefore, this chapter will provide details about those differences.

Note: For each life stage listed, the nutrient needs described refer both to people with diabetes and to the general population unless otherwise specified. Also, keep in mind that these are *general* guidelines based on average size and that individual requirements will vary. *The only good meal plan is one that is tailored to individual needs.*

INFANCY

The period from birth through the first birthday is one of extremely rapid growth, which results in great nutrient needs. The well-nourished infant, in fact, will double in weight by age four to six months and will likely be three times heavier than his or her birthweight by 12 months. The baby will also be about 50 percent taller than birth height by one year of age.

Fortunately, meeting the newborn's nutrient needs is not overly complex. The infant needs primarily human milk or formula (modified cow's milk) for the first four to six months of life. Infants receiving human milk, however, may need to be given supplements of vitamin D beginning at birth. In some instances, doctors may also recommend that parents supplement the infant's

16

diet with fluoride if the substance is not being supplied by another source, such as drinking water.

At four to six months, parents can begin giving the baby solid food in amounts recommended by the doctor, particularly foods that are good sources of iron, such as iron-fortified cereals. For some breast-fed babies it may be desirable to give a supplement with an additional source of energy (calories).

Of course, parents should also continue with milk and formula feedings. Strained vegetables and fruits may also be given as early as 6 months. When introducing new foods, parents should begin with a small amount and continue offering the food to the child for three days.

Parents should introduce finger foods and foods of different textures (such as strained carrots with carrot bits in it) at six to eight months, the sensitive period for learning to chew.

The diabetic infant will have essentially the same needs as the nondiabetic infant, but parents may want to wait until the six-month mark to introduce solid foods. At that time, the baby's insulin dose and/or the timing of injections may need to be adjusted to cover the foods. The best approach is to discuss the individual needs of the baby with your doctor and diet counselor.

As with older insulin users, the diabetic infant needs to have insulin action matched by food. This often means that whoever is doing the feeding will need to gently awaken the baby to keep feedings regular. To be sure that the baby has enough glucose in the blood yet does not develop excessively high blood glucose, parents of diabetic infants usually give the child frequent, small feedings.

As the diabetic child starts to develop a feeding pattern that more closely approximates three meals plus snacks, the doctor may recommend covering some of the meals with added insulin (Regular). When in doubt about the baby's need for food or insulin, parents can test the baby's blood-glucose level by using a heelprick instead of a fingerprick. Blood-testing is especially useful for the parent who is wondering whether the baby's crankiness is due to low blood glucose or merely to being a baby!

TODDLERS (Preschool)

The period of one to six years is one of slower growth than before and of increasing physical activity. As the growth rate slows, the child's appetite will decrease. Children are good judges of the *amount* of food they need, but it is up to the parent to provide the right *kind* of food. Children are born without food prejudice. Their eating patterns are learned. Children who taste new foods each time they are served learn to know and enjoy a wide variety of foods. But introduce only one new food at a meal, perhaps along with a favorite food.

The nutritional needs of the diabetic toddler are no different than those of the nondiabetic, except that the parent of the diabetic child will be more concerned about timing and amounts of food because of the need to match insulin action. For the child who is cared for by a baby sitter, nursery school, or day-care facility, the caretaker should be instructed about the warning signs and treatment of insulin reactions and should be made aware of the child's food needs.

In general, depending on activity levels, the caloric needs of children one to six years old can be estimated using the following rule of thumb:

1000 calories for the first year, plus,
100 calories for each additional year thereafter
    until about 10 years of age

EXAMPLE:

3-year old:	1000	1st year
	200	Years 2 and 3
	1200	Total
5-year old:	1000	1st year
	400	Years 2, 3, 4, and 5
	1400	Total

The bulk of the calories should come from complex carbohydrates, protein, and milk (for calcium and other nutrients), and from good sources of Vitamins C and A and iron. (See table of vitamins and minerals at the end of this chapter for sources and Appendix I for the nutrient and caloric values for food.)

For protein, it is best to emphasize animal proteins (meats, fish, poultry, milk), because they provide the amino acids essential for growth. For variety, vegetable proteins can be combined with small amounts of animal protein (such as milk and cereal) or specific vegetable-vegetable combinations can be formed that together will be as effective as animal proteins. (Discuss options with a dietitian and also see Chapter 15, page 390.)

Iron-rich foods are particularly important at this stage of life to help prevent iron-deficiency anemia, a common result of a child's narrow food intake and reduced appetite. A child who insists on having mostly milk or bread and resists other foods would be a good candidate for this form of anemia.

Of course, children will have "off days" when they are irritable and refuse to eat what you serve. They also go through whimsical phases of alternately liking and disliking certain foods, even rejecting ones they once adored. If you are a parent, try to avoid making a big issue over the child's refusal to eat a given food. If rejecting foods get attention, food dislikes may become permanent, or, worse, the child may use eating as an arena for getting attention.

Children—both diabetic and nondiabetic—in this stage of the life cycle can't hold very much food in the stomach at one time, and they also have short attention spans, both of which contribute to the need for frequent small feedings (four to six) rather than the traditional adult three meals a day. These feedings are important for providing nutrients and should be wholesome rather than sugary even if the child is nondiabetic. Offer the child foods that are easily chewed and swallowed because, at least in the early toddler stage, chewing skills are just developing. Give meats, cheeses, or vegetables that are tender and cut into bite-sized pieces. Snacks high in unrefined carbohydrates and protein (such as crackers with either peanut butter or cheese) are excellent for any child, diabetic or not.

For diabetic children, eating at regular times is generally considered to be critical. Parents should, therefore, be firm and matter-of-fact about the need to eat on time, just as they are firm about insulin injections.

SUGGESTED SNACKS AND FINGER FOODS FOR LITTLE PEOPLE*
(See *Exchange Lists for Meal Planning*
for exchange equivalents, in Appendix I)

Fruits
Apple wedges
Banana slices
Berries
Fresh peach wedges
Fresh pear wedges
Fresh pineapple sticks
Grapefruit sections (seeded)
Grapes
Melon cubes or balls
Orange sections (seeded)
Pitted plums
Tangerine sections

Breads/Cereals
Cold cereals
Toast fingers
Whole-grain crackers

Milk Products
Milk
Yogurt
Puddings made with milk

Vegetables
Cabbage wedges
Carrot sticks
Cauliflowerets
Celery sticks**
Cherry tomatoes
Cucumber slices
Green pepper sticks
Tomato wedges
Turnip sticks
Zucchini or summer squash
  strips

Meats
Cheese cubes
Cooked meat cubes
Hard-cooked eggs
Small sandwiches
  (quartered)

*Adapted from "A Planning Guide for Food Service in Child Care Centers," USDA, FNS-64, Food and Nutrition Service, Washington, D.C., revised 1976.
**May be stuffed with cheese or peanut butter.

SCHOOL AGE AND PREADOLESCENCE

The ages of seven to ten are periods of varying individual growth rates. The caloric needs of children in this age group vary greatly and are influenced by age, body size, and physical activity. Having enough calories is important for the body to be able to effectively use the protein from food for growth. Seven- to ten-year-olds commonly consume from 1,650 to 3,300 calories a day. Thus, a child in the middle of the age range would need about 2,400 calories, the midpoint of the calorie range.

Because this preadolescent stage is one of storing nutrients for the growth spurt of adolescence, some children might become slightly chunky, only to slim down suddenly in the next stage. Again, four to five small meals, or meals plus snacks, are recommended. Children at this age are just beginning to "go with the group," so that if one child dislikes (or likes) a food, he or she may influence others. The best way to combat negativity is to be a good "role model" and eat the foods you want your child to eat. Often the child will imitate adults he or she loves.

The preadolescent person with diabetes may choose to test his or her emerging independence by refusing to eat on schedule and by rejecting previously accepted foods. This can result in insulin reactions. Try to avoid turning mealtime into battle time. Allowing the young diabetic person to develop a list of three to four foods that don't have to be eaten (while all others must) may help to reduce food-related conflict.

Regularity of meals and a matter-of-fact approach may be helpful in reducing potential conflict. Since children with diabetes, like nondiabetic children, are influenced by TV commercials and peers, they may start asking for sugary foods. Allowing limited choices occasionally, such as among cereals that have limited amounts of sugar, may suffice. Some families save sweets for before-exercise snacks. Giving the child food choices can also be used to start teaching the child some of the information he or she will need when taking on some responsibility for self-care.

Preferences for single food items over a period of time are

also common during this stage and will generally pass. This phase might create some problems for the diabetic child if overreliance on the favored food starts to play havoc with diabetes control. A parent's best bet may be to learn how to work the food into the diet to some extent, and to explain to the child that the food is only allowable if other nutrient needs are also met.

As school terms (and gym classes) come and go and the child spends more time in activities with friends, his or her insulin and food schedules may have to be adjusted to adapt to activity-level changes. In addition to discussing insulin dose and timing changes with the doctor as your child's schedule changes, parents will need to give the child guidance in handling insulin reactions solo. When you feel he or she is ready, you can give the child food to carry for use as needed.

Note that the treatment plan—insulin, food, and activity—should promote normal growth in the child. If your child seems unusually short, this may indicate that a change is needed in insulin dose and/or in the amount of food being eaten.

SUGGESTIONS FOR HANDLING THE EASTER CANDY BASKET, TREATS AT HALLOWEEN, AND GRANDPARENTS' GIFTS FOR CHILDREN

EASTER
- □ Use small gifts other than food in Easter basket.
- □ Use sugar-free gum or bubble gum.
- □ If candy is necessary, use dietetic hard candies.

HALLOWEEN
- □ Go trick-or-treating and give candy to a child who is ill and cannot go.
- □ Give candy to children in the hospital.
- □ Collect for UNICEF.
- □ Divide treats with friends, brothers, and sisters.
- □ Take treats to school for children in class.

GRANDPARENTS
□ Ask them to bring treats other than food: clothes, books, small toys.
□ Set quotas in advance if food is to be used as a gift.

ADOLESCENCE (TEEN YEARS)

In the first three stages of the life cycle, the sex of the person makes no difference to recommendations for caloric intake. In the adolescent years, however, sex differences alter the rate of growth and the nutrient needs. The growth spurt of adolescence begins for girls at ages 9 to 10 and for boys at ages 11 to 13. The spurt for boys is more intense and lasts longer than for girls, and boys typically need more calories. (The body composition of males and females begin to differ considerably, too, with girls having a greater percentage of fat compared to muscle, and boys having a greater percentage of muscle.) Common caloric ranges for boys and girls follow. Keep in mind that, in general, children at the younger end of the age range need fewer calories than children at the older end of the range. The exception may be girls ages 15 to 18; sometimes the oldest ones need the fewest calories, in part because they have reached their adult heights. Calorie requirements, however, will also be influenced by body size and activity levels; the greater these are, the more calories the child is likely to need.

Boys ages 11 to 14 tend to require about 2,000 to 3,700 calories a day, with 12- to 13-year-olds needing about 2,700 calories (the midpoint of the calorie range). Boys 15 to 18 years old have a range of 2,100 to 3,900 calories, with the 16- to 17-year-olds requiring about 2,800 calories.

Girls have a somewhat lower caloric requirement. Girls aged 11 to 14 need about 1,500 to 3,000 calories, with 12- to 13-year-olds needing about 2,200 calories. The older girls, 15 to 18 years old, need about 1,200 to 3,000 calories, with the 16- to 17-year-olds needing about 2,100 calories.

Iron-rich foods are very important for adolescent boys and

girls. Boys need iron for their developing muscles and rapidly expanding blood volume. Girls need it because once they begin menstruating they lose blood each month. The iron in meats is used better by the body than iron of plant origin, although eating foods rich in vitamin C (such as citrus fruits or tomatoes) will enhance the availability of vegetable iron when sources of non-meat iron and vitamin C are eaten together.

During this period, the adolescent becomes responsible for his or her own food intake. No longer is the child fed, but rather eats according to what food is available and what foods friends are eating. Snacking, or eating many small meals, is a common pattern for this age group. To help the teenager eat right, parents can keep nutritious, ready-to-eat foods available at all times. (Teenagers are notorious for grabbing food rather than taking the time to go through preparations.) Also, parents will want to encourage the teenager to eat a variety of foods.

Adolescent boys generally eat larger quantities of food than do girls and for that reason may come closer to meeting their nutrient needs. Girls tend to be especially conscious of weight control and may diet unwisely. They should be taught to eat a variety of low-calorie foods to meet their energy and growth needs without gaining a lot of weight.

Teenagers with diabetes may benefit from meeting with a dietitian and a doctor who can help them to set up a weight-loss plan, if desired, or work on adding more variety (including portions of pizza, or even 'burgers and fries if it's important to them) into the meal plan. Some teenagers will benefit from the reminder that more food can be eaten if exercise follows it. Also, discussing the pros and cons of alcohol use with a dietitian may help the teenagers to make wiser choices at parties and to take appropriate precautions if they decide to drink beer or wine. Counseling from someone who understands their need to be like their friends, but who can also help to motivate them to attend to diabetes, may help to prevent some of the teenage rebellion common at this stage. Maintaining some flexibility may also help to prevent binges on sweets that are common during the teen years.

As the teens hit puberty and their bodies change, they may need to have their treatment plans changed once again. Girls may find that they have difficulty managing diabetes during their menstrual cycle because hormones make blood-glucose levels erratic. Self-monitoring of blood glucose (which is more precise than urine testing) can be especially useful during adolescence. Seeing how blood-glucose levels change in response to meals and exercise (and stress) and learning how to adjust food and exercise and, in some instances, insulin in response to blood-glucose changes can help to improve diabetes control.

SNACKS FOR SCHOOLAGERS AND TEENAGERS

STARCH/BREAD
Bread (plain, toasted with margarine)
Sandwiches (with meat or cheese or vegetable fillings)
Crackers (plain, with meat or cheese toppings)
Rolls (with margarine, meat or cheese spreads)
Waffles, pancakes, biscuits
Cereal (dry, with milk, with fruit)
Popcorn (plain, with margarine)
Pizza—toppings provide sources from other groups

MEAT
Meat, fish, peanut butter sandwiches
Chicken, ham, tuna salad (on crackers, vegetables)
Peanut butter (with raw vegetables, raw fruits)
Cheese (cubes, sticks, slices, dips, spreads)
Cottage cheese (plain, with fruit added)

FRUITS AND VEGETABLES
Fruits
Fresh whole fruit (apples, oranges, bananas, pears, peaches, plums, grapefruits, melons, grapes, watermelon, pineapple)

Fruit juice (as a beverage, as an ice)
Fresh fruit added to yogurt, cottage cheese, milkshakes
Fruit on top of waffles, pancakes, biscuits, cereal

Vegetables
Raw vegetables (plain, with cheese dips, peanut butter)
   (cauliflower, broccoli, green pepper, zucchini, carrots,
   celery, turnips, cucumbers, radishes)
Vegetable juice (tomato, carrot)

MILK
Milk (whole, 2%, skim, buttermilk)
Milkshakes (with fruit, ice milk, or just crushed ice to make
   thick)
Yogurt (plain, with fresh fruit, frozen)

FATS
Nuts (peanuts, mixed); olives

FREE SNACKS
Sugar-free carbonated beverages or packaged drink mixes
   (plain or frozen as in ice)
Gelatin (prepared with sugar substitutes, flavorings)
Raw vegetables (½ cup or less)—(lettuce, green pepper,
   cauliflower, broccoli, celery, pickles, cucumbers,
   radishes)

EARLY AND MIDDLE ADULT YEARS

The adult years mark the end of growth and the beginning of a rather stable period as far as nutrient needs are concerned. Recommendations for adults are different for males and females, primarily because of differences in body size and composition. Only in the case of iron do females have a greater need than males because of their monthly blood losses (menstruation). Just as in other periods of life, lifestyle (active or inactive) will have an impact on caloric needs. Weight control continues to be a concern to women and may become a concern to more men when they suddenly notice a new arrival in their lives: the pot belly.

Males ages 19 to 50 generally need about 2,300 to 3,300 calories a day, and females of the same age generally need about 1,600 to 2,500 calories. Men need more protein than women because men are generally bigger.

In adults with diabetes, the daily schedule has usually become more routine because of work and family responsibilities, which makes meal planning easier. Although food habits are well established by the adult years, changes can still be made to improve nutrient intake, manage weight, promote good health, and prevent chronic diseases or manage diabetes. You may be somewhat set in your ways, but human beings have a remarkable capacity for change.

Two important aspects of the adult years that have an impact only on the nutrient needs of women are pregnancy and breast feeding (lactation). The pregnant woman needs to take in about 300 calories extra a day and considerably more protein, and the woman who is breast feeding needs about 500 calories more than her prepregnancy meal plan and less protein than when she was pregnant but more than she needed prior to the pregnancy. The diabetic woman will follow a meal plan much like the non-diabetic woman except, of course, that the diabetic woman will need to pay close attention to blood-glucose levels before *conceiving* and throughout her pregnancy to protect the baby.

LATER ADULT YEARS (ELDERLY)

The adult years were described as a period of stability. The later years are characterized by a great deal of individual variation in body functioning and activity. Generally, however, a person's metabolism slows down and physical activity, sensitivity to taste, and vigor decrease. At the same time, the proportion of fat compared with muscle increases and so does susceptibility to disease. Good nutrition during these years may help to alter the timing, rate, and severity of these processes.

Little nutrition research has been conducted on this older age group and is sorely needed; we are, after all, an aging nation. (A few decades from now, the elderly will make up a much larger proportion of the total population than they do today.) However, one thing is clear: since older people eat less, each calorie eaten must contribute to nutrient requirements. The elderly, in particular, need to eat wholesome foods.

While more research is awaited, a common recommendation for calorie intake in the later adult years is about 2,000 to 2,800 calories for men ages 51 to 75, and 1,650 to 2,450 calories for men older than 76. For women ages 51 to 75, an intake of about 1,400 to 2,200 calories should be adequate, and women older than that should have about 1,200 to 2,000 calories.

Unfortunately, meeting nutrient needs during later life often becomes increasingly difficult, because of such factors as:

1. *Lack of motivation.* Many elderly people live alone and are not motivated to prepare food for themselves. (Group feeding is known to improve food intake for many when it is available, even if it's just once a day.)
2. *Lack of transportation, money, or cooking facilities.*
3. *Poor food habits* that are resistant to change.
4. *Environmental changes* that force different (worse) eating patterns, such as having to move from a rural setting with a garden food supply into a city where only convenience food is easily available.
5. *The presence of chronic illness,* which can reduce appetite and alter taste.
6. *Physical disabilities,* such as missing teeth, poor eyesight, impairment of memory, or confusion.
7. *Isolation.*

Inadequate nutrient intake may lead to irritability, moodiness, depression, and other symptoms that are commonly considered a "natural" part of aging but are not necessarily unavoidable. If elderly people can be encouraged to eat an adequate diet with a variety of foods, they may be able to stay healthy and vigorous and minimize health problems.

For elderly people with diabetes who take pills or insulin—as many do—it is crucial to eat regularly and to have enough food to avoid low blood sugar. If you have an elderly relative with diabetes who lives alone and seems to have trouble in this area, you may need to arrange for home health services. (Contact a dietitian or diet counselor or your local health department for information.)

VITAMINS, MINERALS—AND YOU*

WHY YOU NEED THEM

FOODS THAT SUPPLY THEM

VITAMIN C (Ascorbic Acid): Helps hold body cells together and strengthens walls of blood cells. Helps in wound healing. Helps body to build bones and teeth. Helps in absorption and use of iron.

Cantaloupe, grapefruit, oranges, strawberries, broccoli, cabbage, tomatoes, green leafy vegetables, and fresh potatoes.

THIAMINE (B_1): Helps body cells obtain energy from food. Helps keep nerves in healthy condition. Promotes good appetite and digestion.

Whole-grain and enriched breads and cereals, potatoes, organ meats, pork, other meats, poultry and fish, nuts, milk, green vegetables, dried peas, and beans.

RIBOFLAVIN (B_2): Helps cells use oxygen to release energy from food. Helps keep eyes healthy. Helps keep skin around mouth and nose healthy.

Milk, liver, kidney, heart, lean meat, eggs, green leafy vegetables, enriched and whole-grain breads and cereals.

NIACIN: Helps the cells of the body use oxygen to produce energy. Maintains health of skin, tongue, digestive tract, and nervous system.

Liver, poultry, fish, lean meat, peanuts and peanut butter, beans and peas, and whole-grain and enriched breads and cereals.

VITAMIN B_{12}: Helps with normal functioning of all body cells. Necessary for formation of red blood cells.

Foods of animal origin (such as liver, other organ meats, fish, meat, eggs, shellfish, milk, cottage cheese and other milk products, except butter).

VITAMIN A: Helps keeps eyes healthy and able to adjust to dim light. Keeps skin healthy. Helps keep lining of mouth, nose, throat, and digestive tract healthy and resistant to infection. Promotes growth.

Liver; dark green and deep-yellow vegetables such as broccoli, collards, and other dark-green leafy vegetables; carrots, pumpkin; sweet potatoes; winter squash; tomatoes; green pepper; apricots; cantaloupe; strawberries; papaya; watermelon; butter; and fortified margarine.

VITAMIN D: Promotes growth and lays down minerals for bones and teeth.

Egg yolk, butter, fortified margarine, fortified milk, fatty fish, and liver. Vitamin D is produced in the skin with the stimulus of sunlight.

VITAMIN E: Helps other vitamins and unsaturated fatty acids perform their special functions in the body.

Fats and polyunsaturated oils of vegetable products, safflower oil. Meats and green vegetables contain small amounts. Whole-grain cereals and peanuts.

IRON: Combines with protein to make hemoglobin, the red substance of blood that carries oxygen from the lungs to muscles, brain, and other cells of the body. Helps cells use oxygen. Prevents anemia.

Liver, kidney, heart, oysters, lean meat, egg yolk, dried beans, dried peas, dark-green leafy vegetables, dried fruit, parts of whole-grain and enriched bread and cereals, and prune juice.

CALCIUM: Builds bones and teeth. Helps blood to clot. Helps nerves, muscles, and heart to function properly.

Milk: fortified skim, low-fat, whole, buttermilk, yogurt; cheeses made from skim or partially skim milk (such as mozzarella), whole-milk cheese (such as Cheddar); leafy vegetables, such as collards, dandelion, kale, mustard, and turnip greens.

MAGNESIUM: Activates various enzymes. Aids in erergy production and utilization, contraction of nerves and muscles, and building tissue.

Bananas, whole-grain cereals, dried beans, milk, most dark-green vegetables, meat, nuts, peanuts and peanut butter.

ZINC: Is a constituent of the hormone insulin. Activates various enzymes. Aids in growth, wound healing, taste acuity, and prevention of anemia.

Whole grains, dried beans and peas, nuts, shellfish (particularly oysters), meat, cheese, and cocoa.

SODIUM: Is a key element in regulation of body water and of acid-base balance in the body.

Naturally occurs in most foods, broth, gelatin dessert, table salt, baking soda, and most processed foods.

POTASSIUM: Is a component of lean body tissue. Contributes to growth and muscle strength. Helps regulate body water and acid-base balance. Helps maintain neuromuscular function.

Meats, milk, fruits (especially citrus fruits), bananas, dried dates, cantaloupe, apricots, tomato juice, potatoes, and dark-green leafy vegetables.

*From the book, *The American Diabetes Association/The American Dietetic Association Family Cookbook*, © 1980 by The American Diabetes Association/The American Dietetic Association. Published by Prentice-Hall, Inc., Englewood Cliffs, New Jersey 07632.

4 □ DIET DILEMMAS OF INSULIN USERS

People who take insulin to treat their diabetes have special dietary concerns. The first consideration is, of course, *what* to eat. For this, a careful daily meal plan should be worked up with the help of their physician and dietitian or diet counselor. (See Appendix I for more information on meal plans.) Insulin users also have to pay close attention to the timing of their meals and snacks, and they must be prepared to adjust their diets to compensate for insulin reactions, unusual activity, delayed meals, and illness.

TIMING OF MEALS AND SNACKS. When you take insulin, you have to coordinate the size and scheduling of your meals with the time of your injections. This is to insure a proper balance of the foods you eat with the amount of insulin you receive and the exercise you get. Food raises blood-glucose levels, and insulin and exercise (if diabetes is under control) lower it. Generally speaking, you should eat at regular times and plan meals and snacks to coincide with the greatest insulin activity (see chart).

For example, if you use rapid-acting insulin (Regular) you should eat a half hour after your insulin injection, and if you use an intermediate-acting (such as *NPH* or lente) insulin, you may need a midafternoon snack to cover the peak insulin action. A bedtime snack is used to cover the action of insulin during the night.

In the past, most insulin users ate three meals a day and snacks at midmorning, midafternoon, and bedtime. Today, more

33

INSULIN ACTION

RAPID ACTING (onset 1/2–4 hours, peak action 1–5 hours duration 5–16 hours)

Humulin Regular
Novolin R (Regular)
  (formerly Actrapid Human)
Velosulin (Regular)
Purified Pork S (Semilente)
  (formerly Semitard)

Iletin I Regular
Regular
Iletin I Semilente
Semilente

INTERMEDIATE ACTING (onset 1–4 hours, peak action 4–12 hours, duration 16–28 hours)

Humulin L
Humulin NPH
Insulatard + (NPH)
Novolin L (Lente)
  (formerly Monotard Human)
Novolin N (NPH)
Iletin II Lente
Iletin II NPH
Iletin II Lente
Iletin II NPH

Insulatard (NPH)
Purified Pork Lente
  (formerly Monotard)
Purified Pork N (NPH)
  formerly Protaphane)
Iletin I Lente
Iletin I NPH
NPH

LONG ACTING (onset 4–6 hours, peak action 14–24 hours, duration 36 hours)

Iletin II PZI
Iletin II PZI
Purified Beef U (Ultralente)
  (formerly Ultratard)

Iletin I PZI
Iletin I Ultralente
Ultralente

MIXTURES
Mixtard + 30%
  (30% Regular, 70% NPH)

Source: From *Diabetes Forecast* 39 (3): 1986.

flexibility may be allowed, depending on the timing and number of injections and the type and amount of insulin you use. See your doctor and/or diet counselor for more details on adding flexibility to your life.

INSULIN REACTIONS. These are always a threat for the person with type I diabetes. When you feel a reaction coming on, test your blood glucose to see if it is, indeed, low. If blood testing is not practical, treat yourself as if you were having a reaction. For low blood glucose, take about 15 grams of carbohydrate, such as 1 tablespoon of honey or corn syrup, 2 tablespoons of raisins, ½ cup fruit juice or a *non*dietetic soft drink, or indicated portion of a packaged product for insulin reactions (for example, three glucose tablets). Usually, symptoms will go away within twenty minutes. Retest blood glucose at that point. If symptoms persist, treat again. Carbohydrate eaten to treat insulin reactions that occur at other than meal times generally does not need to be subtracted from the carbohydrate allowance in your meal plan.

EXERCISE. Physical activity burns calories and uses up some glucose for energy. A certain amount of regular exercise is accounted for in your daily meal plan. If you engage in additional exercise, however, you may need to eat a snack before you start or else risk an insulin reaction.

How much extra should you eat before exercising? For light activity, such as walking a half mile at a modest pace, you should not need any additional food. For moderate exercise, such as playing golf without a cart, you may need 10 to 15 grams of carbohydrate for each hour of exercise planned. Eat this snack just before you begin. For vigorous exercise, such as roller skating or running, you may need as much as 20 to 30 grams of carbohydrate for each hour of anticipated activity. After strenuous exercise, it may be necessary to eat again, because the body may have used up the carbohydrate stored in liver and muscle cells during especially heavy workouts, and it needs to be replaced. Remember, these are *rough* guidelines. You may need more or less food, depending on your blood-glucose level, your usual activity level, and past experience. Testing before unplanned exercise is always wise.

Crackers, bread sticks, and fruit are good sources of on-the-spot carbohydrate before exercising. One small apple or pear, for example, will give you 10 grams of carbohydrate. This food is *not counted* toward your meal plan allotment if it is eaten to cover extra exercise; the additional calories should be burned off by the extra exercise.

Although eating carbohydrates as described above is the most common way to compensate for the calories burned in exercise, alternative approaches are available. Consult your dietitian for more details.

DELAYED MEALS. For the times you cannot eat on schedule, 15 to 30 grams of carbohydrates should prevent low blood glucose for one to two hours. Again, crackers or bread sticks are good sources; you can carry them in your pocket or keep some in the glove compartment of your car. (Three graham crackers, for instance, would give you about 15 grams of carbohydrate.) In this case *deduct the amount you eat as a snack* from the total carbohydrate in your delayed meal.

ILLNESS. Many illnesses cause a lack of appetite. And when you eat less, your tendency might be to decrease your insulin. Nevertheless, you *must* take insulin to avoid ketoacidosis if you have insulin-dependent diabetes. In fact, the stress of illness may elevate your blood glucose even when you are eating very little, and you may actually have to *increase* your insulin dose. Additionally, if you take insulin, you must also take in calories to avoid reactions. To be sure you are eating enough, have at least 50 to 75 grams of carbohydrate during every six to eight hours, or the amount your doctor recommends. If you are nauseated, try sipping sweetened ginger ale or soup or eating ice cream or custard.

During illness, test your blood for glucose and urine for ketones, even if you do not normally use these tests. Blood-glucose monitoring combined with multiple injections of Regular insulin (or with an insulin pump if you normally use one) can give you a bit of flexibility in choosing meal and snack times. This is because you will not have to worry about covering long-acting insulin if you don't use any. (For more advice on handling illness, see Volume I, Chapter 13.)

5 □ ON FIGHTING FAT I: WHY LIMIT CALORIES?

Losing weight and keeping it off is a challenge that is little understood by people who are "naturally thin." Unfortunately, nobody can give you a magic key to weight control. But three kinds of information can help you achieve your weight goal:

- □ *An explanation of the biological side of weight loss*, so that you will understand the reasons for restricting calories. It's hard to do something well if you don't understand the logic behind it.
- □ *Practical advice* about steps you can take to make your next effort at weight control more successful.
- □ *A glimpse of the feelings expressed by many people who have type II* diabetes and are struggling to control their weight. Their responses may help you feel less alone.

This chapter deals with the biological side of losing weight. It answers some of the basic questions people have before embarking on a weight-loss program:

- □ What are the benefits of being at your suggested weight and what are the risks of being overweight?
- □ How do you know whether you are too fat?
- □ What happens in the body when you restrict calories?

□ What kind of diet will allow you to lose weight without jeopardizing your health?

□ Once you have lost weight, how do you keep it off?

WHY LOSE WEIGHT?

A prominent researcher, the late Dr. Kelly West, wrote:

Being fat has some advantages, but these are outweighed by major disadvantages. Hard chairs are less uncomfortable for those who are generously padded. Because fat is less dense than muscle or bone, folks with extra fat are particularly good floaters. When obese people go out in the cold, their blankets of fat keep them warmer. Also, obese people are full of calories, so . . . they tolerate prolonged famine well.

On the other hand, fat people move around less comfortably, are hotter in summer, and are often considered less attractive. What's worse, they suffer more and die earlier than slender people. Although fat people are often free of medical difficulties during the first years of obesity, after one or two decades of excess weight, more and more problems appear. Overweight people have more pain in their backs, knees, and hips. They have more gall bladder operations and more lung trouble . . . And, for people more than 40 percent overweight, death rates are three times as high as for people of normal weight.

Obesity (having too much fat) also plays a major role in *causing* diabetes and makes *controlling* diabetes difficult. When you are too fat, your body's insulin works less effectively, because the body's cells "resist" acting on its messages. In addition, the pancreas has to work harder to keep the fat person supplied with enough insulin and sometimes is not up to the task. Losing weight (and fat!) helps the body to use its insulin more effectively and also gives the pancreas a break. In fact, people with type II diabetes who lose enough weight and exercise regularly can often stop taking insulin or diabetes pills, if they get a doctor's approval, of course.

AM I TOO FAT?

Now that you know about the risks of being too heavy, you may be wondering if *your* "baby fat" is excessive enough to cause trouble. (*Note*: It is the excess of fat that causes body cells to "resist" insulin, not extra weight per se. But with the exception of some extremely muscular people, most people who are overweight tend to have too much fat.) Doctors have some very precise methods of measuring fat, including underwater weighing and the use of a device called a caliper, which measures skinfold thickness. In most cases, these tools are not really necessary. To see if you need to shed some pounds, try these simple methods:

THE PINCH TEST. Using your thumb and forefinger, pinch a fold of skin on the back of your upper arm. If the fold is more than an inch thick, you are probably too fat.

THE RULER TEST. Lying on your back, place a 12-inch ruler on your stomach pointing from head to toe. If the ends of the ruler fail to touch your body, you should probably lose weight.

THE BELT TEST. (For men.) Wrap a belt around your middle and note where the notch is. Now place the belt around your chest. If you're wider at the waist than at the chest, you're carrying more fat on your body than you need.

Of course, just weighing yourself and comparing the results to the generally accepted weights for your height and build should give a pretty good idea of where you stand. If you are 20 percent or more heavier than the norm for your height, weight, and sex, you would generally be classified as obese. Use this formula to estimate the suggested weight for your height.

DESIRABLE BODY WEIGHT

Women: 100 pounds for the first five feet,
            5 pounds for each additional inch
Men: 106 pounds for the first five feet,
            6 pounds for each additional inch.

Add 10 percent for large body frame; subtract 10 percent for small body frame.

In general, your weight should fall within a range of 10 percent above or below the accepted weight for your height. (That is, if the appropriate weight for your height is 115, you could weigh between 103 and 127 and be within the normal range.)

YOU ARE WHAT YOU EAT

What has to happen for the fat to flee? Essentially, you have to take in fewer calories than the body needs each day. When you don't provide it with enough energy (calories), the body turns to its stores of fat and breaks them down. In this way, the body gets the fuel it needs and you lose fat . . . and weight.

Of course, if you take in *more* calories than you burn off, the body *stores* the excess as fat for future use. Popular storage depots are just beneath the skin of the waist, stomach, thighs, and upper arms.

To find out how many calories your body needs for weight maintenance, and how many calories to eat each day in order to lose weight, talk to your doctor or dietitian. Your health advisors will give you an individualized set of guidelines, taking into account your activity level, size, sex, and the energy your body needs to maintain its involuntary processes ("basal metabolism"), such as breathing and keeping a normal temperature. Your basal caloric needs are usually highest up to the ages of 19 to 22. After that, basal requirements shift down, with a marked drop at around age 50. Also, as you age, the percentage of body fat (compared to muscle) tends to increase.

For normal adults, basal metabolism uses about 1,300 to 1,700 calories a day. The remainder of your daily calorie supply is used to give you energy for your regular physical activities. The more active you are, the more calories you can have while maintaining your weight. See the chart called "Estimated Caloric Requirements Reflecting Effects of Physical Activity" to get an idea of how many calories you need to sustain your desired weight at any given activity level. But remember, this is just a general guide.

For an example of how to use the chart, let's say your appropriate weight is 120 pounds. To maintain that weight despite

ESTIMATED CALORIC REQUIREMENTS REFLECTING EFFECTS OF PHYSICAL ACTIVITY

Calories per pound of desirable body weight		Level of activity
Up to Age 55	*Older than 55*	
10	9	*Basal* (resting: little or no activity)
12	11	*Sedentary* (usual activity; activities that burn 25–80 calories per hour, such as most done seated or standing, including auto and truck driving, office work, light housework, standing, croquet)
15	14	*Moderate** (activities that burn 150–300 calories per hour; such as carpentry, plastering, weeding, hoeing, scrubbing floors, shopping with a heavy load, cycling, tennis, walking 3–5 miles per hour, rowing with two oars)
18–20	17–19	*Very active** (activities that burn 300+ calories per hour, such as working with a pick and shovel, playing basketball or football, swimming, climbing, skiing, walking up stairs)

*To consider yourself to be moderately or very active, you must participate in activities like the ones listed for an average of at least two hours each day.

having little exercise (being sedentary), you would need about 12 calories × 120, or 1,440 calories a day. If you wanted to eat more, you would have to increase your activity level.

For weight *loss*, you have to cut back 3,500 calories from your "maintenance" food intake to lose one pound of body fat. For example, let's say that 2,000 calories a day keeps your weight fairly constant. To eliminate 3,500 calories—and one pound—in a week, you would have to reduce your calories by 500 a day. This would leave you with a daily intake allowance of 1,500 calories. If you were to add exercise to this weight-loss plan, you would lose that pound more quickly or would lose more weight in one week. (Unfortunately, brain-work doesn't count as calorie-burning exercise!)

WHAT KIND OF DIET?

For a long time, researchers have sought the safest and easiest method for losing weight and keeping it off, but so far no single "right way" has emerged. Some determined people can lose weight slowly but steadily with only a modest reduction in calories. Others need a brief, dramatic cutback to begin. Everyone, however, needs a lifelong commitment to healthful eating habits. Otherwise, weight loss is likely to be temporary.

"Easy" weight-loss schemes will not help you to keep weight off because they do not change your basic eating habits. Fad diets that exclude certain types of food may deprive the body of needed nutrients; they are nutritionally unsound and may be hazardous to your health.

The best results usually come from a balanced low-calorie diet (following the principle of Chapters I and II) combined with planned exercise. Better than diet alone, diet plus exercise gets rid of more fat and builds attractive muscles in place of fat. Because muscle cells need more food than fat cells, your maintenance diet can also be more generous when you are physically fit.

If you want a realistic weight-loss and exercise program

that will help you to change your habits, contact your dietitian or diet counselor. Also get a thorough check-up from your physician before starting.

People who have type I diabetes will have to be especially careful as they switch to a weight-loss meal plan. They will need to work with a dietitian and doctor to be sure that insulin is reduced if necessary and that the low-calorie diet adequately covers the insulin injected.

The weight-loss program suggested to you will probably be fairly low in fat. This is because fat is the most calorie-dense of all the nutrients, with more than twice the calories of an equal measure of protein or carbohydrate. (See the following chart.)

The meal plan will also include foods you like because it will make your commitment easier to keep. High-fiber foods, such as whole-grain cereals and uncooked fruits and vegetables with edible seeds and skins, are valuable because they provide bulk that helps to satisfy hunger. Also, the fiber in these foods needs to be chewed, and chewing is one of the pleasures of eating.

CALORIES IN 1 GRAM OF EACH NUTRIENT

NUTRIENT	CALORIES PER GRAM (28 gm = 1 oz)
Carbohydrate (CHO)	4
Protein (PRO)	4
Fat	9
Alcohol	7
Vitamins	0
Minerals	0
Water	0

CONSOLIDATING YOUR LOSSES

When you have finally reached your goal and brought your weight down to where you want it, you will need a long-term meal plan to help you keep it there. If you remember that proper weight and better health go hand in hand, sticking to this plan will be easier.

As with weight loss, no one formula for weight maintenance works for everyone. For most people, including those with non-insulin-dependent diabetes, a gradual increase in carbohydrate, protein, and fat intake is desirable after reaching the suggested weight range. But if you reach the upper limit of that range, you will have to reduce calories once again. If maintenance is difficult, consult a dietitian or other diet counselor.

SUMMING UP

Especially when you have a weight-related disorder, such as type II diabetes, the earlier you lose weight the better. Of course, there is no guarantee that the improvements that come from weight-loss and exercise will be permanent. However, chances are good that if you lose enough weight *and keep it off,* the benefits of your hard work will stick.

6 □ ON FIGHTING FAT II: KEEPING PRIMED

As Chapter 5 indicates, a nutritionally balanced, low-caloric meal plan is a safe and effective way to lose weight if you follow the plan consistently. But that's a big "if." Setting up a weight-loss plan is easy compared to following it day in, day out. Yes, the market is filled with diet books claiming to be the last word on easy weight control and personal happiness. But don't believe them! Many overlook the hidden factors (such as emotions) that can contribute to weight problems, and even if the diet "works," the success is usually fleeting.

A crucial element in successful weight loss is mental preparation. This, combined with practical strategies for resisting temptations—especially the temptation to go back to your old way of eating—raises your odds for success.

It's best to think in terms of long-term weight control rather than a "diet." Going on a diet indicates that some day you will also be going off it. You may be willing to follow someone else's dictates for a while, but the time will come when you rebel and insist on making your own choices again. This is the time when many a diet falls apart and the weight you lose comes right back. It is not uncommon for people to end a diet and then become even heavier than before.

To develop a new way of eating that frees you from the feast-and-famine cycle (yo-yo dieting), you will need a plan that balances all of your food-related needs: emotional as well as nutritional. Most overweight people have an intense desire to regain control over their bodies and their lives. Balance in your diet and also *in your life* should help to strengthen your sense of control and allow you to persist in your efforts at taking weight off and keeping it off.

Such internal balance does not grow out of a spur-of-the-moment resolution, based on a chance remark or embarrassing situation. Rather, it takes careful introspection as well as planning. Achieving balance also takes motivation, which can only come from within. Slimming down for the beach audience each summer is something you do to impress others; the pounds may come off in June, but they will be back on by October. If you are to make any lasting progress, you will have to decide that it is worth doing for *yourself*, and you will have to set your mind to working on change.

KNOW YOURSELF

A new pattern of eating, if it is to work, must be one you will be able to live with indefinitely. It must be one that is tailored to your style and your needs, not your neighbor's. The first and most important step, therefore, is to understand just what your own nature is. This entails a conscious (and sometimes painful) effort to see yourself as you really are, to observe your present and past eating patterns and your personal and family eating history, including the *emotional* interactions involving food. Once you are able consciously to recognize and *understand* the origins of your eating habits and food-related behavior, you will be better able to come up with a plan to improve, or replace, them with a more positive and healthy approach.

You can start your self-examination by asking yourself what food really means to you emotionally. Is it a means of comfort when you are angry? Upset? Scared? Lonely? Or is it a drug—an ongoing pacifier, or antidepressant? Do you handle strong feelings by swallowing them, along with forkfuls of food? Is food one of your few real joys? There is something in many of us that delights in the forbidden, such as stealing from the cookie jar. If you recognize yourself in any of these questions, you'll have an idea of where your work has to begin. You'll know what emotions are likely to trigger overeating unless you are prepared with other outlets.

You may also gain a better *physiological* understanding of your problem by observing when and how you overeat. When you get "the munchies," what foods, in particular, give you comfort? For some people, certain types of food cause most of their weight troubles. If you can isolate these problem foods, you will have a big advantage when trying to develop an effective meal plan. For example, there are people who can easily follow almost any diet regimen until they have sugar, even a small amount. Then their self-control evaporates. Other people may be thrown off the track by caffeine or chocolate. And some find that they are unable to control weight without first controlling salt intake.

Another aid to self-awareness is to examine your weight changes over time. Take a piece of graph paper and chart your weight since early adolescence. Where are the sharp gains and losses? Do they correspond to significant life events? With severe emotional stress, such as death of a loved one, some people may eat more and gain weight, while others may eat less and lose weight. Positive events—marriage, birth of a child, a promotion—can also be stressful and affect eating habits. Many women put on a layer of fat with each pregnancy, going from light to medium to heavy in three pregnancies. Other women find that staying at home with young children may result in a sharp increase in weight. Retirement or reducing one's workload can also be associated with weight gain. If you know how life changes have affected your weight in the past, you may be able to exercise better control in the future. When stressful events arise, you can recognize—and resist—that impulse to reach for the refrigerator door. There are other means of comfort besides food. Start searching for them.

In family therapy, counselors often ask people to look back further still—to recall what mealtime was like in their childhood, because the habits established early in life are the most powerful and long-lasting. Some people remember mealtime as an ordeal, because parents chose that time to interrogate and criticize. Others feel that eating was the one thing their family had in common, and that food was their sole shared pleasure. Or the mother may have taken it as a personal rejection if her children refused any food. Some families never ate together, and it was a lonely time.

Much can be learned by observing our extended families as well. Many of us are but one or two generations removed from our immigrant predecessors, whose attitudes toward food may have been formed under conditions of scarcity. To them, a layer of fat may have been a sign of health and security, even a status symbol of sorts; being thin may have been indicative of illness. These attitudes may well have been reproduced in our families and in ourselves. Understanding their history will help us to realize that such fears of going without need no longer trouble us today. By looking into your family's and your past, you can begin to evaluate whether old habits that once served a purpose are useful to you today.

LEARNING TO SAVOR YOUR FOOD

Along with introspection you can take other steps to build new habits. It may sound paradoxical, but if you can learn to truly enjoy your food, to concentrate on and savor the act of eating itself, you will probably get more satisfaction while eating less. If, for example, you gulp your food, not only do you need larger quantities before your appetite is satiated, you also miss out on the pleasure of tasting each individual bite. To remedy this, try learning to chew very slowly and carefully. Chewing to the pace of a metronome set to its lowest count may help.

Another solution to mouth-stuffing is to make sure you eat only when you are with others. Even better, place a large mirror in front of yourself when eating alone, and watch closely. Try to eat as calmly and gracefully in front of yourself as you do in front of others. If you don't treat yourself with deference, no one else will.

Make a commitment to yourself not to eat standing up, and never to eat (standing or sitting) at the refrigerator. Some people kid themselves into believing that leftovers have fewer calories. Not so! Don't eat while doing something else (watching TV or reading); with your mind on the book or picture, you won't realize how much you have swallowed.

It takes time to learn to permit yourself to enjoy food. In time, you can eat less and enjoy it more. Ask someone who is permanently slim. (For more behavioral tips, see Chapter 8, on binge eating.)

KEEPING IT UP

To maintain your commitment to your weight-control program, you need to work on accepting yourself. A new way of eating, if it is to be successful, must be predicated upon a new feeling about yourself.

Accepting yourself means acknowledging both your hidden capabilities (your intelligence, generosity, sense of humor, and . . .) and your human limitations.

It also means that there are times for strict dieting, but also times to let up and take a breather. Otherwise, incessant and inflexible demands on yourself for constant perfection may jeopardize the entire enterprise.

For example, you may be one of the many people for whom Christmas is a lonely time of the year. To force yourself to diet rigidly at that point is cruel and unusual punishment; furthermore, it just won't work. If you recognize this, and if you are *not* diabetic, you may be able to compensate by dieting carefully in the preceding month (from the end of the Thanksgiving feast until Christmas Eve). You will then have balanced out your inevitable five-pound gain of the week just prior to the New Year. If you have diabetes, you unfortunately cannot abandon your meal plan safely. However, you *can* talk with your diet counselor and get an alternative meal plan for the holidays.

There may be other times in the year, month, or even day that you have to accept some vulnerability. Remember that there is a vast difference between maintaining and gaining; sometimes, simply holding steady may be progress enough.

Also, although the scale can be a useful reminder of your progress as well as your need to redouble your efforts, don't let it punish you inordinately. There are ways to measure progress other than the scale. We tend to endow the scale with unreasonable powers, allowing it to determine our self-worth. Scales unfortunately register in black and white, leaving no room for mitigating explanations. If only their data could be softened with messages: "You've gained half a pound, but that always happens when you're premenstrual." Or: "You've taken off two pounds overnight. But don't be too quick to celebrate. Saunas will do that every time (dehydration). And drinking water will undo it."

Instead of weighing yourself, you can weigh and measure the foods you eat and keep track in a regular food diary. In this way, you can chart your progress without risking the occasional (but devastating) disapproval of the scale. Or you can use a tape measure or the fit of your clothes as your indicators. At the start of your weight-loss program, choose a favorite dress or pair of well-fitting pants and then try them on at weekly intervals. You'll know how well you are doing by the bagginess of the outfit. When friends and family ask you the inevitable question: "How much have you lost?" give your answer in inches or sizes and save pressure on yourself.

UNDERSTAND THE INFLUENCE OF OTHERS

It is great to have a friend or family member with whom you can share your struggle, who will congratulate you on your progress and offer encouragement when you slip. Just be careful to choose a "cheerleader" who is not too judgmental. If your supporter makes you feel humiliated or depressed, it defeats the purpose. Also beware of relying on people who have a hidden wish to keep you fat. (Sometimes a spouse or friend unconsciously wants you to be heavy.) These people may choose fat spouses or friends because, on some level, it makes them feel more secure. Or they may choose slim mates and then go about fattening them up to fill some kind of inner need.

In the final analysis, however, we are responsible for our own choices and our own fates. It is *our* decision whether or not we are going to let someone else's pastries or pasta determine how we look and feel next week.

Once again, the motivation to lose weight has to be internal. If you have attained some balance within yourself, you will not be so easily tempted by others, nor will you look to others to save you from yourself.

HAVE REALISTIC EXPECTATIONS

If someone were to ask you how you would climb a tall mountain, you would likely answer "very slowly." Probably you would not attempt to climb straight up either; the task would be too hard, and you would quickly become so exhausted that you might have to give up the effort. Similarly, there is no reason to diet as if you were climbing a tall mountain in one day.

Sometimes the circular route is fastest, even if it doesn't seem so at first. Of course, at various plateaus on the mountain you might be tempted to gaze up and dwell on all you have left to accomplish, filling yourself with fear and self-doubt. But if you are a wise traveler, you will re-energize yourself by thinking about the distance you *have already climbed* and about your budding faith in your ability to continue. And you will make steady progress.

Speaking of plateaus, they're very common in people who are working on weight loss. Sometimes you just stop losing weight for a while despite your efforts. Now is not the time to give up. Try on an old pair of slacks and savor the progress you have made. Should you stay at your plateau for a long time, remind yourself that maintaining your slimmed-down weight is indeed progress. You may not have lost more weight, but neither did you fall headlong off your plateau! You have the strength to stick with your weight-control program despite having no obvious reward from the scale for your trouble.

As you embark on your lifelong weight-control plan, keep in mind that losing weight won't change your life in the magical way promised in magazine ads. In fact, getting used to your new, thinner self can be downright disconcerting at first. Just as adolescents feel awkward about their rapidly changing bodies, adults may experience confusion or new vulnerability along with their newly reduced dimensions. People may not recognize you; they may even say disparaging things about your old self (of whom you may have been rather fond). Women may find that men are beginning to make remarks they have never heard directed at them before, and it may seem threatening. There is really no way to know what the changes will be like in advance and to expect the world to adhere to an imagined scenario is to ask for disappointment.

It may be difficult to accept that losing weight will not solve all your problems. But it may be necessary to separate weight-related problems from your old conflicts in order to prevent recurrent relapses of old eating habits. One young man, for example, pudgy since childhood, had always blamed his extra girth for his failure with the opposite sex. But, in actuality, he had developed a needley, porcupiny personality that was much more distancing than his overweight appearance. He finally lost weight—grumpily, in fact—and began woman-hunting with a vengeance. After a year he was no closer to a relationship than he had ever been. He then went from his boyish teddy-bear pudge to true obesity, never acknowledging that it was his manner and not his baby fat that kept the world at bay. Focusing on weight, in other words, can be a form of tunnel vision that shuts out other aspects of ourselves in need of growth and change.

The idea that slim people were born that way and maintain their weight effortlessly is another self-defeating fairy tale. True, there are a few fortunate souls for whom food never presents a problem. Most people, however, *choose* to be the way they are. They have developed an inner control mechanism that helps them to eat more slowly or to be more careful between meals.

When you are finally fully ready to begin a serious weight-control program, keep in mind that you are not alone. As the next chapter will demonstrate, many people travel the same path that you are considering. It can be a great help to find others who are headed in the same direction and who share many of your fears and anxieties. The next chapter is based on experiences of people who have diabetes, but many of the feelings expressed are common to anyone who is overweight.

7 □ ON FIGHTING FAT III: COPING WITH FEELINGS

The combination of diabetes, obesity, and the stress of having to change daily habits can produce anxiety, loneliness, fear, guilt, anger, and depression. Such feelings can take the joy out of life, tarnish a person's self-esteem, and dampen one's interest in diabetes control. It is difficult to succeed at anything—even taking care of yourself—if you do not feel well and if you doubt your value as a person.

This chapter is based on a series of discussions among people with non-insulin-dependent diabetes who are struggling with weight control. Their personal feelings, along with comments by health care professionals specializing in diabetes treatment, are offered here to let you know that you are not alone and to encourage you to hang in there. Try not to let your negative moods get in the way of taking care of your body. If they begin to, you may want to consider sharing your feelings with others who understand. Research has shown that talking about feelings can be an effective form of self-help.

"SO ALONE"

I feel so alone . . . No one's interested in my problem. I just seem to get in everyone's way.

Loneliness is a common feeling among people with either type of diabetes. People who have insulin-dependent (type I) diabetes feel "different" from the rest of the world because they take injections. They also feel that it is unfair that they have to spend so much of their time and energy calculating balances of food, exercise, and insulin. "If I only had to worry about my diet," they often say, "life would be so simple!"

But for overweight people with type II diabetes, losing weight and staying on a meal plan is far from simple. Knowing that other (thin) people think diet control is easy makes them feel isolated and angry. Overweight people have to fight constantly against their hunger, habits, and perhaps an inherited tendency to gain weight. Yet, they are not often praised for their efforts. In fact, they may have to deal with friends and family members who invite them to eat "forbidden" foods and then blame their obesity on self-indulgence. Add to this the fear of developing complications and/or type I diabetes, and you have a heavy emotional burden.

"THEN I FEEL GUILTY"

Sometimes, I make three trips to the candy machine and fight off the urge each time. But then, on the fourth trip, I give in. It's as if the food talks to me, saying, "Come and eat me. I won't hurt your diet just this once."

It's like alcoholism. If I'm invited to a party, my first thought is, "What will be served?" All day long, on or off my diet, I think about food. My hunger has nothing to do with appetite, and I can't tell when I'm full.

I do all right when no one else is home. The trouble is, if anyone offers me a bite, I get a shovel to taste it with, and then I feel guilty.

Research has shown that hunger has both physical and psychological elements and that the balance between them varies with the individual and his or her circumstances. In other words, intense food cravings are not necessarily "all in your head."

Feeling guilty for constantly craving food, or for giving in to cravings, is a waste of time and energy. It would be far better to use that energy to transform your guilt into determination, and to use your time to work on developing your coping skills. Keep in mind that many other people with your problem have learned to distinguish between just wanting to eat and really needing nourishment.

PLATEAUS

I had lost 20 of my 30 extra pounds, and everything was going great, when all of a sudden my progress just stopped. I wasn't eating anything more, and I was doing my exercises, but some days I even seemed to be gaining weight. After a few weeks of this, I got so discouraged that I started straying from my meal plan every now and then.

Some people are slow to lose weight or become stuck at plateaus even if they never succumb to temptation. Not only do they find this frustrating, but they may also be unfairly accused of weakness or lack of will power. Health professionals have come to realize, however, that the scales alone cannot always reflect the tremendous effort people make to lose weight. If you find yourself at a discouraging plateau, don't hesitate to seek help. Overweight people with diabetes need lifelong support just as much as those dependent on insulin do.

Actually, plateaus in weight loss are relatively common. There are three main reasons for these standstills:

First, when a person loses a great deal of weight, the body starts to behave as if it were semistarved. It slows down its "machinery" to conserve energy and, as a result, burns fewer calories than usual. This, in turn, hampers further weight loss.

Second, to compensate for its reduced bulk, the body may conserve more than usual amounts of fluid for future use. In particular, the kidneys retain salt and water. Eventually, however, as you continue to lose fat, the kidneys release the fluid and the pointer on the scale moves downward once again.

Third, exercise replaces fat with muscle tissue, and muscle weighs more than fat. Nevertheless, muscle development is a good sign, indicating that your body's fat level is declining and that you are becoming more fit.

FAMILY UPSETS:
AN OBSTACLE TO CHANGE

. . . and she said, "Mom, can't you please taste just a tiny piece of this apple pie?"

Temptations offered by those you love can be the most painful to resist. In fact, it is not unusual to get subtle discouraging signals from the people you counted on most for support. The diagnosis of diabetes—or the renewed determination to control it through weight loss—can threaten other family members in surprising ways. They may not like the changes!

There are no easy prescriptions for helping family members to adapt to changing behavior and responsibility. But openly acknowledging the feelings and conflicts can be an important first step. Often, family members are not even aware that they are being discouraging.

FEAR OF LOSING
FRIENDS: ANOTHER HURDLE

So much of socializing seems to revolve around eating. I always feel like the odd man out when my friends get together.

Taking control of diabetes involves some difficult trade-offs. But if you feel left out of socializing, consider taking the offensive. Many of your friends and co-workers may also want to lose weight and get in shape. Form a mutual support group, with its own meals and activities. You'll be helping them and easing your own loneliness at the same time.

For those who aren't ready to change, consider making non-food dates—go to a museum or play tennis. Or, meet for a drink and have a glass of sparkling water with a twist. Or, invite friends to your place, where you can control what's served.

IMAGE PROBLEMS: STILL ANOTHER ROADBLOCK

I always saw myself as the food provider in the family. Now that I have to limit what I eat and keep out of the kitchen more, I'm not sure just who I am.

How you picture yourself and your role in life can have a big effect on eating behavior and weight. For example, women in our society today are under great pressure to play several different roles: assertive and successful at business, attractive and yet unthreatening to men, nurturing at home. Some people find these contradictions too much to bear and may subconsciously gain weight or stay heavy to avoid competing for certain kinds of work or for love relationships.

Of course, women are not the only ones who suffer from image problems. Some men may fear losing weight because they will become smaller and, therefore, somehow less masculine.

MOTIVATION

You have to understand what diabetes is really doing to your body, otherwise you won't watch your blood and urine, do your tests, and stay on your diet.

If I go off my diet, at first I think of myself as a no-good person. But if I write it down, somehow, admitting what I've done lessens the guilt. I face up to it and am able to see that my overall effort is really not bad. Then I'm ready to try again.

Truly, motivation is a subtle and individual process. Many people have found that the turning point in their decision to lose weight came when their health professionals sat them down and explained what diabetes could do to them. Others have noted that seeing consistent, near-normal results in blood-glucose tests serves as an incentive to keep on controlling weight.

Maintaining one's motivation can be quite a challenge. In fact, people have to recharge their batteries, so to speak, over and over throughout their lives. Losing motivation does not imply failure if you make an effort to recapture your energy.

Feeling well is the best motivator of all. Yet even success has its pitfalls. If losing weight makes you relax your vigilance, you may find yourself slipping back into old eating habits. Eternal vigilance is the price that has to be paid for good health in both types of diabetes.

CARING AND SHARING

I'm going to be fighting this battle for the rest of my life . . . please keep the caring coming!

It is important both for people with diabetes and for health professionals to recognize the unique qualities of each human being. We each have our own happiness and stress, frustration and accomplishment, loneliness, illness, and health. We all need constantly to re-examine our own progress and motivation and to understand and respect the difficulties that other people face. We need to search out those who succeed and learn from them, and, just as important, we have a responsibility to pass on our own strengths and knowledge to others in need.

Throughout the country, there are already groups set up for people who have diabetes who want to share their feelings and help each other build up strength and confidence. To find out if a group exists in your area, contact your American Diabetes Association affiliate, listed on pages xv-xx.

8 □ HELP FOR COMPULSIVE BINGERS

Almost everyone has gone on an eating binge at one time or another. But for tens of thousands, binge-eating is more than an occasional fall from grace. It is a bewildering and tormenting part of their everyday lives—a compulsion, like alcoholism, and equally hard to conquer.

A compulsive binger is one who feels powerless over food and, as one eating disorder expert puts it, "eats anything that is not nailed down as often as several times a day." Once a binge gets started, it may go on and on and can total thousands of calories.

No one knows just how many compulsive bingers there are in either the general or the diabetic population, in part because people who binge heavily often do so "in the closet" and are too embarrassed to admit it. "I have done this for so long," says one woman, "that I have become a professional at hiding it."

Researchers also have few hard answers to the question of what causes binging. They have observed, however, that many people who binge in this way seem to have particular difficulty handling stress and react by binge-eating, in part because food is so easily available as an outlet for anxiety. There are indications that at least some people who have diabetes binge in response to feelings of deprivation.

The short-term physical consequences of binging—bloat, pain, and so on—can be uncomfortable for anyone, but they spell double trouble for people who have diabetes.

In the aftermath of a binge, people who are not diabetic may feel pretty ill and disgusted. But people with diabetes also have to contend with elevated blood glucose and its effects, such as excessive thirst and constant trips to the bathroom to urinate. Insulin users who try to treat themselves with extra insulin often find that even a large dose can't restore blood-glucose control and can actually disrupt it by causing a severe insulin reaction, which, in turn, sometimes leads to yet another binge (because of hunger and eating to treat the reaction).

Those are just the short-term effects. In the long run, compulsive bingers leave themselves open to increased risks for high blood pressure, heart disease, and other disorders if they become obese as a result of chronic binge-eating. And people with diabetes also run an increased risk of developing diabetic complications if frequent binges lead to chronically uncontrolled diabetes.

BINGE-PURGE CYCLE IS DEADLY

An apparently growing number of people—primarily slender college-aged women as well as athletes and models—try to "undo" their binges and avoid weight gain by coupling their binges with purges. They either cause themselves to vomit, or they take large amounts of diuretics (water pills) and/or laxatives. People who engage in binge-purge behaviors regularly are commonly said to have "bulimia," although, technically, several criteria need to be met and a person may be diagnosed bulimic even if he or she does not purge. The number of people who binge and purge is unknown, but it is clear that at least some people with diabetes are among their numbers.

For anyone, such behavior can be devastating if done regularly. Chronic vomiting, for example, can cause serious damage to the liver, kidneys, esophagus, and teeth. Abuse of laxatives and diuretics can disrupt the normal functioning of the intestinal tract. Purging can also upset the chemical balance in the body and seriously reduce potassium, a loss that can cause severe dehydration and muscle weakness and, in extreme cases, disturbed heart function and even death.

In people with diabetes, a major loss of potassium can also play havoc with an already disturbed metabolism. And vomiting and dehydration added to already poor diabetes control can push a person toward a diabetic coma.

"WHAT SHOULD I DO?":
A QUESTION WITH NO EASY ANSWERS

"You can advise a person not to smoke," says a doctor, "but you can't tell a person not to eat." Treatment for binge-eating has to teach people to cope with almost constant temptation.

Occasional bingers in good health can try some of the self-help tips listed later in this chapter before turning to professional assistance. They may also find help through such reputable diet groups as Weight Watchers. In addition, many people benefit from attending meetings of Overeaters Anonymous (OA), a free self-help group modeled on Alcoholics Anonymous. In many cities, group meetings are available daily, and chapters everywhere offer access to a network of people to call for support when the going gets rough. (Local chapters of OA are listed in the white pages of your phone book.)

However, people who binge frequently and seemingly uncontrollably—or who binge and purge—need professional help, preferably behavior therapy and psychotherapy. This is because compulsive behavior can be extremely difficult to correct on one's own. (See the resource list at the end of this chapter for help in locating professionals.)

By pinpointing the situations and feelings that trigger and reinforce binge-eating, and by making plans to defuse them, behavior therapy can sometimes bring about relatively rapid changes in these habits. And by unearthing and dealing with emotions that encourage binge-eating and/or purging, psychotherapy can help to ensure that these behavior changes are lasting. Other important resources include a diet counselor and, particularly with diabetes, a physician who can monitor any medical problems.

Fortunately, people usually do not have to shop around for several specialists. Once a doctor or therapist familiar with eating disorders is found, he or she can steer the person to other needed resources.

Even with professional help, neither binging nor purging can be shut off like a light switch, and many people with these problems in their past consider themselves to be much like recovered alcoholics. Those bingers who gain control over their eating habits report, however, that giving up the momentary "high" of their binges is well worth the sacrifice.

HELP YOURSELF

To stop binge-eating, you first need the determination to stop. Then, you need some aids to help you avoid taking the "one little bite" that leads to all the rest. The following approaches have helped some people, although none can substitute for the therapy needed by compulsive bingers.

- □ *Keep a log of your food intake* and how you feel before, during, and after binges. This can help you pinpoint why you binge, so you can develop strategies for avoiding eating sprees.
- □ *Keep binge foods out of the house:* Don't buy them yourself, and ask your family to do the same and to avoid eating those foods in front of you.
- □ *Don't skip meals:* You'll get too hungry to control yourself. Resolve to eat only at the table, never standing up or serving yourself from the container.
- □ *Set up a support system:* Have a list of people you can call when cravings begin to overpower you. Decide on your menu in advance and commit yourself to just those foods and portions by announcing your intentions to your companion.
- □ *Stop and think:* Before you grab food, ask yourself, "Am I

really hungry?" Think about how you will feel after the binge.

- □ *Put it off:* Tell yourself you can have the food if you really need it—later. Often the craving will pass.
- □ *Do something . . . anything:* Take a walk. Draw a bath. Jog. Wash the car. Put on music and dance! Have a list of activities you enjoy ready in advance. Exercise (in moderation) has saved many a binger.
- □ *Be on your own side:* For one woman who gained control over binging, the crucial realization came when, "I finally understood that if the diabetic in the family were someone else, I'd do anything to see that the person had a proper diet."
- □ *Change your thinking about food:* Instead of bemoaning the items you cannot eat, think about the foods you *can* have. Find permissible foods (perhaps a favorite fruit) that will feel like a treat whenever you have it. If you hate your meal plan or always feel hungry, perhaps your dietitian can suggest changes to make the diet more appealing to you.
- □ *Eat one portion of a food you enjoy:* Do this when you absolutely must have *something*. But don't choose a food that will lead to an uncontrolled binge. Eat slowly, savoring every bite so you'll feel satisfied. Make a list of problem foods—decide which ones you should avoid and which ones you can learn to eat in limited quantities.
- □ *Be prepared:* Keep cut-up raw vegetables in the refrigerator. And there's always popcorn—three cups cooked with no oil in a hot-air popper are only 80 calories, one Starch/Bread exchange.
- □ *Become involved in activities that make you feel good about yourself:* Feeling good often reduces the need to overeat.
- □ *If you're a teen with diabetes and you binge to rebel and feel normal, consider the words of one of your peers:* "I finally realized that I was so busy worrying about being normal that

I was making myself a real pig! Once I came to my senses, I realized that nowadays teens are worried about *not* eating so much."

□ *See your doctor:* If you have diabetes, perpetual hunger is sometimes a sign that your treatment plan needs adjustment.

□ *Don't be a perfectionist:* For many people, the urge to binge never goes away completely. To think you will never slip is unrealistic and sets you up for failure. If you slip up, do not give up. Forgive yourself and start over.

RESOURCES FOR COMPULSIVE BINGERS

GROUPS FOR PEOPLE WITH BULIMIA

ANAD (Anorexia Nervosa and Associated Disorders), Box 7, Highland Park, IL 60035. (312) 831-3438.

AABA (American Anorexia Bulimia Association), 133 Cedar Lane, Teaneck, NJ 07666. (201) 836-1800.

Both groups offer information on bulimia and have names of health professionals concerned with eating disorders.

EATING DISORDER CLINICS
To find a reputable clinic near you, call the psychology or community-relations department of a local university hospital or medical center.

OTHER
Consult the yellow pages of your phone book for local weight-control programs and get the approval of your dietitian or diet counselor before joining any organization with a diet plan of its own. Your affiliate of the American Diabetes Association may also be able to provide information about community resources.

9 □ EXERCISE: NUTRITION'S IMPORTANT PARTNER

Everyone today seems to be joining an exercise class or fitness club. But not everyone knows exactly what physical fitness is, why it is important, and the best way to achieve it.

Physical fitness is a state of high-level well-being: your body becomes more efficient, and both your endurance and your ability to cope with stress increase as well. On the cellular level, regular, reasonably strenuous exercise (such as jogging) improves the body's ability to transport and use the nutrients and oxygen that our 75 trillion cells need to perform their complex tasks. Exercise also helps to improve the tone, size, and endurance of muscles, and may, along with good nutrition, help to prevent certain disorders, such as heart and blood-vessel disease, high blood pressure, degenerative joint disease, obesity, and type II diabetes. Exercise can strengthen the lungs, heart, and circulatory system while making their work easier. It can also enhance joint flexibility, reduce levels of certain blood fats, and improve the body's ability to use its insulin.

If you are already overweight, regular exercise can help you to lose weight. It does this in part by increasing your *basal metabolic rate* (BMR), the rate at which your body burns fuel (calories) for energy. When you are on a low-calorie diet for a long time, your metabolism eventually adapts to fewer calories and burns them more frugally, so you stop losing weight or lose it more slowly. Speeding up your BMR through exercise helps to keep the needle on the scale moving down.

One way to lose weight is to continue to eat your usual amount of calories while exercising more. For example, a 200-pound person who maintains the same diet but adds a brisk walk of 1½ miles to each day's activity will lose 10 to 14 pounds per year. But your best bet is to increase exercise *and* cut back on calories, because you will lose weight even faster.

If you are overweight *and* diabetic, exercise can benefit you in two ways. By helping you to lose weight, it should help to improve diabetes control. In addition, because exercise helps the body to use its insulin and overcome insulin resistance—and therefore to handle its blood glucose more efficiently—it helps to keep blood glucose levels down. In fact, exercise enhances glucose use by the body for several hours—and sometimes for more than a day—after a workout. This prolonged effect is one reason why regular exercise is highly recommended for most people with diabetes *as long as the precautions outlined later in this chapter are followed.*

(*Note:* Certain people should *not* exercise unless under close medical guidance. Among these are people who have very high fasting levels of blood glucose. When diabetes is so out of control, exercise can make the situation worse. In addition, individuals who have had diabetes for many years or who have diabetic complications may need to avoid some exercises. If you are one of these people, see your doctor for advice.)

NO TIME TO EXERCISE?

Just as a car engine needs a regular maintenance program and performs better tuned than untuned, your body needs regular care, too. Fortunately it is a lot less expensive to keep the body tuned! But it does take work. Physical fitness is not something you can gain by wishing for it. You have to invest energy and time.

Before you say that you cannot make these investments,

consider this perspective: A seven-day week has 168 hours, or a little over 10,000 minutes. To become physically fit, you have to invest only *90 minutes per week of vigorous exercise.* That's just 1 percent of the total time available to you in a week. (Did you know that you spend about a third of your week sleeping?)

PRELIMINARY CONSIDERATIONS

Before starting any exercise routine, see your doctor. Discuss your exercise goals with him or her and get a thorough medical exam-ination. If you are over 40, you should probably get an exercise stress, or tolerance, test. This test consists of taking an electro-cardiogram to record the heart's activity during exercise (usually on a treadmill or a stationary bicycle). It not only provides a good basis for rating your overall fitness but can also indicate the pres-ence of heart disease, high blood pressure, poor circulation, and other chronic conditions. These basic precautions apply to diabetic and nondiabetic individuals alike.

Once you've received your physician's medical approval to exercise, the next step is mental preparation. If you are out of shape, you have to realize that your body did not get so soft and tired overnight, or in just the last couple of weeks or months. Nor are the changes necessarily due to aging. They are caused, in large part, by your body's adaptation to a sedentary lifestyle.

The fact is that most Americans get little vigorous exercise at work or during leisure hours. Today, only a few jobs (i.e., lumberjacking) require real physical exertion. People usually ride in cars or buses rather than walk, take elevators instead of stairs, and sit at home watching television during much of their free time. Recreational activities such as golf with a cart may be enjoy-able, but offer little in the way of physical conditioning. Similarly, spot toning exercises may firm up flab and improve muscle tone in specific areas, but they do not affect overall fitness.

The transition from a sedentary lifestyle to one that includes frequent and demanding exercise should be carried out gradually. Don't expect instant results; it took time to get this far out of shape, and it's going to take time to get back in. Accept from the outset that it may take months before you reap any lasting benefits. In fact, regular physical training is a lifelong project. If you stick to your program, however, you will probably start to notice a difference in the way you *feel*—more energy, less fatigue, better sleep—within a few weeks.

CHOOSING YOUR EXERCISE:
AEROBIC VS. ANAEROBIC

The best exercise for weight loss and all-around conditioning—and for improving blood glucose control in people with diabetes—is called "aerobic" exercise. The word aerobic is of Greek origin and means "to use or be in the presence of oxygen." Aerobic exercise improves the body's ability to transport and process oxygen and, by so doing, builds strength and endurance in the muscle cells. The regular contraction of the muscles in aerobic exercise assists blood circulation and, since the heart itself is a muscle, the entire blood-pumping system is strengthened.

Aerobic activities are rhythmic and continuous, meaning that you should be able to perform them for at least three minutes without experiencing *extreme* fatigue and breathlessness. They also involve large muscle groups, which makes them sufficiently strenuous to increase the heart rate as you do them. Walking, jogging, swimming, dancing, and cycling are some good examples of aerobic exercise.

On the other hand, there are many forms of strenuous exercise that *do not* increase the body's capacity to handle oxygen. These *anaerobic* exercises require bursts of exertion so intense that the muscles are actually deprived of sufficient oxygen. Such extreme exertion can be sustained for only brief periods of time.

Examples of pure anaerobic activities include weight-lifting, sprinting, shot-putting, and high jump. Activities such as basketball, soccer, and middle-distance running events combine elements of both aerobic and anaerobic exercise.

GETTING STARTED

You need at least 20 minutes of moderately vigorous exercise to get a proper aerobic workout. But that doesn't mean that you just put on your exercise outfit and start right in. Each exercise session should be preceded by at least 10 to 15 minutes of warming-up, and followed by an equivalent cooling-down period.

A good warm-up should start with long, slow stretching exercises, which will improve flexibility in the muscles and joints and help to prevent pulls, strains, and sprains. It may also include some light calisthenics to get the heart pumping, and thus, pre-pare the body for the more vigorous activity to follow. In cold weather, a longer warm-up period may be necessary. People whose muscles are normally tight, or who are prone to muscle or bone injuries, may also want to spend more time on their warm-ups.

The cooling-down, or slow-down, period after exercise should be like the warm-up in reverse; again, the purpose is to help your body to adjust to the change in activity level. Stretching the muscles after strenuous exercise will also aid in preventing spasms and charley horse, and will reduce the soreness and stiff-ness that often develops overnight.

For most beginners, 20 minutes of continuous aerobic activity will probably be too much. So, to gradually improve your endurance, you can start off by exercising in work-rest intervals. For example, if jogging is your "thing" you can try a jog-walk routine: 10 sets of 2-minute jogs, each followed by a minute of easy walking. Or, if you are a cyclist, you can pedal hard for two minutes, then coast for a minute, and repeat until you have com-pleted 10 intervals. In this way, you will have gotten in your 20 minutes of aerobic exercise without overextending yourself. And as your aerobic capacity improves, you can gradually remove the rest periods until you are able to exercise for 20 minutes (or more) without a break.

HOW MUCH?

To get the most out of your exercise routine, work out at least three, and at most five, times a week. Try to work up to about 30 to 45 minutes per session.

If you are looking for an aerobic-exercise program that will help you to lose weight, keep in mind that burning calories is more a function of duration than of speed. In other words, the total caloric cost of performing a given task—say, jogging for a half hour—is about the same whether the pace is fast or slow. *It is the length of time* spent at the activity that counts most; increasing or decreasing the speed has little effect on total energy expended. Thus, an aerobic activity that can be performed continuously for an extended period will burn calories and reduce fat, while an all-out anaerobic effect will be too brief to use up a significant number of calories.

HOW MUCH IS TOO MUCH?

Your heart rate, taken sporadically (such as every five minutes) during the aerobic part of your exercise session, is a good indicator of whether or not you are getting the desired training effect from your aerobics program. (You can find out your heart rate by calculating the number of heart beats per minute. A simple way to do this is to find the pulse on your wrist, count the beats in a ten-second interval, and multiply by six.) Find out from your doctor what your "target heart rate" is. This is your safety range, and it varies from person to person according to age, weight, and normal level of activity.

If your heart rate during exercise is in the target range, it means that you are probably getting a good, safe workout. If it is below the target range, you may need to work a little harder; if it is above, you could be overdoing it. Other ways to tell when it is time to ease off are: extreme breathlessness, to the degree that you cannot speak while exercising; extreme muscle weakness or heavy, tired, and burning muscles; lightheadedness; and nausea.

Note that in certain circumstances measuring the heart rate will not be useful. If you have autonomic neuropathy or if you take medicines called beta blockers (such as Inderal) for blood-pressure control or heart disease, measuring your pulse will not warn you that you are overdoing it. Ask your physician or exercise physiologist how to monitor yourself.

To find an organized exercise program run by a true authority on physical fitness, ask your doctor; a member of the physical education department of the local high school, community college, or university; or a program planner at your local "Y" to point you in the right direction. While some neighborhood spas and health clubs might be excellent, others are not.

EXERCISE AND DIABETES

People with diabetes should be aware of the special precautions they may have to take to ensure a sound, safe, and effective exercise regimen. Here are the answers to some common questions about diabetes and exercise:

QUESTION: What is the best time of day for a diabetic individual to exercise?

ANSWER: People who do *not* take insulin can usually exercise whenever they like, although people who are treated with diabetes pills should avoid exercising on an empty stomach.

For insulin users, the best time to exercise is generally one to three hours after a meal, unless insulin is peaking during that time. Be very careful about vigorous exercise before meals (when blood glucose may be falling) or when insulin is likely to be peaking, because you are most likely to have an insulin reaction at those times. For example, in a person who takes a mixed dose of Regular and NPH insulin at 7 A.M., the insulin will peak at about

10 A.M. and 3 P.M. These would probably be poor choices of exercise times. If you must exercise then, be sure to cover yourself with a snack (see next questions for details).

QUESTION: What tests are needed before I exercise?

ANSWER: People with type I diabetes should perform blood-glucose and urine-ketone tests before exercise. The glucose level will give you an idea of whether or not you need the extra pre-exercise snack, and whether blood glucose is too high for safe exercising. The ketone test lets you know if you have enough insulin available to safely exercise.

(Ketones are substances formed when the body breaks down fat, which it does when it lacks insulin. If they appear in the urine *before* you exercise, ketones generally mean that you do not have enough insulin available to exercise safely and that you need to get your diabetes in better control before working out. Unless you have enough insulin in your blood, exercise will not help your body to use its glucose, anyway.)

However, you generally do not have to worry about ketones that appear *after* exercise; this can occur even in nondiabetic individuals. If ketones persist for more than a day, though, contact your doctor.

QUESTION: Should I eat before exercise?

ANSWER: People who do not take insulin generally do not need an extra snack before exercise.

For people who take insulin, it is generally advisable to have an extra snack of carbohydrate *before* you exercise unless a blood test indicates that your glucose is elevated. Have 10 to 30 grams of carbohydrate (depending on the activity, your blood-glucose level, and your past experience) within 15 to 30 minutes before you start each hour of vigorous activity. A small apple or banana or a half cup of juice has about 15 grams of carbohydrate. A snack is particularly important if you must exercise at times when your blood sugar is likely to be at its lowest.

Once exercise becomes a part of your lifestyle and you have worked out insulin and meal-plan adjustments with your health professionals, you will probably have to add very few calories to your usual meal plan unless the training is unusually long or intense.

QUESTION: Do I need to change insulin doses on the day I exercise?

ANSWER: At the start of an exercise training program this is often important. Check with your physician or diabetes specialist concerning changes in insulin dosages. After a few weeks, when your body has adjusted to your new routine, you may not need to make continual changes. In the adjustment period, however, you may have some fluctuations in blood glucose, possibly leading to more reactions than usual.

QUESTION: Where should I inject my insulin?

ANSWER: The injection site may be important because the pumping effect of nearby muscles being exercised tends to move insulin rapidly into the bloodstream, and thus generally increases the risk of an insulin reaction. Therefore, it's usually advisable to use an abdominal injection site before leg exercises, such as running or bicycling. Conversely, when the arms are heavily exercised as in rowing or canoeing, the thigh might be an ideal injection site.

QUESTION: During prolonged exercise, should I cut my insulin dose or eat more food?

ANSWER: For activities lasting over a full day, such as hiking, skiing, canoeing, or biking trips, the insulin dose will usually have to be reduced. In addition, a light snack of 10 to 50 grams of long-acting carbohydrate, such as crackers, bread, or granola, eaten every 20 minutes to an hour for the duration of the activity may help to prevent an insulin reaction. You might also combine the carbohydrate with some meat to delay the carbohydrate's absorption into the bloodstream. It is important to consult your physician prior to altering your insulin dosage.

QUESTION: Do I need to exercise every day to keep blood sugar under control?

ANSWER: A good recommendation is to exercise at least four days a week. Most people with diabetes find that an every-other-day schedule allows for adequate control with little need to adjust the insulin dose. On the days you don't exercise strenuously, you can engage in milder activities such as walking or non-demanding recreational sports. The benefits of proper exercise in controlling blood glucose may last for up to a full day; however, more than two to four days without training often results in increased insulin requirements for people with insulin-dependent diabetes.

ENJOY

One other word of advice: in choosing your exercise program, whatever it is, make sure that it consists of activities you enjoy. Exercising for good health is hard work—but it should also be fun. If it isn't, you aren't likely to keep it up for long. Since the most important part of any exercise routine is sticking to it, pick a program you can at least learn to live with. If jogging bores you, there's always cycling or swimming or, weather permitting, cross-country skiing. If you don't like exercising alone, you may want to consider an aerobic dance class. And for people who just wouldn't feel comfortable participating in any of these activities, the walking program detailed below may be the most pleasant and natural introduction to healthful exercise.

WHY NOT WALK?

Walking is man's best medicine, according to the ancient Greek physician Hippocrates. His statement is as true today as it was in his day when walking was the primary means of transportation.

It's safe. Nearly everyone can do it. You don't need lessons. It doesn't cost a lot. You can do it anywhere, anytime. And, you can start as soon as your doctor gives the word.

According to "Walking for Exercise and Pleasure," a Blue Shield pamphlet, you should strike out at a steady clip that is brisk enough to get your heart beating faster and your lungs working harder. Hold your head erect and keep your back straight and abdomen flat. Point your toes straight ahead and let your arms swing loosely at your sides. Land on the heel of the foot and roll forward to drive off the ball of the foot. Be sure not to walk only on the ball of the foot or in a flat-footed style, as this may cause fatigue and soreness. Take long, easy strides, but don't strain yourself.

Of course, before you begin any exercise program, including a walking program, discuss any precautions with your doctor. Generally, however, a minimum of twenty minutes and a maximum of one hour of walking are recommended. If your pace is too tiring, or too easy, reduce or lengthen your walking time accordingly. Try to fit in at least three walking sessions per week. As your fitness level and staying power increases, set a swifter pace and walk longer distances. The more you walk, the more efficient your exercise program will be. Eventually, you may want to progress to more strenuous activities as well.

Adequate footwear is usually the only special equipment

walking requires. Lighter trail and hiking boots, or casual shoes with heavy rubber or crepe soles, are suitable. Shoes should fit well around the heel with plenty of room at the toes. Make sure your shoes are comfortable and provide support and don't cause blisters or calluses. Consult your podiatrist or the doctor who treats your diabetes before choosing a pair of walking shoes, in case you need special adaptations in your shoes.

Walking generates a lot of body heat, so keep this in mind when dressing for your workout. On hot days, the lighter the better. Cotton is a good choice; it absorbs perspiration and lets excess moisture evaporate. On wet days, choose shoes made of leather or nylon because they shed water better. When it's colder outside, dress in layers. Several thin layers of clothing will help insulate you better than a single thick layer. In addition, you can peel off clothes as you warm up. Wear cotton or silk next to your skin, wool on the outside. A nylon windbreaker over your layers provides the best insulation, as seasoned runners have learned. Don't forget mittens or knit gloves, and always wear a hat on cold and damp days.

THE FIRST STEP

Walking can be as easy as opening up the front door and stepping outside. For some people, however, following a specially designed program is the best way to get motivated. (See the following chart.) Be sure to do plenty of stretching warmup exercises to increase flexibility before you walk. If you have been an exercise dropout in the past, take heart—walking has a low dropout rate! No matter what your age or condition, it's an activity that can make you healthier and happier.

PICK UP THE PACE:
TRY RACEWALKING

If walking is too slow, and jogging or running too strenuous, consider racewalking—a cross between the two. Racewalking

A STEP-BY-STEP WALKING PROGRAM

If you find a particular week's pattern of exercise tiring, repeat it before going on to the next pattern. You do not have to complete the program in 12 weeks. Remember to do stretching warmup exercises before the walking warmup. Check with your doctor before beginning this program.

	WARMUP (Slow walking)	EXERCISE (Brisk walking)	COOL DOWN (Slow walking)	TOTAL TIME
WEEK 1				
Session A	5 min.	5 min.	5 min.	15 min.
Session B	5 min.	5 min.	5 min.	15 min.
Session C	5 min.	5 min.	5 min.	15 min.
Continue with at least three exercise sessions during each week.				
WEEK 2 (each session)	5 min.	7 min.	5 min.	17 min.
WEEK 3 "	5 min.	9 min.	5 min.	19 min.
WEEK 4 "	5 min.	11 min.	5 min.	21 min.
WEEK 5 "	5 min.	13 min.	5 min.	23 min.
WEEK 6 "	5 min.	15 min.	5 min.	25 min.
WEEK 7 "	5 min.	18 min.	5 min.	28 min.
WEEK 8 "	5 min.	20 min.	5 min.	30 min.
WEEK 9 "	5 min.	23 min.	5 min.	33 min.
WEEK 10 "	5 min.	26 min.	5 min.	36 min.
WEEK 11 "	5 min.	28 min.	5 min.	38 min.
WEEK 12 "	5 min.	30 min.	5 min.	40 min.

Designed by the National Heart, Lung, and Blood Institute. Reprinted from the publication, "Exercise and Your Heart."

resembles accelerated "street walking," with more emphasis on the pumping action of the arms. As you stride, the back leg remains straight, and foot contact is maintained with the ground at all times. To aid the forward motion, the arms are bent at right angles and are pumped back and forth. Regular racewalking can give your heart and lungs a good workout without making your feet, ankles, and knees take a beating. Many people are finding it a great way to get fit and stay that way. As with any strenuous exercise, be sure to discuss precautions and proper footwear with your doctor before beginning.

Racewalking burns about as many calories per mile as plain fast walking and doesn't require any special equipment other than a good pair of shoes and clothing that suits the weather. However, you may need a qualified instructor or experienced racewalker to teach you the proper technique. The athletic department of your local high school or college may be able to help. Or, to find a racewalking clinic in your area, write to the New York Walker's Club, Box M, Livingston Manor, NY 12758. (914) 439-5155. (Include a self-addressed, stamped envelope.)

10 □ FIBER: WHAT'S IN IT FOR YOU?

Fiber, the undigestible part of plants, comes in several forms. Some fibers, such as cellulose, make up cell walls and help the plant to hold a firm shape. These are "water-insoluble," or "unfermentable," fibers. That is, bacteria in the digestive tract do not break them down, and they tend to maintain their structure throughout the digestive process. Wheat bran and whole grains, for example, contain such insoluble fibers.

Other forms of fiber repair injuries to the plant. Among these fibers are gums, pectins, and mucilages, which are "water-soluble," or "fermentable." That is, they do not retain their structure but become gummy or gel-like in the digestive tract. These fibers are found in fruits and legumes (dried* beans and peas). The differences are worth noting because some evidence suggests that soluble and insoluble fibers have different effects in the body and may well prove to differ in their impact on blood-glucose and blood-lipid (fat) levels. For instance, it seems that soluble fibers (such as dried beans) may be better for keeping blood glucose down right after a meal.

In reading food charts, you have probably seen fiber referred to as *crude*, *dietary*, or *total*. These terms all refer to laboratory measurement techniques rather than to the chemical makeup of the fiber. *Crude* fiber is measured in an old-fashioned way and tends to underestimate the fiber content. If you see the

---

*Dried beans and peas are ones you soak before cooking. Canned versions may be acceptable but choose carefully; they may be prepared with salt, sugar, and oil.

other terms, you can usually assume that the fiber has been measured by a newer technique that gives higher values, ones more representative of the amount of matter that goes undigested in the human body. However, no measurement approach used today is considered to be the definitive one.

HOW DOES FIBER AFFECT BLOOD GLUCOSE?

As physicians in India suggested 2,000 years ago, high-fiber diets seem capable of improving blood-glucose control, although how fiber does that is still not completely clear. Researchers have several theories, however. One way for overweight people to improve blood-glucose control is to lose weight, and substituting high-fiber carbohydrates for high-fat foods seems to help in this effort. For instance, a plate of high-fiber foods (such as fresh vegetables) is quite filling yet relatively low in calories, assuming you steer clear of sauces, cheese toppings, and the like. Many high-fiber foods (think brown rice or broccoli) are low calorie because, in addition to having a lot of indigestible matter (which provides no calories), they are high in carbohydrate and water and low in fat. (Water, as you know, is calorie-free. Carbohydrate has four calories per gram, in contrast to fat, which has nine.)

In addition to helping control blood glucose by helping you to lose weight, fiber seems to improve control by slowing the rate at which glucose is absorbed into the blood from the intestines. As a result, the blood-glucose rise after eating is less rapid and less high than it might have been. In several studies, when fiber was eaten along with sugar, the sugar was absorbed more slowly than usual, and the blood-glucose rise was not as high.

Researchers do not know exactly how fiber slows absorption. But one mechanism seems to be that it somehow slows the emptying of the stomach and the movement of food through the upper digestive tract, the place where nutrients pass into the blood.

Note: In some people who switch to a high-fiber diet, the

change may cause the need for an adjustment in insulin dosage or oral agents. Never change your diet radically without consulting your doctor and diet counselor.

WHAT OTHER BENEFITS DOES FIBER HAVE?

Fiber can be helpful in the following additional ways:

IT RELIEVES CONSTIPATION. Fiber absorbs water like a sponge, and water makes stools soft and easier to pass. The best sources of natural laxatives are whole-grain (bran-containing) breads and breakfast cereals. Fruits and vegetables are also good.

IT EASES OR PREVENTS HEMORRHOIDS AND DIVERTICULITIS. Hemorrhoids are swollen blood vessels at or near the anus, and diverticula are small bulges in the large intestines that can become infected. (Infected diverticula are referred to as diverticulitis.) By softening stools, fiber allows them to pass more easily through the intestine and out of the body. As a result, less strain is put on the bowel walls and blood vessels. Once again, bran and bran-containing foods are good choices.

IT MAY LOWER CHOLESTEROL AND FAT LEVELS IN THE BLOOD. When eaten as part of a diet high in complex carbohydrate, pectins (found in most fruits), guar gum (found in beans), rolled oats, oat bran, and chick peas have been found to lower cholesterol and fat levels, at least in some studies of animals and people. Wheat bran has not been effective. More study is needed, however, before anything definitive can be said about fiber's impact on blood fats.

WHAT ARE THE DRAWBACKS?

Fiber can cause gas if you eat too much too suddenly. It can also make you feel bloated or nauseous. Furthermore, people who rely too heavily on fiber-rich foods, particularly if they do not vary their choices, may exclude other important nutrients from their diets. In addition, fiber might bind with certain minerals (such as iron and zinc) and so prevent them from being absorbed into the blood, although this has not been conclusively proven. Eating a well-balanced diet, however, should prevent any vitamin and nutrient deficiencies, and increasing fiber *gradually* should prevent discomfort.

DOES THE FORM OF THE FOOD AFFECT FIBER'S IMPACT?

Increasing evidence shows that the way food is prepared can affect fiber's impact on blood sugar. Early reports indicate that raw, whole, and solid foods cause less of a blood-glucose rise than do forms that are cooked, ground, or liquid. For instance, raw potatoes seem to be absorbed into the blood much more slowly than well-cooked mashed potatoes. Beans that are slightly cooked are absorbed more slowly than well-cooked ones. Whole apples cause less of a blood-glucose rise than pureed ones. Oranges cause a lower rise than orange juice. Or so it seems. More study of individual foods and their action is needed.

ANY OVERALL ADVICE?

High-fiber foods seem to be helpful, although researchers still need more information on how fiber does its work, which fibers are best, and how much fiber is optimal for blood-glucose control and other benefits. For the moment, however, it seems prudent to gradually increase the amount of fiber you eat. The best way to do this is to consult a dietitian and doctor to be sure that your diet includes plenty of nutrients, vitamins, and minerals.

GUIDELINES FOR ADDING FIBER TO YOUR MEAL PLAN

"Everything in moderation." Your grandmother probably had this advice in her repertoire. And wise advice it is. The best way to add fiber to your diet is to continue with your balanced meal plan. Don't rely on any one food. Don't bother with fiber supplements or start compulsively to count grams. Just learn to identify high-fiber foods (complex carbohydrates such as whole-grain cereals, beans, vegetables, and fruits are often excellent sources) and substitute a *variety* of them for low-fiber items. Variety is important because nutrients vary from food to food and a mixture will help ensure that you are getting all you need.

OTHER GUIDELINES:
DISCUSS FIBER WITH YOUR DOCTOR AND DIETITIAN BEFORE CHANGING YOUR EATING HABITS. They will tell you if you need to take special precautions. For instance, high-fiber diets sometimes reduce people's insulin needs, so if you take insulin or oral agents, you have to be on the lookout for unusual blood-glucose changes. Your dietitian can help you find high-fiber foods you'll enjoy eating, and the doctor can help you make any needed reductions in medication.

GO FOR CARBOHYDRATES PACKAGED IN THEIR NATURAL FIBROUS COATINGS. Good choices are beans, peas, fruits, and vegetables. Other examples are brown rice instead of white and whole-grain flour instead of white. Increase your intake of whole grain, whole-wheat, or rye breads, crackers, and cereals.

SUBSTITUTE HIGH-FIBER FOODS FOR LOW-FIBER ONES GRADUALLY. A common recommendation—though not gospel—is to *slowly* work up to about 30 to 40 grams of fiber a day. This equals about 20 to 25 grams for every 1,000 calories you eat. The "gradual" part is important because it will cause the fewest side effects. Remember, this is only a guideline.

DRINK MORE FLUIDS WHEN YOU EAT MORE FIBER; otherwise, fiber can be constipating.

WATCH THOSE CALORIES! Keep in mind that fiber is not a medicine. If you eat extra calories by *adding* high-fiber foods to your daily diet instead of *substituting* them for some food choices, you will probably gain weight and cause a blood-glucose rise. To save calories, trim your intake of high-fat, high-caloric foods such as cream, gravies, sauces, and salad dressings. Eat bread and vegetables without margarine or butter; use noncaloric products for "greasing" pans, or use nonstick pans.

TIPS FOR USING LEGUMES, WHOLE GRAINS, AND RICE

You may be under the impression that starches and beans are fattening, but that simply isn't true. It's the gobs of margarine or butter on rice or bread that heap on the calories! Grain products in the raw, brown rice, whole-wheat breads, and legumes (dried beans and peas) give you a lot of value for the calories—they're excellent sources of protein, B vitamins, and iron. (An average slice of bread or ½ cup of rice contains about 80 calories.) Try experimenting with the various foods in these categories, such as barley, brown rice, buckwheat groats (kasha), bulgur (cracked wheat), cornmeal or polenta, and whole-grain flours (whole wheat, rye, or buckwheat).

LEGUMES. Beans, peas, and lentils are among the best sources of fiber and are full of protein. However, when eaten by themselves, they are "incomplete proteins." That is, they lack, or are low in, certain amino acids needed by the body. There are eight to ten amino acids that cannot be made by the body and must come from food. Most beans (except soybeans) are deficient in two of these amino acids, but whole wheat, whole grains, nuts, seeds, and dairy products are rich in them. Therefore, these foods should be combined with legumes in order to provide complete protein to your diet if you substitute legumes for meat. (See chart in Chapter 14 pages 398–399.)

Because legumes may be hard to digest and can cause intestinal gas, especially if you aren't used to eating them, it is best to start with the most easily digested legumes, such as lentils, split peas, and lima beans.

Before cooking beans, make sure you rinse and sort them

thoroughly, since they come directly from the fields. To cut cooking time, soak all beans overnight. (Soybeans should be refrigerated during soaking to prevent fermentation.) Another method
is to put beans and water in a pot, bring the water to a boil,
simmer for two minutes, then remove from heat and allow to
stand covered for one hour. Salt should not be added until the
beans are tender, otherwise they will not cook properly and might
get tough. Also, don't mix different kinds of beans when cooking
unless you are using a slow-cooking pot. (See Bean Cookery Conversion Chart.) Keep beans covered with liquid during cooking.
If you're cooking beans for a salad or any dish where they should
be firm, cook just until tender. For soups, beans may be cooked
much longer.

The following procedures can be used to reduce the amount
of gas (called "flatulence" in medical jargon) that results from
eating beans:

- □ Soak the dried beans for 4 to 5 hours; discard the water.
- □ Add fresh water, cook beans for a half hour, and again
  discard the water.
- □ In each step above, for best results, use 9 cups of water
  for each cup of beans.
- □ If the beans still require cooking, add more water and
  discard after cooking unless otherwise directed by the
  recipe.

The disadvantage of this procedure is that approximately 50 percent of the water-soluble vitamins and a small amount of the
protein is lost.

WHOLE GRAINS. Store whole grains in a cool, dry place
to prevent spoilage. Whole-grain flour keeps best in a refrigerator
or freezer. Because whole-wheat flour is bulkier than white flour,
you'll need to make adjustments when baking with it. For each
cup of white flour in a recipe, you can substitute:

BEAN COOKERY CONVERSION CHART

Bean	Regular Cooking Time	Pressure Cooker Cooking Time	Minimum Cooking Water	Dry Beans	◆	Cooked Beans
Black beans	1½ hrs.	20–25 min.	4 cups	1 cup		2 cups
Black-eyed peas	1 hr.	20–25 min.	3 cups	1 cup		2 cups
Pinto beans	2½ hrs.	20–25 min.	3 cups	1 cup		2 cups
Kidney beans	1½ hrs.	20–25 min.	3 cups	1 cup		2 cups
Soybeans	3 hrs. or more	20–25 min.	3 cups	1 cup		2 cups
Garbanzo beans	3 hrs.	40–45 min.	4 cups	1 cup		4 cups
Lentils and split peas	1 hr.	10–15 min.	3 cups	1 cup		2 ¼ cups
Great Northern beans	2 hrs.	20–25 min.	3½ cups	1 cup		2 cups
Navy beans	1½ hrs.	20–25 min.	3 cups	1 cup		2 cups
Lima beans	1½ hrs.	20–25 min.	2 cups	1 cup		1¼ cups

Source: *Nutrition Action*, Jan/Feb 1983. (Pressure cooking times come from *Recipes for a Small Planet*, by E. Ewald, New York: Ballantine, 1973, p. 310. The rest of the data are from *Laurel's Kitchen*, by L. Robertson, et al. New York: Bantam, 1976, p. 288.)

- [ ] One cup whole-wheat flour minus 2 Tbsp. (Decrease the amount of oil, and increase the liquid, by 1 or 2 Tbsp.); or
- [ ] Three-quarters cup white flour plus either ¼ cup wheat germ or ¼ cup bran; or
- [ ] Half cup of white flour and ¼ cup whole-wheat flour.

BROWN RICE. Brown rice takes longer to cook than white rice, but is relatively easy to prepare. Follow package instructions but, in general, put rice in boiling water in a 1:2 ratio, return to boil, cover, reduce heat, and cook for 45 minutes until the water steams off. When rice is thoroughly cooked, remove from heat and let stand several minutes to allow it to steam and dry. If you have fully cooked the rice, and it still seems hard or tough, add a little boiling water, cover, and continue cooking. To enhance the nutty flavor of the rice, stir washed, uncooked rice in a dry sauce pan over medium heat until the grain is dry and lightly toasted. When cooking, don't add salt until after the rice is cooked. (Salt tends to harden the kernels.) Also don't stir rice or grain while cooking; stirring makes rice pasty and grains gummy.

Now you know the basics of high-fiber eating, but how do you plan your meals? The "Fiber Exchange" with this chapter gives you the approximate fiber content of many foods. Based on that listing, you can easily construct high-fiber menus like this one:

SAMPLE MENU—1500 Calories, High Carbohydrate, High Fiber

Meal Plan	Sample Menu	Fiber
Breakfast:		
½ Skimmed milk	½ cup skim milk	0 gms.
1 Fruit	1 small orange	2 gms.
2 Starch/Bread	1 cup All-Bran	18 gms.
1 Starch/Bread	1 slice whole-wheat toast	2 gms.
1 Fat	1 tsp. margarine	0 gms.

SAMPLE MENU—1500 Calories, High Carbohydrate, High Fiber

Meal Plan	Sample Menu	Fiber
Snack:		
1 Fruit	1 small apple	2 gms.
Lunch:		
1 Skimmed milk	1 cup skim milk	0 gms.
1 Vegetable	2 cups lettuce w/diet dressing	2 gms.
1 Vegetable	1 medium tomato	2 gms.
1 Fruit	15 grapes	2 gms.
	Sandwich	
2 Starch	2 slices whole-wheat bread	4 gms.
2 Meat	2 oz. sliced turkey	0 gms.
1 Fat	1 tsp. margarine	0 gms.
Snack:		
1 Starch	4 squares Ry Krisp	3 gms.
Dinner:		
2 Vegetable	1 cup broccoli	4 gms.
1 Vegetable	2 cups lettuce w/diet dressing	2 gms.
1 Fruit	⅓ cup pineapple chunks	2 gms.
1 Starch	⅓ cup brown rice	3 gms.
3 Meat	3 oz. broiled fish	0 gms.
1 Fat	1 tsp. margarine	0 gms.
Evening Snack:		
1 Starch	3 cups popcorn, no butter	2 gms.
½ Skim milk	½ cup skim milk	0 gms.
Total:		
1,500 calories	210 gms. carbohydrate (57%)	49 gms.
	90 gms. protein (23%)	Fiber
	35 gms. fat (20%)	

Fiber seems to have many benefits and may have special benefits for people with diabetes, so trying to substitute some high-fiber foods for some high-fat items is probably worth the effort. And don't despair if you're one of those people who insist they'd rather starve than eat broccoli. Lots of foods have fiber, so chances are good that you can find a selection you like.

THE FIBER EXCHANGE*

The following is an adaptation of the American Diabetes Association/The American Dietetic Association's *Exchange Lists for Meal Planning.* To the six basic food groups listed there (See Appendix I) have been added the approximate fiber content of foods and guidelines for choosing high-fiber foods. Keep in mind, however, that the nutrient and fiber measures are *averages.* The nutrient and fiber contents of one food on any given list may differ from those of another food on the list and may affect your blood glucose differently. In addition, portion size and the form of food (cooked or raw, for example) can also affect a food's impact on your body. The letters CHO stand for "carbohydrate."

LIST 1: STARCH/BREAD

(This category is subdivided because of wide variations in fiber content and nutrients. The nutrients listed may vary from the ones in the *Exchange Lists* because the lists give an average for *all* of the foods in the category.)

> LEGUMES (BEANS AND PEAS)
> *Nutrients:* 15 gm. CHO; 6 gm. pro.; 1 gm. fat; 90 calories.
> *Serving size:* Beans, peas, lentils (cooked)—⅓ cup; canned
> baked beans (no pork)—¼ cup.
> *Fiber:* 8 gm.

*All servings here represent one "exchange," or portion as listed in the *Exchange Lists for Meal Planning.* The fiber values are from *HCF: A User's Guide to High-Carbohydrate, High-Fiber Diets,* by James W. Anderson *et al.* University of Kentucky Diabetes Fund, Lexington, 1979.

GUIDELINES FOR HIGH-FIBER CHOICES: Fiber is found in cooked or canned dried beans (lima, kidney, navy, pinto, etc.), in dried peas, and in lentils.

> STARCHY VEGETABLES
> *Nutrients:* 15 gm. CHO; 3 gm. pro.; 1 gm. fat; 80 calories.
> *Serving size* (cooked): winter squash and parsnips—¾ cup; corn, barley, peas—½ cup; sweet potatoes or wheat bulgar (cracked wheat)—⅓ cup; baked potato (w/skin)—1 small.
> *Fiber:* 3 gm.

GUIDELINES FOR HIGH-FIBER CHOICES: All above are good.

> CEREALS (BRAN AND WHOLE GRAIN TYPES)
> *Nutrients:* 15 gm. CHO; 3 gm. pro.; 0 fat; 80 calories.
> *Serving size:* Varies
> *Fiber:* 3 gm.

GUIDELINES FOR HIGH-FIBER CHOICES: Cereals can be excellent sources of fiber and make good choices for breakfast. Read labels, though—many bran-type cereals contain a moderate amount of sugar. Some of those can be eaten but should be alternated with ones that contain little or no sugar. (See "Cereals" chart below for the best choices and portion sizes.)

CEREALS: Does high in fiber mean low in sugar?

Although many cereals with "healthy" sounding names are indeed high in fiber and low in sugar, others—especially bran cereals and granolas—can have a lot of sugar. The cereals here are listed in order of how much sugar they contain. Those marked with an asterisk are good choices—low in sugar and high in fiber. Cereals that contain more than 10% sugar should not be eaten every day, and ones higher than 30% sugar should be left on supermarket shelves.

Cereal	Serving size	Sugar (gms)[1]	Fiber (gms)[2]
Cereals containing approximately 10% sugar or less			
Oatmeal, Oats*	½ cup, cooked	—	2.9
Puffed Wheat*	¾ cup	—	3.4
Shredded Wheat*	1 biscuit	—	2.8
Ralston*	½ cup, cooked	1	2.1
Cheerios*	1 cup	1	2.5
Chex, Corn*	⅔ cup	1	2.6
Chex, Wheat*	½ cup	1	2
Corn Flakes*	⅔ cup	1	2.6
Grape Nuts*	3 Tbsp.	1	2.7
Nutri-Grains*	½ cup	1	2
Corn Bran*	½ cup	2	4.4
Grape Nut Flakes*	⅔ cup	2	2.5
Oat Bran*	¼ cup	2	5.3
Total*	¾ cup	2	2.5
Wheaties*	¾ cup	2	2.6
Cereals containing approximately 10 to 30% sugar			
40% Bran Flakes*	⅔ cup	4	3
Bran Chex*	½ cup	4	4.1
Most*	⅓ cup	4	3
All-Bran*	⅓ cup	5	9
Honey Bran	⅔ cup	5	2.4
Frosted Mini-Wheats	2½ biscuits	5	1.3
Cracklin' Bran	⅓ cup	5	3
Raisin Bran	¾ cup	8	3.4
Cereals containing approximately 30 to 40% sugar			
Wheat and Raisin Chex	½ cup	6	2
Bran Buds	⅓ cup	8	8

[1]Source: USDA Nutrient Composition Laboratory of the Nutrition Institute, Human Nutrition Center, Beltsville, MD. *Journal of Food Science* 45 (1): 138–141, 1980.
[2]Sources: Anderson, J. W., *et al.*, *Plant Fiber in Foods*, HCF Diabetes Research Foundation, Inc., Lexington, KY; Kellogg's; Ralston Purina.

BREADS AND GRAINS
Nutrients: 15 gm. CHO; 3 gm. pro.; 0 fat; 80 calories.
Serving size: Breads—1 slice; graham crackers—3 squares;
popcorn—3 cups.
Fiber: 2 gm.

GUIDELINES FOR HIGH-FIBER CHOICES: Choose items made from grains that retain their natural fibrous coatings. (Beware: "wheat flour" on an ingredients list is usually white flour.) Good choices are whole-grain breads or crackers, such as cracked wheat, whole meal (stone ground), whole wheat, or rye bread; rye crackers; and bran muffins.

LIST 2: (MEDIUM-FAT MEAT)

FROM ANIMAL SOURCES (LEAN MEATS)
Nutrients: 0 CHO; 7 gm. pro.; 5 gm. fat; 75 calories.
Serving size: Mostly 1 oz. (cooked).
Fiber: 0 gm.

LIST 3: VEGETABLE

Nutrients: 5 gm. CHO; 2 gm. pro.; 0 fat; 25 calories.
Serving size: ½ cup cooked, or 1 cup raw.
Fiber: 2–3 gm.

GUIDELINES FOR HIGH-FIBER CHOICES: Pick foods with edible skins and seeds. May be fresh, frozen, or canned but should not have added fat, sauces, glazes, cheese, etc. (*Note:* Cooking reduces volume and destroys some nutrients but does not alter fiber content.)

LIST 4: FRUIT

Nutrients: 15 gm. CHO; 0 pro.; 0 fat; 60 calories.
Serving size: Varies (see *Exchange Lists*).
Fiber: 2 gm.

GUIDELINES FOR HIGH-FIBER CHOICES: Fruits should be raw, canned in their own juice, unsweetened, or artificially sweetened with a sugar substitute. Select fruits with edible skins and seeds. Eat more whole fruits instead of fruit juice.

LIST 5: MILK

Nutrients: 12 gm. CHO; 8 gm. pro.; trace fat; 90 calories.
Serving size: 1 cup (skim-milk products).
Fiber: 0 gm.

LIST 6: FAT

Nutrients: 0 CHO, 0 pro.; 5 gm. fat; 45 calories.
Serving size: Varies (see *Exchange Lists*).
Fiber: 0 gm.

NOTE: All varieties of nuts contain fiber, as do pumpkin seeds, sesame seeds, and sunflower seeds. Fiber is usually 3 grams per 1-ounce serving.

11 □ RECIPES

Recipes in this book were selected to complement the collection in the first *Family Cookbook*. They emphasize dishes that combine foods from different groups and include several ethnic and regional dishes.

Prior to recipe development and testing, a list of characteristics that each final recipe should have were established—characteristics based on the nutritional guidelines for diabetes as well as the guidelines for all health-conscious people. As a result, the final recipes are generally:

□ Reduced in total fat and saturated fat;
□ Limited to ½ egg per serving when the recipe includes eggs;
□ Limited in salt and sodium-rich ingredients;
□ Limited to about ½ teaspoon of sugar, honey, or molasses when a recipe includes these ingredients.

Note, too, that the preponderance of recipes use low-fat meats, vegetables, dried beans and peas, pasta, and whole grains, rather than fatty meats or processed foods.

RECIPE DEVELOPMENT AND TESTING

Recipes were analyzed, adjusted, and tested in a test kitchen by a registered dietitian experienced in recipe development. The final products were served to customers in a restaurant and only recipes that met with their approval were accepted.

Most recipes are for six, and sometimes two, servings, except soups and items that require long preparation and cooking times. These usually yield eight or more servings. Extra servings may be packaged and frozen, and reheated for later meals. This type of preparation is particularly useful for those who have microwave ovens.

Portion sizes for items that are part of a typical meal pattern are the traditional ⅓ to ½ cup. Portion sizes for combination-type dishes are generally 1 to 1½ cups, as they are intended to be the major item in the meal.

INGREDIENTS

Information about basic ingredients found in the first *Family Cookbook* (Volume I) applies to this book as well. Recipe calculations are based on skim milk, fat-free broth,* large eggs, unsifted all-purpose flour, and unsalted water for cooking rice, pasta, vegetables, and the like, unless otherwise specified. For shortening, vegetable oils and margarines were generally used. In your own cooking, choose among those made from corn, cottonseed, safflower, soybean, and/or sunflower oils.

Sugar, when used in recipes, has been calculated in the recipes' total carbohydrate content, as before. Additionally, in this volume, each recipe with added sugar (exceptions: recipes with trace amounts of sugar per serving) has a note describing the amount of refined sugar, honey, or molasses, and the calories from these sources. Discuss the use of the recipes with your dietitian before trying them. Sugar substitutes have been used in some recipes. (See Chapter 14, "The New Sweetener: Aspartame," about uses and limitations of this new sugar substitute.)

In general, granular sugar substitutes are packaged to provide the sweetness of two teaspoons of sugar. Most products also contain about one gram of carbohydrate. But check each product's label before using.

Specialty canned items, such as water chestnuts, ripe olives, mushrooms, green chilies, and pimientos are used in some recipes. Often a whole can is not required; therefore, freeze the remainder of the can for future use or refrigerate and use within a day or two. These can be nice additions to omelets or other recipes.

*Use of homemade broth will reduce sodium content for those who must limit sodium in the diet.

Items such as miller's bran, tofu, wheat germ, pearl barley, and sprouts are usually available in large supermarkets. Growing your own sprouts, however, can be fun. (See the directions on page 277.)

In some areas of the country where miller's bran is not available, you can use all-bran and sugar-free bran breakfast cereal.

Chicken is used extensively in these recipes. If a whole chicken is not required, you can buy breasts, thighs, or quarters of chickens. If buying a whole chicken, keep in mind that a three-pound chicken with bones will yield about 2 to 2½ cups (about 1½ pounds) of diced cooked chicken. To cook chicken, follow the recipe for cold chicken or use the traditional method of simmering until the meat falls from the bones. Chicken parts bought individually will be larger than those from a 2¾- to 3-pound chicken.

SEASONINGS

Most of the seasonings used here are available in large supermarkets. Find fresh ginger root and fresh basil in the fresh vegetable section. Picante sauce and green chili salsa with no added sugar are available in the Mexican food section. (See recipe section for homemade picante sauce, page 321.) They are excellent for seasoning foods in place of catsup. Garlic powder, fresh garlic, and black pepper are very good flavor enhancers and may be increased in recipes to reduce salt content.

"EXCHANGES" AND "ESTIMATED NUTRIENTS" PER SERVING

As in the first *Family Cookbook*, the exchanges and selected estimated nutrients are given for one serving of each recipe. However, in this volume, grams of dietary fiber are listed in addition to the estimated calories, grams of carbohydrate, protein, and fat, and milligrams of sodium, potassium, and cholesterol. The nutrients per serving are expressed in abbreviations and symbols as follows:

Calories (CAL)   Sodium (Na)
Carbohydrates (CHO)   Potassium (K)
Protein (PRO)   Fiber (Fiber)
Fat (FAT)   Cholesterol (Chol)

Optional ingredients and dashes of ingredients were not included in the nutrient analysis. If a choice of ingredients was offered, the first listed was included in the nutrient analysis.

If a given serving size is too large for your meal plan, you can divide the serving size and the listed calculations in half. Similarly, you can double serving sizes if necessary and multiply all calculations by two to find the exchange and nutrient value of the enlarged serving.

The exchanges and nutrients per serving were derived by computer.

RECIPE ANALYSIS*

The data base for the recipe analysis program contains more than seven hundred foods, including all of the ingredients in this cookbook. For each food, the data base includes twenty-eight different nutrients. Of those, the amount per serving of protein, fat, carbohydrate, sodium, potassium, cholesterol, and total dietary fiber appears for each recipe. Nutrient analysis information for calories and the first six nutrients is from the United States Department of Agriculture, Handbook 8 and Handbooks 8-1 through 8-14. Nutrient information for foods not available in these sources was obtained from provisional information or from the producers of the products. Total dietary fiber analysis is from a published source.

The recipe analysis program, developed by Lawrence A. Wheeler, M.D., Ph.D., was written in Pascal and runs on IBM type

---

*The recipe analysis was performed by Madelyn L. Wheeler, M.S., R.D., C.D.E.

computers. The program not only analyzes recipes for individual nutrients per serving (as described above) but also:

1. Provides "exchanges" for an individual serving based on the 1986 edition of *Exchange Lists for Meal Planning*, so that the exchange value of the serving is close to the actual nutrient content.

2. "Flags" key nutrients. A "key nutrient" is defined as a nutrient in a single serving that will provide more than 75 percent of the Recommended Daily Allowance (USRDA).

For some recipes, there were several possible combinations of exchanges that yielded good nutritional approximations. Combinations that might have been "best" in terms of reflecting the actual nutrient content of the recipe, but which seemed inappropriate (for example, a milk exchange in a recipe that did not contain a milk product) were eliminated.

REFERENCES

1. American Diabetes Association. 1987. Nutritional Recommendations and Principles for Individuals with Diabetes Mellitus: 1986, *Diabetes Care* 10: 126–32

2. Anderson, J. W.: 1986. *Plant Fiber in Foods*. Lexington, KY: HCF Diabetes Research Foundation, Inc.

3. United States Department of Agriculture and Health and Human Services. 1985. *Dietary Guidelines for Americans*. Washington, DC: HHS.

4. United States Department of Agriculture Handbook. 1976–86. *8-1: Dairy and Egg Products; 8-2: Spices & Herbs; 8-4: Fats & Oils; 8-5: Poultry Products; 8-6: Soups, Sauces & Gravies; 8-7: Sausages & Luncheon Meats; 8-8: Breakfast Cereals; 8-9: Fruits and Fruit Juices; 8-10: Pork Products; 8-11: Vegetables and Vegetable Products; 8-12: Nut and Seed Products; 8-13: Beef Products; 8-14: Beverages.* Washington, DC: HHS.

5. Watt, B. K., and A. C. P. Merrill. 1984. *Composition of Foods: Raw, Processed, Prepared. USDA Agriculture Handbook No. 8.* Washington, DC: Government Printing Office.
6. Wheeler, L. A., M. L. Wheeler, and P. Ours. 1985. Computer Selected Exchange Lists Approximations for Recipes. *J. Am. Diet. Assoc.* 85:700–703.

Best-Bet Breakfasts

Orange Juice Milk Drink

Yield: 4 servings
Serving Size: 1 cup
Exchange List Approximation:
    Fruit 1
    Milk, low-fat ½

Nutrient Content Per Serving:
CAL: 135   PRO: 4.8 (gm)
FAT: 2.7 (gm)   CHO: 23.4 (gm)
Na: 49.5 (mg)   K: 469.2 (mg)
Fiber: 0   Chol: 73 (mg)

Ingredients

1   6-OUNCE CAN FROZEN CONCENTRATED ORANGE
     JUICE
1   CUP WATER
1   CUP 2% MILK
1   EGG
6   PACKETS SUGAR SUBSTITUTE
8   ICE CUBES

Method

1. Place all ingredients in blender or food processor.
2. Blend until smooth.
Note: You can cut this recipe in half, but continue to use a
    whole egg. The change in nutrients per serving is
    negligible.

Stick-to-the-Ribs Oatmeal

Yield: 1 serving
Serving Size: 1 recipe
Exchange List Approximation:
    Starch/Bread 2
    Meat, lean 1
    Fruit $\frac{1}{2}$

Nutrient Content Per Serving:
CAL: 255   PRO: 14.5 (gm)
FAT: 3.7 (gm)   CHO: 42.2 (gm)
Na: 360.4 (mg)   K: 279 (mg)
Fiber: 4.7 (gm)   Chol: 5 (mg)

Ingredients

⅔ CUP WATER
½ CUP OATMEAL
1/16 TEASPOON SALT
⅓ CUP UNSWEETENED CRUSHED PINEAPPLE
¼ CUP LOW-FAT COTTAGE CHEESE
¼ TEASPOON COCONUT EXTRACT

Method

1. Bring water to a boil, add oatmeal and salt. Stir and cook 1 minute.
2. Stir in pineapple, cottage cheese, and flavoring. Bring to a boil.
3. Serve with sweetener and milk as meal plan permits.

Everyday Oatmeal-Plus

Yield: 1 serving
Serving Size: 1 cup
Exchange List Approximation:
   Starch/Bread 2
   Meat, lean 1

Nutrient Content Per Serving:
CAL: 205   PRO: 14.2 (gm)
FAT: 3.6 (gm)   CHO: 29.1 (gm)
Na: 359.4 (mg)   K: 196 (mg)
Fiber: 4 (gm)   Chol: 5 (mg)

Ingredients

1 CUP WATER
½ CUP OATMEAL (QUICK)
1/16 TEASPOON SALT
¼ CUP LOW-FAT COTTAGE CHEESE
¼ TEASPOON COCONUT EXTRACT OR 2 TEASPOONS SHERRY

Method

1. Bring water to boil. Add oatmeal and salt. Stir. Bring to a boil. Reduce heat, cover, and cook about 3 minutes.
2. Stir in cottage cheese and bring to a boil.
3. Add flavoring and serve with sweetener and milk, if meal plan permits.

Raisin-Apple Oatmeal-Plus-Egg

Yield: 1 serving
Serving Size: 1 recipe
Exchange List Approximation:
    Starch/Bread 1
    Meat, medium-fat 1
    Fruit 2

Nutrient Content Per Serving:
CAL: 271   PRO: 10.9 (gm)
FAT: 7.7 (gm)   CHO: 41.8 (gm)
Na: 72 (mg)   K: 348.2 (mg)
Fiber: 5.3 (gm)   Chol: 274 (mg)

Ingredients

½ SMALL APPLE DICED OR ¼ CUP UNSWEETENED
   APPLESAUCE
1 TABLESPOON RAISINS
1 CUP WATER
⅓ CUP OATMEAL (QUICK)
1 EGG, BEATEN
⅛ TEASPOON CINNAMON
   DASH NUTMEG

Method

1. Combine diced apple or applesauce, raisins, and water in small saucepan. Bring to boil, cover, and simmer until apple is tender.
2. Stir in oatmeal, bring to a boil, and cook 1 minute.
3. Gradually add half of oatmeal to beaten egg. Add mixture back to oatmeal and cook about 10 seconds. Egg may be added directly to oatmeal if desired.
4. Stir in cinnamon and nutmeg.
5. Serve with milk and sweetener, as meal plan permits.

Fluffy High-Fiber, Low-Fat Pancakes

Yield: 8 4-inch pancakes
Serving Size: 1 pancake
Exchange List Approximation:
 Starch/Bread 1

Nutrient Content Per Serving:
CAL: 68   PRO: 3.7 (gm)
FAT: 1.6 (gm)   CHO: 11.3 (gm)
Na: 217.5 (mg) K: 145.4 (mg)
Fiber: 2.3 (gm) Chol: 35 (mg)

Ingredients

1   CUP BUTTERMILK OR SOUR MILK (ADD 1 TBSP.
    LEMON JUICE PER 1 CUP MILK)
½   CUP ROLLED OATS (QUICK)
⅔   CUP MILLER'S BRAN (UNPROCESSED, UNCOOKED
    WHEAT BRAN)
1   EGG
¼   CUP WHOLE-WHEAT FLOUR
½   TEASPOON SUGAR
¼   TEASPOON SALT
¾   TEASPOON SODA

Method

1. Combine buttermilk, oats, and bran in large mixing bowl.
    Let stand 5 minutes. Add egg and beat until blended.
2. Mix whole-wheat flour, sugar, salt, and baking soda until
    blended.
3. Add to bran mixture and blend until all flour is moistened.
4. Pour about ¼-cup batter on lightly greased, preheated 375°
    F griddle or frying pan. Cook about 3 minutes or until
    bubbles form and the edge of pancake is dry. Turn and
    cook 2 minutes longer. This is a "fat" pancake.
5. Serve with sugar-free jam or jelly.

Spicy Whole-Wheat Pancakes

Yield: 6 servings
Serving Size: 3 small or 2 large
Exchange List Approximation:
    Starch/Bread 1
    Fat 1

Nutrient Content Per Serving:
CAL: 124   PRO: 5 (gm)
FAT: 4.6 (gm)   CHO: 16.6 (gm)
Na: 225.3 (mg)   K: 149.7 (mg)
Fiber: 1.9 (gm)   Chol: 49 (mg)

Ingredients

1 CUP WHOLE-WHEAT FLOUR
2 TEASPOONS BAKING POWDER
½ TEASPOON CINNAMON
¼ TEASPOON SALT
1 CUP LOW-FAT MILK
1 EGG
1 TABLESPOON VEGETABLE OIL

Method

1. Mix dry ingredients. Add remaining ingredients. Mix until blended.
2. Drop by 1½ tablespoons for small pancakes and 2 tablespoons for large pancakes on hot, lightly greased griddle or frying pan (375° F). Cook until bubbles form on top and the edge appears dry. Turn and cook until lightly browned.
3. Serve with warm applesauce (recipe in Volume I).

Scrambled Tofu

Yield: 6 or 2 servings
Serving Size: ½ cup
Exchange List Approximation:
    Meat, medium-fat 1

Nutrient Content Per Serving:
CAL: 76   PRO: 8.1 (gm)
FAT: 4.3 (gm)   CHO: 2.9 (gm)
Na: 529.3 (mg)   K: 49.7 (mg)
Fiber: 0   Chol: 0

Ingredients

Six servings

1-POUND 4-OUNCE PACKAGE TOFU
½ TEASPOON ONION POWDER
2 CUBES CHICKEN BOUILLON (OR 2 TEASPOONS INSTANT BOUILLON)
¼ TEASPOON SEASONED SALT
VEGETABLE COOKING SPRAY

Two servings

6⅔ OUNCES
⅛ TEASPOON
1 CUBE
1/16 TEASPOON

Method

1. Spray skillet with vegetable cooking spray.
2. Dice tofu and place in skillet. Add remaining ingredients to tofu and brown lightly. Turn occasionally while cooking.
3. Serve like scrambled eggs for breakfast.

*To reduce sodium content, substitute herb blend recipe (from Chapter 15) for bouillon and seasoned salt.

Breakfast on the Run

Yield: 2 servings
Serving Size: 1¼ cup
Exchange List Approximation:
    Starch/Bread 1
    Fruit 1
    Milk, skim 1

Nutrient Content Per Serving:
CAL: 239   PRO: 12.7 (gm)
FAT: 3.2 (gm)   CHO: 44 (gm)
Na: 108.6 (mg)   K: 931 (mg)
Fiber: 4.9 (gm)   Chol: 6 (mg)

Ingredients

1⅓ CUPS SLICED RIPE BANANAS, FROZEN (ABOUT 2
     WHOLE)
  1 CUP SKIM MILK
  ½ CUP PLAIN LOW-FAT YOGURT
  ¼ CUP WHEAT GERM
  1 EGG (OPTIONAL)*
  2 TEASPOONS VANILLA
  1 PACKET SUGAR SUBSTITUTE (IF DESIRED)

Method

1. Slice bananas and freeze overnight.
2. Place ingredients in blender and blend until smooth.
3. Garnish with nutmeg.

*If egg is added, count as an extra ½ Meat, medium-fat.

Crunchy Granola

Yield: 16 servings ($5\frac{1}{2}$ cups)
Serving Size: $\frac{1}{3}$ cup
Exchange List Approximation:
    Starch/Bread $1\frac{1}{2}$
    Fat $1\frac{1}{2}$

Nutrient Content Per Serving:
CAL: 188   PRO: 5 (gm)
FAT: 8.9 (gm)   CHO: 24 (gm)
Na: 9.2 (mg)   K: 176.3 (mg)
Fiber: 3.7 (gm)   Chol: 0

Ingredients

$3\frac{1}{2}$ CUPS OLD-FASHIONED OATS
½ CUP WHEAT GERM
½ CUP COCONUT
¼ CUP SESAME SEEDS
¼ CUP ALMONDS
¼ CUP SUNFLOWER SEEDS OR MILLET SEEDS
¼ CUP HONEY
¼ CUP OIL
1 TABLESPOON VANILLA
½ CUP RAISINS, RESERVE

Method

1. Mix all together with electric mixer, spread evenly on 2 baking sheets with edges, and bake in 250° F oven until golden brown (45 to 60 minutes).
2. Turn and stir after 30 minutes.
3. Remove from oven and add raisins. Cool and store in plastic bag. This is very good with milk for breakfast.

Note: Approximately ¾ teaspoon of honey (12 calories) per serving.

Whole-Wheat Granola

Yield: 28 servings
Serving Size: ½ cup
Exchange List Approximation:
  Starch/Bread 1
  Fruit 1
  Fat 2

Nutrient Content Per Serving:
CAL: 227*   PRO: 4.7 (gm)
FAT: 11.9 (gm)* CHO: 27.9 (gm)
Na: 98.4 (mg)   K: 189.1 (mg)
Fiber: 4 (gm)   Chol: 0

Ingredients

4   CUPS REGULAR OATS, UNCOOKED
3   CUPS WHOLE-WHEAT FLOUR
2   CUPS WHEAT GERM
1   TABLESPOON CINNAMON
1   TEASPOON SALT (OPTIONAL)
1   CUP VEGETABLE OIL
1   CUP HONEY OR SUBSTITUTE
½   CUP ORANGE JUICE
1   CUP FLAKED COCONUT
½   CUP SLICED ALMONDS
1   CUP RAISINS

Method

1. Mix first 5 ingredients in electric mixer.
2. Combine oil, honey, and juice and pour over mixture. Mix
    until completely blended.
3. Spread evenly in 4 shallow pans and bake in 250° F oven
    for 45 minutes.
4. Stir in coconut and almonds and bake 30 minutes more.
5. Cool and stir in raisins.

*To cut calories and fat, reduce the coconut and oil by a third.

Yeast Breads, Quick Breads, Muffins

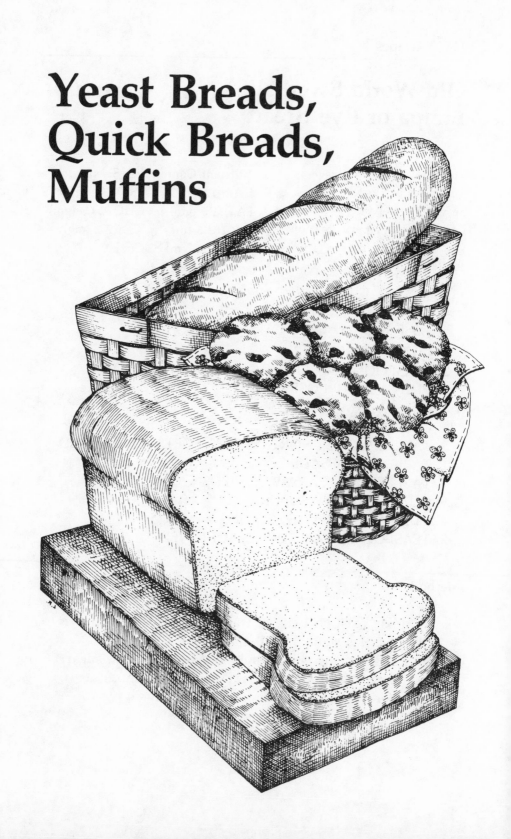

Old World Swedish Limpa or Rye Bread

Yield: 36 servings (2 loaves,
  18 slices per loaf)
Serving Size: 1 slice
Exchange List Approximation:
  Starch/Bread $1\frac{1}{2}$

Nutrient Content Per Serving:
CAL: 125   PRO: 3.4 (gm)
FAT: 1.6 (gm)   CHO: 24.3 (gm)
Na: 181.5 (mg)   K: 117.2 (mg)
Fiber: 1.5 (gm)   Chol: 0

Ingredients

  2 ¼-OUNCE PACKAGES ACTIVE DRY YEAST
  1 CUP WARM WATER
  2 TEASPOONS SUGER
  2 CUPS ALL-PURPOSE FLOUR
1½ CUPS WARM WATER (85° F)
  ½ CUP LIGHT MOLASSES
  3 TABLESPOONS SHORTENING, VEGETABLE, MELTED
  1 TABLESPOON SALT
  1 TABLESPOON CARAWAY SEEDS
1½ CUPS DARK RYE FLOUR
  4 CUPS ALL-PURPOSE FLOUR
  2 TEASPOONS MARGARINE, SOFTENED

Method

  1. Sprinkle yeast on 1-cup of warm water (100–110° F). Stir to
     dissolve. Let stand 5 to 10 minutes.
  2. In a large mixing bowl, combine dissolved yeast, sugar,
     and 2 cups flour. Beat by hand or mix with mixer at
     number 3 speed until smooth and stretchy.

3. Cover with a cloth. Let rise until double in bulk in a warm place (80° F) free from drafts, approximately 20 minutes.

4. In a separate mixing bowl, thoroughly mix water, molasses, shortening, salt, and caraway seeds. Transfer this mixture to the bowl containing the yeast "sponge." Mix together.

5. To this mixture, add rye and all-purpose flours. Beat by hand or mix on number 2 speed on mixer. Dough will be soft, not stiff.

6. Lightly grease top of dough. Cover with cloth. Let rise until double in bulk in a warm place (80° F) free from drafts.

7. Grease heavily 2 loaf pans, 9¼- by 5¼- by 2¾-inches. Punch down dough. Place soft dough on a floured board. Divide in half. Shape into loaves the size of the pans. Place in greased pans and push down all around the sides so no air is trapped.

8. Cover and let rise until double in size.

9. Preheat oven to 375° F.

10. Place loaves in oven on middle shelf. Bake 45 to 50 minutes. If browning too fast, cover with aluminum foil tent. To check for doneness after 45 minutes, tap top of loaf. It will sound hollow if done. The loaf will shrink from the sides of the pans.

11. Remove from oven. Brush tops with melted margarine. Cool briefly. Carefully remove from pans and cool loaves on wire rack.

Note: Each serving has less than ¾-teaspoon sugar (10 to 11 calories).

Whole-Wheat Batter Bread

Yield: 3 loaves (20 slices per loaf) Nutrient Content Per Serving:
Serving Size: 1 slice CAL: 80 PRO: 2.6 (gm)
Exchange List Approximation: FAT: 1.7 (gm) CHO: 13.9 (gm)
    Starch/Bread 1 Na: 129 (mg) K: 74.2 (mg)
      Fiber: 1 (gm) Chol: 9 (mg)

Ingredients

  3 CUPS WHOLE-WHEAT FLOUR
  2 PACKAGES ACTIVE DRY YEAST
2½ CUPS SOUR MILK (2½ CUPS SKIM MILK + 1
    TEASPOON LEMON JUICE OR VINEGAR)
  ¼ CUP MOLASSES
  ¼ CUP HONEY
  1 TABLESPOON SALT
  ⅓ CUP MARGARINE
1½ CUP REGULAR ROLLED OATS
  2 EGGS
3–3½ CUPS UNSIFTED ALL-PURPOSE FLOUR
  1 TABLESPOON MELTED MARGARINE TO BRUSH ON
    DOUGH

Method

1. Combine whole-wheat flour and yeast.
2. Heat margarine, sour milk, molasses, honey, and salt until
    warm. Pour into 3-quart bowl.
3. Add oats, whole-wheat flour-yeast mixture and eggs.
    Blend at low speed with electric mixer until moistened.
    Beat 3 minutes at high speed.
4. Stir in enough white flour to make a stiff dough.

5. Brush with melted margarine.
6. Cover and let rise in a warm place until doubled (about 1 hour).
7. Punch down and shape into 3 loaves. Place in 3 9- by 5-inch loaf pans, greased.
8. Cover loaves and let rise in a warm place until doubled in size (about 45 minutes to 1 hour).
9. Heat oven to 375° F last 10 to 15 minutes of rising time.
10. Bake 25 to 35 minutes or until loaf sounds hollow when tapped.

Note: Each slice of bread has less than ½ teaspoon sugar (6 calories).

Whole-Wheat French Bread

Yield: 3 loaves (8 slices per loaf)
Serving Size: 1 slice
Exchange List Approximation:
    Starch/Bread 1

Nutrient Content Per Serving:
CAL: 88   PRO: 3.3 (gm)
FAT: 0.4 (gm)   CHO: 18.7 (gm)
Na: 178.8 (mg)   K: 87.2 (mg)
Fiber: 2 (gm)   Chol: 0

Ingredients

3½–4 CUPS WHOLE-WHEAT FLOUR
  1 CUP UNBLEACHED WHITE FLOUR
  2 PACKAGES DRY YEAST
  2 TEASPOONS SALT
  2 TEASPOONS HONEY
  2 CUPS WARM WATER
     CORNMEAL

Method

1. Combine 2 cups flour, salt, and dry yeast; stir well. Mix warm water with honey and add to flour mixture. Mix well. Let rest 5 minutes.
2. Add remaining flour, 1 cup at a time. Knead about 10 minutes on floured surface. Cover with inverted bowl, and let rise 1 hour.
3. Punch down dough and divide into thirds. Roll each third into 10- by 14-inch rectangle. With long end facing you, roll tightly into a jelly roll shape.
4. Sprinkle baking sheet with corn meal and place loaves, seam side down, on the baking sheet. Make 4 diagonal slashes on top of each loaf.

5. Place baking sheet in middle of cold oven. Place a pan of hot water on rack below the baking sheet. Let loaves rise about 20 minutes; remove pan of water and brush top of each loaf with cold water.
6. Bake at 425° F oven for 35 to 40 minutes. Do not preheat oven.

Blueberry Banana Bread

Yield: 1 loaf (22 slices)
Serving Size: 2 slices
Exchange List Approximation:
    Starch/Bread 1
    Fruit 1
    Fat $\frac{1}{2}$

Nutrient Content Per Serving:
CAL: 168   PRO: 3.9 (gm)
FAT: 4.3 (gm)   CHO: 30 (gm)
Na: 167.6 (mg)   K: 165 (mg)
Fiber: 2.6 (gm)   Chol: 25 (mg)

Ingredients

  1 CUP WHOLE-WHEAT FLOUR
  ¾ CUP ALL-PURPOSE FLOUR
  1 TEASPOON BAKING SODA
  ½ TEASPOON CINNAMON
  ¼ TEASPOON SALT
  ½ CUP QUICK-COOKING ROLLED OATS
  3 TABLESPOONS MARGARINE
  ⅓ CUP SUGAR
  1 EGG
  1 CUP MASHED BANANAS (ABOUT 2 WHOLE)
  1 TABLESPOON LEMON JUICE
  1 CUP FRESH OR FROZEN BLUEBERRIES, THAWED
     (ABOUT 4 OUNCES)

Method

1. Preheat oven to 350° F and lightly grease 8½- by 4½-inch
    loaf pan.
2. Mix flour, soda, salt, and cinnamon. Stir in oats and set aside.
3. Cream margarine and sugar. Whip in egg, add bananas
    and lemon juice. Stir until blended.
4. Fold in blueberries.
5. Add dry ingredients and mix until just moistened.
6. Pour batter in loaf pan and bake for about 1 hour.
7. Let bread cool in pan for 10 minutes. Turn out on wire rack
    to cool. Wrap and refrigerate several hours before slicing.

Variation: Double recipe and use canned blueberries; 1 15-ounce
can blueberries, drained. Reserve ½ cup juice. Add blueberries
and juice in step 4.

Note: Two-slice serving contains less than 1½ teaspoons sugar
(approximately 22 calories).

Burgess's Bran Bread

Yield: 2 loaves (20 slices per loaf)
Serving Size: 1 slice
Exchange List Approximation:
    Starch/Bread $\frac{1}{2}$

Nutrient Content Per Serving:
CAL: 40   PRO: 1.2 (gm)
FAT: 1.2 (gm)   CHO: 7.4 (gm)
Na: 498.7 (mg) K: 130 (mg)
Fiber: 1.3 (gm) Chol: 0

Ingredients

1 PACKAGE ACTIVE DRY YEAST
¾ CUP WARM WATER
1 CUP WARM SKIM MILK
⅓ CUP MOLASSES
2 TABLESPOONS SHORTENING
1 TABLESPOON SALT
3 CUPS WHOLE-WHEAT FLOUR
1 CUP UNPROCESSED BRAN

Method

1. Dissolve yeast in warm water. Add warm milk, molasses, shortening, and salt.
2. Mix in bran and enough flour to make a soft dough. Knead until smooth, about 3 minutes.
3. Place in greased bowl, cover, and let rise until double in size; about 2 hours.
4. Punch down and shape into 2 loaves.
5. Place in greased 9- by 5-inch loaf pans.
6. Cover and let rise until doubled in bulk; about 1½ hours.
7. Preheat oven to 375° F last 15 minutes of rising time.
8. Bake for 40 minutes.

Variation: Replace 3 Tablespoons flour with 3 Tablespoons wheat germ.

Basic Rolls

Yield: 8 rolls
Serving Size: 1 roll
Exchange List Approximation:
  Meat, medium-fat $\frac{1}{2}$

Nutrient Content Per Serving:
CAL: 46   PRO: 4 (gm)
FAT: 2.9 (gm)   CHO: 0.5 (gm)
Na: 79.2 (mg)   K: 39.2 (mg)
Fiber: 0   Chol: 138 (mg)

Ingredients

4 EGGS (SEPARATED)
   PINCH EACH: SALT AND CREAM OF TARTAR
4 TABLESPOONS LOW-FAT COTTAGE CHEESE, MASHED
1 PACKET SUGAR SUBSTITUTE

Method

1. Separate egg whites, whip until foamy, add pinch of salt
   and cream of tartar. Whip until firm peaks are formed.
2. Mix egg yolks, cottage cheese, and sugar substitute.
3. Add slowly to whites while mixing with folding motion.
4. Spray a cookie sheet with vegetable pan spray. Apportion
   mixture into 8 mounds, bun shaped.
5. Bake in 300° F oven for 1 hour. Lower heat to 250° F if rolls
   become too brown. This is an unusual item that can be
   used for sandwiches or hamburger.

Variation: Add 6 packets sugar substitute, 2 teaspoons cinnamon,
and ¼ cup chopped nuts for cookie-type rolls. Nutrient information is as follows:

Exchange List Approximation:
  Meat, medium-fat $\frac{1}{2}$
  Fat $\frac{1}{2}$

Nutrient Content Per Serving:
CAL: 71   PRO: 4.6 (gm)
FAT: 5.4 (gm)   CHO: 1.3 (gm)
Na: 79.7 (mg)   K: 59.2 (mg)
Fiber: 0.2 (gm) Chol: 138 (mg)

Banana Date-Nut Bread

Yield: 2 loaves (16 slices per loaf)
Serving Size: 2 slices
Exchange List Approximation:
    Starch/Bread $1\frac{1}{2}$
    Fat $1\frac{1}{2}$

Nutrient Content Per Serving:
CAL: 174   PRO: 4 (gm)
FAT: 9.4 (gm)   CHO: 21.1 (gm)
Na: 210.9 (mg)   K: 225.6 (mg)
Fiber: 3 (gm)   Chol: 34 (mg)

Ingredients

1½ CUPS WHOLE WHEAT FLOUR
1 CUP UNPROCESSED BRAN FLAKES
¼ CUP WHEAT GERM (ABOUT 1 OUNCE)
2½ TEASPOONS BAKING POWDER
½ TEASPOON BAKING SODA
¼ TEASPOON SALT
½ CUP MARGARINE (1 STICK)
2 EGGS
1 TEASPOON VANILLA
2 TEASPOONS BROWN SUGAR SUBSTITUTE
1½ CUPS MASHED BANANAS (ABOUT 12 OUNCES)
½ CUP CHOPPED WALNUTS OR PECANS (ABOUT 2 OUNCES)
½ CUP CHOPPED DATES (ABOUT 3 OUNCES)

Method

1. In a medium mixing bowl place whole-wheat flour, bran flakes, and wheat germ. Sift baking powder, soda, and salt over flour and mix all together. Set aside.
2. In a large mixing bowl, cream together margarine and brown-sugar substitute. Add eggs and vanilla; mix thoroughly.

3. Add flour mixture to creamed mixture alternately with mashed bananas. Blend completely after each addition.
4. Fold in nuts and dates.
5. Pour into 2 lightly greased loaf pans and bake for 50 minutes to 1 hour in 350° F oven.

Southern Cornbread

Yield: 6 servings
Serving Size: 1 wedge
Exchange List Approximation:
    Starch/Bread $1\frac{1}{2}$
    Fat $\frac{1}{2}$

Nutrient Content Per Serving:
CAL: 143   PRO: 4.5 (gm)
FAT: 3.6 (gm)   CHO: 22.7 (gm)
Na: 263.6 (mg) K: 104 (mg)
Fiber: 2.2 (gm) Chol: 47 (mg)

Ingredients

1 CUP CORNMEAL
2 TABLESPOONS FLOUR
1 TEASPOON BAKING POWDER
½ TEASPOON BAKING SODA
¼ TEASPOON SALT
1 CUP BUTTERMILK OR SOUR SKIM MILK (ADD 1 TBSP. LEMON JUICE PER 1 CUP MILK)
1 EGG
1 TABLESPOON VEGETABLE SHORTENING

Method

1. Combine dry ingredients in a bowl.
2. Add milk and egg. Stir until blended and set aside 30 minutes to soften cornmeal.
3. Place shortening in 8-inch ovenproof skillet (preferably iron) or cake pan. Place in oven and heat to 425° F.
4. When shortening is very hot, add to batter, stir, and immediately pour into skillet.
5. Bake in 425° F oven 20 to 25 minutes.

Note: Cornbread is very good with stew, beans, or black-eye peas.
Variation: Add 2 Tablespoons chopped green chilies to batter to make Mexican Cornbread.

Apple-Raisin Muffins

Yield: 12 servings
Serving Size: 1 muffin
Exchange List Approximation:
    Starch/Bread 1
    Fruit $\frac{1}{2}$
    Fat 1

Nutrient Content Per Serving:
CAL: 154   PRO: 3.5 (gm)
FAT: 4.5 (gm)   CHO: 25.2 (gm)
Na: 134.9 (mg)   K: 105.7 (mg)
Fiber: 1.5 (gm)   Chol: 23 (mg)

Ingredients

  2 CUPS ALL-PURPOSE FLOUR
  1 TABLESPOON BAKING POWDER
  ¼ TEASPOON SALT
  1 TEASPOON CINNAMON
  3 PACKETS SUGAR SUBSTITUTE
  1 EGG
  3 TABLESPOONS CORN OIL
  ½ CUP SKIM MILK
  1 CUP UNSWEETENED APPLESAUCE
  ½ CUP RAISINS, WASHED AND DRAINED

Method

1. Preheat oven to 400° F. Prepare 2½-inch muffin tins with vegetable pan spray or grease lightly.
2. Combine dry ingredients in mixing bowl and mix thoroughly.
3. Beat egg and whip in oil, milk, and applesauce.
4. Add to dry ingredients and mix until flour is moistened. Stir in raisins.
5. Fill muffin tins ⅔ full. Bake for 25 minutes. Remove from tin immediately.

Banana Muffins

Yield: 12 servings
Serving Size: 1 muffin
Exchange List Approximation:
    Starch/Bread 1
    Fat $\frac{1}{2}$

Nutrient Content Per Serving:
CAL: 102   PRO: 2.3 (gm)
FAT: 4.6 (gm)   CHO: 14.3 (gm)
Na: 101.4 (mg)   K: 164.9 (mg)
Fiber: 1.5 (gm)   Chol: 23 (mg)

Ingredients

  3 TABLESPOONS VEGETABLE OIL
  1 EGG
 ¼ CUP SKIM MILK
1⅓ CUPS MASHED, VERY RIPE BANANAS (ABOUT 3 MEDIUM)
  1 CUP WHOLE-WHEAT FLOUR
  2 TEASPOONS BAKING POWDER
 ¼ TEASPOON BAKING SODA
 ⅛ TEASPOON SALT

Method

1. Preheat oven to 400° F. Spray 12-cup muffin tin or 3 miniature muffin tins (12 each) with vegetable cooking spray or grease lightly.
2. Beat egg, oil, and milk. Stir in bananas.
3. Mix dry ingredients together and stir into banana mixture until flour is moistened.
4. Fill tins ½ to ⅔ full.
5. Bake about 23 minutes (15 to 18 minutes for small muffins).
6. Let cool about 15 minutes before removing from pans to let texture firm up.

Fresh Peach Muffins

Yield: 12 muffins
Serving Size: 1 muffin
Exchange List Approximation:
    Starch/Bread 1
    Fruit $\frac{1}{2}$
    Fat 1

Nutrient Content Per Serving:
CAL: 151   PRO: 3.9 (gm)
FAT: 5.8 (gm)   CHO: 21.6 (gm)
Na: 139.3 (mg)   K: 132.3 (mg)
Fiber: 1.7 (gm)   Chol: 23 (mg)

Ingredients

1 CUP UNPEELED, CHOPPED FRESH PEACHES
1 TEASPOON LEMON JUICE
1 CUP ALL-PURPOSE FLOUR
1 CUP WHOLE-WHEAT FLOUR
1 TABLESPOON BAKING POWDER
2 TABLESPOONS SUGAR
3 PACKETS SUGAR SUBSTITUTE
½ TEASPOON MACE
¼ TEASPOON SALT
1 EGG
¼ CUP VEGETABLE OIL
1 CUP SKIM MILK

Method

1. Heat oven to 400° F. Lightly grease 12-cup muffin pan.
2. Add lemon juice to peaches. Set aside.
3. Combine sugar, sugar substitute, and remaining dry ingredients and mix thoroughly.
4. Beat egg, oil, and milk together.
5. Add to dry ingredients. Stir until flour is just moistened.

6. Fold in peaches. Fill muffin cups ⅔ full. (Paper baking cups may be used.)
7. Bake about 25 minutes or until brown. Remove from pan immediately.

Note: Each muffin has ½ teaspoon sugar (8 calories).

Bran-Fruit Muffins

Yield: 12 muffins	Nutrient Content Per Serving:
Serving Size: 2 muffins	CAL: 228 PRO: 7.6 (gm)
Exchange List Approximation:	FAT: 9 (gm) CHO: 34.9 (gm)
Starch/Bread 2	Na: 356.5 (mg) K: 410.7 (mg)
Fat $1\frac{1}{2}$	Fiber: 7.2 (gm) Chol: 46 (mg)

Ingredients

1 CUP ALL-BRAN CEREAL
⅓ CUP CHOPPED DATES (OR RAISINS)
1¼ CUPS SKIM MILK
3 TABLESPOONS VEGETABLE OIL
1 EGG
1 CUP WHOLE-WHEAT FLOUR
1 TABLESPOON BAKING POWDER

Method

1. Preheat oven to 400° F and prepare 12-cup muffin pan;
    lightly grease or spray with vegetable pan spray or line
    with paper baking cups.
2. Mix bran cereal and fruit in mixing bowl. Add milk, stir,
    and let stand several minutes.
3. Add oil and egg. Beat well.
4. Mix flour and baking powder. Add to bran mixture. Stir
    until flour is just blended or moistened.
5. Spoon mixture into 12 muffin cups.
6. Immediately place in oven. Bake 15 minutes.
7. Remove from pan immediately.

Orange-Bran Muffins

Yield: 12 servings
Serving Size: 1 muffin
Exchange List Approximation:
    Starch/Bread 1

Nutrient Content Per Serving:
CAL: 80   PRO: 3.3 (gm)
FAT: 2.1 (gm)   CHO: 14.1 (gm)
Na: 161.9 (mg)   K: 175.1 (mg)
Fiber: 2.6 (gm)   Chol: 24 (mg)

Ingredients

- 1 CUP WHOLE-WHEAT FLOUR
- ¾ CUP MILLER'S BRAN (UNPROCESSED, UNCOOKED WHEAT BRAN)
- ¾ TEASPOON SODA
- ⅛ TEASPOON SALT
- 1 TABLESPOON GRATED ORANGE RIND
- 1 EGG
- 1 TABLESPOON VEGETABLE OIL
- 2 TABLESPOON DARK MOLASSES
- 1 CUP BUTTERMILK
- ½ CUP RAISINS (OPTIONAL)

Method

1. Preheat oven to 350° F. Spray muffin pan with vegetable pan spray.
2. Combine whole-wheat flour, bran, soda, salt, and orange rind.
3. Beat egg and whip in oil, molasses, and buttermilk.
4. Add dry ingredients and stir until just blended. Fold in raisins.
5. Spoon mixture into 12 muffin cups.
6. Bake for 25 minutes.

Note: Muffin contains ½ teaspoon sugar (8 calories).

Meat

Beef Burgundy

Yield: 4 servings
Serving Size: 1 cup
Exchange List Approximation:
    Meat, lean $2\frac{1}{2}$
    Vegetable 2

Nutrient Content Per Serving:
CAL: 185   PRO: 22 (gm)
FAT: 5.9 (gm)   CHO: 10.1 (gm)
Na: 610.9 (mg)   K: 552.5 (mg)
Fiber: 2.3 (gm)   Chol: 55 (mg)
Key Source Nutrients:
    Vitamin A: 7754 (IU)

Ingredients

- ¾ POUND BEEF ROUND, WELL-TRIMMED, CUT IN 1-INCH CUBES
- ½ TEASPOON SALT
- ⅛ TEASPOON PEPPER
- 1 BAY LEAF
- ⅛ TEASPOON THYME LEAVES
- 1½ CUPS WATER
- 1½ CUPS DICED POTATOES
- 1 CUP SLICED CARROTS
- ½ CUP DICED CELERY
- ⅓ CUP CHOPPED ONION
- 1 CUP SLICED FRESH MUSHROOMS
- 3 TABLESPOONS FLOUR
- ¼ CUP WATER
- ⅓ CUP RED BURGUNDY WINE
  PARSLEY (TO GARNISH)

Method

1. Brown beef cubes in hot frypan.
2. Add salt, pepper, bay leaf, thyme, and 1½ cups water.
3. Simmer, covered, until beef is almost tender, about 1¾ hours.

4. Remove bay leaf.
5. Add potatoes, carrots, celery, onion, and mushrooms. Simmer, covered, until vegetables are tender, about 20 minutes.
6. Mix flour with ¼ cup water until smooth. Add slowly to meat mixture, stirring gently; cook until thickened.
7. Stir in wine.
8. Garnish with parsley.

Stir-Fried Beef and Broccoli

Yield: 4 or 2 servings
Serving Size: 1 cup
Exchange List Approximation:
 Meat, lean 2
 Vegetable 2
 Fat 2

Nutrient Content Per Serving:
CAL: 259   PRO: 19 (gm)
FAT: 17.2 (gm)   CHO: 8.3 (gm)
Na: 585.7 (mg)* K: 559.8 (mg)
Fiber: 3.3 (gm)   Chol: 44 (mg)
Key Source Nutrients:
 Ascorbic acid: 65 (mg)

Ingredients

Four Servings	Two Servings
¾ POUND ROUND OR FLANK STEAK	6 OUNCES
2 TEASPOONS CORNSTARCH	1 TEASPOON
2 TABLESPOONS SOY SAUCE	1 TABLESPOON
3 CUPS BROCCOLI, PEELED, CUT IN STRIPS 1 INCH × ¼ INCH	1½ CUPS
3 CUPS WATER	2 CUPS
2 TABLESPOONS VEGETABLE OIL	1 TABLESPOON
1 CUP WEDGE-CUT ONION	½ CUP
1 TABLESPOON MINCED GINGER ROOT	1½ TEASPOONS
1 TABLESPOON SHERRY (OPTIONAL)	½ TEASPOON
2 TABLESPOONS WATER	1 TABLESPOON

Method

1. Trim fat from steak, slice across the grain in thin slices 1 inch by ¼ inch.

2. Sprinkle with cornstarch and soy sauce. Mix and set aside.
3. Bring water to a boil, add broccoli, stir; bring to a boil and cook 2 minutes. Drain immediately. Set aside.
4. Heat oil in wok or large skillet until very hot. Add onion and ginger root. Stir-fry about 30 seconds.
5. Add steak and stir-fry about 2 minutes.
6. Add broccoli, sherry, and water. Stir contantly until steaming, about 1 minute.
7. Serving suggestion: Serve with rice (½ cup cooked rice = 1 Bread Exchange).

Note: Broccoli may be cooked in hot oil in wok (or skillet) before onions. Stir-fry 3 minutes and remove. This recipe tastes very good. Broccoli is firmer in wok, but color is more attractive when boiled.

*To reduce sodium content, use mild soy sauce or cut back on the quantity of soy sauce used.

Beef Ragout

Yield: 8 or 2 servings
Serving Size: $\frac{2}{3}$ cup
Exchange List Approximation:
    Meat, lean $3\frac{1}{2}$
    Vegetable 1

Nutrient Content Per Serving:
CAL: 211   PRO: 26.9 (gm)
FAT: 9 (gm)   CHO: 4.8 (gm)
Na: 342.6 (mg)   K: 534.2 (mg)
Fiber: 1.9 (gm)   Chol: 74 (mg)

Ingredients

Eight Servings			*Two Servings*	
2	POUNDS BEEF, LEAN, CUBED		½	POUND
1	TABLESPOON MARGARINE		1	TEASPOON
2	CUPS CHOPPED ONION		½	CUP
1	TABLESPOON MINCED GARLIC		¾	TEASPOON
2	BAY LEAVES		1	
2	TABLESPOONS CHOPPED PARSLEY		1½	TEASPOONS
1	TABLESPOON CHOPPED FRESH ORANGE PEEL		¾	TEASPOON
1	TEASPOON CRUSHED ROSEMARY		¼	TEASPOON
1	TEASPOON CINNAMON		¼	TEASPOON
½	TEASPOON SALT		⅛	TEASPOON
½	CUP WATER		¼	CUP
2	CUPS SLICED FRESH MUSHROOMS		½	CUP
1	CUP SLICED GREEN PEPPER		¼	CUP

Method

1. Heat margarine in large skillet. Add one layer of beef
   cubes, brown over high heat, and remove to stew pot.
   Continue until all beef is brown.

2. Lower heat and add onions and garlic, stir and cook about 2 minutes. Remove to stew pot.
3. Add bay leaves, parsley, orange peel, rosemary, cinnamon, salt, and water to stew pot.
4. Cover and simmer 1½ hours or until tender. Add a little water if beef becomes dry. Remove bay leaves.
5. Add mushrooms and green pepper, stir, cover, and cook about 5 minutes.
6. Serving suggestion: Serve over noodles (½ cup cooked noodles = 1 Bread Exchange).

Zesty Sauerbraten

Yield: 8 servings
Serving Size: 2 slices meat and
$\frac{1}{2}$ cup sauce
Exchange List Approximation:
Starch/Bread 1$\frac{1}{2}$
Meat, lean 4
Vegtable 2

Nutrient Content Per Serving:
CAL: 381   PRO: 40.5 (gm)
FAT: 11.9 (gm)   CHO: 32.3 (gm)
Na: 256.6 (mg)   K: 856.6 (mg)
Fiber: 6.5 (gm) Chol: 113 (mg)

Ingredients

 3 POUNDS BONELESS BEEF ROAST (CHUCK, RUMP, OR ROUND)
 2 CUPS WATER
 2 CUPS CIDER VINEGAR
 1 CUP SLICED ONION
 ½ CUP SLICED CARROTS
 ¼ CUP SLICED CELERY
10 PEPPERCORNS
 6 WHOLE ALLSPICE
 4 WHOLE CLOVES
 2 BAY LEAVES
1½ TEASPOONS CHOPPED FRESH GINGER ROOT
1½ CUPS BRAN CEREAL, SUCH AS ALL-BRAN, BRAN-CHEX, OR CRACKLIN' BRAN)
 1 TEASPOON GROUND GINGER
 ½ TEASPOON GROUND CINNAMON
 ¼ TEASPOON GROUND ALLSPICE
 2 TABLESPOONS UNSULPHURED MOLASSES
 1 6-OUNCE CAN FROZEN CONCENTRATED APPLE JUICE
 2 TEASPOONS CORNSTARCH

Method

1. Trim fat from roast and place in stainless steel bowl or large plastic bag with secure closure.
2. Heat water to boiling and add vinegar, vegetables, and spices. Cool slightly and add to beef. Cover or close bag securely. Refrigerate 24 to 36 hours. Turn meat after 12 hours.
3. Remove meat and bay leaves. Reserve marinade.
4. Drain meat and pat dry. Brown well on all sides in fat-free pan or 425° F oven or under broiler.
5. Place meat on rack in Dutch oven. Add marinade. Cover tightly and braise 2 to 2½ hours. May be covered and cooked in 325° F oven. Cool.
6. Drain cooking liquid and reserve for sauce. Refrigerate meat until firm enough to slice.
7. Prepare sauce. Remove excess fat from cooking liquid, strain, and bring to a boil. Add bran cereal and remaining ingredients. Cook until blended and thickened, stirring constantly.
8. Slice chilled meat. Arrange in baking pan. Cover with sauce. Cover and heat in 300° F oven for 1 hour.

Pepper Steak

Yield: 4 or 2 servings
Serving Size: 1 cup
Exchange List Approximation:
  Meat, lean 3
  Vegetable 1
  Fat 2

Nutrient Content Per Serving:
CAL: 281   PRO: 22.4 (gm)
FAT: 17.8 (gm)   CHO: 8.2 (gm)
Na: 297.8 (mg)   K: 664.2 (mg)
Fiber: 2.9 (gm)   Chol: 58 (mg)
Key Source Nutrients:
  Ascorbic acid: 77 (mg)

Ingredients

Four Servings
1 POUND ROUND OR FLANK STEAK
2 TEASPOONS SOY SAUCE
1 TEASPOON MINCED GARLIC
2 CUPS GREEN PEPPERS, SLICED IN STRIPS
2 CUPS CELERY, CUT DIAGONALLY
⅔ CUP CHOPPED GREEN ONIONS
4 TEASPOONS VEGETABLE OIL
¼ CUP WATER
1 TABLESPOON CORNSTARCH

Two Servings
½ POUND

1 TEASPOON
½ TEASPOON
1 CUP

1 CUP

⅓ CUP
2 TEASPOONS
2 TABLESPOONS
1½ TEASPOONS

Method

1. Trim all fat from steak, cut across grain in slices about 1 inch by ¼ inch.
2. Add soy sauce and garlic, stir, and set aside.
3. Prepare vegetables.
4. Heat half of oil until very hot in large skillet.
5. Add vegetables and stir-fry 2 minutes; remove from skillet to warm pan.

6. Add remaining oil to skillet, heat, add steak and stir-fry 2 minutes.
7. Mix cornstarch with water, add to steak. Cook, stirring constantly until thickened.
8. Add vegetables, mix thoroughly.
9. Serving suggestion: Serve over brown rice (1/3 cup cooked rice = 1 Starch/Bread Exchange).

Italian Ground Beef and Macaroni

Yield: 4 servings
Serving Size: 1⅓ cup
Exchange List Approximation:
    Starch/Bread 2
    Meat, medium-fat 2
    Vegetable 1

Nutrient Content Per Serving:
CAL: 330   PRO: 22.3 (gm)
FAT: 11.3 (gm)   CHO: 35.7 (gm)
Na: 679.5 (mg)*   K: 855.7 (mg)
Fiber: 2.6 (gm)   Chol: 53 (mg)
Key Source Nutrients:
    Ascorbic acid: 54 (mg)

Ingredients

¾ POUND GROUND BEEF, EXTRA LEAN
½ CUP CHOPPED ONION
¼ CUP CHOPPED GREEN PEPPER
¼ CUP CHOPPED CELERY
1 16-OUNCE CAN TOMATOES
1 10¾-OUNCE CAN TOMATO PUREE
1 TEASPOON OREGANO LEAVES
1 TEASPOON BASIL LEAVES
¼ TEASPOON SALT
⅛ TEASPOON PEPPER
3 CUPS COOKED ELBOW MACARONI, UNSALTED (ABOUT 1 CUP UNCOOKED)

Method

1. Cook beef, onion, green pepper, and celery in large frypan until beef is lightly browned and onion is clear. Drain.
2. Break up large pieces of tomatoes.
3. Add tomatoes, tomato puree, and seasonings to beef mixture. Simmer 15 minutes to blend flavors.
4. Stir in macaroni. Heat to serving temperature.

*To reduce sodium content, use unsalted tomato products and eliminate the ¼ teaspoon of salt. Try herb blend (from Chapter 15) for extra seasoning.

Verhalen Trainwreck (Burrito Filling)

Yield: 8 servings
Serving Size: $\frac{1}{3}$ cup
Exchange List Approximation:
    Starch/Bread 1
    Meat, medium-fat $1\frac{1}{2}$

Nutrient Content Per Serving:
CAL: 194   PRO: 15 (gm)
FAT: 7.7 (gm)   CHO: 16.3 (gm)
Na: 90.2 (mg)   K: 415.6 (mg)
Fiber: 4.7 (gm)   Chol: 34 (mg)

Ingredients

1 POUND LEAN GROUND BEEF
½ CUP CHOPPED ONION
1 10-OUNCE CAN TOMATOES AND GREEN CHILIES
1 3- OR 4-OUNCE CAN GREEN CHILIES (OPTIONAL)
1 15-OUNCE CAN WESTERN-STYLE PINTO BEANS
   DASH TABASCO SAUCE

Method

1. Cook ground beef in large skillet until it starts to brown. Add onions and cook until limp. Drain excess fat.
2. Add can of tomatoes and green chilies, beans, and Tabasco. Add can of green chilies, if desired. Stir to mix and simmer uncovered 30 minutes, stirring occasionally.
3. Serve on either flour tortillas or corn tortillas.
4. Garnish with shredded cheese, chopped onion, and shredded lettuce.

Mexican Bake with Yogurt

Yield: 6 servings
Serving Size: 1 cup
Exchange List Approximation:
    Starch/Bread $2\frac{1}{2}$
    Meat, medium-fat 3

Nutrient Content Per Serving:
CAL: 409   PRO: 27.9 (gm)
FAT: 16 (gm)   CHO: 39.2 (gm)
Na: 687.2 (mg)   K: 673 (mg)
Fiber: 6.7 (gm)   Chol: 53 (mg)

Ingredients

- 6 OUNCES LEAN GROUND BEEF
- ½ CUP CHOPPED ONION
- ½ TEASPOON CUMIN
- ¼ TEASPOON GARLIC POWDER
- ½ TEASPOON CHILI POWDER
- ⅛ TEASPOON CRUSHED RED PEPPER
- 1 8-OUNCE CAN TOMATO SAUCE
- 1 15-OUNCE CAN RANCH-STYLE PINTO BEANS IN TOMATO AND CHILI SAUCE
- 1 CUP LOW-FAT COTTAGE CHEESE
- 1 8-OUNCE CONTAINER LOW-FAT PLAIN YOGURT
- ¼ CUP CHOPPED GREEN CHILIES (ABOUT ½ 4-OUNCE CAN)
- 4 FLOUR TORTILLAS
- 1½ CUPS SHREDDED CHEDDAR CHEESE (ABOUT 6 OUNCES)

Method

1. Cook ground beef and onions until crumbly. Drain off any excess fat.
2. Add spices and mix thoroughly with meat.
3. Add tomato sauce and beans. Mix well.

4. In separate bowl, mix yogurt, cottage cheese, and chilies.
5. Bake tortillas on cookie sheet in 400° F oven until crisp and beginning to brown, about 5 minutes. Break tortillas into large pieces.
6. Put half the tortillas in bottom of a 2½-quart casserole. Spoon half the meat mixture evenly over tortillas. Add half of the yogurt mixture and sprinkle with half the cheese. Repeat, ending with the cheese.
7. Bake, covered, in 350° F oven for 30 to 35 minutes.

Variation: Use ¾ cup of sour cream in place of 8-ounce container low-fat plain yogurt. If sour cream is used, nutritional information is as follows:

Serving Size: 1 cup
Exchange List Approximation:
    Starch/Bread $2\frac{1}{2}$
    Meat, medium-fat 3
    Fat $\frac{1}{2}$

Nutrient Content Per Serving:
CAL: 437   PRO: 26.8 (gm)
FAT: 20.4 (gm)   CHO: 37.5 (gm)
Na: 672.7 (mg)* K: 618.5 (mg)
Fiber: 6.7 (gm) Chol: 61 (mg)

*To reduce sodium content, use unsalted ingredients.

Breaded Veal Cutlets

Yield: 4 or 2 servings
Serving Size: 1 serving
Exchange List Approximation:
    Starch/Bread 1
    Meat, medium-fat 3
    Fat $\frac{1}{2}$

Nutrient Content Per Serving:
CAL: 319   PRO: 30.7 (gm)
FAT: 19.1 (gm) CHO: 10.4 (gm)
Na: 272.4 (mg) K: 620.4 (mg)
Fiber: 0.3 (gm) Chol: 62 (mg)

Ingredients

Four Servings	Two Servings
1 POUND CHOPPED AND FORMED VEAL CUTLETS (4)	8 OUNCES (2)
4 TABLESPOONS TOMATO JUICE SPRINKLE EACH OF SALT, PEPPER, AND GARLIC POWDER	2 TABLESPOONS SPRINKLE
½ TEASPOON OREGANO	¼ TEASPOON
½ CUP SEASONED BREAD CRUMBS	¼ CUP
2 TEASPOONS VEGETABLE OIL	1 TEASPOON
4 SLICES LEMON	2 SLICES

Method

1. Place cutlets on pan. Spoon tomato juice over cutlets. Sprinkle each side lightly with salt, pepper, garlic powder, and oregano.
2. Spread crumbs on wax paper and press cutlets in crumbs to coat.
3. Heat iron skillet or grill. Grease lightly with vegetable oil. Reduce heat and cook cutlets about 5 minutes per side over medium heat.
4. Serve with lemon slice.

Curried Ham and Vegetable Pie

Yield: 4 servings
Serving Size: $\frac{1}{4}$ pie
Exchange List Approximation:
    Starch/Bread 1$\frac{1}{2}$
    Meat, lean 2
    Fat $\frac{1}{2}$

Nutrient Content Per Serving:
CAL: 253   PRO: 18.5 (gm)
FAT: 9.2 (gm)   CHO: 25.9 (gm)
Na: 1222.7 (mg)   K: 556.7 (mg)
Fiber: 4.6 (gm)   Chol: 47 (mg)

Ingredients

½ CUP BEEF BROTH OR WATER
2 TEASPOONS CORNSTARCH
½ TEASPOON CURRY POWDER
2 CUPS DICED COOKED HAM
1 10-OUNCE PACKAGE FROZEN MIXED VEGETABLES, THAWED
2 CUPS MASHED POTATOES
   DASH PAPRIKA

Method

1. In medium bowl blend broth, cornstarch, and curry powder. Stir in ham and vegetables. Pour into a greased 10-inch pie plate.
2. Spread potatoes evenly to cover filling; sprinkle with paprika. Bake in preheated oven at 425° F for 25 minutes or until potatoes are lightly browned.

*This recipe is high in sodium and may not be suitable for some people.

Herbed Pork Kabobs

Yield: 4 servings
Serving Size: 1 serving
Exchange List Approximation:
    Meat, lean 4
    Fat 1

Nutrient Content Per Serving:
CAL: 263   PRO: 32.4 (gm)
FAT: 14.1 (gm)   CHO: 0.3 (gm)
Na: 174.3 (mg)   K: 607.5 (mg)
Fiber: 0   Chol: 103 (mg)

Ingredients

1¼ POUNDS PORK TENDERLOIN
¼ CUP DRY WHITE WINE
¼ TEASPOON DRY MARJORAM LEAVES
¼ TEASPOON DRY ROSEMARY LEAVES
1 MINCED GARLIC CLOVE
3 TABLESPOONS MARGARINE, SOFTENED
½ TEASPOON DRY MARJORAM LEAVES
½ TEASPOON DRY ROSEMARY LEAVES
¼ TEASPOON SALT (OPTIONAL)
PINCH PEPPER

Method

1. Combine trimmed pork, wine, ¼ teaspoon marjoram, ¼ teaspoon rosemary, and garlic in medium-size bowl; toss to coat. Let stand at room temperature 20 minutes.
2. Cream margarine, ½ teaspoon marjoram, ½ teaspoon rosemary, salt, and pepper.
3. Drain pork; reserve marinade. Beat marinade into margarine mix.
4. Cut pork into 1½-inch cubes and thread on 4 skewers.
5. Place on wire rack over shallow baking dish. Broil 4 inches from heat. Turn frequently; baste occasionally with herb-butter mix until brown on all sides. Serve with lemon wedges.

Cantonese Pork

Yield: 6 servings

Serving Size: 7 meat balls and $\frac{2}{3}$ cup sauce

Exchange List Approximation:
    Starch/Bread 1
    Meat, medium-fat $1\frac{1}{2}$
    Vegetable $\frac{1}{2}$

Nutrient Content Per Serving:

CAL: 235	PRO: 19.5 (gm)
FAT: 7.6 (gm)	CHO: 23.3 (gm)
Na: 355.1 (mg)	K: 664.3 (mg)
Fiber: 2.5 (gm)	Chol: 48 (mg)

Ingredients

  1 POUND LEAN GROUND PORK
 ¼ TEASPOON SALT
 ⅛ TEASPOON PEPPER'
 ¼ CUP FINELY CHOPPED ONIONS
 ¼ CUP EVAPORATED SKIM MILK

Sweet and Sour Sauce

  1 15½-OUNCE CAN PINEAPPLE TIDBITS, UNSWEETENED JUICE
 ¼ CUP VINEGAR
  1 TABLESPOON SUGAR
  1 TABLESPOON SOY SAUCE
 ½ CUP WATER
  2 TABLESPOONS CORNSTARCH
  1 TEASPOON MARGARINE
 ¼ CUP SLIVERED TOASTED ALMONDS
  1 CUP SLICED CELERY
 ½ CUP SLICED GREEN ONIONS
 ½ CUP GREEN PEPPER STRIPS
  2 MEDIUM TOMATOES, CUT IN 6 WEDGES

Method

1. Mix pork, salt, pepper, onions, and milk together
    thoroughly. Place on board and roll out in rectangle. Cut
    into 42 pieces. Roll each piece into a ball.
2. Place in shallow pan and bake in 350° F oven 30 to 40
    minutes. Turn after 15 minutes.
3. Drain juice from pineapple and combine with vinegar,
    sugar, soy sauce, water, and cornstarch in 2-quart
    saucepan. Bring to a boil, stirring constantly, and cook until
    clear and thickened. Add margarine.
4. Ten minutes before serving, add almonds and vegetables.
    Heat until vegetables are just heated through.
5. Serve meat balls over rice and cover with ⅔ cup sauce (⅓ cup
    cooked rice = 1 Starch/Bread Exchange).

Note: Approximately ½ teaspoon sugar (8 calories) per serving.

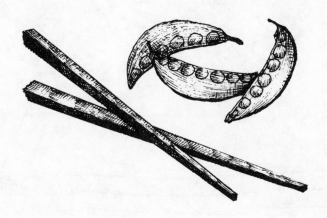

Poultry

Cold Chicken

Yield: 4 servings
Serving Size: breast half or
   leg quarter
Exchange List Approximation:
    Meat, lean 3

Nutrient Content Per Serving:
CAL: 154   PRO: 25 (gm)
FAT: 5.1 (gm)   CHO: 0
Na: 98.1 (mg)   K: 194.5 (mg)
Fiber: 0   Chol: 75 (mg)

Ingredients

3 POUNDS FRYING CHICKEN, CUT UP
1 TEASPOON MINCED GARLIC
1 TEASPOON SALT
3 QUARTS WATER
8 WHOLE PEPPERCORNS
1 TEASPOON CHOPPED FRESH GINGER ROOT
1 SLICED GREEN ONION
2 TEASPOONS DRY SHERRY (OPTIONAL)

Method

1. Remove excess fat from chicken, wash, rub with garlic and salt, set aside.
2. Bring water to a boil in heavy pot.
3. Rinse chicken and add with peppercorns to water.
4. Heat until water is summering, turn off heat, and let stand 30 minutes.
5. Repeat process and let stand 1 hour.
6. Remove chicken; cool enough to handle. Remove skin and discard.
7. Remove breast meat and leg quarters. Bone remaining chicken pieces for later use.
8. Place meat of breast, and leg quarters in refrigerator container.

9. Add ginger, onion, sherry, and enough hot broth to cover. Chill.

10. Serving suggestion: Serve cold breast or leg quarter with green salad or hot vegetables. (See Appendix I for exchange values of salad ingredients or vegetables.) Sprinkle chicken with picante sauce.

*To reduce sodium, eliminate the salt.

Greek Chicken Salad

Yield: 6 or 2 servings
Serving Size: 1 cup
Exchange List Approximation:
Starch/Bread 1
Meat, lean 1
Vegetable 1
Fat 1

Nutrient Content Per Serving:
CAL: 200   PRO: 13 (gm)
FAT: 6.9 (gm)   CHO: 21.6 (gm)
Na: 148.3 (mg)   K: 414.2 (mg)
Fiber: 2.8 (gm)   Chol: 32 (mg)

Ingredients

Six Servings		Two Servings	
2	CUPS COOKED BROWN RICE	⅔	CUP
1½	CUPS COOKED, DICED CHICKEN	½	CUP
⅛	TEASPOON SALT		DASH
½	CUP PLAIN LOW-FAT YOGURT	3	TABLESPOONS
2	TABLESPOONS MAYONNAISE	2	TEASPOONS
1	MINCED GARLIC CLOVE	⅓	
1	CUP SLICED CELERY	⅓	CUP
2	CUPS SHREDDED RAW SPINACH	⅔	CUP
¼	CUP CHOPPED GREEN ONIONS	1	TABLESPOON
1	CUP DICED TOMATO	⅓	CUP
2	TABLESPOONS LEMON JUICE	2	TEASPOONS

Method

1. Combine rice and chicken. Sprinkle with salt and chill.
2. Combine yogurt, mayonnaise, and garlic. Mix with rice and chicken.
3. Add remaining ingredients and toss lightly.
4. Serve on lettuce with Greek- or ripe-olive garnish.

Note: Very good salad. Serving is slightly more than a cup.

Chicken Paprika

Yield: 4 or 2 servings
Serving Size: $\frac{1}{2}$ breast plus
    $\frac{1}{2}$ cup sauce
Exchange List Approximation:
    Starch/Bread $\frac{1}{2}$
    Meat, lean $3\frac{1}{2}$
    Vegetable 1

Nutrient Content Per Serving:
CAL: 262   PRO: 32.5 (gm)
FAT: 9 (gm)   CHO: 11.5 (gm)
Na: 266.4 (mg)   K: 528.9 (mg)
Fiber: 3 (gm)   Chol: 85 (mg)

Ingredients

Four Servings		*Two Servings*
4	CHICKEN BREAST HALVES, SKINNED AND BONED	2
1	CLOVE GARLIC, MINCED	½ CLOVE
2	CUPS CHOPPED ONIONS	1 CUP
1	TABLESPOON MARGARINE	1½ TEASPOON
2	TABLESPOONS LEMON JUICE	1 TABLESPOON
1	TEASPOON PAPRIKA	½ TEASPOON
¼	TEASPOON SALT	⅛ TEASPOON
⅛	TEASPOON PEPPER	SPRINKLE
1	TABLESPOON FLOUR	1½ TEASPOON
⅔	CUP SKIM MILK	⅓ CUP
¼	CUP SOUR CREAM	2 TABLESPOONS
1	CUP SLICED FRESH MUSHROOMS (ABOUT 2 OUNCES)	½ CUP

Method

1. Mix chicken with garlic and set aside.
2. Cook onions in margarine in a large skillet for 2 or 3 minutes.

3. Push onions to one side and cook chicken breasts about 3 minutes.
4. Sprinkle chicken with lemon juice, paprika, salt, and pepper.
5. Cover tightly and cook over low heat until tender, about 30 minutes.
6. Remove chicken to another pan.
7. Make sauce by sprinkling flour over onions, stir, and cook about 1 minute. Add milk, stir, and cook until thickened.
8. Stir in sour cream and mushrooms. Add chicken and heat to serving temperature. Do not boil.
9. Serve over noodles (½ cup cooked noodles = 1 Starch/Bread Exchange).

Lemon Barbecued Chicken

Yield: 6 or 2 servings
Serving Size: 1 breast half
Exchange List Approximation:
    Meat, medium-fat 3

Nutrient Content Per Serving:
CAL: 237   PRO: 29.2 (gm)
FAT: 12.6 (gm)   CHO: 0
Na: 157.6 (mg) K: 240.7 (mg)
Fiber: 0   Chol: 83 (mg)

Serving Size: 1 leg
Exchange List Approximation:
    Meat, medium-fat 4
    Fat $\frac{1}{2}$

Nutrient Content Per Serving:
CAL: 320   PRO: 30.2 (gm)
FAT: 21.2 (gm)   CHO: 0
Na: 180.9 (mg) K: 219.2 (mg)
Fiber: 0   Chol: 105 (mg)

Ingredients

Six Servings		*Two Servings*	
6	CHICKEN BREASTS, HALVES OR LEGS AND THIGHS	2	
1	TEASPOON GRATED LEMON RIND	½	TEASPOON
1½	TEASPOONS SALT	¾	TEASPOON
½	TEASPOON DRY MUSTARD	¼	TEASPOON
½	TEASPOON DRIED OREGANO LEAVES	¼	TEASPOON
½	CUP LEMON JUICE	¼	CUP
½	CUP SALAD OIL	¼	CUP
2	TABLESPOONS CHOPPED SCALLIONS	1	TABLESPOON
1	TEASPOON WORCESTERSHIRE SAUCE	½	TEASPOON

Method

1. Mix lemon rind, salt, dry mustard, oregano, and Worcestershire sauce in small bowl.
2. Gradually stir in lemon juice, then oil, and scallions.
3. Pour over chicken in large bowl; marinate in refrigerator for 2 hours.
4. Remove chicken from marinade and place skin-side down on grill.
5. Set 3 to 6 inches from charcoal that has reached light gray stage.
6. Cook for 45 minutes to 1 hour, turning once.

Note: Marinade imparts a very good flavor and drains from the chicken, so probably no more than 5 grams of oil remain on each piece. For the two-serving quantity, the marinade ingredients are only cut in half to provide enough to cover chicken.

*To reduce sodium, eliminate the 1½ teaspoon of salt.

Chicken Curry

Yield: 4 servings
Serving Size: $\frac{1}{4}$ recipe
Exchange List Approximation:
    Meat, lean 3
    Vegetable 1

Nutrient Content Per Serving:

CAL: 198	PRO: 25.7 (gm)
FAT: 6.6 (gm)	CHO: 7.9 (gm)
Na: 190.3 (mg)	K: 463.2 (mg)
Fiber: 1.8 (gm)	Chol: 72 (mg)

Ingredients

2½ CUPS DICED COOKED CHICKEN
  1 CUP CHOPPED ONION
 ½ TEASPOON SALT (OPTIONAL)
  2 TEASPOONS CURRY POWDER
  1 TEASPOON CHILI POWDER
  1 TEASPOON MINCED DEHYDRATED GARLIC
 ½ TEASPOON PEPPER
 ½ CUP LOW-FAT YOGURT
  1 CUP CANNED TOMATOES

Method

1. Cook onion in water (sufficient to cover) until transparent.
2. Add chicken and remaining ingredients. Mix thoroughly and simmer 15 minutes.
3. Serve on rice or toast points.

*Sodium content of salt is not included in the nutrient estimate.

Oven-Fried Chicken

Yield: 6 or 2 servings
Serving Size: ½ breast
Exchange List Approximation:
    Starch/Bread ½
    Meat, lean 3

Nutrient Content Per Serving:
CAL: 230   PRO: 31.3 (gm)
FAT: 7.3 (gm)   CHO: 7.4 (gm)
Na: 341.1 (mg)   K: 287.8 (mg)
Fiber: 0.3 (gm)   Chol: 81 (mg)

Ingredients

Six Servings		*Two Servings*	
6	CHICKEN BREAST HALVES, SKINNED	2	
18	SALTINE CRACKER SQUARES, CRUSHED	6	
2	TABLESPOONS GRATED PARMESAN CHEESE	2	TEASPOONS
¾	TEASPOON PEPPER	¼	TEASPOON
½	TEASPOON EACH: BASIL, CELERY SEED, ONION POWDER, OREGANO, PAPRIKA	⅛	TEASPOON
⅜	TEASPOON SALT	⅛	TEASPOON
¼	CUPS EVAPORATED SKIM MILK	1½	TABLESPOONS
1	TABLESPOON VEGETABLE OIL	1	TEASPOON

Method

1. Combine cracker crumbs, cheese, pepper, basil, celery seed, onion powder, oregano, paprika, and salt in bowl.
2. Dip chicken in evaporated milk and then coat with crumb mixture. Place in lightly greased shallow roasting pan.
3. Bake in 400° F oven for 30 minutes. Brush with oil and bake 10 minutes longer.

Mock Chicken Kiev

Yield: 4 or 2 servings
Serving Size: ½ breast
Exchange List Approximation:
    Starch/Bread ½
    Meat, lean 3

Nutrient Content Per Serving:
CAL: 218   PRO: 30.6 (gm)
FAT: 6.2 (gm)   CHO: 7.5 (gm)
Na: 177.3 (mg)   K: 273.1 (mg)
Fiber: 0.3 (gm)   Chol: 84 (mg)

Ingredients

Four Servings		*Two Servings*	
4	CHICKEN BREAST HALVES, SKINNED, BONED	2	
4	TABLESPOONS SOUR CREAM	2	TABLESPOONS
2	TABLESPOONS CHOPPED PARSLEY	1	TABLESPOON
¼	TEASPOON OREGANO	⅛	TEASPOON
¼	TEASPOON MARJORAM	⅛	TEASPOON
	SPRINKLE SALT		SPRINKLE
	SPRINKLE PEPPER		SPRINKLE
6	TABLESPOONS DRY BREAD CRUMBS	3	TABLESPOONS

Method

1. Place chicken breast halves between sheets of waxed paper and pound to flatten.
2. Mix sour cream, parsley, oregano, and marjoram.
3. Salt and pepper chicken breasts and brush with sour cream mixture.
4. Roll up, beginning at long side, and secure with toothpicks. Brush remaining sour cream mixture on outside of the rolls and roll in dry bread crumbs.

5. Place rolls in shallow pan or casserole which has been sprayed with vegetable pan spray.
6. Cover and bake in 350° F oven for 45 minutes; uncover and bake 15 minutes longer.

Chicken Peanut Pasta

Yield: 6 or 3 servings
Serving Size: 1 cup
Exchange List Approximation:
    Starch/Bread 1½
    Meat, lean 3
    Fat ½

Nutrient Content Per Serving:
CAL: 304   PRO: 25.9 (gm)
FAT: 11.1 (gm)   CHO: 24.4 (gm)
Na: 399.8 (mg)   K: 302.1 (mg)
Fiber: 1.6 (gm)   Chol: 53 (mg)

Ingredients

Six Servings		*Three Servings*	
3	CUPS SPAGHETTI, BROKEN IN 2-INCH LENGTHS (ABOUT 6 OUNCES)	1½	CUPS (ABOUT 3 OUNCES)
2	QUARTS WATER	1	QUART
4	CHICKEN BREAST HALVES, SKINNED AND BONED	2	
1	EGG WHITE, BEATEN UNTIL FOAMY	1	
¼	TEASPOON WATER	¼	TEASPOON
2	TEASPOONS CORNSTARCH	1	TEASPOON
2	TEASPOONS MINCED GARLIC CLOVE	1	TEASPOON
2	TEASPOONS CHOPPED FRESH GINGER ROOT	1	TEASPOON
4	TEASPOONS VEGETABLE OIL	2	TEASPOONS

Six Servings	*Three Servings*
SPRINKLE CRUSHED RED PEPPER	SPRINKLE
2 TABLESPOONS SOY SAUCE	1 TABLESPOON
⅓ CUP VIRGINIA PEANUTS, COCKTAIL TYPE (ABOUT 1½ OUNCES)	¾ OUNCE
¼ CUP WHITE WINE OR WATER	2 TABLESPOONS
2 TEASPOONS SESAME SEED OIL	1 TEASPOON

Method

1. Cook spaghetti in boiling water about 12 minutes while preparing chicken.
2. Cut chicken into bite-size pieces.
3. Combine egg white, water, and cornstarch. Mix with chicken pieces.
4. Heat oil in wok or large skillet over medium heat. Add garlic and ginger root. Stir, then add half of chicken. Stir constantly until chicken meat turns white, about 2 minutes. Place in serving bowl. Stir-fry remaining chicken.
5. Return cooked chicken to skillet. Sprinkle lightly with crushed red pepper.
6. Add soy sauce, peanuts, and wine or water. Stir.
7. Drain spaghetti, add to chicken. Sprinkle with sesame seed oil, toss, and serve.
8. Garnish with chopped parsley.

Chicken Breasts in Sour Cream

Yield: 6 or 2 servings

Serving Size: 1 breast half plus
$\frac{1}{3}$ cup sauce

Exchange List Approximation:
Starch/Bread $\frac{1}{2}$
Meat, lean 4

Nutrient Content Per Serving:

CAL: 252	PRO: 31.4 (gm)
FAT: 10.3 (gm)	CHO: 6 (gm)
Na: 561.4 (mg)	K: 377.1 (mg)
Fiber: 0.4 (gm)	Chol: 87 (mg)

Ingredients

Six Servings		*Two Servings*	
6	CHICKEN BREAST HALVES, SKINNED	2	
¼	TEASPOON GARLIC POWDER	DASH	
1	10½-OUNCE CAN CREAM OF MUSHROOM SOUP	⅓	OF CAN
½	CUP SKIM MILK	3	TABLESPOONS
½	CUP SOUR CREAM	3	TABLESPOONS
¼	CUP SHERRY	1	TABLESPOON
1	4-OUNCE CAN MUSHROOM STEMS AND PIECES, DRAINED PAPRIKA	⅓	OF CAN

Method

1. Place chicken breasts in baking pan so they do not overlap. Sprinkle with garlic powder.
2. Mix soup, milk, sour cream, sherry, and drained mushrooms to make a sauce.
3. Spread over chicken. Sprinkle paprika lightly over top.
4. Bake in 375° F oven 45 minutes or until tender.
5. Serve with noodles or over whole-wheat toast (½ cup cooked noodles or 1 slice toast = 1 Starch/Bread Exchange).

Deviled Chicken Thighs

Yield: 6 or 2 servings
Serving Size: 1 thigh
Exchange List Approximation:
    Meat, lean 2

Nutrient Content Per Serving:

CAL: 113	PRO: 14.2 (gm)
FAT: 4.8 (gm)	CHO: 2.5 (gm)
Na: 179.8 (mg)	K: 178.6 (mg)
Fiber: 0.3 (gm)	Chol: 57 (mg)

Ingredients

Six Servings		*Two Servings*	
6	CHICKEN THIGHS, SKINNED	2	
1	TABLESPOON MARGARINE	1	TEASPOON
1	TABLESPOON PREPARED MUSTARD	1	TEASPOON
1	TABLESPOON VINEGAR	1	TEASPOON
½	TEASPOON PAPRIKA	⅛	TEASPOON
¼	TEASPOON BLACK PEPPER	¹⁄₁₆	TEASPOON
⅛	TEASPOON SALT		DASH
½	CUP FRESH BREAD CRUMBS (1 SLICE WHOLE-WHEAT BREAD)	3	TABLESPOONS

Method

1. Wash and dry chicken thighs.
2. Mix softened margarine with mustard, vinegar, and spices.
3. Place thighs meaty side up on shallow baking pan.
4. Spread mixture evenly over chicken.
5. Sprinkle with crumbs.
6. Bake in 425° F oven for 25 minutes. Do not overbake.

Key Lime Chicken Thighs

Yield: 4 or 2 servings
Serving Size: 2 thighs
Exchange List Approximation:
    Meat, lean 3

Nutrient Content Per Serving:
CAL: 175   PRO: 27.3 (gm)
FAT: 6.4 (gm)   CHO: 0.8 (gm)
Na: 219 (mg)   K: 328.5 (mg)
Fiber: 0   Chol: 114 (mg)

Ingredients

Four Servings		*Two Servings*	
8	CHICKEN THIGHS, SKINNED (ABOUT 2 POUNDS)	4	
1	TEASPOON MARGARINE	½	TEASPOON
2	TABLESPOONS LIME JUICE (1 LIME)	1	TABLESPOON
¼	TEASPOON ROSEMARY, CRUSHED	⅛	TEASPOON
¼	TEASPOON POULTRY SEASONING	⅛	TEASPOON
¼	TEASPOON CHICKEN BOUILLON GRANULES	⅛	TEASPOON
¼	TEASPOON PEPPER	⅛	TEASPOON
¼	TEASPOON PAPRIKA	⅛	TEASPOON

Method

1. Lightly grease baking pan. Space chicken thighs, meat side up, on pan. Do not overlap.
2. Squeeze lime juice over chicken.
3. Sprinkle seasonings evenly over chicken.
4. Bake in 425° F oven for 25 minutes. Do not overbake.
5. Remove chicken. Deglaze baking pan with about ⅓ cup water. Serve as sauce over chicken.

Oriental Chicken with Vegetables

Yield: 6 or 2 servings
Serving Size: 1 cup
Exchange List Approximation:
    Meat, lean 2
    Vegetable 2
    Fat 1

Nutrient Content Per Serving:
CAL: 209   PRO: 19.4 (gm)
FAT: 9.5 (gm)   CHO: 11.3 (gm)
Na: 574.1 (mg)   K: 476.5 (mg)
Fiber: 3.8 (gm)   Chol: 50 (mg)

Ingredients

Six Servings		*Two Servings*	
¾	CUP THINLY SLICED ONION	¼	CUP
2	TABLESPOONS VEGETABLE OIL	2	TEASPOONS
3	CUPS DIAGONALLY SLICED CELERY	1	CUP
1½	TEASPOONS MINCED FRESH GINGER	½	TEASPOON
1	CUP UNCOOKED PEAS OR HALF 10-OUNCE PACKAGE FROZEN PEAS	⅓	CUP
1½	CUPS CHICKEN BROTH OR BOUILLON	½	CUP
3	TABLESPOONS CORNSTARCH	1	TABLESPOON
1	TABLESPOON SOY SAUCE	1	TEASPOON
2	3-OUNCE CANS MUSHROOM CROWNS WITH BROTH	1	CAN
¾	POUND DICED, COOKED CHICKEN	¼	POUND

Method

1. In large, deep skillet, cook onion in oil until transparent. Stir in celery and ginger and cook for 1 minute. Stir in

peas, cover, and cook for about 4 minutes. Vegetables should be bright and tender-crisp. Remove vegetables and set aside.

2. Combine broth from one can of mushrooms, chicken broth, soy sauce, and cornstarch; pour into skillet. Cook, stirring constantly, until sauce thickens.

3. Stir in mushrooms, vegetables, and chicken; toss gently until all ingredients are covered with sauce. Cover and cook over moderate heat until meat is hot, about 5 minutes.

4. Serving suggestion: Serve over hot rice (1/3 cup cooked rice = 1 Starch/Bread Exchange).

*To reduce the sodium content, use salt-free broth and cut back on the amount of soy sauce used.

Smoked Fruity Roast Chicken

Yield: 4 servings

Serving Size: $\frac{1}{4}$ chicken and $\frac{1}{2}$ cup stuffing

Exchange List Approximation:
    Starch/Bread $1\frac{1}{2}$
    Meat, medium-fat 6
    Fruit 1

Nutrient Content Per Serving:

CAL: 640	PRO: 57 (gm)
FAT: 28.6 (gm)	CHO: 39.9 (gm)
Na: 406.8 (mg)*	K: 754.3 (mg)
Fiber: 4.2 (gm)	Chol: 234 (mg)

Key Source Nutrients:
    Protein: 57 (gm)
    Niacin: 17.2 (mg)

Ingredients

  4 SLICES WHOLE-WHEAT BREAD
1½ CUPS UNPEELED, DICED APPLES (WINESAP OR ROME)
  ½ CUP RAISINS
  ¼ CUP CHICKEN BROTH
  2 TABLESPOONS UNSWEETENED APPLE CIDER
  1 TEASPOON CINNAMON
  1 EGG, BEATEN
  1 BROILER-FRYER CHICKEN, 3 TO 3½ POUNDS
  ⅓ CUP LIQUID HICKORY SMOKE
  ¼ TEASPOON MONOSODIUM GLUTAMATE*
     SPRINKLE PAPRIKA

Method

1. Prepare stuffing for chicken. Tear bread into pieces and mix with apples, raisins, broth, cider, and cinnamon. Lightly stir in egg.
2. Spoon stuffing mix into cavity of cleaned whole chicken. Hook wing tips back and tie legs together.
3. Place in a shallow baking pan on rack. Brush liquid smoke

over chicken and sprinkle with paprika and monosodium glutamate.
4. Bake uncovered in 350° F oven about 1½ hours or until legs move freely when lifted or turned.
5. When chicken is done, brush again with liquid smoke.

*If you eliminate monosodium glutamate, sodium content will be reduced.

NOTE: If chicken is skinned, nutrient information is as follows:

Exchange List Approximation:
  Starch/Bread 1½
  Meat, lean 5
  Fruit 1

Nutrient Content Per Serving:
  CAL: 457   PRO: 45.8 (gm)
  FAT: 13.1 (gm)   CHO: 39.9 (gm)
  Na: 377.9 (mg)*   K: 671.1 (mg)
  Fiber: 4.2 (gm)   Chol: 192 (mg)

Chicken with Tortilla Dressing

Yield: 6 servings
Serving Size: 1 cup
Exchange List Approximation:
  Starch/Bread 1
  Meat, lean 2
  Vegetable 2
  Fat $\frac{1}{2}$

Nutrient Content Per Serving:
CAL: 255   PRO: 18.2 (gm)
FAT: 8.9 (gm)   CHO: 25.6 (gm)
Na: 556.9 (mg)   K: 331.9 (mg)
Fiber: 2.8 (gm)   Chol: 42 (mg)

Ingredients

2½ POUNDS FRYING CHICKEN, FAT REMOVED
 3 CUPS WATER
 1 10½-OUNCE CAN CREAM OF MUSHROOM SOUP
 1 CUP DICED CELERY
 1 CUP CHOPPED ONION
 1 TEASPOON POULTRY SEASONING
 ½ TEASPOON PEPPER
 9 CORN TORTILLAS

Method

1. Place chicken and water in large saucepan. Bring to a boil. Cover and simmer about 1 hour until tender.
2. Remove chicken and boil stock gently about 5 minutes to concentrate. There should be 2½ to 3 cups.
3. Stir in soup, celery, onions, and seasonings.
4. Skin and bone chicken. Cut into large pieces (about 2 cups).
5. Pour ½ cup of stock into 2½-quart casserole.
6. Dip tortillas (one at a time) in stock. Break into pieces and place layer of 3 in casserole.

7. Add layer of chicken, cup of stock, layer of tortillas, layer of chicken, and stock; top with layer of tortillas.
8. Pour remaining stock over top. Cover and bake in 350° F oven for 30 minutes. Remove cover. Bake another 10 minutes.

Two-Way Chicken Enchiladas

Yield: 6 servings
Serving Size: 2 enchiladas or
  1 piece, 4½ by 4 inches
Exchange List Approximation:
    Starch/Bread 2½
    Meat, lean 4
    Fat 1

Nutrient Content Per Serving:

CAL: 466	PRO: 35.6 (gm)
FAT: 20.2 (gm)*	CHO: 36.3 (gm)
Na: 999.2 (mg)*	K: 546.4 (mg)
Fiber: 3.7 (gm)	Chol: 97 (mg)

Ingredients

  4 CHICKEN BREAST HALVES
    WATER TO COVER
  ¼ TEASPOON SALT
  1 16-OUNCE CAN TOMATOES, CHOPPED
  1 10½-OUNCE CAN CREAM OF CHICKEN SOUP
  1 4-OUNCE CAN CHOPPED GREEN CHILIES
  1 TEASPOON GROUND CUMIN
    SCANT ½ TEASPOON GARLIC POWDER
  1 CUP CHOPPED ONION
  2 CUPS SHREDDED CHEDDAR CHEESE
 12 CORN TORTILLAS

Method

1. Cover chicken with water and simmer 30 minutes. Remove chicken and reserve broth.
2. Skin and bone chicken. Cut each half into 3 strips. Sprinkle with salt and set aside.
3. Mix tomatoes, soup, chilies, cumin, and garlic powder.
4. Assemble each enchilada individually: dip tortilla in warm broth to soften and place in a flat plan. Place strip of chicken on tortilla, add 2 Tablespoons cheese, 1 teaspoon chopped onion, and 1 teaspoon sauce. Roll up and place seam side down in baking pan.
5. Sprinkle with onion, pour remaining sauce evenly over enchiladas and sprinkle with remaining cheese.
6. Bake in 350° F oven for 35 minutes or until bubbly.

Variation in Method

1. For Casserole: follow directions 1 to 3 above, then dip half of tortillas in warm broth to soften, break into pieces and place in a layer in 9-inch × 13-inch baking pan.
2. Spread chicken evenly over tortillas. Sprinkle with half the onions. Spread with layer of sauce and half the cheese.
3. Dip remaining tortillas in broth, break apart, and layer over sauce. Sprinkle with onion.
4. Pour sauce over casserole. Sprinkle with remaining cheese.
5. Bake in 350° F oven for 40 minutes or until bubbly.
6. Let cool 5 minutes. Cut casserole 2 by 3 into pieces 4½ inches × 4 inches each.

*This recipe is high in fat and sodium. You may want to reserve it for occasional use only.

Chicken Tacos

Yield: 12 tacos
Serving Size: 1 taco
Exchange List Approximation:
    Starch/Bread 1
    Meat, medium-fat 2
    Vegetable 1

Nutrient Content Per Serving:
CAL: 256   PRO: 20.5 (gm)
FAT: 10.5 (gm)   CHO: 19.2 (gm)
Na: 152.8 (mg)   K: 199.8 (mg)
Fiber: 1.3 (gm)   Chol: 56 (mg)

Ingredients

 1 PACKAGE FLOUR TORTILLAS (12 6-INCH)
 1 CHICKEN (3 TO 3½ POUNDS)
 1 PACKAGE TACO SEASONING MIX
 6 OUNCES CHEDDAR CHEESE, SHREDDED
12 TABLESPOONS SOUR CREAM (OPTIONAL)*
   SHREDDED LETTUCE
   CHOPPED TOMATO
   CHOPPED ONION

Method

1. Remove skin from chicken and simmer until meat falls off the bone. Cut meat into small pieces.
2. In a skillet combine cooked chicken, taco seasoning, and 1½ cups water. Bring to a boil then simmer to desired consistency (10 to 15 minutes).
3. Shred cheese. Heat tortillas in microwave or iron skillet. Place 2 ounces chicken mix in the center of each tortilla. Top with ½ ounce cheddar cheese, 1 Tablespoon sour cream,* shredded lettuce, chopped tomato, and chopped onion. Roll up.

*If sour cream is used, add ½ Fat to exchanges, and 2 grams fat and 20 calories to estimated nutrients.

Chicken Green-Bean Casserole

Yield: 6 or 2 servings
Serving Size: 1 cup
Exchange List Approximation:
    Starch/Bread 1
    Meat, lean 1
    Vegetable 1
    Fat 1

Nutrient Content Per Serving:
CAL: 210   PRO: 13.2 (gm)
FAT: 9.4 (gm)   CHO: 19.8 (gm)
Na: 377.8 (mg)   K: 256.4 (mg)
Fiber: 3.2 (gm)   Chol: 36 (mg)

Ingredients

Six Servings		*Two Servings*
½	CUP LONG-GRAIN AND WILD RICE	3 TABLESPOONS
2	CUPS WATER	1 CUP
½	10½-OUNCE CAN CREAM OF CELERY SOUP	3 TABLESPOONS
½	CUP SKIM MILK	3 TABLESPOONS
3	TABLESPOONS MAYONNAISE	1 TABLESPOON
1½	CUPS COOKED, DICED CHICKEN	½ CUP
1	16-OUNCE CAN FRENCH-STYLE GREEN BEANS, DRAINED	⅓ CUP
½	CUP DICED ONION	3 TABLESPOONS
¾	CUP SLICED WATER CHESTNUTS (ABOUT 4 OUNCES)	¼ CUP
4	TABLESPOONS CHOPPED PIMENTO	4 TEASPOONS

Method

1. Add rice to boiling water; bring to a boil, cover, reduce heat, and simmer until tender, 30 minutes to 1 hour. Water will be absorbed. Do not use seasoning packet.

2. Add remaining ingredients to rice. Mix well.
3. Pour in lightly greased 2½ quart casserole.
4. Cover and bake in 350° F oven 30 minutes.

Note: This casserole is so good, make 6 servings, package extra servings, and freeze for later use.

Fanny's Chicken and Rice

Yield: 6 or 2 servings
Serving Size: 1 breast half
  or 1 leg
Exchange List Approximation:
  Starch/Bread 1
  Meat, lean 3½
  Vegetable 2

Nutrient Content Per Serving:
CAL: 322   PRO: 32.8 (gm)
FAT: 9 (gm)   CHO: 26.4 (gm)
Na: 373.3 (mg)   K: 574.5 (mg)
Fiber: 4.4 (gm)   Chol: 79 (mg)

Ingredients

Six Servings		*Two Servings*	
¾	CUP BROWN RICE	¼	CUP
3	CUPS WATER	1	CUP
3	CHICKEN BREASTS, SPLIT AND SKINNED	1	BREAST
or			
6	CHICKEN LEG QUARTERS, SKINNED	2	
1	TABLESPOON VEGETABLE OIL	1	TEASPOON
1	CUP CHOPPED ONIONS	⅓	CUP
¾	CUP CHOPPED GREEN PEPPER	¼	CUP
¾	TEASPOON MINCED GARLIC	¼	TEASPOON

Six Servings	Two Servings
2 TEASPOONS CURRY POWDER	¾ TEASPOON
½ TEASPOON SALT	⅛ TEASPOON
½ TEASPOON THYME	⅛ TEASPOON
1 16-OUNCE CAN TOMATOES	⅓ CAN (ABOUT ⅔ CUP)
1 TABLESPOON CHOPPED PARSLEY	1 TEASPOON
2 TABLESPOONS CURRANTS	2 TEASPOONS
¼ CUP TOASTED ALMONDS (ABOUT 1 OUNCE)	1 TABLESPOON

Method

1. Cook rice while preparing chicken and sauce. Add to boiling water, cover, and simmer 1 hour.
2. Place chicken in 2-inch-deep baking pan. Bake chicken in 425° F oven, 25 minutes. Do not overbake.
3. Make sauce. Saute onion, peppers, and garlic in oil, add spices and blend thoroughly. Add tomatoes and parsley. Heat.
4. Pour sauce over chicken, sprinkle with currants. Cover and bake at 350° F for 30 minutes.
5. Arrange chicken serving with ½ cup rice on plate. Pour ½ cup sauce over rice. Sprinkle 2 teaspoons almonds over chicken.

Chicken Livers Oregano

Yield: 6 or 2 servings
Serving Size: ½ cup
Exchange List Approximation:
    Meat, medium-fat 1
    Vegetable ½

Nutrient Content Per Serving:
CAL: 84   PRO: 12.2 (gm)
FAT: 2.8 (gm)   CHO: 2.3 (gm)
Na: 302.4 (mg) K: 111.4 (mg)
Fiber: 1.3 (gm) Chol: 307 (mg)
Key Source Nutrients:
    Vitamin A: 8103 (IU)
    Folacin: 387 (mcg)
    Vitamin B$_{12}$: 9 (mcg)

Ingredients

Six Servings
1 POUND CHICKEN LIVERS
SCANT ½ TEASPOON SALT
SCANT ½ TEASPOON OREGANO
    SPRINKLE PEPPER
1 CUP WATER
1¾ CUPS CUT GREEN BEANS,
    DRAINED (ABOUT 1 16-OUNCE
    CAN)

Two Servings
5 OUNCES
⅛ TEASPOON
⅛ TEASPOON
SPRINKLE
⅓ CUP
½ CUP

Method

1. Wash and trim chicken livers.
2. Place in skillet. Sprinkle with seasonings. Add water. Bring to a simmer, cover tightly, and simmer 10 minutes, turning occasionally.
3. Remove liver. Bring broth to a boil. Add green beans and heat to a simmer. Add livers and stir to mix.
4. Serving suggestion: Serve ½ cup over cooked rice or toasted bread points (⅓ cup cooked rice or 1 full slice of bread = 1 Starch/Bread Exchange).

Duke of Kent Chicken

Yield: 6 or 2 servings
Serving Size: 1 cup
Exchange List Approximation:
    Starch/Bread 2
    Meat, lean 2
    Fat 1

Nutrient Content Per Serving:
CAL: 312   PRO: 19.7 (gm)
FAT: 13.6 (gm)   CHO: 28.7 (gm)
Na: 319.9 (mg)   K: 321.1 (mg)
Fiber: 3.5 (gm)   Chol: 48 (mg)

Ingredients

Six Servings	Two Servings
¾ CUP BROWN RICE	¼ CUP
2¼ CUPS WATER OR CHICKEN STOCK	1 CUP
½ 10½-OUNCE CAN CREAM OF MUSHROOM SOUP	3 TABLESPOONS
½ CUP SKIM MILK	3 TABLESPOONS
3 TABLESPOONS LEMON JUICE	1 TABLESPOON
2 CUPS COOKED, DICED CHICKEN	⅔ CUP
4 TABLESPOONS PIMENTO, CHOPPED	4 TEASPOONS
½ CUP SLIVERED ALMONDS	2½ TABLESPOONS
¾ CUP WATER CHESTNUTS, SLICED (ABOUT ½ 8-OUNCE CAN)	¼ CUP
½ CUP SHREDDED CHEDDAR CHEESE	3 TABLESPOONS

Method

1. Place brown rice in boiling chicken stock; bring back to a boil, reduce heat, cover, and cook 50 minutes.

2. Combine soup and milk and stir in lemon juice.
3. Add chicken, pimento, almonds, chestnuts, and rice. Toss together to mix.
4. Place in a 2½-quart casserole sprayed with vegetable spray.
5. Sprinkle shredded cheese over top, cover, and bake 30 minutes at 350° F.

*May be too high in salt for frequent use, but ideal for entertaining.

Veggie Fried Rice

Yield: 6 or 2 servings
Serving Size: 1½ cup
Exchange List Approximation:
   Starch/Bread 1¼
   Meat, lean 2
   Vegetable 1

Nutrient Content Per Serving:

CAL: 260	PRO: 18.8 (gm)
FAT: 7.2 (gm)	CHO: 29.6 (gm)
Na: 749.1 (mg)	K: 366.9 (mg)
Fiber: 2 (gm)	Chol: 87 (mg)

Key Source Nutrients:
   Vitamin A: 3772 (IU)

Ingredients

Six Servings		Two Servings	
1	TABLESPOON VEGETABLE OIL	1	TEASPOON
4	TABLESPOONS SOY SAUCE	4	TEASPOONS
2	TEASPOONS CIDER VINEGAR OR LEMON JUICE	½	TEASPOON
1	TEASPOON BROWN SUGAR	¼	TEASPOON
¼	TEASPOON CRUSHED RED PEPPER		SPRINKLE
SCANT ½	TEASPOON CHINESE 5-SPICE	⅛	TEASPOON
½	CUP CHOPPED GREEN ONIONS	3	TABLESPOONS
1	TEASPOON MINCED GARLIC CLOVE	⅓	TEASPOON

Six Servings	*Two Servings*
½ CUP THINLY SLICED CARROTS	3 TABLESPOONS
1½ CUPS BROCCOLI PIECES, CUT INTO ½" CHUNKS	½ CUP
2 CUPS DICED, COOKED CHICKEN (ABOUT 10 OUNCES)	⅔ CUP
1 EGG, LIGHTLY BEATEN	⅓
3 CUPS COOKED RICE	1 CUP

Method

1. In a wok or large skillet, add oil and coat surface. Add soy sauce, vinegar, sugar, and spices. Heat over medium heat.
2. Add vegetables and stir-fry 2 to 3 minutes.
3. Add chicken and egg. Stir-fry until egg is cooked.
4. Add rice, toss, and cook until heated through.

*To reduce sodium content, use mild soy sauce or cut back on the amount of soy sauce used.

Chicken Livers Oregano with Wild Rice

Yield: 6 or 2 servings
Serving Size: $\frac{1}{6}$ recipe
Exchange List Approximation:
    Starch/Bread $\frac{1}{2}$
    Meat, medium-fat 1
    Vegetable 2

Nutrient Content Per Serving:
CAL: 155   PRO: 15.1 (gm)
FAT: 2.9 (gm)   CHO: 17.4 (gm)
Na: 303.9 (mg)   K: 155.4 (mg)
Fiber: 2.8 (gm)   Chol: 307 (mg)
Key Source Nutrients:
    Vitamin A: 8103 (IU)
    Folacin: 390 (mcg)
    Vitamin B$_{12}$: 9 (mcg)

Ingredients

Six Servings	Two Servings
¾ CUP LONG-GRAIN AND WILD RICE	¼ CUP
3 CUPS WATER	1 CUP
1 POUND CHICKEN LIVERS	⅓ POUND
SCANT ½ TEASPOON SALT	⅛ TEASPOON
SCANT ½ TEASPOON OREGANO	⅛ TEASPOON
SPRINKLE PEPPER	SPRINKLE
1 CUP WATER	⅓ CUP
1¾ CUPS CUT GREEN BEANS, DRAINED (ABOUT 1 16-OUNCE CAN)	½ CUP

Method

1. Wash rice. Add water, bring to a boil, reduce heat, cover, and cook until water is absorbed, about 1 hour.
2. Wash and trim livers.
3. Place in skillet. Sprinkle with seasonings, toss. Add water. Bring to a boil, cover tightly, and simmer 10 minutes, turning once.

4. Remove liver. Bring broth to a boil, add beans, and heat to a simmer.
5. Add rice and livers. Toss and heat.

Turkey and Wild-Rice Casserole

Yield: 6 servings
Serving Size: $\frac{1}{6}$ recipe
Exchange List Approximation:
    Starch/Bread $1\frac{1}{2}$
    Meat, lean 2

Nutrient Content Per Serving:
CAL: 233   PRO: 22.2 (gm)
FAT: 7.7 (gm)   CHO: 20 (gm)
Na: 415.2 (mg)   K: 412.8 (mg)
Fiber: 2.6 (gm)   Chol: 45 (mg)

Ingredients

- ½ CUP NATURAL LONG-GRAIN AND WILD RICE (ABOUT 3 OUNCES)
- 2 CUPS WATER
- ¼ TEASPOON SALT
- 8 OUNCES FRESH MUSHROOMS, SLICED
- 1 TABLESPOON MARGARINE
- 2 TABLESPOONS FLOUR
- 1 CUP SKIM MILK
- 1 TEASPOON CHICKEN BOUILLON GRANULES
- 1/16 TEASPOON PEPPER
- 2 CUPS CUBED, COOKED TURKEY (ABOUT 12 OUNCES)
- 4 TABLESPOONS SLICED PIMENTO
- ½ CUP SLICED WATER CHESTNUTS (ABOUT 2 OUNCES)
- ¼ CUP SLICED ALMONDS (ABOUT 1 OUNCE)

Method

1. Wash rice. Add water and salt, bring to boil, cover, and simmer about 1 hour until water is absorbed.
2. In large skillet, saute mushrooms in margarine about 3 minutes. Stir in flour. Add milk, bouillon and pepper. Cook until thickened, stirring constantly.
3. Add turkey, pimento, water chestnuts, and rice. Mix and pour into 7- by 11-inch baking dish. Sprinkle with sliced almonds.
4. Cover and bake in 350° F oven for 30 minutes. Uncover and bake about 3 minutes. Cut into 6 servings, 2 inches by 3 inches.

Ground Turkey Loaf

Yield: 1 loaf (12 slices)
Serving Size: 1 slice
Exchange List Approximation:
    Meat, medium-fat 2
    Fat ½

Nutrient Content Per Serving:
CAL: 167   PRO: 14.4 (gm)
FAT: 11.4 (gm)   CHO: 2.2 (gm)
Na: 595.1 (mg)   K: 240.3 (mg)
Fiber: 0.2 (gm)   Chol: 88 (mg)

Ingredients

2 POUNDS GROUND TURKEY, UNCOOKED
⅓ CUP OATMEAL
¼ CUP CATSUP
2 TABLESPOONS CHOPPED ONION
½ TEASPOON SALT
½ TEASPOON OREGANO
½ TEASPOON PEPPER
2 EGGS

Method

1. Place ingredients, except turkey, in mixing bowl. Mix thoroughly and let stand a few minutes.
2. Mix in turkey until well blended.
3. Shape into loaf. Place in 5- by 9-inch loaf pan or in shallow pan with a little water.
4. Bake in 325° F oven for 1 hour or until meat thermometer registers 160° to 165° F.
5. Cool to set loaf. Slice into ½-inch slices. Extra slices may be used for sandwiches.

Fish

Twenty-Minute Bouillabaise

Yield: 4 servings (4½ cups)
Serving Size: 1 cup
Exchange List Approximation:
    Meat, lean 2
    Vegetable 2

Nutrient Content Per Serving:
CAL: 160   PRO: 24.1 (gm)
FAT: 3.9 (gm)   CHO: 7 (gm)
Na: 468.8 (mg)   K: 569.9 (mg)
Fiber: 1.5 (gm)   Chol: 77 (mg)

Ingredients

  2 TEASPOONS VEGETABLE OIL
  ½ CUP CHOPPED ONION
  ½ TEASPOON MINCED GARLIC CLOVE (ABOUT ½)
    PINCH THYME
  1 TEASPOON CHOPPED FRESH BASIL (OPTIONAL)
  1 15-OUNCE CAN TOMATOES
  ½ CUP WATER
  ½ CUP WHITE WINE OR WATER
  ½ POUND ROCK COD, BUTTERFISH, OR TURBOT
  ¼ POUND COOKED SHRIMP
  1 6¼-OUNCE CAN CHOPPED CLAMS

Method

1. Saute onion, garlic, and herbs in oil until tender, about 5 minutes.
2. Add can of tomatoes, water, and wine. Simmer 5 minutes, stirring to break up tomatoes.
3. Cut fish into 1-inch pieces and add to tomatoes. Bring to a boil and simmer 5 to 7 minutes until fish is done.
4. Add shrimp and clams with juice. Heat thoroughly.
5. Serve immediately or hold over very low heat. Salt and pepper may be added to taste.

Poached Fish and Peas

Yield: 6 or 2 servings
Serving Size: 1 cup
Exchange List Approximation:
    Starch/Bread $\frac{1}{2}$
    Meat, lean $3\frac{1}{2}$

Nutrient Content Per Serving:
CAL: 232   PRO: 27.8 (gm)
FAT: 9.1 (gm)   CHO: 8.1 (gm)
Na: 285 (mg)   K: 651.9 (mg)
Fiber: 3.1 (gm)   Chol: 60 (mg)

Ingredients

Six Servings		*Two Servings*	
1	TABLESPOON MARGARINE	1	TEASPOON
½	CUP CHOPPED ONION	3	TABLESPOONS
1	TEASPOON MINCED GARLIC CLOVE	¼	TEASPOON
½	CUP CARROTS, CUT INTO 1-INCH STRIPS	3	TABLESPOONS
2¼	CUPS FROZEN PEAS (ABOUT 1 10-OUNCE PACKAGE)	¾	CUP
1	BAY LEAF	⅓	
¾	TEASPOON TARRAGON OR MINT	¼	TEASPOON
¼	TEASPOON SALT	⅟₁₆	TEASPOON
¼	TEASPOON PEPPER	⅟₁₆	TEASPOON
½	CUP WHITE WINE	3	TABLESPOONS
½	CUP WATER	3	TABLESPOONS
6	STUFFED SPANISH OLIVES (OPTIONAL)	2	
1½	POUNDS FRESH OR FROZEN FISH, CUT INTO 2-INCH PIECES	8	OUNCES

Method

1. Use a large skillet or saucepan. Cook onions and garlic in margarine about 2 minutes.
2. Add remaining ingredients except fish. Bring to a boil, cover, and simmer about 8 minutes.
3. Add fish, bring to a simmer. Cover and poach (just below boiling) for about 5 minutes.
4. Serve over rice or in soup bowls. (⅓ cup cooked rice = 1 Starch/Bread Exchange).

Tomato-Glazed Fish Fillets

Yield: 4 servings
Serving Size: 1 fillet and
$\frac{1}{2}$ cup sauce
Exchange List Approximation:
    Meat, lean 3
    Vegetable 1

Nutrient Content Per Serving:
CAL: 175   PRO: 30.1 (gm)
FAT: 2.2 (gm)   CHO: 8.7 (gm)
Na: 658.7 (mg)   K: 714.6 (mg)
Fiber: 1.6 (gm)   Chol: 42 (mg)

Ingredients

  1 MEDIUM ONION, THINLY SLICED
  1 TEASPOON VEGETABLE OIL
  1 4-OUNCE CAN MUSHROOMS, STEMS AND PIECES, DRAINED
  1 POUND COD OR HADDOCK FILLETS
  ½ TEASPOON GARLIC SALT*
  ½ TEASPOON GRATED LEMON RIND
  ¼ TEASPOON DILL WEED
1½ CUPS TOMATO JUICE
  4 TEASPOONS LEMON JUICE

1 TABLESPOON FLOUR
1 PACKET SUGAR SUBSTITUTE (OPTIONAL)
1 TABLESPOON CHOPPED PARSLEY

Method

1. Heat oil in large skillet. Add onions and saute about 5 minutes. Add mushrooms.
2. Arrange fish over onions. Sprinkle with garlic salt, lemon rind, and dill weed. Add tomato juice.
3. Bring to a simmer, cover, and cook over moderate heat 10 minutes or until fish is easily flaked with a fork. Remove fish to a heated platter.
4. Blend lemon juice and flour together. Gradually add ½ cup of tomato sauce. Stir back into sauce.
5. Add sweetener, stir, and cook over moderate heat until thickened, about 2 minutes.
6. Serve ½ cup sauce over each fillet and sprinkle with parsley.

*To reduce sodium content, substitute fresh garlic or garlic powder for garlic salt.

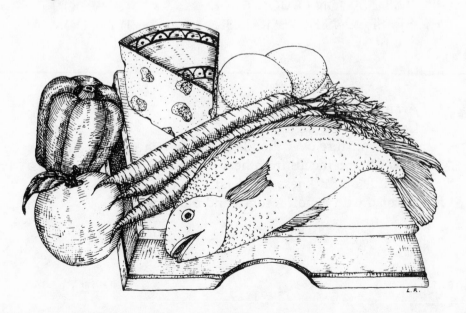

Broiled Fillet of Sole with Parmesan Sauce

Yield: 6 or 2 servings
Serving Size: $\frac{1}{6}$ recipe
Exchange List Approximation:
    Meat, lean $2\frac{1}{2}$

Nutrient Content Per Serving:

CAL: 148	PRO: 29.5 (gm)
FAT: 1.8 (gm)	CHO: 1.6 (gm)
Na: 297.8 (mg)	K: 594.5 (mg)
Fiber: 0.1 (gm)	Chol: 45 (mg)

Ingredients

Six Servings	Two Servings
1½ POUNDS SOLE OR FLOUNDER (FRESH OR FROZEN)	½ POUND
6 TABLESPOONS PLAIN LOW-FAT YOGURT	2 TABLESPOONS
2 TABLESPOONS GRATED PARMESAN CHEESE	2 TEASPOONS
1 TABLESPOON DIJON-STYLE MUSTARD	1 TEASPOON
1 TABLESPOON LEMON JUICE	1 TEASPOON
1½ TEASPOONS HORSERADISH	½ TEASPOON

Method

1. Arrange fish on broiler pan.
2. Combine sauce ingredients.
3. Spread mixture over the fillets in a thin layer.
4. Broil about 8 inches from heat for about 6 minutes (time depends on thickness of fillets).
5. Garnish with lemon wedges and dill sprigs.

Fish-Tomato Sauce for Rice

Yield: 6 or 2 servings
Serving Size: $\frac{2}{3}$ cup sauce plus
  $\frac{1}{2}$ cup rice
Exchange List Approximation:
  Starch/Bread 2
  Meat, lean $1\frac{1}{2}$
  Vegetable 1

Nutrient Content Per Serving:
CAL: 273   PRO: 24.2 (gm)
FAT: 3.5 (gm)   CHO: 36.1 (gm)
Na: 613.5 (mg)   K: 930.3 (mg)
Fiber: 2.3 (gm)   Chol: 31 (mg)

Ingredients

Six Servings
1½ CUPS SLICED ONION
  1 TEASPOON MINCED GARLIC
     CLOVE
  1 TABLESPOON OLIVE OIL
  1 8-OUNCE CAN TOMATO SAUCE
  1 6-OUNCE CAN TOMATO PASTE
 ¾ CUP WATER
  1 POUND FILLET OF SOLE OR
     FLOUNDER (6 PIECES)
  3 CUPS COOKED RICE

Two Servings
 ½ CUP
 ⅓ TEASPOON

  1 TEASPOON
 ⅓ CAN
 ⅓ CAN
 ¼ CUP
  5 OUNCES (2)

  1 CUP

Method

1. Saute sliced onion and garlic in olive oil in deep pan about
   10 minutes. Do not burn garlic.
2. Add tomato sauce, paste, and water. Stir. Bring to a
   simmer and cook 10 minutes, stirring occasionally.
3. Add fish and cook until tender, about 5 minutes. Stir
   occasionally. Fish breaks apart. Do not overcook fish as it
   will become tough.
4. Serve ⅔ cup sauce over ½ cup cooked rice.

Variation: Fish-tomato sauce is also good served over spaghetti.

Oven-Fried Catfish

Yield: 4 servings
Serving Size: $\frac{1}{4}$ recipe
Exchange List Approximation:
    Starch/Bread $\frac{1}{2}$
    Meat, lean 2

Nutrient Content Per Serving:
CAL: 155   PRO: 19 (gm)
FAT: 5.8 (gm)   CHO: 5.3 (gm)
Na: 379.5 (mg) K: 363.8 (mg)
Fiber: 0.2 (gm) Chol: 75 (mg)

Ingredients

1¼ POUNDS WHOLE, HEADLESS CATFISH (4)
  2 TABLESPOONS LOW-FAT YOGURT
  2 TEASPOONS VEGETABLE OIL
1½ TEASPOONS LEMON JUICE
 ¼ TEASPOON PAPRIKA
 ½ TEASPOON SALT
 ⅛ TEASPOON PEPPER
  4 TABLESPOONS DRY WHOLE-WHEAT BREAD CRUMBS

Method

1. Wash and drain fish.
2. Combine yogurt, oil, lemon juice, and seasonings in shallow dish.
3. Sprinkle bread crumbs on wax paper.
4. Dip fish in yogurt mixture, then press in crumbs, lightly coating both sides.
5. Place fish on lightly greased cookie sheet or shallow baking pan.
6. Bake in 475° F oven for 10 minutes or until done.

Note: One pound flounder or sole fillets may be used. Reduce baking time to 8 minutes.

Fish-Spinach Birds

Yield: 6 servings
Serving Size: 1 fillet
Exchange List Approximation:
    Meat, lean 2
    Vegetable 2

Nutrient Content Per Serving:
CAL: 169   PRO: 26.1 (gm)
FAT: 1.8 (gm)   CHO: 11.5 (gm)
Na: 551.7 (mg)   K: 720.5 (mg)
Fiber: 1.8 (gm)   Chol: 36 (mg)

Ingredients

1 10-OUNCE PACKAGE FROZEN CHOPPED SPINACH
½ CUP DRY BREAD CRUMBS
1 4-OUNCE CAN MUSHROOMS, STEMS AND PIECES
6 TABLESPOONS LIGHT ITALIAN SALAD DRESSING
   (DIVIDED)
1¼ POUNDS FLOUNDER FILLETS (ABOUT 6 PIECES)
10 OUNCES FRESH TOMATOES (ABOUT 3 SMALL)

Method

1. Thaw spinach and drain thoroughly. Chop mushrooms and combine with spinach, bread crumbs, and 4 tablespoons salad dressing.
2. Spread mixture equally over fillets. Roll and secure with toothpicks.
3. Place in lightly greased baking dish. Drizzle with remaining 2 tablespoons salad dressing.
4. Bake in 350° F oven for 10 minutes. Add tomatoes, cut into wedges. Bake 10 minutes, or until fish flakes.

Swordfish or Salmon Kabobs

Yield: 4 servings
Serving Size: $\frac{1}{4}$ recipe
Exchange List Approximation:
    Meat, lean $2\frac{1}{2}$
    Vegetable 2

Nutrient Content Per Serving:
CAL: 191   PRO: 22 (gm)
FAT: 5.9 (gm)   CHO: 12.9 (gm)
Na: 93.5 (mg)   K: 711.6 (mg)
Fiber: 5 (gm)   Chol: 33 (mg)
Key Source Nutrients:
    Ascorbic acid: 46 (mg)

Ingredients

¾ POUND SWORDFISH, CUBED, OR SALMON
1 SMALL ONION, CHOPPED
⅛ TEASPOON GROUND BLACK PEPPER
3 TABLESPOONS LEMON JUICE
10 BAY LEAVES
4 SMALL ONIONS OR WEDGES
4 GREEN-PEPPER SQUARES
1 TOMATO, CUT INTO 4 WEDGES
4 ZUCCHINI WEDGES
4 MUSHROOM CAPS

Method

1. Combine onion, pepper, salt,* lemon juice, and fish cubes. Marinate for 4 to 6 hours in refrigerator.
2. One hour before cooking time, pour a cup of boiling water over bay leaves. Let stand.
3. On skewers, alternate: fish, bay leaves, vegetable cubes. Pour marinade over skewered food.
4. Barbecue or broil 8 to 10 minutes, turning once, until fish is golden brown and flakes easily. Discard bay leaves.
5. Serving suggestion: Serve on rice (⅓ cup cooked rice = 1 Starch/Bread Exchange).

*Note: Salt only if desired.

Tasty Cod

Yield: 6 servings
Serving Size: $\frac{1}{6}$ recipe
Exchange List Approximation:
    Meat, lean 2
    Vegetable 1

Nutrient Content Per Serving:
CAL: 140   PRO: 29.1 (gm)
FAT: 0.8 (gm)   CHO: 2.9 (gm)
Na: 214.4 (mg)   K: 540.3 (mg)
Fiber: 1.1 (gm)   Chol: 42 (mg)
Key Source Nutrients:
    Vitamin A: 5351 (IU)

Ingredients

1½ POUNDS FROZEN COD FILLET
¼ TEASPOON SALT
¼ TEASPOON PEPPER
1 TEASPOON TARRAGON
1 TABLESPOON LEMON JUICE
1 CUP CHOPPED MUSHROOMS
1 CUP THINLY SLICED CARROTS
½ CUP CHOPPED CELERY
2 TABLESPOONS FRESH CHOPPED PARSLEY

Method

1. Place the frozen fish on a sheet of aluminum foil; lightly salt and pepper.
2. Sprinkle with tarragon and lemon juice. Add all the chopped vegetables and the fresh parsley. Dot with butter and wrap well.
3. Bake at 350° F for 35 to 45 minutes.

Note: Fillet may be cut into 6 pieces and individual servings wrapped in foil before baking.

Tuna- or Salmon-Rice Pie

Yield: 6 servings
Serving Size: $\frac{1}{6}$ pie
Exchange List Approximation:
    Starch/Bread 1
    Meat, lean 2
    Fat $\frac{1}{2}$

Nutrient Content Per Serving:
CAL: 222   PRO: 16.5 (gm)
FAT: 9.4 (gm)   CHO: 17.2 (gm)
Na: 273.1 (mg)   K: 268.6 (mg)
Fiber: 2.8 (gm)   Chol: 118 (mg)

Ingredients

- ⅓ CUP RICE
- 1 CUP WATER
- ⅛ TEASPOON SALT
- 1 TEASPOON MARGARINE
- 2 EGGS (DIVIDED)
- 1 6½-OUNCE CAN WATER-PACKED TUNA OR SALMON, DRAINED
- ¾ CUP SKIM MILK
- 2 CUPS FROZEN PEAS
- ½ TEASPOON PARSLEY FLAKES
- ¼ TEASPOON PEPPER
- ⅛ TEASPOON NUTMEG
- 4 SLICES LOW-FAT SWISS CHEESE

Method

1. Bring rice to boil in salted water, cover, and simmer 14 minutes. Mix with fork and stir in margarine and 1 beaten egg.
2. Place in 9-inch pie pan sprayed with vegetable pan spray. Press against sides and bottom of pan to make crust.
3. Spread tuna or salmon evenly over rice.
4. Heat milk and peas to a simmer. Add seasonings.

5. Beat remaining egg. Gradually stir in milk mixture. Pour over tuna.
6. Layer slices of cheese over top. Bake in 350° F oven for 25 minutes.

Mock Lobster Salad

Yield: 6 or 2 servings
Serving Size: ½ cup
Exchange List Approximation:
   Meat, lean 2
   Vegetable 1

Nutrient Content Per Serving:
CAL: 131   PRO: 19.4 (gm)
FAT: 4.3 (gm)   CHO: 3.1 (gm)
Na: 177.1 (mg) K: 332 (mg)
Fiber: 0.3 (gm) Chol: 31 (mg)

Ingredients

Six Servings		*Two Servings*
1	POUND SCROD OR COD FILLETS	⅓ POUND
	WATER TO COVER	
1	TABLESPOON VINEGAR	1 TEASPOON
½	CUP FINELY CHOPPED CELERY	3 TABLESPOONS
2	TABLESPOONS MAYONNAISE	2 TEASPOONS
2	TABLESPOONS CATSUP	2 TEASPOONS
1	TABLESPOON LEMON JUICE	1 TEASPOON
1	TABLESPOON LOW-FAT YOGURT	1 TEASPOON
1	TABLESPOON PICKLE RELISH	1 TEASPOON
1	TEASPOON HORSERADISH	½ TEASPOON
¼	TEASPOON ONION POWDER	1/16 TEASPOON
⅛	TEASPOON PEPPER	1/16 TEASPOON

Method

1. Wash fish, place in shallow pan. Cover with water. Bring
   to a simmer. Do not boil. Cook about 4 minutes or until
   fish changes to white and flakes.
2. Drain fish, rinse with cold water. Drain and flake into large
   pieces.
3. Add remaining ingredients. Mix lightly and chill.
4. Serving suggestion: Serve on slit rolls or lettuce (½
   hamburger-type roll = 1 Starch/Bread Exchange; lettuce is
   free).

Dad's Shrimp Over Pasta

Yield: 6 or 2 servings

Serving Size: 1 cup pasta and
$\frac{2}{3}$ cup sauce

Exchange List Approximation:
　　Starch/Bread 3
　　Meat, lean 2

Nutrient Content Per Serving:

CAL: 308	PRO: 20.6 (gm)
FAT: 4.8 (gm)	CHO: 44.1 (gm)
Na: 566.1 (mg)	K: 189.2 (mg)
Fiber: 1.4 (gm)	Chol: 90 (mg)

Ingredients

Six Servings		Two Servings	
12	OUNCES PASTA (VERMICELLI OR LINGUINE)	4	OUNCES
2	QUARTS WATER	3	CUPS
1	TABLESPOON MARGARINE	1	TEASPOON
1½	TEASPOONS CHICKEN BOUILLON GRANULES	½	TEASPOON
1	TABLESPOON MINCED GARLIC CLOVE (ABOUT 3)	1	TEASPOON

SCANT ½ TEASPOON EACH: PAPRIKA AND OREGANO	⅛ TEASPOON
⅓ CUP CHOPPED ITALIAN PARSLEY (OR AMERICAN)	2 TABLESPOONS
1 BAY LEAF	⅓
3 CUPS WATER	1 CUP
12 OUNCES COOKED SHRIMP*	4 OUNCES
6 TABLESPOONS GRATED PARMESAN CHEESE	2 TABLESPOONS

Method

1. Cook pasta in unsalted water about 12 minutes while preparing sauce. Drain.
2. In a saucepan, combine all ingredients except shrimp and cheese. Bring to a simmer and cook about 5 minutes.
3. Wash shrimp to remove excess salt. Add to simmering sauce, cover, remove from heat, and let stand 5 minutes. Remove bay leaf.
4. Serve ⅔ cup shrimp sauce over 1 cup pasta. Sprinkle with 1 Tablespoon cheese.

*One pound shelled, deviled, raw shrimp may be used; add to sauce and cook 7 minutes.

Pasta with Clam Sauce

Yield: 2 servings
Serving Size: $1\frac{1}{4}$ cup
Exchange List Approximation:
    Starch/Bread 3
    Meat, lean 1
    Fat 1

Nutrient Content Per Serving:

CAL: 338	PRO: 15.2 (gm)
FAT: 10.2 (gm)	CHO: 45.5 (gm)
Na: 459.3 (mg)	K: 167.1 (mg)
Fiber: 2 (gm)	Chol: 27 (mg)

Ingredients

  2 CUPS SPAGHETTI, BROKEN INTO 2-INCH LENGTHS (ABOUT 4 OUNCES)
1½ QUARTS WATER
  1 TABLESPOON VEGETABLE OIL
 ¼ CUP CHOPPED ONION
  2 TEASPOONS MINCED GARLIC CLOVE
 ½ CUP CHOPPED PARSLEY
 ½ TEASPOON OREGANO
1/16 TEASPOON PEPPER
  1 6½-OUNCE CAN MINCED CLAMS
  2 TABLESPOONS WHITE WINE OR WATER
  1 TABLESPOON GRATED PARMESAN CHEESE

Method

1. Cook spaghetti in boiling water about 15 minutes while preparing sauce.
2. Saute onions and garlic in oil about 2 minutes.
3. Add parsley, oregano, pepper, and juice drained from clams. Add wine and simmer about 5 minutes.
4. Add clams and heat about 1 minute.
5. Drain spaghetti. Add to sauce and toss until mixed.
6. Sprinkle each serving with Parmesan cheese before serving.

Note: Recipe may be doubled.

Noodle Supreme Salad

Yield: 6 or 2 servings
Serving Size: 1 cup
Exchange List Approximation:
    Starch/Bread $1\frac{1}{2}$
    Meat, lean 1
    Vegetable 1

Nutrient Content Per Serving:
CAL: 196   PRO: 14.3 (gm)
FAT: 3.4 (gm)   CHO: 26.4 (gm)
Na: 547.3 (mg)   K: 279.2 (mg)
Fiber: 2.2 (gm)   Chol: 47 (mg)

Ingredients

Six Servings	Two Servings
6 OUNCES NOODLES	2 OUNCES
¾ CUP FROZEN PEAS	¼ CUP
2 QUARTS WATER	3 CUPS
⅔ CUP CREAM OF MUSHROOM SOUP (ABOUT HALF 10½-OUNCE CAN)	3 TABLESPOONS
1 6½-OUNCE CAN TUNA FISH PACKED IN WATER	2 OUNCES
½ CUP SHREDDED RED CABBAGE	2 TABLESPOONS
1 CUP DICED TOMATOES (ABOUT 1 LARGE)	¼ CUP
⅛ TEASPOON SALT	SPRINKLE
SPRINKLE PEPPER	SPRINKLE

Method

1. Bring water to a boil. Add noodles and peas. Cook uncovered 5 minutes. Drain.
2. Combine noodles, peas, soup, and drained tuna. Mix lightly. Cool.
3. Add red cabbage and tomatoes. Sprinkle with salt and pepper.
4. Serve on lettuce leaf and garnish with chopped green onion.

Note: Some noodles require longer cooking. Check package.

Tuna Cakes

Yield: 3 servings
Serving Size: 2 cakes
Exchange List Approximation:
    Starch/Bread 1
    Meat, lean 2
    Vegetable 1

Nutrient Content Per Serving:
CAL: 205   PRO: 22.7 (gm)
FAT: 5.9 (gm)   CHO: 15.4 (gm)
Na: 916.6 (mg)   K: 388.9 (mg)
Fiber: 3 (gm)   Chol: 130 (mg)

Ingredients

1 CUP SHREDDED ZUCCHINI (ABOUT 4 OUNCES)
2 TABLESPOONS CHOPPED ONION
½ TEASPOON MINCED GARLIC CLOVE
2 TEASPOONS MARGARINE
1 6½-OUNCE CAN TUNA PACKED IN WATER
1 EGG
1½ CUPS WHOLE-WHEAT BREAD CUBES (ABOUT 3 SLICES)
¼ TEASPOON SALT
¼ TEASPOON PEPPER

Method

1. Saute zucchini, onion, and garlic in 1 teaspoon margarine about 5 minutes.
2. Mix with remaining ingredients until blended.
3. Form into 6 patties and brown in margarine in large skillet over medium heat, about 3 minutes per side.
4. Serve with lemon or horseradish dip (see recipe, page 308).

Salmon-Noodle Bake

Yield: 6 or 2 servings
Serving Size: 1 cup
Exchange List Approximation:
    Starch/Bread 2
    Meat, medium-fat 2
    Fat $\frac{1}{2}$

Nutrient Content Per Serving:
CAL: 326   PRO: 22.3 (gm)
FAT: 13.2 (gm)   CHO: 28 (gm)
Na: 403.7 (mg)   K: 484.1 (mg)
Fiber: 1.2 (gm)   Chol: 58 (mg)

Ingredients

Six Servings	Two Servings
6 OUNCES NOODLES	2 OUNCES
2 QUARTS WATER	3 CUPS
2 TABLESPOONS MARGARINE	2 TEASPOONS
3 TABLESPOONS FLOUR	1 TABLESPOON
2 CUPS SKIM MILK	⅔ CUP
3 TABLESPOONS CHOPPED ONION	1 TABLESPOON
¼ TEASPOON PEPPER	¹⁄₁₆ TEASPOON
1 15½-OUNCE CAN SALMON	4 OUNCES
2 TABLESPOONS MAYONNAISE	2 TEASPOONS

Method

1. Cook noodles according to package directions and drain.
2. Prepare sauce in small saucepan. Melt margarine, stir in flour, and cook 1 minute. Add milk, stir until blended, bring to a boil, and cook 2 minutes, stirring constantly.
3. Add onion and pepper to sauce.
4. Drain salmon and reserve juice. Remove bones and flake salmon.
5. Add 6 tablespoons juice, mayonnaise, and sauce. Stir. Add noodles and mix.

6. Pour into a lightly greased 2-quart casserole. Bake in 350° F oven for 30 minutes.

Variation: Twelve ounces of chicken or tuna may be used instead of salmon.

Vegetarian
Main-Meal
Dishes

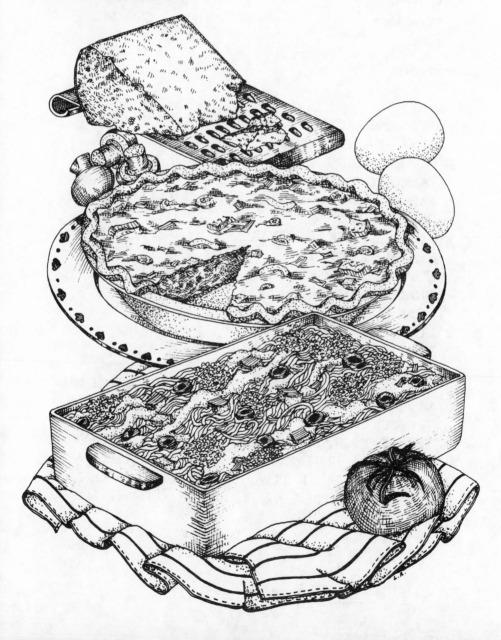

Vegetable Medley

Yield: 6 or 2 servings
Serving Size: 1 cup
Exchange List Approximation:
    Starch/Bread 2
    Vegetable 1
    Fat 1

Nutrient Content Per Serving:
CAL: 229   PRO: 10
FAT: 7.1 (gm)   CHO: 35.2 (gm)
Na: 164.1 (mg)   K: 414.2 (mg)
Fiber: 6.7 (gm)   Chol: 10 (mg)

Ingredients

Six Servings	Two Servings
3 OUNCES SPAGHETTI, BROKEN INTO 1-INCH LENGTHS	1 OUNCE
2 QUARTS WATER	1 QUART
1 TABLESPOON VEGETABLE OIL	1 TEASPOON
3 TABLESPOONS CHOPPED ONION	1 TABLESPOON
1 6-OUNCE PACKAGE FROZEN CHINESE PEA PODS	⅓ PACKAGE
1 CUP FROZEN CORN OR DRAINED WHOLE-KERNEL CANNED CORN	⅓ CUP
2 CUPS GARBANZO BEANS, DRAINED (ABOUT 1 15-OUNCE CAN)	⅔ CUP
2 TABLESPOONS WHITE-WINE VINEGAR	2 TEASPOONS
½ TEASPOON SUGAR	⅛ TEASPOON
½ TEASPOON BASIL	⅛ TEASPOON
½ TEASPOON OREGANO	⅛ TEASPOON
¼ TEASPOON GARLIC POWDER	⅛ TEASPOON
⅛ TEASPOON PEPPER	DASH

1 TABLESPOON CHOPPED
  PIMENTO (OPTIONAL)

1 TEASPOON

2 OUNCES CHEDDAR CHEESE,
  CUT INTO ¼-INCH CUBES
  (ABOUT ½ CUP)

⅔ OUNCE (ABOUT 3
  TABLESPOONS)

Method

1. Add spaghetti to boiling water, stir, and cook about 12 minutes until just tender. Drain and rinse with cold water.
2. In a large skillet, heat oil. Add onions and stir-fry about 1 minute. Add pea pods and stir-fry about 1 minute. Add corn and stir-fry until steaming, about 2 minutes.
3. Place in large mixing bowl. Add remaining ingredients and spaghetti.
4. Toss to mix well. Cover and chill several hours.
5. Place serving on large lettuce leaf.

Variation: If you prefer raw vegetables, combine oil, onions, corn, and pea pods with remaining ingredients. This recipe is delicious both ways.

Ratatouille II*

Yield: 6 servings
Serving Size: $\frac{3}{4}$ cup
Exchange List Approximation:
    Vegetable 2
    Fat 1

Nutrient Content Per Serving:
CAL: 82   PRO: 1.9 (gm)
FAT: 4.9 (gm)   CHO: 9.3 (gm)
Na: 97.6 (mg)   K: 413.9 (mg)
Fiber: 3.9 (gm)   Chol: 0

Ingredients

- 2 TABLESPOONS OLIVE OIL
- 1 CUP SLICED ONION (ABOUT 1 LARGE ONION)
- 1 TEASPOON MINCED GARLIC
- 3 CUPS DICED EGGPLANT (ABOUT 1 SMALL)
- 2½ CUPS SLICED ZUCCHINI (ABOUT 2 SMALL)
- ¾ CUP GREEN PEPPER, CUT INTO STRIPS (ABOUT 1 MEDIUM)
- 2 CUPS TOMATOES, PEELED AND CUBED (ABOUT 2 MEDIUM)
- 1 TEASPOON SWEET BASIL
- ¼ TEASPOON SALT
- ⅛ TEASPOON PEPPER

Method

1. Heat oil in large frying pan. Add onions and garlic; stir-fry about 2 minutes.
2. Add eggplant, stir-fry about 2 minutes. Add layer of zucchini, green pepper, and tomato.
3. Sprinkle basil, salt, and pepper over tomatoes. Cover and simmer 30 minutes over low heat.
4. Uncover, stir gently, and simmer 10 minutes.
5. Serve over brown rice or chill and serve with crackers or as a vegetable or relish.

Note 1: 1 16-ounce can of tomato wedges, drained, may be used for fresh tomatoes. Use juice if needed. Ratatouille is delicious cold. Make the whole recipe.

Note 2: This is a complete meal when served with tofu.

*Ratatouille I can be found in Volume I.

Garden Stir-Fry

Yield: 3 servings (2 cups)
Serving Size: $\frac{2}{3}$ cup
Exchange List Approximation:
    Meat, medium-fat 1
    Vegetable 1
    Fat 2

Nutrient Content Per Serving:
CAL: 181   PRO: 6.4 (gm)
FAT: 14.9 (gm)* CHO: 7.1 (gm)
Na: 81.1 (mg)   K: 356.4 (mg)
Fiber: 2.9 (gm) Chol: 183 (mg)
Key Source Nutrients:
    Vitamin A: 6270 (IU)
    Ascorbic acid: 64 (mg)

Ingredients

  2 TABLESPOONS SALAD OIL
  1 LARGE CLOVE GARLIC, MINCED OR PRESSED
  1 CUP BROCCOLI FLOWERETS, CUT INTO ½" CHUNKS
  1 CUP CAULIFLOWER FLOWERETS, CUT INTO ½" CHUNKS
  3 TABLESPOONS WATER
  ½ CUP CARROTS, CUT INTO ½-INCH SLANTING SLICES
  ¼ CUP RED BELL PEPPER, CUT INTO ¼-INCH STRIPS
    SALT (OPTIONAL)
  ⅛ TEASPOON PEPPER
  2 TEASPOONS WHOLE CASHEWS
  2 EGGS
  1 TABLESPOON SKIM MILK
  1 TABLESPOON SOY SAUCE (OPTIONAL)

Method

1. Place wok over high heat. When wok is hot, add 1 tablespoon of the oil. When oil is hot, add garlic and stir-fry for 30 seconds. Reduce heat to medium.
2. Add broccoli and cauliflower and stir-fry for 1 minute. Add 2 tablespoons water; cover and cook, stirring frequently for about 3 minutes. Remove from wok and set aside.
3. Add remaining 1 tablespoon oil to wok. When oil is hot, add carrots and red pepper. Stir-fry for 1 minute. Add remaining 1 tablespoon water; cover and cook, stirring frequently, for about 2 minutes or until vegetables are tender-crisp.
4. Return broccoli and cauliflower to wok and stir-fry to heat through (about 1 minute).
5. Combine eggs, milk, salt, and pepper. Beat until foamy and well-blended.
6. Pour egg mixture over vegetables. Cook, stirring from bottom until eggs are done.
7. Serve with garnish of cashews and sprinkle with soy sauce.

Note: This is a complete meal when served with tofu.

*To reduce fat content, cut back on the oil and add some broth for stir-frying.

Vegetable Platter with Peanut Sauce

Yield: 16 party or 8 main-meal
servings (party = ¾ vegetables
with ¼ cup sauce; main
meal = 1½ cups vegetables
with ½ cup sauce)

Serving Size: 1/16 recipe

Exchange List Approximation:
Vegetable 2
Fat 2

Nutrient Content Per Serving:

CAL: 135 PRO: 6.7 (gm)
FAT: 9.2 (gm) CHO: 9.8 (gm)
Na: 93 (mg) K: 458.9 (mg)
Fiber: 4.4 (gm) Chol: 0

Key Source Nutrients:
Vitamin A: 4692 (IU)
Ascorbic acid: 49 (mg)

Ingredients

4 CUPS FRESH BROCCOLI, PEELED AND CUT INTO 3-INCH LENGTHS
2 CUPS FRESH GREEN BEANS, CUT INTO 2-INCH LENGTHS
2 CUPS CARROTS, CUT INTO 2-INCH STRIPS
4 CUPS CAULIFLOWER, CUT INTO FLOWERETS
3 CUPS YELLOW SUMMER SQUASH, CUT INTO 2½-INCH PIECES
2 CUPS CUCUMBER, CUT INTO 2½-INCH STICKS
8 RADISHES, SLICED
2 TEASPOONS VEGETABLE OIL
½ CUP CHOPPED ONION
2 TEASPOONS MINCED GARLIC CLOVES
3½ CUPS HOT WATER OR VEGETABLE STOCK
1 CUP PEANUT BUTTER
2 TEASPOONS CHOPPED FRESH HOT PEPPER OR 1 TEASPOON HOT SAUCE

2 TEASPOONS LEMON JUICE
1 TEASPOON GRATED LEMON RIND
1 TEASPOON CHOPPED FRESH GINGER ROOT
1 BAY LEAF

Method

1. Steam the first five vegetables until crisp-tender; drain stock for use in sauce.
2. Arrange vegetables on 2 platters while making sauce.
3. Garnish with cucumber sticks and radishes.
4. Prepare sauce in large skillet. Heat oil, add onions and garlic. Stir-fry about 2 minutes.
5. Add remaining ingredients; stir until blended; simmer for 15 minutes, stirring occasionally. Taste for seasoning; ½ teaspoon salt may be added if diet permits.
6. Pour in 2 bowls and place in center of vegetable platters.
7. For main meal, arrange vegetables in portions on 8 plates with mound of hot rice (⅓ cup cooked rice = 1 Starch/Bread Exchange). Serve ½ cup sauce over vegetables. Extra vegetable servings may be combined with sauce, packaged, and frozen.

Impossible Garden Pie

Yield: 6 servings
Serving Size: $\frac{1}{6}$ recipe
Exchange List Approximation:
    Starch/Bread 1
    Meat, medium-fat 1
    Vegetable 1

Nutrient Content Per Serving:
CAL: 175   PRO: 10.2 (gm)
FAT: 7 (gm)   CHO: 18 (gm)
Na: 390 (mg)   K: 373.7 (mg)
Fiber: 2.8 (gm)   Chol: 144 (mg)

Ingredients

  2 CUPS ZUCCHINI, QUARTERED AND SLICED
1½ CUPS DICED TOMATOES
  ½ CUP CHOPPED ONION
  ½ CUP GRATED PARMESAN CHEESE
  ¼ TEASPOON PEPPER
1½ CUPS SKIM MILK
  ¾ CUP BISCUIT MIX (BISQUICK-TYPE)
  3 EGGS

Method

1. Heat oven to 400° F. Lightly grease 7- by 11-inch ovenproof glass or ceramic dish.
2. Place layer of zucchini, tomatoes, and onion in dish.
3. Sprinkle Parmesan cheese and pepper evenly over vegetables.
4. Combine milk, biscuit mix, and eggs. Beat until smooth, about 1 minute, and pour over vegetables.
5. Bake about 30 minutes.
6. Let set 5 minutes before cutting.

Quiche I (Broccoli)

Yield: 6 or 3 servings
Serving Size: $\frac{1}{6}$ recipe
Exchange List Approximation:
  Starch/Bread 1
  Meat, medium-fat 2
  Vegetable 1
  Fat 1

Nutrient Content Per Serving:
CAL: 291   PRO: 18.2 (gm)
FAT: 15.3 (gm)   CHO: 20 (gm)
Na: 555.9 (mg)   K: 249.4 (mg)
Fiber: 2 (gm)   Chol: 190 (mg)

Ingredients

Six Servings
  1 16-OUNCE CONTAINER LOW-FAT COTTAGE CHEESE
  ½ CUP SKIM MILK
  4 EGGS
  ¼ CUP CHOPPED ONION
  1 10-OUNCE PACKAGE BROCCOLI, THAWED
     SPRINKLE APPLE-PIE SPICE
  1 9-INCH PIE SHELL OR 6 TART SHELLS

Three Servings
  1 8-OUNCE
  ¼ CUP
  2
  2 TABLESPOONS
  5 OUNCES

     SPRINKLE
  1 SMALL PIE SHELL OR 3 TART SHELLS

Method

1. Place cottage cheese, milk, and eggs in blender. Blend about 30 seconds until mixture is smooth. Stir in onion.
2. Distribute broccoli evenly in pie shell. Pour cottage cheese mixture over it. Sprinkle with apple-pie spice.
3. Bake in 400° F oven for 50 minutes.

Variation: If recipe is made without the crust, nutrient information is as follows:

Exchange List Approximation:
    Meat, lean 2
    Vegetable 1

Nutrient Content Per Serving:
CAL: 141   PRO: 16.4 (gm)
FAT: 5.3 (gm)   CHO: 6.8 (gm)
Na: 373.3 (mg)   K: 234.8 (mg)
Fiber: 1.3 (gm)   Chol: 190

Quiche II (Vegetable)

Yield: 6 servings
Serving Size: $\frac{1}{6}$ recipe
Exchange List Approximation:
    Starch/Bread 1
    Meat, medium-fat 1
    Vegetable 1
    Fat $1\frac{1}{2}$

Nutrient Content Per Serving:
CAL: 243   PRO: 13.5 (gm)
FAT: 13 (gm)   CHO: 18.3 (gm)
Na: 291.6 (mg)   K: 225.1 (mg)
Fiber: 1.4 (gm)   Chol: 158 (mg)

Ingredients

    1   CUP SHREDDED CHEDDAR CHEESE
    ½   CUP CHOPPED ONION
    ½   CUP DICED TOMATOES
    1   CUP TOFU, DICED
    ½   CUP ZUCCHINI, DICED
    3   EGGS
    ¼   TEASPOON SALT
    ½   TEASPOON PEPPER
    1   CUP SKIM MILK
    1   TABLESPOON VEGETABLE OIL
    ¾   CUP ALL-PURPOSE FLOUR
    ½   TEASPOON BAKING POWDER

Method

1. Sprinkle cheese, onion, tomatoes, tofu, and zucchini in 9-inch pie plate that has been sprayed with nonstick vegetable spray.
2. Combine eggs, salt, pepper, milk, and oil in small bowl and mix well.
3. Combine flour and baking powder; add to milk and egg mixture. Beat with an egg beater or small hand mixer until smooth.
4. Pour above mixture evenly over ingredients in pie plates.
5. Bake at 400° F for 30 minutes. Let stand 5 minutes before serving.

Spinach Cheese Bake

Yield: 6 or 3 servings
Serving Size: $\frac{3}{4}$ cup
Exchange List Approximation:
    Meat, medium-fat 1
    Vegetable 2
    Fat $\frac{1}{2}$

Nutrient Content Per Serving:
CAL: 152   PRO: 13.9 (gm)
FAT: 6.7 (gm)   CHO: 9.2 (gm)
Na: 407.8 (mg)   K: 209.3 (mg)
Fiber: 1 (gm)   Chol: 150 (mg)

Ingredients

Six Servings		*Three Servings*
1	10-OUNCE PACKAGE FRESH SPINACH	½ PACKAGE
3	EGGS	1
¼	CUP ALL-PURPOSE FLOUR	2 TABLESPOONS
1	TEASPOON MINCED GARLIC	½ TEASPOON
1½	CUPS SMALL-CURD LOW-FAT COTTAGE CHEESE (1½% TO 2% MILKFAT)	¾ CUP

½ CUP CRUMBLED FETA CHEESE   ¼ CUP
(OR SHREDDED JALAPENO
CHEESE)
1 TEASPOON MARGARINE   ½ TEASPOON

Method

1. Cut spinach into small pieces. If garden spinach is used, wash and drain dry.
2. Beat eggs, add cheese, mix well; add flour and mix.
3. Add garlic and spinach; mix well.
4. Pour into lightly greased 2- or 2½-quart casserole. Cover loosely with foil and bake in 350° F oven for 35 to 40 minutes.

Vegetarian Lasagna

Yield: 6 servings
Serving Size: 4½-by-4-inch piece
Exchange List Approximation:
    Starch/Bread 2
    Meat, medium-fat 2½
    Vegetable 1
    Fat ½

Nutrient Content Per Serving:
CAL: 392   PRO: 24.7 (gm)
FAT: 16.8 (gm)   CHO: 36.8 (gm)
Na: 887.9 (mg)   K: 775.9 (mg)
Fiber: 4.1 (gm)   Chol: 129 (mg)
Key Source Nutrients:
    Vitamin A: 11847 (IU)

Ingredients

6 LASAGNA NOODLES (ABOUT 4 OUNCES)
2 QUARTS WATER
2 TABLESPOONS VEGETABLE OIL
1 CUP CHOPPED ONION
1½ CUPS ⅛-INCH BIAS-CUT CARROTS (ABOUT 4 MEDIUM)

2 TEASPOONS MINCED GARLIC (ABOUT 1 CLOVE)
1¾ CUPS SPAGHETTI SAUCE (ABOUT 1 15-OUNCE JAR)
½ CUP WATER
1 TEASPOON BASIL
½ TEASPOON OREGANO
2 EGGS
2 CUPS LOW-FAT (½% MILKFAT) COTTAGE CHEESE
   (ABOUT ONE 16-OUNCE CARTON)
4 TABLESPOONS PARMESAN CHEESE
1 10-OUNCE PACKAGE FROZEN CHOPPED SPINACH,
   THAWED AND DRAINED
1 CUP SLICED MUSHROOMS
1 CUP QUARTERED AND SLICED ZUCCHINI
1 CUP SHREDDED PART-SKIM MOZZARELLA CHEESE
   (ABOUT 4 OUNCES)
¼ CUP SLICED BLACK OLIVES (OPTIONAL)

Method

1. Cook lasagna noodles in boiling water about 12 minutes. Drain, rinse, and cover with cold water.
2. Heat vegetable oil in sauce pan. Add onions, carrots, and garlic. Saute until carrots are tender, about 10 minutes.
3. Add spaghetti sauce, water, and spices. Bring to a simmer.
4. Beat eggs and blend in cottage cheese, Parmesan cheese, and vegetables.
5. Spread a thin layer of sauce over bottom of 9- by 13-inch baking pan. Cover with layer of noodles, spoon half of cheese mixture over noodles. Cover with half of sauce. Repeat.
6. Cover with foil and bake at 350° F oven for 35 minutes.
7. Remove foil. Arrange olive slices over top and sprinkle with cheese. Bake uncovered about 15 minutes, or until center is bubbly.
8. Let cool about 10 minutes to set layers. Cut 2 by 3 into 4½- by 4-inch pieces.

Lasagne with Tofu

Yield: 6 or 2 servings
Serving Size: $\frac{1}{6}$ recipe
Exchange List Approximation:
    Starch/Bread 1$\frac{1}{2}$
    Meat, lean 2
    Vegetable 1
    Fat 1$\frac{1}{2}$

Nutrient Content Per Serving:
CAL: 317   PRO: 19.4 (gm)
FAT: 15.8 (gm)   CHO: 26.6 (gm)
Na: 730.9 (mg)   K: 623.2 (mg)
Fiber: 2.1 (gm)   Chol: 43 (mg)

Ingredients

Six Servings		Two Servings	
6	LASAGNA NOODLES	2	
2	QUARTS WATER	1	QUART
1	TEASPOON VEGETABLE OIL	1	TEASPOON
1	8-OUNCE PACKAGE MUSHROOMS, SLICED	1⅓	CUPS
¾	CUP CHOPPED ONION	¼	CUP
2	TABLESPOONS VEGETABLE OIL	2	TEASPOONS
1	8-OUNCE CAN TOMATO SAUCE	1	8-OUNCE CAN
1	6-OUNCE CAN TOMATO PASTE		OMIT
1	CUP WATER	⅓	CUP
¾	TEASPOON GARLIC POWDER	¼	TEASPOON
¾	TEASPOON BASIL	¼	TEASPOON
¾	TEASPOON OREGANO	¼	TEASPOON
¼	TEASPOON PEPPER	¹⁄₁₆	TEASPOON
1	BAY LEAF	⅓	LEAF
1	TABLESPOON PARSLEY, FRESH, CHOPPED	1	TEASPOON
8	OUNCES TOFU (SOY CHEESE), DRAINED, CRUMBLED	⅔	CUP

Six Servings	*Two Servings*
6 TABLESPOONS PARMESAN CHEESE, GRATED	2 TABLESPOONS
2 CUPS SHREDDED, LOW-MOISTURE, PART-SKIM MOZZARELLA CHEESE	⅔ CUP

Method

1. Cook lasagna noodles in boiling water containing oil about 12 minutes. Drain, rinse, and cover with cold water.
2. Prepare sauce. Saute onions and mushrooms in oil about 2 minutes. Add tomato sauce and paste. Rinse cans with water and add. Add spices and parsley. Simmer over low heat 30 minues.
3. Mash tofu and combine with ¾ ounce of Parmesan cheese (reserve rest for topping).
4. Spread thin layer of sauce over bottom of baking dish. Cover with layer of cooked noodles, spoon half the tofu mixture over noodles, sprinkle with half of cheese. Cover with 1 cup sauce; repeat. Top with layer of noodles and remaining sauce. Omit top layer in small casserole. Sprinkle with Parmesan cheese.
5. Bake in 350° F oven for 30 minutes or until sauce is bubbling.
6. Let cool about 10 minutes to set layers. Cut lasagna 2 by 3 into 3½- by 3¾-inch pieces.
7. Serve with green salad.

Note: Lasagna may be prepared in 9- by 13-inch pan with 2 layers of noodles.

Pasta Primavera

Yield: 6 or 2 servings
Serving Size: 1½ cup
Exchange List Approximation:
    Starch/Bread 2
    Vegetable 1
    Fat 1

Nutrient Content Per Serving:
CAL: 222   PRO: 8 (gm)
FAT: 5.5 (gm)   CHO: 35.8 (gm)
Na: 295 (mg)   K: 337.5 (mg)
Fiber: 4.2 (gm)   Chol: 2 (mg)

Ingredients

Six Servings		Two Servings	
8	OUNCES THIN SPAGHETTI, 2-INCH LENGTHS	2⅔	OUNCE (ABOUT 1 CUP)
6	CUPS WATER	2	CUPS
2	TABLESPOONS MARGARINE	2	TEASPOONS
1	CUP ONION, CUT INTO THIN WEDGES	⅓	CUP
2	CUPS BROCCOLI, CUT INTO FLOWERETS AND PEELED STALKS, SLICED	⅔	CUP
1	CUP CARROTS, THINLY SLICED	⅓	CUP
1	CUP ZUCCHINI, THINLY SLICED	⅓	CUP
1	CUP YELLOW SUMMER SQUASH, DICED	⅓	CUP
¾	CUP WATER	¼	CUP
¾	TEASPOON CHICKEN BOUILLON GRANULES	¼	TEASPOON
6	TABLESPOONS PARSLEY, CHOPPED	2	TABLESPOONS
3	TABLESPOONS LEMON JUICE	1	TABLESPOON
1½	TEASPOONS BASIL	½	TEASPOON
¼	TEASPOON PEPPER	¹⁄₁₆	TEASPOON
3	TABLESPOONS GRATED PARMESAN CHEESE	1	TABLESPOON

Method

1. Bring water to a boil, add spaghetti, stir, and boil gently until tender, about 10 minutes. Meanwhile prepare vegetables.
2. Heat margarine in a large skillet. Add onion. Stir-fry about 1 minute.
3. Add vegetables. Stir. Add water and chicken bouillon. Stir. Cover and simmer about 6 minutes.
4. Add parsley, lemon juice, basil, and pepper. Stir and cook 1 minute.
5. Drain spaghetti and add to vegetables.
6. Sprinkle with parmesan cheese, toss to mix well.

Manicotti Crepes

Yield: 6 servings
Serving Size: 2 crepes
Exchange List Approximation:
    Starch/Bread 2
    Meat, medium-fat 3
    Vegetable 1
    Fat 1

Nutrient Content Per Serving:
CAL: 448   PRO: 28.7 (gm)
FAT: 22.6 (gm)   CHO: 32.2 (gm)
Na: 986.9 (mg) K: 528.1 (mg)
Fiber: 0.6 (gm)   Chol: 278 (mg)

Ingredients

Crepes
- ¾ CUP WATER
- ¾ CUP FLOUR
- ⅛ TEASPOON SALT
- 2 EGGS

Filling
- 2 CUPS LOW-FAT RICOTTA CHEESE
- 1¾ CUPS LOW-FAT MOZZARELLA CHEESE, GRATED
- ¼ TEASPOON SALT
- 3 EGGS*
- 2 CUPS SPAGHETTI SAUCE (CANNED) OR TOMATO SAUCE (CANNED)
- ½ CUP PARMESAN CHEESE

Method

1. Combine first four ingredients and beat or mix in blender until smooth.
2. Heat 5-inch skillet or crepe pan until moderately hot. Film with shortening or margarine. Ladle a few tablespoons of batter into the skillet; tilt quickly to cover pan with thinnest possible layer.

3. Cook until bottom is lightly browned and edges lift easily. Turn and cook for a few minutes on other side. Remove crepe to plate. Film pan with shortening or margarine prior to adding batter. Make 12 crepes.
4. To make filling, beat eggs* and combine with ricotta and mozzarella cheese and salt.
5. Spoon filling down center of each crepe and roll it.
6. Cover bottom of 9- by 13-inch baking dish with about half of the spaghetti sauce. Arrange filled crepes in dish. Cover top with remaining spaghetti sauce. Sprinkle Parmesan cheese on top.
7. Bake at 350° F for 30 minutes.

*To reduce cholesterol, use egg whites as egg replacement.
Nutrient information is as follows:

Exchange List Approximation:
   Starch/Bread 2
   Meat, medium-fat 3
   Vegetable 1
   Fat $\frac{1}{2}$

Nutrient Content Per Serving:
CAL: 425   PRO: 29 (gm)
FAT: 19.8 (gm)   CHO: 32.3 (gm)
Na: 1002.4 (mg) K: 540.6 (mg)
Fiber: 0.6 (gm)   Chol: 141 (mg)

Pasta with Hot and Cold Sesame-Peanut Sauce

Yield: 6 or 2 servings
Serving Size: $\frac{1}{4}$ cup sauce and
$\frac{3}{4}$ cup spaghetti
Exchange List Approximation:
   Starch/Bread 2$\frac{1}{2}$
   Meat, medium-fat 1$\frac{1}{2}$
   Fat 3

Nutrient Content Per Serving:
CAL: 441   PRO: 18.1 (gm)
FAT: 25.5 (gm)   CHO: 39.1 (gm)
Na: 208.2 (mg)   K: 346.2 (mg)
Fiber: 4.5 (gm)   Chol: 0

Ingredients

Six Servings		*Two Servings*
1	CUP CRUNCHY PEANUT BUTTER	⅓ CUP
1	TABLESPOON SESAME SEED OIL	1 TEASPOON
1	TABLESPOON SESAME SEEDS	1 TEASPOON
2	TABLESPOONS CIDER VINEGAR	2 TEASPOONS
3	TABLESPOONS CHOPPED GREEN ONION	1 TABLESPOON
⅜	TEASPOON CAYENNE PEPPER	⅛ TEASPOON
½	CUP COLD WATER	3 TABLESPOONS
9	OUNCES SPAGHETTI, BROKEN	3 OUNCES
3	QUARTS WATER	1 QUART

Method

1. Blend peanut butter, oil, seeds, vinegar, onions, and pepper together.
2. Beat in cold water gradually, using fork, until sauce has consistency of thick mayonnaise.
3. Cook spaghetti in boiling water about 15 minutes.

4. Serve ¼ cup sauce on ¾ cup spaghetti.
5. Sauce may be served hot or cold on seafoods and vegetables.

*This is a high-fat dish and should be limited to occasional use.

Tofu Balls

Yield: 6 or 2 servings
Serving Size: 4 balls
Exchange List Approximation:
    Starch/Bread 1
    Meat, medium-fat 1
    Fat 1

Nutrient Content Per Serving:
CAL: 200   PRO: 11 (gm)
FAT: 12.4 (gm)   CHO: 12.5 (gm)
Na: 277.7 (mg)   K: 113.2 (mg)
Fiber: 0.7 (gm)   Chol: 137 (mg)

Ingredients

Six Servings	*Two Servings*
1 POUND TOFU	5½ OUNCES
BOILING WATER	
1 TEASPOON MARGARINE	½ TEASPOON
3 TABLESPOONS GRATED ONION	1 TABLESPOON
⅓ CUP FINELY SHREDDED CARROTS	1½ TABLESPOONS
3 EGGS, BEATEN	1
¾ CUP DRY, SEASONED BREAD CRUMBS	¼ CUP
⅜ TEASPOON SALT	⅛ TEASPOON
¼ TEASPOON PEPPER	1/16 TEASPOON
1 TABLESPOON CHOPPED PARSLEY	1 TEASPOON

Method

1. Cut tofu in large cubes. Place in sieve and rinse with boiling water. Drain well. Mash fine or process in a food processor.
2. Braise onion and carrot in margarine for about 2 minutes.
3. Mix with tofu and remaining ingredients. Place in refrigerator for at least 2 hours for flavors to blend.
4. Form in walnut-size balls about 1 ounce each. Deep-fat fry in 350° F fat until brown, about 4 minutes.
5. Serve with tartar sauce.

Variation: Five slices of whole-wheat bread can be dried and ground for bread crumbs. Add ⅛ teaspoon each of thyme and garlic powder.

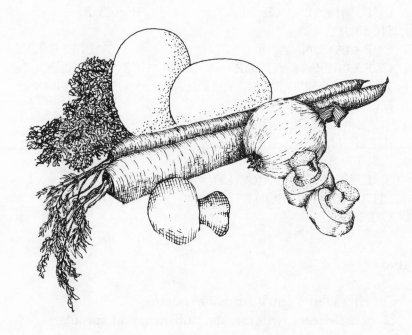

Cheese-and-Sprouts Pita Sandwich

Yield: 6 or 1 serving
Serving Size: 1 sandwich
Exchange List Approximation:
    Starch/Bread 2
    Meat, lean 1
    Vegetable 2
    Fat 1$\frac{1}{2}$

Nutrient Content Per Serving:
CAL: 328   PRO: 17 (gm)
FAT: 12.4 (gm)   CHO: 38.2 (gm)
Na: 846 (mg)   K: 500.8 (mg)
Fiber: 6.9 (gm)   Chol: 23 (mg)
Key Source Nutrients:
    Vitamin A: 5413 (IU)

Ingredients

Six Servings	One Serving
6 SLICES LOW-FAT CHEESE (ABOUT 6 OUNCES)	1 SLICE
1 CUP SHREDDED CARROTS	3 TABLESPOONS
12 SLICED RADISHES	2
2 CUPS ALFALFA OR BEAN SPROUTS	⅓ CUP
¼ CUP MAYONNAISE	2 TABLESPOONS
¾ CUP LOW-FAT YOGURT	2 TABLESPOONS
1 TEASPOON DIJON OR REGULAR MUSTARD	1/16 TEASPOON
½ TEASPOON CURRY POWDER (OPTIONAL)	⅛ TEASPOON
12 SLICED SALAD ONIONS, THIN-SLICED AND SEPARATED	2 SLICES
6 PITA BREAD (ABOUT 12 OUNCES)	1 (ABOUT 2 OUNCES)

Method

1. Cut cheese into small strips or squares.
2. Combine cheese with carrots, radishes, and sprouts.

3. Mix dressing of mayonnaise, yogurt, mustard, and curry powder.
4. Cut each pita in half to make sandwich pockets. Spread inside with dressing.
5. Fill with cheese-vegetable filling and lay onion slices on top.

Chick Peas and Green Pepper

Yield: 4 servings (3 cups)
Serving Size: $\frac{3}{4}$ cup
Exchange List Approximation:
    Starch/Bread 1
    Vegetable 2
    Fat 1

Nutrient Content Per Serving:
CAL: 179   PRO: 7.9 (gm)
FAT: 5.6 (gm)   CHO: 26 (gm)
Na: 15.2 (mg)   K: 451.2 (mg)
Fiber: 6.6 (gm)   Chol: 0

Ingredients

1 TABLESPOON VEGETABLE OIL
½ CUP CHOPPED ONION (ABOUT 1 SMALL)
½ TEASPOON CHOPPED FRESH GINGER
1 TEASPOON CUMIN SEEDS
1 TEASPOON CORIANDER, GROUND
¼ TEASPOON PEPPER
⅛ TEASPOON SALT (OPTIONAL)
1 CUP CHOPPED GREEN PEPPER
1 15-OUNCE CAN CHICK PEAS (GARBANZO), DRAINED
1 CUP CHOPPED FRESH TOMATOES (ABOUT 2)
2 TABLESPOONS LEMON JUICE

Method

1. Saute onions and ginger in oil.
2. Add seasonings and stir for 1 minute.
3. Add chopped green pepper and chick peas. Cook about 5 minutes.
4. Add tomatoes and lemon juice. Cook about 2 minutes, stirring frequently.
5. Serve hot on flour tortilla (1 Starch/Bread Exchange) or in pita bread (1 Starch/Bread Exchange) with shredded fresh lettuce.

Cheese Enchiladas

Yield: 6 servings
Serving Size: 2 enchiladas
Exchange List Approximation:
   Starch/Bread 2
   Meat, medium-fat 2
   Fat 1½

Nutrient Content Per Serving:
CAL: 371   PRO: 19 (gm)
FAT: 20.8 (gm) CHO: 29.6 (gm)
Na: 668.2 (mg) K: 409.4 (mg)
Fiber: 3.8 (gm) Chol: 60 (mg)

Ingredients

Sauce

- 1 8-OUNCE CAN TOMATO SAUCE, SPANISH STYLE, NO SUGAR ADDED
- 1 4-OUNCE CAN CHOPPED GREEN CHILIES
- 1 CUP CHOPPED, PEELED TOMATO (ONE 7-OUNCE CAN OR ONE CUP FRESH TOMATO)
- 1 TABLESPOON DEHYDRATED MINCED ONION
- 1 TEASPOON MINCED GARLIC CLOVE (ABOUT 1)
- 1 TEASPOON GROUND CUMIN
- ½ TEASPOON OREGANO
- PINCH SUGAR SUBSTITUTE

Enchiladas

- 12 CORN TORTILLAS (ABOUT 10-OUNCE PACKAGE)
- 4 CUPS SHREDDED CHEDDAR CHEESE (ABOUT 12 OUNCES)
- 1½ CUPS CHOPPED ONIONS

Method

1. Combine ingredients for sauce in small saucepan. Bring to boil, cover, and simmer 15 minutes. For smooth sauce, whip in blender.

2. Prepare enchiladas one at a time. Heat tortilla in skillet sprayed with vegetable pan spray.
3. Pour part of sauce in a plate. Place tortilla on sauce and flip to other side.
4. Place 2 Tablespoons cheese and 1 Tablespoon onion on one edge of tortilla and roll up. Place flap-side down in a 9- by 13-inch baking pan spread with a thin layer of sauce.
5. Continue until all tortillas are filled and rolled.
6. Spread remaining sauce over tortillas. Be sure all edges are moistened.
7. Sprinkle remaining cheese evenly over rolls.
8. Bake, uncovered, in 350° F oven until cheese melts and starts to bubble, 15 to 20 minutes.
9. Sprinkle the rest of chopped onions over enchiladas. Serve with garnish of shredded lettuce.

Variation: Sauce used on top of enchiladas may be thinned with ½ cup sour cream, if diet permits. Nutrient information is as follows:

Exchange List Approximation:	Nutrient Content Per Serving:	
Starch/Bread 2	CAL: 406	PRO: 19.5 (gm)
Meat, medium-fat 2	FAT: 24.1 (gm)	CHO: 30.3 (gm)
Fat 2½	Na: 676.2 (mg)	K: 432.1 (mg)
	Fiber: 3.8 (gm)	Chol: 67 (mg)

High-Fiber Main Meals and Side Dishes

To turn many of the lower-calorie dishes into satisfying main meals, simply double the serving size. Just be sure to double the nutrient and exchange information as well.

Soybean Vegetable Casserole

Yield: 6 servings (4 cups)
Serving Size: $\frac{2}{3}$ cup
Exchange List Approximation:
    Starch/Bread 1
    Meat, medium-fat 1
    Vegetable $\frac{1}{2}$

Nutrient Content Per Serving:
CAL: 170   PRO: 12.9 (gm)
FAT: 7.3 (gm)   CHO: 16.5 (gm)
Na: 143.2 (mg)   K: 830 (mg)
Fiber: 6.3 (gm)   Chol: 0

Ingredients

1 CUP DRY SOYBEANS
4 CUPS WATER
1 TEASPOON VEGETABLE OIL
¼ CUP CHOPPED ONION
1 CUP DICED CELERY
¼ CUP CHOPPED GREEN PEPPER
1 16-OUNCE CAN TOMATOES

Method

1. Wash soybeans and soak overnight. Bring to a boil, cover, and simmer until tender, about 2 hours. Add water as needed. Drain and reserve liquid.
2. Saute onion, celery, and peppers in a little oil, about 5 minutes.
3. Add beans, 1 cup bean liquid, and canned tomatoes. Stir to mix and break up tomatoes.
4. Pour into 1½-quart casserole and bake in 350° F oven for 1 hour.

Beans and Sausage Casserole

Yield: 6 or 2 servings
Serving Size: $\frac{1}{6}$ recipe
Exchange List Approximation:
  Starch/Bread $2\frac{1}{2}$
  Meat, lean 1
  Fat 1

Nutrient Content Per Serving:
CAL: 302   PRO: 17.8 (gm)
FAT: 9.4 (gm)   CHO: 38 (gm)
Na: 827.2 (mg)   K: 940.1 (mg)
Fiber: 9.5 (gm)   Chol: 23 (mg)

Ingredients

Six Servings		*Two Servings*	
1½	CUPS DRAINED, COOKED PINTO BEANS	½	CUP
1½	CUPS DRAINED, COOKED LIMA BEANS	½	CUP
1½	CUPS DRAINED, COOKED NAVY OR GREAT NORTHERN BEANS	½	CUP
¾	POUND BULK SAUSAGE (BEEF OR TURKEY MAY BE SUBSTITUTED)	¼	POUND
½	CUP BEEF BROTH (CANNED OR BOUILLON)	¼	CUP
1	8-OUNCE CAN TOMATO SAUCE	⅓	CUP
1	TEASPOON GROUND CUMIN (OPTIONAL)	½	TEASPOON
3	TABLESPOONS RED WINE OR COOKING SHERRY (OPTIONAL)	1	TABLESPOON
½	TEASPOON SALT		DASH
½	TEASPOON PEPPER		DASH
1	TEASPOON MINCED FRESH GARLIC	½	TEASPOON
1	CUP FINELY CHOPPED ONION	⅓	CUP

Method

1. Combine beans in a 2½-quart casserole and set aside.
2. Shape sausage into about 24 small balls and brown in a skillet. Drain fat.
3. While the sausage browns, add beef broth, tomato sauce, cumin, wine, salt, and pepper to the beans.
4. Add browned sausage balls to beans.
5. Saute garlic and onions in sausage drippings. Add to ingredients in the casserole and stir.
6. Cover casserole and bake in 325° F oven for 1 hour.

Red Beans and Brown Rice

Yield: 6 or 2 servings
Serving Size: $\frac{2}{3}$ cup
Exchange List Approximation:
    Starch/Bread $1\frac{1}{2}$

Nutrient Content Per Serving:
CAL: 118   PRO: 5.3 (gm)
FAT: 2.6 (gm)   CHO: 18.7 (gm)
Na: 38.3 (mg)   K: 292.9 (mg)
Fiber: 4.8 (gm)   Chol: 3 (mg)

Ingredients

Six Servings
  ½ CUP BROWN RICE
1½ CUPS WATER
  1 SLICE BACON, DICED
  1 CUP CHOPPED ONIONS
  ½ CUP DICED CELERY
  ½ CUP DICED GREEN PEPPER
  1 15-OUNCE CAN RED KIDNEY
    BEANS (NEW ORLEANS STYLE),
    OR PINTO BEANS, OR BLACK-
    EYE PEAS
¼-½ TEASPOON HOT SAUCE
  ⅛ TEASPOON PEPPER

Two Servings
  3 TABLESPOONS
  ⅔ CUP
  ⅓ SLICE
  ⅓ CUP
  3 TABLESPOONS
  2 TABLESPOONS
  ⅓ CAN

  2 DROPS
    DASH

Method

1. Bring rice and water to a boil, cover tightly, reduce heat, and cook until water is absorbed, about 1 hour.
2. In large skillet, cook diced bacon, onion, celery, and green peppers slowly over low heat, about 10 minutes.
3. Add undrained canned beans or peas and seasonings. Bring to a boil, cover, and simmer 5 minutes.

4. Add cooked rice and mix lightly. Add a little water, if mixture is too dry.

Variation: Season pinto beans or black-eye peas and rice with 2 teaspoons Picante sauce. Refer to page 321.

Green-Pea Curry with Rice

Yield: 6 or 2 servings
Serving Size: $\frac{3}{4}$ cup
Exchange List Approximation:
    Starch/Bread $3\frac{1}{2}$

Nutrient Content Per Serving:
CAL: 286   PRO: 12.2 (gm)
FAT: 1.9 (gm)   CHO: 55.8 (gm)
Na: 17.4 (mg)   K: 503 (mg)
Fiber: 8.1 (gm) Chol: 0

Ingredients

Six Servings		*Two Servings*	
1½	CUPS GREEN SPLIT PEAS (ABOUT 12 OUNCES)	½	CUP
3	CUPS WATER	1	CUP
1½	TEASPOONS VEGETABLE OIL	½	TEASPOON
1	CUP CHOPPED ONION	⅓	CUP
1	TABLESPOON CURRY POWDER	1	TEASPOON
¾	TEASPOON GROUND GINGER	¼	TEASPOON
3	TABLESPOONS RAISINS	1	TABLESPOON
¼	TEASPOON SALT (OPTIONAL)		PINCH
1	CUP WATER	½	CUP
3	CUPS COOKED RICE	1	CUP

Method

1. Wash peas, add water, bring to boil. Cover, remove from heat and let stand 1 hour.
2. Heat oil in sauce pan. Add onions and saute until limp. Add spices and raisins. Stir to blend.
3. Add green peas and water as needed to cover. Stir. Bring to a boil. Cover and simmer 1 hour.
4. Serve over ½ cup cooked rice.
5. Garnish with any of the following as diet permits: chutney (on average, 1 tablespoon = ½ Fruit Exchange), finely diced hard-cooked eggs, shredded fresh coconut, chopped olives, chopped nuts. (For remaining exchanges, see Appendix I.)

Variation: One or combination of the following may be used.

Six Servings		*Two Servings*	
¾	TEASPOON CINNAMON	¼	TEASPOON
¾	TEASPOON CUMIN	¼	TEASPOON
1	TABLESPOON TOASTED SESAME SEEDS	1	TEASPOON

Marinated Beans and Corn

Yield: 6 main meal or 12
  salad servings
Serving Size: 1 cup
Exchange List Approximation:
    Starch/Bread 4
    Meat, lean 1
    Vegetable $\frac{1}{2}$

Nutrient Content Per Serving:

CAL: 390	PRO: 19.4 (gm)
FAT: 7.8 (gm)	CHO: 64.8 (gm)
Na: 130.5 (mg)	K: 826 (mg)
Fiber: 14.5 (gm)	Chol: 8 (mg)

Serving Size: $\frac{1}{2}$ cup
Exchange List Approximation:
    Starch/Bread $1\frac{1}{2}$
    Vegetable $1\frac{1}{2}$

Nutrient Content Per Serving:

CAL: 156	PRO: 8.2 (gm)
FAT: 2.3 (gm)	CHO: 27.9 (gm)
Na: 20.1 (mg)	K: 471.9 (mg)
Fiber: 7.3 (gm)	Chol: 0

Ingredients

1 15-OUNCE CAN RED KIDNEY BEANS, DRAINED
1 15-OUNCE CAN PINK BEANS, DRAINED; RESERVE ¼ CUP SAUCE
1 15-OUNCE CAN GARBANZO BEANS, DRAINED
1 10-OUNCE PACKAGE FROZEN WHOLE-KERNEL CORN
1 CUP SLICED CELERY (ABOUT 2 LARGE STALKS)
⅓ CUP WINE VINEGAR
1 TABLESPOON VEGETABLE OIL
1 TABLESPOON CHOPPED FRESH PARSLEY
2 TEASPOONS MINCED GARLIC CLOVES (ABOUT 2)
¼ TEASPOON CHILI POWDER

Method

1. Drain beans and save ¼ cup sauce.
2. Cook corn according to packaged directions. Drain.
3. Combine beans and corn in large mixing bowl.
4. Combine all other ingredients and bean sauce. Pour over bean-and-corn mixture. Toss lightly to mix.
5. Cover and refrigerate overnight.
6. For salad, serve ½-cup portions on lettuce. Garnish with onion slice and tomato wedge.
7. For main meal, serve 1-cup portion on heated flour tortilla. Sprinkle with shredded cheese, chopped onion, and shredded lettuce.

New Mexico Green-Chili Zucchini

Yield: 6 servings
Serving Size: $\frac{1}{6}$ recipe
Exchange List Approximation:
    Meat, lean 2
    Vegetable 2

Nutrient Content Per Serving:
CAL: 159   PRO: 19.5 (gm)
FAT: 4.9 (gm)   CHO: 10.2 (gm)
Na: 181.7 (mg) K: 712.4 (mg)
Fiber: 4.6 (gm)   Chol: 45 (mg)

Ingredients

  1 POUND LEAN BEEF, CUBED
  1 CUP CHOPPED ONION
  1 7-OUNCE CAN GREEN CHILIES
  4 MEDIUM ZUCCHINI, QUARTERED AND SLICED
  2 TEASPOONS MINCED GARLIC CLOVE (ABOUT 2)
  1 16-OUNCE CAN TOMATOES
 ½ CUP WATER
 ½ CUP SHREDDED MONTEREY JACK CHEESE (ABOUT 2 OUNCES)

Method

1. Use large electric skillet or other large skillet. Spray with vegetable pan spray.
2. Saute beef until lightly browned; add onions and garlic. Cook about 5 minutes. Add chilies.
3. Add zucchini, toss, and cook until just tender.
4. Chop tomatoes and add. Heat to a simmer. Mixture should be soupy. Add water if needed.
5. Serve in soup bowls with 1½ Tablespoons cheese on top.
6. Serving suggestion: Serve with Southern Cornbread (see recipe on page 125).

Western-Style Beans

Yield: 9 servings (6 cups)
Serving Size: $\frac{2}{3}$ cup
Exchange List Approximation:
  Starch/Bread 2
  Vegetable 1

Nutrient Content Per Serving:
CAL: 190   PRO: 11.8 (gm)
FAT: 1.5 (gm)   CHO: 33.8 (gm)
Na: 160.9 (mg) K: 682.7 (mg)
Fiber: 9.1 (gm) Chol: 0

Ingredients

1   POUND DRIED BEANS (PINTO, RED, PINK, OR NAVY)
1   TEASPOON VEGETABLE OIL
1   CUP CHOPPED ONION
2   TEASPOONS CHILI POWDER
½   TEASPOON SALT
5   CUPS WATER
1   CUP GREEN CHILIES SAUCE (SEE RECIPE PAGE 322)

Method

1. Wash and pick over beans. Cover with water and soak overnight. Drain.
2. Heat oil in cooking pot. Add onion and saute until tender, about 5 minutes.
3. Add chili powder, salt, beans, and water.
4. Bring to a boil. Reduce heat, cover, and cook until beans are tender, 1 to 1½ hours.
5. Add Green Chilies Sauce, stir, and simmer uncovered 30 minutes longer. Beans should not be too soupy.

Note: Extra servings can be packaged and frozen.

Simmered Black-Eye Peas

Yield: 10 servings (6⅔ cups)
Serving Size: ⅔ cup
Exchange List Approximation:
    Starch/Bread 1
    Meat, medium-fat ½

Nutrient Content Per Serving:
CAL: 117   PRO: 6.5 (gm)
FAT: 2.7 (gm)   CHO: 17.8 (gm)
Na: 156.8 (mg) K: 306 (mg)
Fiber: 12.2 (gm) Chol: 2 (mg)

Ingredients

1 POUND DRIED BLACK-EYE PEAS
2 QUARTS COLD WATER
1 SLICE SALT PORK OR BACON (ABOUT 1 OUNCE)
½ TEASPOON SALT
1 LARGE ONION, SLICED

Method

1. Wash peas and place in large pot. Add water, pork, and salt.
2. Bring to a boil, cover, and cook slowly for 2 hours. Water should cook down so peas are just covered. Add more water if needed.
3. Serve peas with juice and slices of onion. Pepper sauce may be served with peas. Cornbread is a good accompaniment. Peas may be used in salads or to make dip.

Rum-Baked Black Beans

Yield: 6 servings (4 cups)
Serving Size: ⅔ cup
Exchange List Approximation:
    Starch/Bread 2

Nutrient Content Per Serving:
CAL: 172   PRO: 9.2 (gm)
FAT: 2.6 (gm)   CHO: 29.4 (gm)
Na: 142.8 (mg)   K: 564.8 (mg)
Fiber: 11.3 (gm)   Chol: 0

Ingredients

½ POUND DRIED BLACK BEANS
3 CUPS WATER
¾ CUP CHOPPED ONION
1 CUP FINELY CHOPPED CELERY
⅔ CUP CHOPPED CARROTS
1 TEASPOON MINCED GARLIC CLOVE (ABOUT 1)
1 SMALL BAY LEAF
2 TABLESPOONS CHOPPED FRESH PARSLEY
¾ TEASPOON THYME LEAVES
¼ TEASPOON SALT
¼ TEASPOON PEPPER
1 TABLESPOON MARGARINE
2 TABLESPOONS DARK RUM
1 ORANGE, CUT INTO 6 WEDGES

Method

1. Wash beans. Cover with 4 cups water. Soak overnight. Drain.
2. Place beans, 3 cups water, and ingredients except margarine, rum, and orange in cooking pot. Bring to a boil, cover, and simmer until beans are mealy, about 1 hour.
3. Transfer beans and juice to bean pot. Stir in margarine and rum. Cover and bake in 325° F oven 2 hours.

4. Remove cover and bake 30 minutes longer.
5. Serve with wedge of orange and rice.

Cheese-y Lima Beans

Yield: 3 servings
Serving Size: 1 cup
Exchange List Approximation:
    Starch/Bread $1\frac{1}{2}$
    Meat, lean $2\frac{1}{2}$

Nutrient Content Per Serving:
CAL: 255   PRO: 23.2 (gm)
FAT: 7.8 (gm)   CHO: 23 (gm)
Na: 440.1 (mg)   K: 533.8 (mg)
Fiber: 5.6 (gm)   Chol: 112 (mg)

Ingredients

1 10-OUNCE PACKAGE FROZEN LIMA BEANS OR 1 16-OUNCE CAN LIMA BEANS, DRAINED
1 EGG
¾ CUP POT OR FARMER'S CHEESE OR DRAINED LOW-FAT COTTAGE CHEESE
¾ CUP SHREDDED SKIMMED MILK MOZZARELLA CHEESE OR MUENSTER OR SWISS (DIVIDED)
2 TABLESPOONS CHOPPED ONIONS
2 TABLESPOONS CHOPPED PARSLEY
SPRINKLE PEPPER

Method

1. Cook frozen lima beans according to package directions. Drain. If canned beans are used, drain.
2. Beat egg, add pot cheese, and ½ cup shredded cheese.
3. Combine with beans. Add onions and parsley. Pour in lightly greased 1-quart casserole. Sprinkle with pepper.
4. Bake in 350° F oven for 20 minutes. Sprinkle with ¼ cup shredded cheese. Place under broiler to brown.

Spanish Beans

Yield: 6 servings
Serving Size: 1 cup
Exchange List Approximation:
    Starch/Bread 3
    Meat, medium-fat $1\frac{1}{2}$
    Vegetable 1

Nutrient Content Per Serving:
CAL: 381   PRO: 21.5 (gm)
FAT: 11.5 (gm)   CHO: 49.8 (gm)
Na: 261.1 (mg)   K: 1248.1 (mg)
Fiber: 11.4 (gm)   Chol: 24 (mg)

Ingredients

1   POUND DRY BABY LIMA BEANS
⅛   TEASPOON CRUSHED RED PEPPER
6   CUPS WATER
1   TEASPOON CHILI POWDER
¼   TEASPOON GARLIC POWDER
1   TEASPOON OLIVE OIL
1   CUP DICED ONIONS
1   CUP DICED CELERY
¾   CUP RED SWEET PEPPER
⅔   CUP SLICED, PITTED RIPE OLIVES
1⅓ CUPS SHREDDED MONTEREY JACK CHEESE

Method

1. Add beans and red pepper to water. Bring to a boil, cover, remove from heat and let stand 1 hour. Bring to boil and simmer 1 hour.
2. Drain beans and save ⅔-cup liquid.
3. Sprinkle beans with chili powder and garlic powder. Add reserved liquid.
4. Saute onions, celery, and red pepper in hot olive oil until onions start to brown, about 3 minutes.

5. Add beans, olives, and one half the cheese to vegetables. Mix well.
6. Pour into a 3-quart casserole. Sprinkle remaining cheese over beans.
7. Bake in 375° F oven until bubbly, about 30 minutes.
8. Serving suggestion: Serve with brown rice (1/3 cup cooked rice = 1 Starch/Bread Exchange) and a tossed salad.

Variation: If red sweet pepper is not available, use green pepper and 2 Tablespoons minced pimento.

Note: Extra beans may be packaged in 1 cup servings and frozen for later use.

Mexi-Greek Beans

Yield: 6 or 3 servings
Serving Size: 1 cup
Exchange List Approximation:
    Starch/Bread 1
    Meat, medium-fat 2
    Vegetable 2
    Fat 2

Nutrient Content Per Serving:
CAL: 376   PRO: 24.3 (gm)
FAT: 22.3 (gm)   CHO: 24.6 (gm)
Na: 473.5 (mg)   K: 1040.1 (mg)
Fiber: 10.1 (gm)   Chol: 25 (mg)

Ingredients

Six Servings	*Three Servings*
2 CUPS DRY SOYBEANS (ABOUT 12 OUNCES)	1 CUP (ABOUT 6 OUNCES)
8 CUPS WATER	4 CUPS
4 TEASPOONS VEGETABLE OIL	2 TEASPOONS
1 CUP CHOPPED ONION	½ CUP
½ CUP CHOPPED RED OR GREEN PEPPER	¼ CUP
1 TEASPOON MINCED GARLIC CLOVE	½ TEASPOON
1 4-OUNCE CAN CHOPPED GREEN CHILIES	2 OUNCES
½ TEASPOON CUMIN	¼ TEASPOON
¾ CUP CRUMBLED FETA CHEESE (ABOUT 6 OUNCES)	6 TABLESPOONS
1 CUP GREEK OLIVES OR PITTED RIPE OLIVES	½ CUP

Method

1. Wash soybeans and soak overnight. Bring to a boil, cover, and simmer until tender and almost dry, about 2 hours. Add water as needed.

2. Saute onion and peppers in vegetable oil until limp, about 5 minutes.
3. Add garlic, chilies, and cumin. Mix. Add to beans and heat.
4. Serve 1 cup beans in soup bowl. Sprinkle 1 ounce (2 Tablespoons) feta cheese over serving. Garnish with 5 olives.

Dried Beans in Seasoned Tomato Sauce

Yield: 12 servings
Serving Size: 1 cup
Exchange List Approximation:
    Starch/Bread 2
    Vegetable 1

Nutrient Content Per Serving:
CAL: 182   PRO: 10.1 (gm)
FAT: 3.1 (gm)   CHO: 30.3 (gm)
Na: 112.2 (mg)   K: 579.9 (mg)
Fiber: 8.8 (gm)   Chol: 0

Ingredients

1 POUND DRIED MARROW OR PINTO BEANS
6 CUPS WATER
1 TABLESPOON OLIVE OIL
1 TABLESPOON VEGETABLE OIL
1 TABLESPOON MINCED FRESH GARLIC (ABOUT 3 CLOVES)
1½ POUNDS ONIONS, THICKLY SLICED (ABOUT 4 MEDIUM)
¼ TEASPOON MARJORAM OR OREGANO
¼ TEASPOON THYME
1 BAY LEAF, CRUMBLED

2 TABLESPOONS CHOPPED FRESH PARSLEY
1 28-OUNCE CAN TOMATOES OR 4 LARGE FRESH
   TOMATOES
2 TEASPOONS SALT (OPTIONAL)*

Method

1. Wash beans and soak overnight. Bring to a boil, cover, and
    simmer 1 hour. Drain thoroughly and wash with cold
    water.
2. Heat oils in a heavy iron pot. Add garlic, onions, and
    herbs. Saute until onions are soft but not brown, about 5
    minutes.
3. Stir in tomatoes and simmer until well blended.
4. Add drained beans, salt,* and just enough water to cover.
    Bring to a boil, reduce heat, and simmer uncovered 1 hour.

*Optional salt is not accounted for in nutrient analysis.

Refried Beans

Yield: 6 servings (3 cups)
Serving Size: $\frac{1}{2}$ cup
Exchange List Approximation:
    Starch/Bread 1$\frac{1}{2}$

Nutrient Content Per Serving:
CAL: 124   PRO: 7.8 (gm)
FAT: 0.5 (gm)   CHO: 23 (gm)
Na: 135.5 (mg) K: 380 (mg)
Fiber: 6.8 (gm)   Chol: 0

Ingredients

- 1 CUP DRIED PINTO BEANS (ABOUT 6 OUNCES)
- 4 CUPS WATER
- 1 CUP CHOPPED ONIONS
- 1 TEASPOON MINCED GARLIC CLOVE
- ¼ TEASPOON SALT
- ½ TEASPOON GROUND CUMIN OR CUMINO
- ¼ CUP TACO SAUCE (MILD, MEDIUM, OR HOT TO TASTE)

Method

1. Soak beans overnight in water to cover.
2. Drain beans and place in heavy saucepan with 4 cups water, onions, garlic, salt and cumin. Bring to a boil, then simmer 1½ to 2 hours until beans are soft enough to mash.
3. Mash or blend beans in blender to desired consistency.
4. Mix in taco sauce and reheat in lightly greased skillet.
5. Serve as vegetable or in burrito (1 6-inch flour tortilla = 1 Starch/Bread).

Lentil Bake

Yield: 4 servings
Serving Size: 1½ cup
Exchange List Approximation:
    Starch/Bread 3
    Meat, lean ½
    Vegetable 1

Nutrient Content Per Serving:
CAL: 290   PRO: 16.2 (gm)
FAT: 4.1 (gm)   CHO: 48.8 (gm)
Na: 302.1 (mg)   K: 739.9 (mg)
Fiber: 10.4 (gm) Chol: 5 (mg)

Ingredients

- 1 CUP LENTILS
- 3 CUPS WATER
- ⅓ CUP RICE
- 1 CUP WATER
- 4 SLICES BACON, CHOPPED
- 2 TABLESPOONS CHOPPED GREEN PEPPER
- 1 CUP CHOPPED ONION (ABOUT 1 MEDIUM)
- 1 16-OUNCE CAN TOMATOES

Method

1. Wash and sort lentils. Add water, bring to a boil, and simmer until tender, about 30 minutes.
2. Bring water to a boil, add rice; cover and cook over low heat about 15 minutes.
3. In a Dutch oven, fry chopped bacon until nearly done. Add green pepper and onion. Continue to cook until onions start to brown. Drain fat from mixture.
4. Add tomatoes to onions and stir until tomatoes are broken up. Add rice and lentils. Mix gently.
5. Bake covered in 350° F oven 45 minutes.

Foul Madamis (Beans)

Yield: 4 servings
Serving Size: $\frac{1}{3}$ cup
Exchange List Approximation:
    Starch/Bread 1
    Vegetable $\frac{1}{2}$
    Fat $1\frac{1}{2}$

Nutrient Content Per Serving:
CAL: 162   PRO: 5.5 (gm)
FAT: 8.9 (gm)   CHO: 16.7 (gm)
Na: 68.7 (mg)   K: 346.3 (mg)
Fiber: 4.8 (gm)   Chol: 0

Ingredients

- 1 CUP COOKED FRIZOL, SMALL FAVA BEANS, OR PINTO BEANS
- 1 TABLESPOON TAHINI (SESAME SEED PASTE)
- ¾ CUP DICED TOMATO (ABOUT 1 MEDIUM)
- ¾ CUP CHOPPED ONION (ABOUT 1 MEDIUM)
- 2 TABLESPOONS OLIVE OIL (DIVIDED)
- 1 TABLESPOON TOMATO PASTE
- 1 TEASPOON CUMIN
- PINCH EACH: GINGER, PEPPER, AND SALT

Method

1. Blend beans in a food processor until big chunks disappear (alternately, mash beans). Add tahini and mix well. Set aside.
2. Saute tomato and onion in 1 Tablespoon olive oil about 5 minutes. Stir in tomato paste and spices.
3. Combine with bean mixture.
4. Spread serving on plate and sprinkle with 1 Tablespoon olive oil. Serve with pita bread.

Cowpoke Beans

Yield: 8 cups

Serving Size: 1 cup

Exchange List Approximation:
 Starch/Bread 2½
 Vegetable 1

Nutrient Content Per Serving:

CAL: 226   PRO: 14.4 (gm)

FAT: 0.9 (gm)   CHO: 41.9 (gm)

Na: 365.9 (mg)   K: 742.7 (mg)

Fiber: 12.2 (gm)   Chol: 0

Ingredients

1 POUND DRIED PINTO BEANS
2 QUARTS WATER
1 TEASPOON SALT
½ TEASPOON CRUSHED RED PEPPER
1 CUP CHOPPED ONION
1 TEASPOON MINCED GARLIC
1 16-OUNCE CAN TOMATOES
2 TEASPOONS GROUND CUMIN
1 TABLESPOON CHILI POWDER

Method

1. Presoak beans in water overnight or use quick-cook method on the package.
2. After soaking, add red pepper and salt, and bring beans to a boil; reduce heat, cover, and simmer gently for 2+ hours or until beans are tender.
3. Add remaining ingredients during last hour of cooking and continue to simmer.
4. Serve. Freeze leftover portions and reheat for another meal.

Lentils Italiano

Yield: 8 servings
Serving Size: 1 cup
Exchange List Approximation:
    Starch/Bread 2
    Meat, medium-fat ½

Nutrient Content Per Serving:
CAL: 197   PRO: 10.8 (gm)
FAT: 4.7 (gm)   CHO: 30.3 (gm)
Na: 1258.5 (mg)   K: 652 (mg)
Fiber: 7.1 (gm)   Chol: 1 (mg)

Ingredients

  1 MEDIUM ONION, CHOPPED
  1 CLOVE GARLIC, MINCED
  2 TABLESPOONS OIL
1½ CUPS DRIED LENTILS, WASHED
  ½ TEASPOON CRUSHED RED PEPPER
  1 TEASPOON SALT
  ½ TEASPOON PEPPER
  4 CUPS WATER
  2 CUBES BEEF BOUILLON OR 4 TEASPOONS INSTANT
    BEEF BOUILLON OR 4 CUPS FAT-SKIMMED BEEF
    BROTH (IF USED, OMIT 4 CUPS WATER)
  ¼ TEASPOON DRIED CRUSHED BASIL
  ¼ TEASPOON DRIED CRUSHED OREGANO
  1 16-OUNCE CAN TOMATOES
  1 6-OUNCE CAN TOMATO PASTE
  1 TABLESPOON VINEGAR
  1 CUP WATER

Method

1. In heavy 4-quart pot, saute onion and garlic in oil for 5 minutes.
2. Add lentils, red pepper, salt, pepper, bouillon, and water. Cover and simmer for 30 minutes.

3. Add remaining ingredients and simmer uncovered for about 1 hour. Stir occasionally.
4. Serve as a bowl of beans or as a sauce over noodles or rice (½ cup cooked noodles or ⅓ cup rice = 1 Starch/Bread Exchange).

Note: Package extra servings and freeze for later use.

Soups

Russian Cabbage Borscht

Yield: 16 servings
Serving Size: $\frac{1}{4}$ cup meat and
  1 cup vegetable
Exchange List Approximation:
    Starch/Bread $\frac{1}{2}$
    Meat, lean $1\frac{1}{2}$
    Vegetable 1

Nutrient Content Per Serving:
CAL: 151   PRO: 13 (gm)
FAT: 5.7 (gm)   CHO: 13.3 (gm)
Na: 458 (mg)   K: 604.6 (mg)
Fiber: 2.4 (gm)   Chol: 36 (mg)
Key Source Nutrients:
    Vitamin A: 3958 (IU)
    Ascorbic acid: 46 (mg)

Ingredients

2¾ POUND CHUCK ROAST, BONE IN
  1 TEASPOON SALT
 ¼ TEASPOON PEPPER
  2 CUPS CHOPPED ONION
  1 2-POUND HEAD OF CABBAGE, SHREDDED
  1 28-OUNCE CAN TOMATO PUREE
  1 28-OUNCE CAN TOMATOES
  1 CUP DICED GREEN PEPPER
1½ CUPS SLICED CARROTS
  1 TEASPOON SUGAR
  1 CUP PLAIN LOW-FAT YOGURT

Method

1. Trim fat from meat.
2. Place meat in 6-quart pot. Add salt, pepper, and onions.
3. Add water to cover meat; bring to a boil, reduce heat, cover, and simmer 1 hour.
4. Add vegetables in order listed, and sugar.
5. Cover and cook at a simmer for 2½ hours.
6. Cool and refrigerate overnight.
7. To serve, remove meat, slice or cut in 1½-ounce servings (2 slices, about ¼ cup).

8. Heat vegetables and serve 1 cup over meat.
9. Top with 1 tablespoon yogurt.
10. Serve with black bread (1 slice of bread = 1 Starch/Bread Exchange).

Turkey (or Chicken) Gumbo Soup

Yield: 8 servings
Serving Size: 1 cup
Exchange List Approximation:
    Starch/Bread 1
    Meat, lean ½

Nutrient Content Per Serving:

CAL: 107	PRO: 7.7 (gm)
FAT: 2.8 (gm)	CHO: 13.2 (gm)
Na: 406.3 (mg)	K: 318.5 (mg)
Fiber: 2 (gm)	Chol: 14 (mg)

Ingredients

    ROAST TURKEY CARCASS OR MEAT AND BONES
    FROM CHICKEN
    WATER
1 TEASPOON SALT
1 TABLESPOON MARGARINE
1 CUP SLICED OKRA, FRESH OR FROZEN
1 CUP SLICED CELERY
½ CUP CHOPPED ONION
¼ CUP DICED GREEN PEPPER
1 TEASPOON MINCED GARLIC CLOVE
2 TABLEPOONS FLOUR
1 16-OUNCE CAN TOMATOES
1½ QUARTS TURKEY BROTH
¼ CUP UNCOOKED RICE
2 TABLESPOONS CHOPPED PARSLEY

¼ TEASPOON EACH: CUMIN, PEPPER, TABASCO SAUCE, THYME
1 CUP CHOPPED, COOKED TURKEY

Method

1. Place turkey (or chicken) carcass in large pot, add any uncooked parts (neck, back, wings). Cover with water. Add salt. Simmer about 2 hours.
2. Pour broth into container and chill. Skim off fat. Remove meat from bones and reserve.
3. Saute okra in margarine until it starts to brown, about 5 minutes.
4. Add celery, onion, green pepper, and garlic. Saute for about 2 minutes while stirring.
5. Sprinkle with flour. Stir until blended and starting to brown.
6. Add tomatoes. Stir, break into pieces, and cook until thickened.
7. Add broth, rice, and seasonings.
8. Simmer 30 minutes. Add meat and heat 5 minutes. Serve.

Valley Forge Pepperpot Soup

Yield: 8 servings (2 quarts)
Serving Size: 1 cup
Exchange List Approximation:
    Starch/Bread $\frac{1}{2}$
    Vegetable 1
    Fat 1

Nutrient Content Per Serving:
CAL: 113   PRO: 3.6 (gm)
FAT: 6.7 (gm)   CHO: 10 (gm)
Na: 668.1 (mg)   K: 247.9 (mg)
Fiber: 1.1 (gm)   Chol: 2 (mg)

Ingredients

1¼ CUPS DICED POTATOES
¼ CUP FINELY CHOPPED ONION
½ CUP JULIENNED GREEN PEPPER
½ CUP THINLY SLICED CELERY
4 TABLESPOONS MARGARINE
1½ QUARTS CHICKEN BROTH, CANNED
    (ABOUT 1 46-FLUID-OUNCE CAN)
¼ CUP ALL-PURPOSE FLOUR
½ CUP WHOLE MILK
1 TEASPOON DICED PIMENTO

Method

1. In a soup pot, cook potatoes in 1 quart of the broth until half done. Reserve 2 cups broth for step 3.
2. Add onion, green pepper, and celery. Simmer for 15 minutes.
3. In another pan melt margarine; stir in flour. Add the reserved 2 cups of broth while stirring constantly. Simmer 5 minutes. Stir in milk.
4. Add thickened broth to the cooking vegetables. Add pimento.
5. Simmer 3 to 5 minutes, stirring frequently until smooth and slightly thickened consistency is achieved.

Mulligatawny Soup

Yield: 8 or 2 servings
Serving Size: 1 cup
Exchange List Approximation:
    Meat, lean 1
    Vegetable 2

Nutrient Content Per Serving:
CAL: 109   PRO: 7.4 (gm)
FAT: 4.2 (gm)   CHO: 10.9 (gm)
Na: 424.1 (mg)   K: 268.3 (mg)
Fiber: 1.6 (gm)   Chol: 24 (mg)

Ingredients

Eight Servings		Two Servings	
4	CHICKEN DRUMSTICKS, FAT REMOVED	1	
1½	QUARTS WATER	2	CUPS
1	TEASPOON SALT	¼	TEASPOON
¼	TEASPOON PEPPER	1⁄16	TEASPOON
2	TABLESPOONS MARGARINE	1½	TEASPOONS
¼	CUP CHOPPED ONION	1	TABLESPOON
¼	CUP CARROTS, THINLY SLICED	1	TABLESPOON
¼	CUP CELERY, THINLY SLICED	1	TABLESPOON
3	TABLESPOONS FLOUR	2	TEASPOONS
1	TEASPOON CURRY POWDER	¼	TEASPOON
1	16-OUNCE CAN TOMATOES, DICED, WITH JUICE	½	CUP
1	CUP PEELED, DICED APPLE	¼	CUP
1	TABLESPOON PARSLEY, FRESH, CHOPPED	1	TEASPOON

Method

1. Cook chicken legs in seasoned water in large pot about 45 minutes while preparing vegetables.
2. Heat margarine in saucepan. Add vegetables and cook about 5 minutes. Do not burn.

3. Stir flour and curry powder and cook about 2 minutes. Set aside.
4. Remove chicken from broth. Cool slightly, skin, bone, and cut up (yields 1 cup chicken).
5. Add chicken, vegetables, and tomatoes to broth. Bring to a boil while stirring. Cover and simmer 20 minutes.
6. Add apples and parsley, stir, and simmer uncovered for 10 minutes.

Variation: 1 cup of cup-up chicken and 5½ cups of stock may be used. Omit salt.

Fresh Vegetable Chowder

Yield: 8 servings
Serving Size: 1 cup
Exchange List Approximation:
   Starch/Bread 1
   Meat, medium-fat $\frac{1}{2}$
   Vegetable 1
   Fat $\frac{1}{2}$

Nutrient Content Per Serving:
CAL: 160   PRO: 9.1 (gm)
FAT: 6.5 (gm)   CHO: 18.2 (gm)
Na: 798.6 (mg)*   K: 511.3 (mg)
Fiber: 4 (gm)   Chol: 16 (mg)

Ingredients

  1 POUND ZUCCHINI
  1 TABLESPOON MARGARINE
  ½ CUP CHOPPED ONION
  2 TABLESPOONS CHOPPED PARSLEY
  ½ TEASPOON BASIL LEAVES
  3 TABLESPOONS ALL-PURPOSE FLOUR
2½ CUPS WATER
  2 TEASPOONS CHICKEN BOUILLON GRANULES
  1 TEASPOON LEMON JUICE
  ½ TEASPOON PEPPER
  1 CUP FROZEN WHOLE-KERNEL CORN
  1 16-OUNCE CAN TOMATOES
  1 13-OUNCE CAN EVAPORATED SKIM MILK
  1 CUP AMERICAN CHEESE, CUBED (ABOUT 4 OUNCES)

Method

1. Cut zucchini lengthwise in half and slice into ¼-inch pieces.
2. Heat margarine in 3- to 6-quart saucepan. Add zucchini, onion, parsley, and basil. Cook for about 6 minutes, stirring occasionally.

3. Add flour and stir until mixed.
4. Add water, bouillon, lemon juice, and pepper. Stir while heating to a boil.
5. Add corn, bring to a boil, stirring to prevent scorching.
6. Drain tomatoes. Reserve juice for another use. Dice tomatoes and add to chowder.
7. Add milk and heat to just boiling.
8. Add cheese. Stir until melted. Do not boil.

*To reduce sodium content, use salt-free bouillon or substitute an herb blend from Chapter 15 for the bouillon.

Black Bean Soup

Yield: 8 cups (8 servings)
Serving Size: 1 cup
Exchange List Approximation:
    Starch/Bread 2½
    Meat, lean 1

Nutrient Content Per Serving:
CAL: 241   PRO: 13.3 (gm)
FAT: 4.4 (gm)   CHO: 38.8 (gm)
Na: 815.5 (mg)* K: 682.9 (mg)
Fiber: 15.7 (gm) Chol: 0

Ingredients

  1 POUND DRIED BLACK BEANS
  2 QUARTS WATER
  3 TEASPOONS SALT
  2 TABLESPOONS OLIVE OIL
  2 CUPS CHOPPED ONIONS
  1 CUP CHOPPED GREEN PEPPER (OPTIONAL)
  2 TEASPOONS MINCED GARLIC
  1 TEASPOON GROUND CUMIN
  1 TEASPOON OREGANO
 ¼ TEASPOON DRY MUSTARD
  1 TABLESPOON LEMON JUICE

Method

1. Presoak beans in water overnight or use quick-cook method on package.
2. After soaking beans, add 2 teaspoons salt and bring to a boil; cover and simmer on low heat for 2 hours.
3. Heat oil, add onions, and saute about 5 minutes. Add green pepper and sauté until onions are tender.
4. Stir in remaining ingredients. Add about ¾ cup hot bean liquid, cover, and simmer 10 minutes.

5. Add onion seasoning mixture to beans and continue to cook 1 hour, stirring occasionally.
6. Serve over cooked brown rice (½ cup cooked rice = 1 Bread Exchange) and top with chopped green onions. Freeze leftovers and reheat for another meal.

*To reduce sodium content, cut back on, or eliminate, the salt.

Fish Chowder with Black Olives

Yield: 8 servings (8 cups)
Serving Size: 1 cup
Exchange List Approximation:
    Starch/Bread 1
    Meat, lean 1

Nutrient Content Per Serving:
CAL: 137   PRO: 12.6 (gm)
FAT: 2.8 (gm)   CHO: 15.9 (gm)
Na: 335.7 (mg)   K: 504.7 (mg)
Fiber: 2.5 (gm)   Chol: 16 (mg)

Ingredients

  3 CUPS DICED POTATOES
  ½ TEASPOON SALT
  ¼ TEASPOON PEPPER
3½ CUPS WATER
  1 TABLESPOON MARGARINE
  1 CUP CHOPPED ONION
  2 TEASPOONS MINCED GARLIC CLOVE (ABOUT 2)
  1 16-OUNCE CAN TOMATOES
  ¼ CUP CHOPPED PARSLEY
  1 TEASPOON THYME
  1 BAY LEAF

¾ POUND COD OR HADDOCK, CUT INTO 1-INCH
   CUBES
¼ CUP QUARTERED, PITTED BLACK OLIVES
½ TEASPOON WORCESTERSHIRE SAUCE (OPTIONAL)

Method

1. Place potatoes in large pot (3-quart). Add salt, pepper, and water. Bring to a boil, cover, and cook about 20 minutes.
2. Saute onions in margarine in saucepan, about 5 minutes. Add garlic and cook 1 minute.
3. Add tomatoes, parsley, thyme, and bay leaf. Mash tomatoes while cooking over moderate heat, about 15 minutes.
4. Add tomato mixture, fish, and olives to potatoes. Cook over low heat 6 to 8 minutes. Add more water, if needed to make 8 cups.
5. Garnish with parsley or capers.

Indiana Senate Bean Soup

Yield: 8 servings
Serving Size: 1 cup
Exchange List Approximation:
    Starch/Bread 2½
    Meat, lean 1½

Nutrient Content Per Serving:
CAL: 278   PRO: 20.1 (gm)
FAT: 6.7 (gm)   CHO: 35.4 (gm)
Na: 478 (mg)   K: 819.3 (mg)
Fiber: 9.6 (gm)   Chol: 20 (mg)

Ingredients

- 1 POUND GREAT NORTHERN BEANS, DRIED
- 3 QUARTS WATER
- ¼ CUP DICED SALT PORK (ABOUT 1½ OUNCES)
- ½ TEASPOON BLACK PEPPER
- ½ TEASPOON WORCESTERSHIRE SAUCE
- 1¾ CUPS DICED LEAN HAM (ABOUT 8 OUNCES)
- 1 CUP THINLY SLICED CELERY
- ¼ CUP CHOPPED ONION

Method

1. Wash beans thoroughly in cold water. Remove any discolored beans or trash.
2. Place beans in 4- to 6-quart pot. Add water. Let set overnight or bring the beans to a boil, cover, turn off heat, and let stand 1 hour.
3. Add diced salt pork, pepper, and Worcestershire sauce. Bring to a boil and simmer covered for 1 hour.
4. Add ham, celery, and onion. Cover and simmer 1½ to 2 hours longer, until beans are tender and liquid is thickened. Stir occasionally. Add water if needed. Adjust yield to 2 quarts.
5. Garnish with chopped onion.

Cream of Tomato Soup

Yield: 6 servings
Serving Size: $\frac{2}{3}$ cup
Exchange List Approximation:
    Starch/Bread 1
    Fat 1

Nutrient Content Per Serving:
CAL: 122   PRO: 6 (gm)
FAT: 4.3 (gm)   CHO: 15.7 (gm)
Na: 487.8 (mg)   K: 476.5 (mg)
Fiber: 1.1 (gm)   Chol: 2 (mg)

Ingredients

3 CUPS COOKED TOMATOES (ABOUT 1 28-OUNCE CAN)
1 TABLESPOON MINCED ONION
½ TEASPOON SALT
¼ TEASPOON PEPPER
    DASH CAYENNE OR TABASCO SAUCE
2 TEASPOONS SUGAR
2 TABLESPOONS MARGARINE
2 TABLESPOONS FLOUR
1 13-OUNCE CAN EVAPORATED SKIM MILK

Method

1. Cook tomatoes, onions, salt, pepper, cayenne, and sugar together for 15 minutes. Strain into large liquid measuring cup or bowl.
2. Melt margarine in a 2-quart saucepan. Blend in flour. Cook until bubbly. While stirring, gradually add milk and cook until thickened.
3. Add tomato mixture, stirring constantly. Heat just to a simmer. Do not boil.

Variation: 4 cups of chopped fresh tomatoes may be used for canned tomatoes.

Note: Less than ½ teaspoon of sugar per serving (5 calories).

Zucchini Soup

Yield: 8 or 4 servings
Serving Size: 1 cup
Exchange List Approximation:
    Starch/Bread 1
    Vegetable 1

Nutrient Content Per Serving:
CAL: 106   PRO: 4.8 (gm)
FAT: 2.6 (gm)   CHO: 16.9 (gm)
Na: 397.5 (mg)   K: 376.1 (mg)
Fiber: 4.6 (gm)   Chol: 1 (mg)

Ingredients

Eight Servings	*Four Servings*
1 TABLESPOON OLIVE OIL	1½ TEASPOONS
1 CUP CHOPPED ONION	½ CUP
1 TEASPOON MINCED GARLIC CLOVE	½ TEASPOON
½ CUP EACH: DICED CARROTS, CELERY, POTATOES	¼ CUP
2 BOUILLON CUBES	1
1 TEASPOON OREGANO	½ TEASPOON
½ TEASPOON BASIL	¼ TEASPOON
⅛ TEASPOON PEPPER	¹⁄₁₆ TEASPOON
6 CUPS WATER	3 CUPS
1 CUP RED OR PINTO BEANS, DRAINED (ABOUT ⅔ 15-OUNCE CAN)	½ CUP
4 CUPS ZUCCHINI, QUARTERED AND SLICED, ⅜ INCH (ABOUT 1 POUND)	2 CUPS
½ CUP ELBOW MACARONI (ABOUT 2 OUNCES)	¼ CUP
2 TABLESPOONS GRATED PARMESAN CHEESE	1 TABLESPOON

Method

1. Saute onion and garlic in olive oil in 3- to 4-quart saucepan until lightly browned, about 5 minutes.
2. Add carrots, celery, potatoes, and seasonings. Stir. Add water. Cover and simmer about 15 minutes.
3. Add beans and zucchini. Bring to a boil. Add macaroni. Stir. Cover and simmer 15 minutes.
4. Sprinkle each serving with ¾ teaspoon Parmesan cheese.

Salads and
Side Dishes

Sprouts

Yield: 6 servings
Serving Size: $\frac{1}{3}$ cup
Exchange List Approximation:
 Free food

Nutrient Content Per Serving:
CAL: 3   PRO: 0.4 (gm)
FAT: 0.1 (gm) CHO: 0.4 (gm)
Na: 0.7 (mg)   K: 8.6 (mg)
Fiber: 0.3 (gm) Chol: 0

Ingredients

 1 TABLESPOON ALFALFA SEEDS
or
 2 TABLESPOONS DRIED BEANS (LENTILS, MUNG, SOY,
  OR BLACK)

Method

1. Use clean wide-mouth, quart, clear-glass jar with mesh or cheese-cloth cover.
2. Place seeds or beans in jar, cover with water, and soak overnight at room temperature.
3. Pour off water, rinse seeds thoroughly, and drain well. Place jar on side away from light at room temperature.
4. Repeat process every morning. Seeds will start sprouting after 2 days, beans after 3 days.
5. Rinsing will remove hulls and prevent souring. In hot, humid climates, the sprouts should be rinsed twice a day.
6. Allow about 6 to 7 days for sprouts' growth. Use in salad or stir-fry recipes.

Note: Sprouts tend to grow best in darkness; however, place alfalfa, mustard, radish, cabbage, and clover in indirect light to develop chlorophyll the last 2 days of growth.

Sprouts Salad

Yield: 6 or 2 servings
Serving Size: 1 cup
Exchange List Approximation:
    Vegetable 1
    Fat 2

Nutrient Content Per Serving:
CAL: 124*   PRO: 3.1 (gm)
FAT: 11.3 (gm)*   CHO: 3.8 (gm)
Na: 61 (mg)   K: 180.1 (mg)
Fiber: 1.1 (gm)   Chol: 46 (mg)

Ingredients

Six Servings		Two Servings
4	TABLESPOONS SUNFLOWER SEEDS	4 TEASPOONS
2	CUPS ALFALFA SPROUTS	⅔ CUP
or		
1½	CUPS BEAN SPROUTS	½ CUP
½	CUP SLICED RADISHES	3 TABLESPOONS
¾	CUP CUCUMBER, QUARTERED AND SLICED	¼ CUP
¼	CUP SLICED GREEN ONIONS	2 TABLESPOONS
4	CUPS BITE-SIZED PIECES SALAD GREENS	1¼ CUPS
3	TABLESPOONS SALAD OIL	1 TABLESPOON
2	TABLESPOONS VINEGAR	2 TEASPOONS
⅛	TEASPOON SALT	PINCH
⅛	TEASPOON GARLIC POWDER	PINCH
⅛	TEASPOON BASIL	PINCH
¹⁄₁₆	TEASPOON BLACK PEPPER	SPRINKLE
1	SLICED HARD-COOKED EGG	⅓

Method

1. Place sunflower seeds in dry skillet. Toast by stirring over medium heat for about 3 minutes (optional).

2. Combine sunflower seeds, sprouts, radishes, cucumbers, and onions in large salad bowl. Add cold, dry salad greens and toss. Cover and chill.
3. Prepare dressing by mixing salad oil, vinegar, salt, garlic powder, basil, and pepper.
4. When ready to serve, pour over salad and toss. Garnish with slices of hard-cooked egg.

*To reduce fat and calories, cut back on the sunflower seeds.

Summer Night Salad

Yield: 6 servings
Serving Size: 1 cup
Exchange List Approximation:
    Meat, medium-fat 1
    Vegetable 2
    Fat 3

Nutrient Content Per Serving:
CAL: 262*   PRO: 10.6 (gm)
FAT: 21.5 (gm)* CHO: 9.3 (gm)
Na: 642.2 (mg) K: 448 (mg)
Fiber: 3 (gm)   Chol: 165 (mg)

Ingredients

1 CUP FRESH BROCCOLI CUT INTO FLOWERETS
1 CUP FRESH CAULIFLOWER CUT INTO FLOWERETS
1 CUP FRESH YELLOW SQUASH IN STRIPS
1 CUP ZUCCHINI IN STRIPS
3 HARD-COOKED EGGS, DICED
½ CUP CHOPPED PECANS
½ CUP CHOPPED COOKED HAM
½ CUP CHOPPED CHEDDAR CHEESE
¼ CUP MAYONNAISE
¼ CUP CREAM, LIGHT
1 TABLESPOON VINEGAR
1 TEASPOON SALT
1 TEASPOON SUGAR
2 TOMATOES, CUT INTO WEDGES

Method

1. Steam vegetables together just until broccoli turns bright green, about 5 minutes.
2. Drain and pour into large bowl.
3. Combine mayonnaise, cream, vinegar, salt, and sugar for dressing.
4. Toss vegetables and remaining ingredients with dressing and chill for several hours.

5. Arrange 1-cup serving and garnish with 2 tomato wedges.

*To reduce fat and calories, use low-calorie dressing instead of following step 3 and making your own.

Three-Bean Salad
(Mexican Bean Salad)

Yield: 6 servings (3 cups)
Serving Size: ½ cup
Exchange List Approximation:
    Starch/Bread 1
    Meat, medium-fat ½

Nutrient Content Per Serving:
CAL: 118   PRO: 5.2 (gm)
FAT: 3.4 (gm)   CHO: 17.9 (gm)
Na: 62.2 (mg)   K: 254.5 (mg)
Fiber: 4.7 (gm)   Chol: 0

Ingredients

1 CUP CUT GREEN BEANS (ABOUT ONE HALF 16-OUNCE CAN)
¾ CUP RED KIDNEY OR PINTO BEANS (ABOUT ONE HALF 15-OUNCE CAN)
⅞ CUP GARBANZOS OR CHICK PEAS (ABOUT ONE HALF 15-OUNCE CAN)
¼ CUP FINELY CHOPPED ONION
¼ CUP CHOPPED GREEN PEPPER
3 TABLESPOONS VINEGAR
¼ CUP WATER
1 TABLESPOON VEGETABLE OIL
2 TEASPOONS SUGAR
¼ TEASPOON OREGANO
1 GARLIC CLOVE

Method

1. Combine drained beans, onion, and green pepper.
2. Mix vinegar, water, oil, sugar, oregano, and garlic clove.
   Pour over beans. Toss to mix.
3. Cover and chill about 4 hours or overnight before serving.
   Remove garlic clove.

Variation: For Mexican Bean Salad, omit oregano and add 1 Tablespoon Picante sauce (see recipe page 321). Soy beans, navy beans, black-eye peas, or lima beans may be substituted for garbanzos.

Barley Salad

Yield: 6 servings (3 cups)
Serving Size: $\frac{2}{3}$ cup
Exchange List Approximation:
    Starch/Bread 1
    Fat 1

Nutrient Content Per Serving:
CAL: 111   PRO: 1.9 (gm)
FAT: 5.2 (gm)   CHO: 15.2 (gm)
Na: 93.6 (mg)   K: 123.6 (mg)
Fiber: 2.6 (gm)   Chol: 0

Ingredients

½ CUP QUICK PEARL BARLEY
1½ CUPS WATER
¼ TEASPOON SALT
1 CUP SLICED FRESH MUSHROOMS
⅓ CUP THINLY SLICED CARROTS
⅓ CUP THINLY SLICED ZUCCHINI (OR YELLOW SQUASH)
3 TABLESPOONS SLICED GREEN ONION
3 TABLESPOONS FINELY CHOPPED PARSLEY
3 TABLESPOONS LEMON JUICE
2 TABLESPOONS VEGETABLE OIL
¼ TEASPOON GARLIC POWDER
½ TEASPOON BASIL (OR 1 TEASPOON FRESH BASIL)
⅛ TEASPOON SALT

Method

1. Add barley to boiling salted water; stir. Add drop of oil to prevent boiling over; cover, lower heat, and cook until tender, about 1 hour for regular barley.
2. Drain and chill.
3. Add vegetables.

4. Combine lemon juice, oil, and spices. Add to salad. Toss lightly to coat ingredients. Sprinkle with salt.
5. Chill at least 3 hours or overnight.
6. Serve on lettuce and garnish with tomato wedges, if desired.

Note: This salad will keep well in refrigerator for several days.

Broccoli-Cauliflower Salad with Dressing

Yield: 6 or 2 servings
Serving Size: $\frac{1}{6}$ recipe
Exchange List Approximation:
    Vegetable 1
    Fat $\frac{1}{2}$

Nutrient Content Per Serving:
CAL: 52   PRO: 3.1 (gm)
FAT: 2.5 (gm)   CHO: 5.2 (gm)
Na: 50.4 (mg)   K: 250.4 (mg)
Fiber: 1.7 (gm)   Chol: 4 (mg)

Ingredients

Six Servings	*Two Servings*
2 CUPS BROCCOLI, PEELED, QUARTERED, CUT INTO BITE-SIZED PIECES	⅔ CUP
1 CUP CAULIFLOWER, SLICED INTO BITE-SIZED PIECES	⅓ CUP
2 TABLESPOONS CHOPPED GREEN ONION	2 TEASPOONS
⅛ TEASPOON PEPPER	SPRINKLE

Horseradish Dressing

1 TABLESPOON PREPARED HORSERADISH	1 TEASPOON
1 TABLESPOON MAYONNAISE	1 TEASPOON
1 8-OUNCE CONTAINER PLAIN LOW-FAT YOGURT	4 TABLESPOONS

Method

1. Mix broccoli, cauliflower, onion, and pepper. Chill.
2. Mix horseradish and mayonnaise until blended. Carefully fold into yogurt.
3. Pour over vegetables and mix lightly.

Banana-Yogurt Mold

Yield: 8 servings
Serving Size: $\frac{1}{2}$ cup
Exchange List Approximation:
    Fruit 1

Nutrient Content Per Serving:
CAL: 59   PRO: 3.4 (gm)
FAT: 0.6 (gm)   CHO: 11.1 (gm)
Na: 32.7 (mg)   K: 250.1 (mg)
Fiber: 0.7 (gm)   Chol: 2 (mg)

Ingredients

- 1 ENVELOPE UNFLAVORED GELATIN
- 2 TABLESPOONS WATER
- ⅓ CUP ORANGE JUICE
- 1⅓ CUPS MASHED BANANAS (ABOUT 3 SMALL)
- 1 TEASPOON VANILLA
- 1 8-OUNCE CARTON PLAIN LOW-FAT YOGURT
- 2 EGG WHITES
- 6 PACKETS SUGAR SUBSTITUTE

Method

1. Sprinkle gelatin on water in custard cup; place in pan of hot water; heat until gelatin melts.
2. Place orange juice, bananas, gelatin, and vanilla in mixer bowl. Whip until mixture is smooth. (May be whipped in blender or food processor.)
3. Use wire whip to gently fold in yogurt. Refrigerate while whipping egg whites.
4. Beat egg whites until foamy, add sweetener, and whip until stiff. Fold into yogurt mixture.
5. Spoon into 8 individual serving containers, cover, and freeze.

Variation: Frozen Banana Yogurt. Following step 3, freeze mixture in shallow metal pan. Break into pieces and beat until smooth in electric mixer or food processor. Add whipped egg whites and beat until just blended.

Apple-Cabbage Slaw

Yield: 4 servings
Serving Size: $\frac{1}{2}$ cup
Exchange List Approximation:
  Vegetable $\frac{1}{2}$
  Fruit $\frac{1}{2}$

Nutrient Content Per Serving:
CAL: 42   PRO: 1.3 (gm)
FAT: 0.4 (gm) CHO: 9.2 (gm)
Na: 154.3 (mg) K: 170.4 (mg)
Fiber: 1.5 (gm) Chol: 1 (mg)

Ingredients

- ¼ CUP PLAIN LOW-FAT YOGURT
- ¼ TEASPOON SALT
  DASH PEPPER
- 2 TEASPOONS VINEGAR
- ¼ TEASPOON PREPARED MUSTARD
- 1 CUP APPLES, UNPARED, THINLY SLICED
- 2 CUPS CABBAGE, SHREDDED

Method

1. Mix yogurt, salt, pepper, vinegar, and mustard thoroughly.
2. Lightly mix apples and cabbage.
3. Pour yogurt mixture over apple-cabbage mixture; toss lightly.
4. Serve immediately.

Wine Salad

Yield: 12 servings (6 cups)
Serving Size: $\frac{1}{2}$ cup
Exchange List Approximation:
    Fruit 1
    Fat 1

Nutrient Content Per Serving:
CAL: 101   PRO: 1.8 (gm)
FAT: 3.2 (gm)   CHO: 17.6 (gm)
Na: 34.4 (mg)   K: 122.4 (mg)
Fiber: 0.8 (gm) Chol: 0

Ingredients

1 PACKAGE RASPBERRY LOW-CALORIE GELATIN DESSERT POWDER
1 ENVELOPE PLAIN GELATIN
1 CUP JELLIED CRANBERRY SAUCE (ABOUT ONE HALF 16-OUNCE CAN)
1¾ CUPS BOILING WATER
¾ CUP PORT WINE
2¼ CUPS CRUSHED PINEAPPLE IN UNSWEETENED JUICE (ABOUT 1 20-OUNCE CAN)
⅔ CUP CHOPPED CELERY
½ CUP CHOPPED NUTS

Method

1. Mix gelatin and cranberry sauce.
2. Add boiling water and stir until gelatin and sauce are dissolved.
3. Add wine, pineapple and juice, celery, and nuts. Stir and chill until slightly thickened.
4. Mix and pour into 12 individual molds or one large mold. Chill until firm.

Note: This salad may be prepared for 6 servings; use raspberry dessert powder and one half of ingredients.

Garden Green-Salad Mold

Yield: 6 servings
Serving Size: ½ cup
Exchange List Approximation:
    Free food

Nutrient Content Per Serving:
CAL: 15   PRO: 1.2 (gm)
FAT: 0   CHO: 2.3 (gm)
Na: 136.5 (mg)   K: 104.2 (mg)
Fiber: 1 (gm)   Chol: 0

Ingredients

1	ENVELOPE LOW-CALORIE LIME-FLAVORED GELATIN
1	CUP BOILING WATER
1	CUP COLD WATER
1	TABLESPOON LEMON JUICE
¼	TEASPOON SALT
½	TEASPOON HORSERADISH
½	TEASPOON FINELY CHOPPED JALAPENO PEPPER (OPTIONAL)
2½	CUPS FINELY SHREDDED CABBAGE
⅓	CUP THINLY SLICED GREEN ONIONS
⅓	CUP SLICED RADISHES

Method

1. Add boiling water to gelatin. Stir until dissolved.
2. Add cold water and chill until thickened.
3. Add seasonings and vegetables. Mix thoroughly.
4. Pour into 1 quart mold or individual molds and chill until firm.
5. Serve on lettuce or as relish on salad plate.

Jellied Vegetable Salad

Yield: 4 servings
Serving Size: $\frac{2}{3}$ cup
Exchange List Approximation:
    Vegetable 1

Nutrient Content Per Serving:
CAL: 29   PRO: 2.1 (gm)
FAT: 0.1 (gm)   CHO: 6.2 (gm)
Na: 149.4 (mg)   K: 174.9 (mg)
Fiber: 1.1 (gm)   Chol: 0
Key Source Nutrients:
    Vitamin A: 4262 (IU)

Ingredients

1	ENVELOPE UNFLAVORED GELATIN
¼	CUP WATER
1½	CUPS BOILING WATER
2	TABLESPOONS TARRAGON VINEGAR
¼	TEASPOON SALT
½	TABLESPOON HONEY
¾	CUP FINELY SHREDDED CABBAGE
½	CUP SHREDDED CARROTS
¼	CUP CHOPPED CELERY
½	CUP PARED, DICED CUCUMBER
1	TABLESPOON CHOPPED GREEN ONION
1	TABLESPOON FINELY CHOPPED PIMENTO
	SALAD GREENS (AS DESIRED)

Method

1. Soften gelatin in ¼ cup water for 5 minutes.
2. Add softened gelatin to boiling water. Stir until gelatin is dissolved.
3. Stir in vinegar, salt, and honey.
4. Chill until mixture begins to thicken.
5. Fold in remaining ingredients except salad greens.
6. Pour into 1-quart mold or 8-inch square pan.
7. Chill until set.
8. Unmold and serve on crisp salad greens.

Pineapple Salad

Yield: 8 servings (4 cups)
Serving Size: ½ cup
Exchange List Approximation:
    Fruit ½
    Fat ½

Nutrient Content Per Serving:
CAL: 50   PRO: 1 (gm)
FAT: 1.8 (gm)   CHO: 6.7 (gm)
Na: 43 (mg)   K: 56.6 (mg)
Fiber: 0.2 (gm) Chol: 0

Ingredients

1 PACKAGE LEMON OR LIME LOW-CALORIE GELATIN DESSERT
1 CUP BOILING WATER
1 8-OUNCE CAN CRUSHED PINEAPPLE IN UNSWEETENED PINEAPPLE JUICE
½ 12-OUNCE CAN CITRUS OR LEMON-LIME SUGAR-FREE CARBONATED BEVERAGE
4 OUNCES WHIPPED TOPPING (ABOUT ONE HALF 8-OUNCE CONTAINER)

Method

1. Add boiling water to gelatin dessert. Stir until dissolved.
2. Add juice from pineapple and beverage.
3. Chill until medium stiff. Whip with mixer until foamy.
4. Gradually whip into whipped topping. Fold in pineapple.
5. Pour into mold and chill until set.

Variation: Orange or raspberry low-calorie gelatin dessert and 1 cup of other unsweetened fruits may be used, such as peaches, apricots, etc.

Vegetable Salad en Gelée

Yield: 8 servings (4 cups)
Serving Size: $\frac{1}{2}$ cup
Exchange List Approximation:
    Vegetable 1
    Fat $\frac{1}{2}$

Nutrient Content Per Serving:
CAL: 46   PRO: 1 (gm)
FAT: 2.8 (gm)   CHO: 4.6 (gm)
Na: 27.8 (mg)   K: 88.5 (mg)
Fiber: 0.5 (gm)   Chol: 2 (mg)

Ingredients

1 ENVELOPE UNFLAVORED GELATIN
1 12-OUNCE CAN SUGAR-FREE CARBONATED GRAPEFRUIT-LEMON BEVERAGE
1 6½-OUNCE CAN UNSWEETENED CRUSHED PINEAPPLE
2 TABLESPOONS MAYONNAISE
1 CUP SHREDDED OR FINELY CHOPPED CABBAGE
⅓ CUP SHREDDED OR FINELY CHOPPED CARROTS

Method

1. Sprinkle gelatin over beverage. Let set 1 minute to soften. Heat over low heat until gelatin is dissolved.
2. Stir in remaining ingredients.
3. Pour into individual molds or into pan. Refrigerate until set.

Cheesy Grits

Yield: 6 or 2 servings
Serving Size: 1 cup
Exchange List Approximation:
    Starch/Bread $1\frac{1}{2}$
    Meat, medium-fat 1
    Fat 2

Nutrient Content Per Serving:
CAL: 286   PRO: 12.3 (gm)
FAT: 15.4 (gm)*   CHO: 24.1 (gm)
Na: 253.5 (mg)   K: 124 (mg)
Fiber: 2.2 (gm)   Chol: 122 (mg)

Ingredients

Six Servings		Two Servings	
4	CUPS WATER	2	CUPS
1	CUP QUICK GRITS	½	CUP
1½	CUPS PROCESSED CHEDDAR CHEESE, CHOPPED	¾	CUP
2	TABLESPOONS MARGARINE	1	TABLESPOON
¼	CUP CHOPPED GREEN CHILIES (ABOUT 2 OUNCES) OR PICANTE SAUCE	2	TABLESPOONS
2	EGGS (SEPARATED)	1	
½	CUP SKIM MILK	¼	CUP

Method

1. Bring water to a boil in heavy sauce pan. Stir in grits. Bring to a boil. Reduce heat, partially cover, and cook 5 minutes. Stir occasionally.
2. Add cheese, margarine, and chilies. Stir until cheese is melted.
3. Beat egg yolks with milk and stir into grits.
4. Whip egg whites until stiff and fold into mixture.
5. Pour into lightly greased 7- × 11-inch baking dish (5- × 5-inch casserole for 3 servings) and bake in 350° F oven for 1 hour. Let set 5 minutes before cutting.

*To reduce fat, use half servings. If full servings are used, limit this dish to occasional use.

Cottage Cheese Baked Potatoes

Yield: 4 servings
Serving Size: $\frac{1}{2}$ potato
Exchange List Approximation:
    Starch/Bread $1\frac{1}{2}$

Nutrient Content Per Serving:
CAL: 131   PRO: 6.5 (gm)
FAT: 0.7 (gm)   CHO: 24.9 (gm)
Na: 263.7 (mg)   K: 435.8 (mg)
Fiber: 2.7 (gm)   Chol: 3 (mg)

Ingredients

  2 8-OUNCE BAKING POTATOES
  ½ CUP LOW-FAT COTTAGE CHEESE
  ¼ CUP SKIM MILK
  ¼ TEASPOON SALT
  ⅛ TEASPOON PEPPER
     PAPRIKA (USE AS DESIRED)

Method

1. Wash potatoes well. Prick skins in several places. Bake at
    425° F (hot oven) until tender, 50 to 60 minutes.
2. Remove from oven; cut in half. Scoop out insides of
    potatoes, leaving skins intact; save skins. Mash potatoes
    thoroughly.
3. Add remaining ingredients except paprika. Beat until fluffy.
4. Put mashed potato mixture into potato skins. Sprinkle
    paprika over the tops.
5. Bake at 425° F until heated through and tops are lightly
    browned, about 10 minutes.

Brown Rice Pilaf

Yield: 6 servings
Serving Size: ¾ cup
Exchange List Approximation:
    Starch/Bread 2
    Fat ½

Nutrient Content Per Serving:
CAL: 167   PRO: 4.4 (gm)
FAT: 5.1 (gm)   CHO: 26.8 (gm)
Na: 264.9 (mg)*   K: 94.6 (mg)
Fiber: 2.1 (gm)   Chol: 0

Ingredients

- 1 TABLESPOON MARGARINE
- ½ CUP VERMICELLI, BROKEN INTO ½-INCH LENGTHS
- ¾ CUP BROWN RICE
- 3 CUPS WATER
- 1 CUBE BOUILLON
- 3 TABLESPOONS CHOPPED TOASTED NUTS (ALMONDS, PECANS, PINE NUTS)

Method

1. Heat margarine in large skillet. Add vermicelli. Stir until it starts to brown.
2. Add rice. Stir until rice starts to brown.
3. Add water and bouillon cube. Stir. Bring to a boil, cover, and cook over low heat until rice is tender, about 45 minutes.
4. Add nuts and stir with fork to fluff.

Note: Extra servings can be packaged and frozen for later use.

*Na content minimal if low-sodium bouillon cube used.

Stove-Top Yams and Apples

Yield: 6 or 2 servings
Serving Size: $\frac{2}{3}$ cup
Exchange List Approximation:
    Starch/Bread 1 $\frac{1}{2}$
    Fruit 1
    Fat $\frac{1}{2}$

Nutrient Content Per Serving:
CAL: 202   PRO: 1.6 (gm)
FAT: 4.2 (gm)   CHO: 41.3 (gm)
Na: 96 (mg)   K: 750.2 (mg)
Fiber: 5.3 (gm)   Chol: 0

Ingredients

Six Servings	Two Servings
1½ POUNDS YAMS	½ POUND
1 CUP WATER	½ CUP
2 TABLESPOONS MARGARINE	2 TEASPOONS
1 TABLESPOON SUGAR	1 TEASPOON
⅛ TEASPOON SALT	PINCH
3 TART APPLES	1
SPRINKLE CINNAMON	SPRINKLE
1 PACKET SUGAR SUBSTITUTE	1 PACKET

Method

1. Peel and cut yams into ¼-inch slices. Place in large skillet.
2. Pour water over potatoes. Dot with margarine. Sprinkle with salt and sugar. Cover, bring to boil, and cook over moderate heat 20 minutes.
3. Wash, core, and slice apples (peel if desired). Spread over potatoes, sprinkle with cinnamon; cover, and cook 10 minutes longer.
4. Remove cover and cook until sauce is absorbed, about 5 minutes.
5. Sprinkle with sweetener; stir gently.

Vegetables

Broccoli with Mustard-Dill Sauce

Yield: 4 servings
Serving Size: 2 stalks broccoli
 and 2 tablespoons sauce
Exchange List Approximation:
 Vegetable 1
 Fat ½

Nutrient Content Per Serving:
CAL: 50   PRO: 3.2 (gm)
FAT: 1.6 (gm)   CHO: 6.5 (gm)
Na: 273.4 (mg)   K: 169 (mg)
Fiber: 1.8 (gm) Chol: 1 (mg)

Ingredients

    1 10-OUNCE PACKAGE FROZEN BROCCOLI SPEARS OR
       FRESH BROCCOLI SPEARS, 4 INCHES LONG
    ½ CUP WATER WITH ¼ TEASPOON SALT
    ¼ TEASPOON SALT
 1½   TEASPOONS MARGARINE
    1 TABLESPOON FLOUR
    ½ CUP SKIM MILK
 1½   TEASPOONS PREPARED MUSTARD
    ¼ TEASPOON DILL WEED

Method

1. Bring broccoli spears and salted water to boil, cover, and
   cook until just tender, about 6 minutes.
2. Melt margarine in small saucepan, add flour, and cook
   about 1 minute, stirring constantly. Add milk, mustard,
   salt, and dill weed. Stir until smooth, bring to a simmer,
   and cook 2 minutes while stirring.
3. Spoon 2 Tablespoons sauce over each serving of broccoli
   (2 spears).

Jade-Green Broccoli

Yield: 10 servings
Serving Size: ½ cup
Exchange List Approximation:
    Vegetable 1
    Fat 1

Nutrient Content Per Serving:
CAL: 82   PRO: 2.5 (gm)
FAT: 6.2 (gm)   CHO: 5.2 (gm)
Na: 239.1 (mg)   K: 131.1 (mg)
Fiber: 1.8 (gm) Chol: 0
Key Source Nutrients:
    Riboflavin: 147.3 (mg)

Ingredients

1 BUNCH BROCCOLI (ABOUT 2 POUNDS)
1 CLOVE GARLIC, MINCED
1 TABLESPOON CORNSTARCH
2 TABLESPOONS SOY SAUCE
½ CUP WATER OR CHICKEN STOCK
¼ CUP VEGETABLE OIL
⅛ TEASPOON SALT
2 TABLESPOONS SHERRY

Method

1. Wash broccoli in cold water. Drain, peel stems, and cut the stems on a slant into ⅛-inch slices.
2. Mix together cornstarch, soy sauce, and chicken stock; put aside.
3. Heat wok or pan hot and dry. Add the oil, then the salt.
4. Turn heat to medium and add the garlic. When garlic is golden brown, add the broccoli. Turn heat up and stir-fry for 3 minutes.
5. Add the sherry and cover wok or pan quickly. Cook, covered, 2 minutes longer.
6. Add cornstarch, soy sauce, and chicken stock. Stir constantly until gravy has thickened.

Green Beans with Sunflower Seeds

Yield: 6 or 2 servings
Serving Size: $\frac{1}{2}$ cup
Exchange List Approximation:
    Vegetable 1
    Fat $\frac{1}{2}$

Nutrient Content Per Serving:
CAL: 51   PRO: 2.2 (gm)
FAT: 2.2 (gm)   CHO: 7.1 (gm)
Na: 45.1 (mg)   K: 244.7 (mg)
Fiber: 2.6 (gm)   Chol: 0

Ingredients

Six Servings		*Two Servings*	
1	POUND FRESH GREEN BEANS	⅓	POUND
½	CUP CHOPPED ONIONS	3	TABLESPOONS
1	TEASPOON MINCED GARLIC	⅓	TEASPOON
⅛	TEASPOON SALT		PINCH
⅛	TEASPOON PEPPER		PINCH
	SHAKE CRUSHED RED PEPPER (OPTIONAL)		SHAKE
⅓	CUP WATER	2	TABLESPOONS
3	TABLESPOONS SUNFLOWER SEEDS	1	TABLESPOON
¼	TEASPOON OREGANO		SPRINKLE

Method

1. Snap ends off beans and break into ½" lengths. If very young, leave whole. Wash and place in saucepan.
2. Sprinkle onion, garlic, salt, and pepper over beans. Add water.
3. Cover tightly. Cook on high until steaming, reduce heat, and cook about 20 minutes until beans are crisp-tender.
4. Remove lid. Pour off excess liquid.
5. Sprinkle sunflower seeds and oregano over beans. Mix lightly.

Peas and Celery

Yield: 6 or 2 servings
Serving Size: $\frac{1}{2}$ cup
Exchange List Approximation:
    Starch/Bread $\frac{1}{2}$
    Vegetable $\frac{1}{2}$

Nutrient Content Per Serving:
CAL: 54   PRO: 2.6 (gm)
FAT: 1.5 (gm)   CHO: 8.4 (gm)
Na: 113.3 (mg)   K: 163.3 (mg)
Fiber: 3.4 (gm)   Chol: 0

Ingredients

Six Servings		Two Servings
2	TEASPOONS MARGARINE	¾ TEASPOON
1	CUP CELERY, ⅛-INCH BIAS CUT SLICES	⅓ CUP
2	TABLESPOONS FINELY CHOPPED ONION	2 TEASPOONS
½	TEASPOON SAVORY	⅛ TEASPOON
½	CUP WATER	¼ CUP
1	10-OUNCE PACKAGE FROZEN PEAS	¾ CUP
⅓	CUP SLICED CANNED MUSHROOMS, DRAINED	2 TABLESPOONS
2	TABLESPOONS CHOPPED PIMENTO	2 TEASPOONS
	SPRINKLE BLACK PEPPER	SPRINKLE

Method

1. Heat margarine in a saucepan. Add celery, onion, and savory. Stir-fry about 2 minutes.
2. Add water, bring to a boil, cover, and simmer 5 minutes.
3. Add frozen peas, mushrooms, and pimento. Sprinkle with black pepper. Bring to a simmer, cover, and cook over low heat about 5 minutes, until peas are just tender.

Squash Puff

Yield: 6 or 2 servings
Serving Size: $\frac{1}{2}$ cup
Exchange List Approximation:
  Starch/Bread $1\frac{1}{2}$

Nutrient Content Per Serving:
CAL: 125   PRO: 4.4 (gm)
FAT: 2.9 (gm)   CHO: 22.4 (gm)
Na: 173.5 (mg)   K: 372.7 (mg)
Fiber: 3.9 (gm)   Chol: 137 (mg)

Ingredients

Six Servings

 3 CUPS ACORN SQUASH,
   COOKED AND MASHED (ABOUT
   3 POUNDS)
 3 TABLESPOONS HONEY
 3 TABLESPOONS WHOLE-WHEAT
   FLOUR
 ⅜ TEASPOON SALT
 ¼ TEASPOON EACH: CINNAMON,
   GINGER, NUTMEG
 3 EGGS, SEPARATED

Two Servings

 1 CUP (ABOUT 1
   POUND)

 1 TABLESPOON
 1 TABLESPOON

 ⅛ TEASPOON
 ¹⁄₁₆ TEASPOON

Method

1. Cut acorn squash and scoop out seeds. Steam or bake in 350° F oven until tender. Remove from skin and mash.
2. Combine with honey, flour, salt, spices, and egg yolks. Whip until blended.
3. Beat egg whites until stiff (not dry). Fold into squash mixture.
4. Pour into 1½-quart baking dish, sprayed with nonstick vegetable spray.
5. Bake in 350° F oven until crusty, about 45 minutes.

Note: One serving contains approximately 1½ teaspoons honey (24 calories).

Dilled Zucchini

Yield: 4 servings
Serving Size: $\frac{1}{2}$ cup
Exchange List Approximation:
    Vegetable 1

Nutrient Content Per Serving:
CAL: 19   PRO: 0.8 (gm)
FAT: 0   CHO: 4.6 (gm)
Na: 66.2 (mg)   K: 249.8 (mg)
Fiber: 3.1 (gm)   Chol: 0

Ingredients

  1 POUND ZUCCHINI
  ⅓ CUP CHOPPED ONION
  ¼ CUP BOILING WATER
  ⅛ TEASPOON SALT
  ½ TEASPOON PAPRIKA
  ½ TEASPOON DILL WEED
  1 TABLESPOON VINEGAR

Method

1. Remove ends from zucchini; cut into strips or slices.
2. Add zucchini and onion to boiling salted water. Cover and boil gently until tender, about 10 minutes. Drain.
3. Add paprika, dill weed, and vinegar. Stir gently.

Stir-Fry Zucchini

Yield: 4 or 2 servings
Serving Size: $\frac{3}{4}$ cup
Exchange List Approximation:
    Vegetable 1
    Fat 1

Nutrient Content Per Serving:
CAL: 75	PRO: 1.7 (gm)
FAT: 5 (gm)	CHO: 7.2 (gm)
Na: 239.3 (mg)	K: 308.9 (mg)
Fiber: 4.1 (gm)	Chol: 0

Ingredients

Four Servings		*Two Servings*	
1	TABLESPOON VEGETABLE OIL	1½	TEASPOONS
4	CUPS ZUCCHINI, CUT INTO 1½-INCH STRIPS (ABOUT 1 POUND)	2	CUPS
1	CUP ONION, CUT IN WEDGES, SEPARATED	½	CUP
1	TABLESPOON SESAME SEEDS	1	TEASPOON
2	TEASPOONS SOY SAUCE	1	TEASPOON
⅛	TEASPOON SALT		SPRINKLE
½	TEASPOON SESAME SEED OIL (OPTIONAL)	¼	TEASPOON

Method

1. Heat vegetable oil in large skillet over medium heat.
2. Add zucchini and onion. Stir-fry about 5 to 8 minutes.
3. Sprinkle with sesame seeds, soy sauce, salt, and sesame seed oil. Stir until blended.

Summer Squash Pudding

Yield: 6 or 3 servings
Serving Size: $\frac{1}{3}$ cup
Exchange List Approximation:
    Vegetable 1
    Fat 1

Nutrient Content Per Serving:
CAL: 81   PRO: 3.7 (gm)
FAT: 4.4 (gm)   CHO: 7.7 (gm)
Na: 154.5 (mg)   K: 286.2 (mg)
Fiber: 1.1 (gm) Chol: 92 (mg)

Ingredients

Six Servings		*Three Servings*	
4	SUMMER SQUASH, LARGE (ABOUT 2 POUNDS)	1	(ABOUT 1 POUND)
½	CUP WATER	¼	CUP
¼	TEASPOON SALT	⅛	TEASPOON
2	EGGS	1	
2	TABLESPOONS LOW-FAT YOGURT	1	TABLESPOON
½	TEASPOON PEPPER	¼	TEASPOON
1	TABLESPOON MARGARINE, DIVIDED	1½	TEASPOONS
2	TABLESPOONS SEASONED BREAD CRUMBS	1	TABLESPOON

Method

1. Slice squash, add to salted water; cover, bring to a boil, and cook until tender, about 20 minutes. Mash.
2. Beat eggs. Stir in yogurt, pepper, and mashed squash.
3. Grease 2-quart casserole with 1 teaspoon margarine. Mix remaining margarine with seasoned crumbs.
4. Pour squash mixture into casserole. Sprinkle crumbs over top.
5. Bake in 350° F oven for 20 minutes.

Dips and Dressings

Delicious Dip

Yield: 8 servings
Serving Size: 3 tablespoons
Exchange List Approximation:
    Milk, skim $\frac{1}{2}$

Nutrient Content Per Serving:
CAL: 36   PRO: 3.6 (gm)
FAT: 0.8 (gm)   CHO: 3.5 (gm)
Na: 105.6 (mg)   K: 105.8 (mg)
Fiber: 0.1 (gm) Chol: 3 (mg)

Ingredients

  1   CUP PLAIN LOW-FAT YOGURT
  ½   CUP LOW-FAT COTTAGE CHEESE
  ¼   MINCED GREEN PEPPER
  1   TABLESPOON CATSUP
  1½ TEASPOONS PREPARED HORSERADISH
  1   TEASPOON WORCESTERSHIRE SAUCE
  ⅛   TEASPOON MINCED GARLIC
  ½   TEASPOON DRY MUSTARD

Method

1. Mix yogurt and cottage cheese.
2. Stir in remaining ingredients.
3. Cover and chill 2 hours to blend flavors.
4. Serve as a dip for crackers, chips, or raw vegetable pieces.
   Or serve as dressing for lettuce wedge or green salad.

Horseradish Dip

Yield: 1 cup
Serving Size: 1⅓ tablespoons
Exchange List Approximation:
    Free food

Nutrient Content Per Serving:
CAL: 17   PRO: 0.7 (gm)
FAT: 1.1 (gm)   CHO: 1 (gm)
Na: 16.6 (mg)   K: 33.9 (mg)
Fiber: 0.1 (gm)   Chol: 2 (mg)

Ingredients

1 8-OUNCE CONTAINER PLAIN LOW-FAT YOGURT
1 TABLESPOON MAYONNAISE
2 TEASPOONS PREPARED HORSERADISH

Method

1. Mix well and serve as dip for raw vegetables.

Spinach Dip for Raw Vegetables

Yield: 16 servings
Serving Size: $2\frac{1}{2}$ tablespoons
Exchange List Approximation:
    Vegetable $\frac{1}{2}$
    Fat 1

Nutrient Content Per Serving:
CAL: 62   PRO: 1.1 (gm)
FAT: 5.8 (gm)   CHO: 1.8 (gm)
Na: 66.6 (mg)   K: 73.4 (mg)
Fiber: 0.3 (gm)   Chol: 5 (mg)

Ingredients

  1 10-OUNCE PACKAGE FROZEN CHOPPED SPINACH
 ½ CUP MAYONNAISE
  1 CUP LOW-FAT YOGURT
 ¼ CUP CHOPPED PARSLEY OR 2 TABLESPOONS
     PARSLEY FLAKES
 ¼ CUP FINELY CHOPPED ONION
     PINCH DILL WEED
     PINCH SALT

Method

1. Thaw spinach and drain thoroughly.
2. Combine with remaining ingredients.
3. Cover and chill to let blend.

Black-Eye Pea Dip

Yield: 10 servings
Serving Size: ¼ cup
Exchange List Approximation:
    Starch/Bread 1
    Fat ½

Nutrient Content Per Serving:
CAL: 113   PRO: 5.4 (gm)
FAT: 3.4 (gm)   CHO: 16.2 (gm)
Na: 94.5 (mg)   K: 319.9 (mg)
Fiber: 6.1 (gm)   Chol: 0

Ingredients

  3 CUPS COOKED, DRY BLACK-EYE PEAS
  ½ CUP CHOPPED ONION
  ½ CUP CHOPPED GREEN PEPPER
  ½ CUP TOMATO SAUCE
  ¼ CUP VINEGAR
  2 TABLESPOONS VEGETABLE OIL
  2 PACKETS SUGAR SUBSTITUTE
  1 TABLESPOON WORCESTERSHIRE SAUCE
  ¼ TEASPOON PEPPER
  ¼ TEASPOON GARLIC POWDER

Method

1. Place all ingredients in blender or food processor. Blend for 2 to 3 seconds. Pieces of pea should be present.

Variation: For relish, combine ingredients and add 1 small jalapeno pepper, chopped.

Garbanzo Spread

Yield: 6 servings
Serving Size: $\frac{1}{4}$ cup
Exchange List Approximation:
    Starch/Bread 1
    Fat $\frac{1}{2}$

Nutrient Content Per Serving:
CAL: 112   PRO: 5.4 (gm)
FAT: 4 (gm)   CHO: 14.9 (gm)
Na: 50.8 (mg)   K: 208.2 (mg)
Fiber: 3.7 (gm)   Chol: 0

Ingredients

1¾ CUPS GARBANZO BEANS, DRAINED (ABOUT 15 OUNCES)
¼ CUP TOASTED SESAME SEEDS
4 TABLESPOONS LEMON JUICE
2 TABLESPOONS CHOPPED ONION
¼ TEASPOON MINCED GARLIC
¾ TEASPOON BASIL
⅛ TEASPOON PEPPER
⅛ TEASPOON SALT

Method

1. Drain beans and reserve liquid.
2. Place all ingredients in blender or food processor.
3. Blend to a smooth paste. Add a little bean liquid (about 1 Tablespoon) to get desired consistency.
4. Serve on lettuce with wedge of onion and whole wheat toast or crackers. Also can be served as dip for raw vegetables.

Note: If your diet permits, sprinkle a little olive oil over spread.

Chick Peas and Sesame-Seed-Paste Dip

Yield: 6 servings
Serving Size: $\frac{1}{4}$ cup
Exchange List Approximation:
    Starch/Bread 1
    Fat 1

Nutrient Content Per Serving:
CAL: 133   PRO: 6.9 (gm)
FAT: 3.7 (gm)   CHO: 19.4 (gm)
Na: 9.3 (mg)   K: 261.8 (mg)
Fiber: 4.7 (gm)   Chol: 0

Ingredients

1¾ CUPS CHICK PEAS (GARBANZO BEANS, ABOUT 1 15-OUNCE CAN)
2 TABLESPOONS TAHINI (SESAME SEED PASTE)
2 TABLESPOONS LEMON JUICE
1 SMALL GARLIC CLOVE
½ TEASPOON GROUND CORIANDER
¼ TEASPOON CUMIN
¹⁄₁₆ TEASPOON CAYENNE PEPPER

Method

1. Place all ingredients in blender or food processor. Blend to a smooth paste.
2. Serve as a vegetable dip or sandwich spread.

Ranch Salad Dressing

Yield: 32 servings
Serving Size: 1 tablespoon
Exchange List Approximation:
   Fat ½

Nutrient Content Per Serving:
CAL: 20   PRO: 0.7 (gm)
FAT: 1.6 (gm)   CHO: 0.9 (gm)
Na: 31.1 (mg)   K: 30 (mg)
Fiber: 0   Chol: 2 (mg)

Ingredients

1¾ CUPS PLAIN LOW-FAT YOGURT
 ¼ CUP MAYONNAISE
 1 TEASPOON DRIED PARSLEY FLAKES
 1 TEASPOON DRIED MINCED ONION
 ½ TEASPOON ONION POWDER
 ½ TEASPOON GARLIC POWDER
 ½ TEASPOON DILL WEED
 ¼ TEASPOON PAPRIKA
 ¼ TEASPOON PEPPER
 ¼ TEASPOON CELERY SALT
 ⅛ TEASPOON MONOSODIUM GLUTAMATE

Method

1. Place ingredients in mixing bowl. Stir until blended and smooth.
2. Pour into container and refrigerate 1 hour to blend flavors. Can be stored for several weeks.
3. Use on salad greens or as dip for raw vegetables.

*Exchanges for less than 1 Tablespoon serving are Free.

Mock French Dressing

Yield: 8 servings
Serving Size: 2 tablespoons
Exchange List Approximation:
    Free food

Nutrient Content Per Serving:
CAL: 18   PRO: 0
FAT: 0   CHO: 4.7 (gm)
Na: 66.7 (mg)   K: 7.5 (mg)
Fiber: 0   Chol: 0

Ingredients

1½ TABLESPOONS CORNSTARCH
2 TABLESPOONS SUGAR
1 CUP WATER
¼ CUP VINEGAR
¼ TEASPOON SALT
½ TEASPOON DRY MUSTARD
½ TEASPOON PAPRIKA
⅛ TEASPOON ONION POWDER
    DASH GARLIC POWDER

Method

1. Mix cornstarch and sugar in saucepan; stir in water.
2. Cook over low heat, stirring constantly, until thickened.
3. Cool slightly.
4. Add remaining ingredients. Mix thoroughly.
5. Chill.

Note: One serving contains ¾ teaspoon sugar (12 calories).

Yogurt-Dill Dressing

Yield: 8 servings
Serving Size: 2 tablespoons
Exchange List Approximation:
    Free food

Nutrient Content Per Serving:
CAL: 18   PRO: 1.5 (gm)
FAT: 0.4 (gm)   CHO: 2.1 (gm)
Na: 20 (mg)   K: 68.2 (mg)
Fiber: 0   Chol: 2 (mg)

Ingredients

1 8-OUNCE CARTON PLAIN LOW-FAT YOGURT
2 TEASPOONS VERY FINELY CHOPPED ONION
1 TEASPOON LEMON JUICE
½ TEASPOON CRUSHED DILL WEED
¼ TEASPOON DRY MUSTARD
⅛ TEASPOON GARLIC POWDER

Method

1. Mix all ingredients thoroughly.
2. Chill until served.
3. Serve over tossed green salad.

Condiments, Spreads, Sauces, Toppings

California Salad Seasoning

Yield: 24 servings (1 cup)
Serving Size: 2 teaspoons
Exchange List Approximation:
    Free food

Nutrient Content Per Serving:
CAL: 12   PRO: 1.1 (gm)
FAT: 0.8 (gm)   CHO: 0.1 (gm)
Na: 91 (mg)   K: 3.2 (mg)
Fiber: 0   Chol: 2 (mg)

Ingredients

¾ CUP GRATED PARMESAN CHEESE
¼ CUP PARSLEY FLAKES
1 TEASPOON GARLIC POWDER
½ TEASPOON FRESHLY GROUND PEPPER
1 TEASPOON CHIVES
1 TEASPOON BELL PEPPER FLAKES
1 TEASPOON BASIL
½ TEASPOON SALT

Method

1. Mix all ingredients together.
2. Sprinkle on salad and garlic bread.

Diet Catsup
(from Tomato Juice)

Yield: 48 servings
Serving Size: 1 tablespoon
Exchange List Approximation:
    Free food

Nutrient Content Per Serving:
CAL: 5   PRO: 0.2 (gm)
FAT: 0   CHO: 1.3 (gm)
Na: 105.7 (mg)   K: 65.5 (mg)
Fiber: 0   Chol: 0

Ingredients

1 46-OUNCE CAN TOMATO JUICE
¼ CUP VINEGAR
⅛ TEASPOON EACH: DRY MUSTARD, ALLSPICE, CINNAMON, CELERY SEED
1 TEASPOON ONION POWDER
6 PACKETS SUGAR SUBSTITUTE

Method

1. Combine all ingredients except sweetener in large, shallow saucepan. Simmer about 1½ hours until thickened.
2. Remove from heat. Stir in substitute sweetener. Store in refrigerator.

Diet Catsup
(from Tomato Sauce)

Yield: 1½ cups
Serving Size: 1 tablespoon
Exchange List Approximation:
    Free food

Nutrient Content Per Serving:
CAL: 6   PRO: 0.2 (gm)
FAT: 0   CHO: 1.5 (gm)
Na: 114.4 (mg) K: 72.6 (mg)
Fiber: 0.2 (gm) Chol: 0

Ingredients

2 8-OUNCE CANS TOMATO SAUCE WITHOUT
   DEXTROSE OR OTHER SUGARS
¼ CUP VINEGAR
⅛ TEASPOON EACH: DRY MUSTARD, ALLSPICE,
   CINNAMON, AND CELERY SEED
1 TEASPOON ONION POWDER
   DASH CAYENNE PEPPER
6 PACKETS SUGAR SUBSTITUTE

Method

1. Combine all ingredients except sugar substitute in saucepan.
2. Simmer 30 minutes until thickened.
3. Remove from heat. Stir in sugar substitute. Store in refrigerator.

Texas-Style Barbecue Sauce

Yield: 6 servings
Serving Size: 3 tablespoons
Exchange List Approximation:
    Free food

Nutrient Content Per Serving:

CAL: 11	PRO: 0.5 (gm)
FAT: 0.1 (gm)	CHO: 2.5 (gm)
Na: 453.7 (mg)	K: 111.2 (mg)
Fiber: 0	Chol: 0

Ingredients

- 4 TABLESPOONS TOMATO PASTE
- 1 TABLESPOON DEHYDRATED ONION FLAKES
- 1 TEASPOON WORCESTERSHIRE SAUCE
- 1 TEASPOON LEMON JUICE
- 1 TEASPOON SALT
- 1 TEASPOON MINCED GARLIC CLOVE
-    DASH CAYENNE PEPPER
- 1 CUP SUGAR-FREE COLA

Method

1. In a small saucepan, mix ingredients in order listed.
2. Bring to a boil, reduce heat, and simmer for 5 minutes.
3. Serve over grilled chicken, beef, pork, or frankfurters.

Texas Picante Sauce (Fresh or Canned)

Yield: 6 servings
Serving Size: 1 tablespoon
Exchange List Approximation:
    Free food

Nutrient Content Per Serving:
CAL: 4   PRO: 0.2 (gm)
FAT: 0   CHO: 0.9 (gm)
Na: 11.4 (mg)   K: 35.1 (mg)
Fiber: 0.2 (gm)   Chol: 0

Ingredients

  5 POUNDS RIPE TOMATOES (ABOUT 9 TO 10 LARGE)
  1 LARGE ONION (ABOUT 10 OUNCES)
  ½ CUP CHOPPED CARROTS (ABOUT 1 SMALL)
  ½ CUP CHOPPED JALAPENO PEPPER, DISCARD SEEDS
     (ABOUT 3)
  ½ CUP CHOPPED CHILI PEPPERS, DISCARD SEEDS
  ¼ TEASPOON PEPPER
  ¾ TEASPOON PICKLING SALT
  2 TEASPOONS MINCED GARLIC CLOVE (ABOUT 2)

Method

1. Cut tomatoes, onion, and carrot. Place in food processor
    and blend until chunky. Place in cooking pot.
2. Handle peppers carefully when chopping. Cut off stem,
    slit, remove seeds, and chop into large pieces.
3. Place in processor and blend to small chunks.
4. Add peppers, pepper, pickling salt, and garlic to tomatoes.
    Bring to boil and cook slowly 30 minutes.
5. Fill into clean, sterile jars (4 1-pint). Leave ½ inch head
    space. Cap and seal.
6. Process in water bath for 15 minutes. (Place in large pot
    with rack, fill with hot water to cover, bring to boil, and
    boil 15 minutes.)

Green Chilies Sauce

Yield: 20 servings (2½ cups)
Serving Size: 2 tablespoons
Exchange List Approximation:
    Free food

Nutrient Content Per Serving:

CAL: 7	PRO: 0.3 (gm)
FAT: 0.1 (gm)	CHO: 1.7 (gm)
Na: 37.1 (mg)	K: 56.8 (mg)
Fiber: 0.4 (gm)	Chol: 0

Ingredients

½ CUP CHOPPED ONION
1 16-OUNCE CAN TOMATOES
1 4-OUNCE CAN GREEN CHILIES
2 TEASPOONS CHILI POWDER
½ TEASPOON GARLIC POWDER
¼ TEASPOON GROUND CUMIN
¼ TEASPOON GROUND OREGANO

Method

1. Spray saucepan with vegetable pan spray.
2. Add onions and saute until tender, about 5 minutes.
3. Add tomato juice. Chop tomatoes and add.
4. Add green chilies and spices. Stir.
5. Bring to a boil, cover, and simmer 10 minutes.
6. Pour into clean jar and store in refrigerator. Use to season beans and other foods such as eggs and hamburgers where catsup might otherwise be used.

Earle's Fire Sauce (Hot Sauce)

Yield: 16 servings (4 cups)
Serving Size: 4 tablespoons
Exchange List Approximation:
    Vegetable 1

Nutrient Content Per Serving:

CAL: 24	PRO: 1 (gm)
FAT: 0.2 (gm)	CHO: 5.4 (gm)
Na: 187.5 (mg)	K: 220 (mg)
Fiber: 1.2 (gm)	Chol: 0

Ingredients

  6 JALAPENO PEPPERS*, ENDS CUT OFF AND QUARTERED
  4 TABLESPOONS WATER
  2 CUPS TOMATO SAUCE, SPANISH STYLE (ABOUT 1 16-OUNCE CAN)
  2 TOMATOES, MEDIUM, CHOPPED
  1 WHITE ONION, LARGE, DICED
  1 TEASPOON MINCED GARLIC CLOVE (ABOUT 1)
  1 TEASPOON MEXICAN CHILI POWDER
  1 TEASPOON LEMON JUICE
  ½ TEASPOON BLACK PEPPER

Method

1. Exercising caution, cut ends off jalapeno peppers, quarter, and remove seeds. Place in blender or food processor, add water, and liquefy. Pepper juice may burn unless well washed off hands.
2. Add tomato sauce, chopped tomatoes, diced onion, minced garlic clove, and remaining ingredients.
3. Gently blend for *short* period. Sauce should have small pieces of tomato and onion in it.

*This sauce is hot. For a milder version, use only 4 peppers.

Dried Fruit Spread(s)

Yield = number of 1-Tablespoon servings in fruit recipe selected.

Exchanges are based upon 1-Tablespoon serving for each fruit spread.

Fruit	APPLE	APRICOT	PEACH	PRUNE
Yield	32	20	24	16
CAL	17	26	31	34
FAT (gm)	0	0	0.1	0.1
Na (mg)	6.3	0.9	1.0	0.6
Fiber (gm)	1.0	2.7	2.3	2.3
PRO (gm)	0.1	0.4	0.5	0.4
CHO (gm)	4.7	6.9	7.9	8.8
K (mg)	32.0	153.7	128.1	104.6
Chol (mg)	0	0	0	0
Exchanges	½ Fruit	½ Fruit	½ Fruit	½ Fruit

Ingredients

  1 8-OUNCE PACKAGE OF THE DRIED FRUIT SELECTED (APPLE OR APRICOT OR PEACH OR PRUNES, pitted)

2–6 PACKETS SUGAR SUBSTITUTE

Method

1. Select the dried fruit for the spread desired.
2. Cover dried fruit with water and simmer until soft and most of water is absorbed.
3. Put in blender and blend until smooth. Add more water if needed to get spreading consistency.
4. Add sweetener to taste.
5. Store in covered container in refrigerator.

Variation: For spiced spread, add ½ teaspoon mace or nutmeg.

Apple Butter

Yield: 10 servings
Serving Size: 2 tablespoons
Exchange List Approximation:
Fruit $\frac{1}{2}$

Nutrient Content Per Serving:
CAL: 36   PRO: 0.1 (gm)
FAT: 0.1 (gm)   CHO: 9.4 (gm)
Na: 1.7 (mg)   K: 72.2 (mg)
Fiber: 1.1 (gm)   Chol: 0

Ingredients

1 20-OUNCE JAR UNSWEETENED APPLESAUCE
1 CUP SWEET CIDER (NO SUGAR ADDED)
1 TEASPOON GROUND CINNAMON
½ TEASPOON GROUND CLOVES
½ TEASPOON ALLSPICE
2 PACKETS SUGAR SUBSTITUTE

Method

1. Combine applesauce, cider, and spices in electric frying pan, or in iron or cast aluminum skillet or pot.
2. Simmer slowly, stirring frequently, 2 to 3 hours until spreading consistency is reached.
3. Cool and sweeten to taste.
4. Store in covered container in refrigerator.

Sugarless Grape Jam

Yield: 2⅔ cups
Serving Size: 1 tablespoon
Exchange List Approximation:
    Free food

Nutrient Content Per Serving:
CAL: 13   PRO: 0.1 (gm)
FAT: 0   CHO: 3.2 (gm)
Na: 0.5 (mg)   K: 16.3 (mg)
Fiber: 0   Chol: 0

Ingredients

    2 CUPS UNSWEETENED GRAPE JUICE
    1 CUP WATER
    ½ CUP QUICK TAPIOCA
       SUGAR SUBSTITUTE EQUIVALENT TO 3 CUPS SUGAR

Method

1. Combine grape juice, water, and tapioca in saucepan. Let set 5 minutes to soften tapioca.
2. Add sweetener. Bring to a boil and boil hard for 1 minute.
3. Pour into clean jars, seal, and store in refrigerator.

Strawberry Jam

Yield: 1¼ cups
Serving Size: 1 tablespoon
Exchange List Approximation:
Free food

Nutrient Content Per Serving:
CAL: 4   PRO: 0.2 (gm)
FAT: 0   CHO: 0.5 (gm)
Na: 12.9 (mg)   K: 12.4 (mg)
Fiber: 0.2 (gm)   Chol: 0

Ingredients

1 CUP SLICED STRAWBERRIES UNSWEETENED (ABOUT 5 TO 6 OUNCES)
¾ CUP SUGAR-FREE STRAWBERRY SODA
1 PACKAGE STRAWBERRY LOW-CALORIE GELATIN DESSERT
3 PACKETS SUGAR SUBSTITUTE

Method

1. Mash strawberries. Add soda and bring to a boil. Cook 1 minute.
2. Remove from heat. Stir in gelatin dessert until dissolved. Stir in sweetener.
3. Pour into clean hot jars, seal, and store in refrigerator.

Mock Sour Cream

Yield: 5 servings ($\frac{2}{3}$ cup)
Serving Size: 2 tablespoons
Exchange List Approximation:
   Meat, medium-fat $\frac{1}{2}$

Nutrient Content Per Serving:
CAL: 44   PRO: 2.9 (gm)
FAT: 3.2 (gm)   CHO: 0.9 (gm)
Na: 66.1 (mg)   K: 24.2 (mg)
Fiber: 0   Chol: 1 (mg)

Ingredients

½ CUP COTTAGE CHEESE, UNCREAMED (DRY)
¼ CUP BUTTERMILK
1 TABLESPOON OIL
1 TEASPOON LEMON JUICE
⅛ TEASPOON SALT

Method

1. Put all ingredients into blender container; cover. Blend until smooth.
2. Serve over baked potatoes or other vegetables.

Low-Calorie Whipped Topping

Yield: 8 servings
Serving Size: ¼ cup
Exchange List Approximation:
    Free food

Nutrient Content Per Serving:
CAL: 20   PRO: 1.5 (gm)
FAT: 0   CHO: 3.4 (gm)
Na: 20.1 (mg) K: 69.9 (mg)
Fiber: 0   Chol: 1 (mg)

Ingredients

  1 TEASPOON UNFLAVORED GELATIN
  2 TEASPOONS WATER
  ¼ CUP INSTANT NONFAT DRY MILK
  ½ CUP SKIM MILK
  ½ TEASPOON VANILLA
  1 TABLESPOON SUGAR

Method

1. Soften gelatin in water for 5 minutes.
2. Stir nonfat dry milk into skim milk in saucepan. Heat to simmering. Add softened gelatin. Stir until gelatin is dissolved.
3. Add vanilla and sugar.
4. Chill until mixture begins to thicken.
5. Beat with electric mixer or rotary beater until very thick and light.
6. Serve on fresh fruit.

Note: Less than ½ teaspoon sugar per serving (6 calories).

Whipped Topping

Yield: 12 servings (1½ cups)
Serving Size: 2 tablespoons
Exchange List Approximation:
   Meat, lean ½

Nutrient Content Per Serving:
CAL: 21   PRO: 1.7 (gm)
FAT: 0.8 (gm)   CHO: 1.6 (gm)
Na: 21.3 (mg)   K: 20.5 (mg)
Fiber: 0   Chol: 3 (mg)

Ingredients

2 EGG WHITES
¼ TEASPOON CREAM OF TARTAR
1 TABLESPOON SUGAR
½ CUP PART SKIM RICOTTA CHEESE
½ TEASPOON VANILLA

Method

1. Whip egg whites until foamy, add cream of tartar, and whip until peaks fold over.
2. Gradually add sugar while whipping. Whip until stiff peaks are formed.
3. Add vanilla to Ricotta cheese and whip until smooth.
4. Fold whites into cheese. Keep refrigerated until served.

Note: This topping tastes like cheesecake. Serve on blueberry-banana bread.

Dream Desserts

Wheat-Germ Gems

Yield: 60 cookies (1-inch
    diameter, approximately)
Serving Size: 2 cookies
Exchange List Approximation:
    Starch/Bread 1
    Fat $\frac{1}{2}$

Nutrient Content Per Serving:
CAL: 104   PRO: 2.2 (gm)
FAT: 5.5 (gm)   CHO: 12 (gm)
Na: 38.2 (mg)   K: 46.2 (mg)
Fiber: 1 (gm)·   Chol: 9 (mg)

Ingredients

- 2 CUPS FLOUR
- 1 CUP TOASTED WHEAT GERM
- ¾ CUP SHORTENING
- ½ CUP SUGAR
- 1 EGG
- 1 TEASPOON GRATED ORANGE RIND
- 1 TEASPOON VANILLA
- ½ TEASPOON SALT

Method

1. Combine all ingredients in mixing bowl. Repeat at low speed until well mixed.
2. Chill dough. Roll into 1-inch balls. Roll in wheat germ.
3. Place on cookie sheet and bake at 350° F for 12 to 15 minutes.

Note: Approximately ¾ teaspoon sugar (13 to 14 calories) per 2-cookie serving.

Date Cookies

Yield: 48 cookies (2-inch diameter) Nutrient Content Per Serving:

Serving Size: 2 cookies	CAL: 72	PRO: 1.4 (gm)
Exchange List Approximation:	FAT: 2.5 (gm)	CHO: 11.7 (gm)
Fruit 1	Na: 62.9 (mg)	K: 80.1 (mg)
Fat $\frac{1}{2}$	Fiber: 0.9 (gm)	Chol: 23 (mg)

Ingredients

1   CUP RAISINS
½   CUP CHOPPED DATES
1   CUP WATER
2   EGGS
¼   CUP MARGARINE
1   TABLESPOON LIQUID SUGAR SUBSTITUTE
1   TEASPOON VANILLA
¼   TEASPOON CINNAMON
1   CUP FLOUR
1   TEASPOON BAKING SODA

Method

1. Combine in saucepan raisins, dates, and water. Boil 3 minutes, stirring constantly. Cool.
2. Cream together eggs, margarine, liquid sugar substitute, and vanilla.
3. Sift together cinnamon, flour, and soda.
4. Add dry ingredients to creamed mixture alternately with date mixture. Beat well. Chill several hours.
5. Drop from teaspoon onto greased baking pan. Bake at 350° F for 10 to 12 minutes.

Chewy Cookies

Yield: 24 cookies
Serving Size: 1 cookie
Exchange List Approximation:
    Starch/Bread $\frac{1}{2}$
    Fat $\frac{1}{2}$

Nutrient Content Per Serving:
CAL: 61   PRO: 0.9 (gm)
FAT: 3.7 (gm)   CHO: 6.4 (gm)
Na: 50 (mg)   K: 38 (mg)
Fiber: 0.5 (gm)   Chol: 11 (mg)

Ingredients

- ⅓ CUP VEGETABLE OIL
- 2 PACKETS SUGAR SUBSTITUTE
  BROWN SUGAR SUBSTITUTE FOR ¾ CUP BROWN SUGAR
- 1 TEASPOON VANILLA
- 1 EGG
- 1 CUP WHEAT-FLAKE CEREAL
- ½ CUP ALL-PURPOSE FLOUR
- ¼ CUP WHOLE-WHEAT FLOUR
- ½ TEASPOON BAKING POWDER
- 2 TABLESPOONS WHEAT GERM
- ½ CUP CHOPPED RAISINS
- ½ TEASPOON BAKING SODA
- 1 TABLESPOON WATER

Method

1. Mix ingredients in order given, adding soda that has been dissolved in water last.
2. Drop by teaspoon on ungreased cookie sheet.
3. Bake in 350° F oven 8 to 12 minutes.

Sugarless Raisin Cookies

Yield: 24 cookies

Serving Size: 2 cookies

Exchange List Approximation:

    Starch/Bread 1

    Fat $\frac{1}{2}$

Nutrient Content Per Serving:

CAL: 93	PRO: 2 (gm)
FAT: 2.5 (gm)	CHO: 15.9 (gm)
Na: 99.4 (mg)	K: 85.2 (mg)
Fiber: 1 (gm)	Chol: 23 (mg)

Ingredients

¾ CUP RAISINS

⅔ CUP WATER

1 TABLESPOON LIQUID SUGAR SUBSTITUTE

1 TEASPOON CINNAMON

¼ TEASPOON NUTMEG

2 TABLESPOONS MARGARINE

1 EGG

1 CUP FLOUR

1 TEASPOON BAKING POWDER

¼ TEASPOON SALT

Method

1. Combine raisins, water, sweetener, spices, and margarine in saucepan. Bring to a boil and cook 3 minutes. Cool.
2. Stir in egg.
3. Mix flour, baking powder, and salt. Add to fruit mixture and mix well.
4. Drop by teaspoon onto a lightly greased baking sheet. Bake in 350° F oven for 9 to 10 minutes until light brown.

Date Prune Bars

Yield: 18 servings
Serving Size: 1 bar
Exchange List Approximation:
    Starch/Bread 1
    Fat 1

Nutrient Content Per Serving:
CAL: 124   PRO: 2.2 (gm)
FAT: 5.4 (gm)   CHO: 17.9 (gm)
Na: 113.4 (mg)   K: 144.2 (mg)
Fiber: 2.4 (gm)   Chol: 30 (mg)

Ingredients

- ½ CUP QUARTERED DATES
- ½ CUP PITTED CHOPPED PRUNES (ABOUT 16)
- ½ CUP RAISINS
- 1 CUP WATER
- ¼ CUP MARGARINE
- 1 CUP FLOUR
- 1 TEASPOON BAKING SODA
- ¼ TEASPOON SALT
- ½ TEASPOON CINNAMON
- ¼ TEASPOON NUTMEG
- 2 EGGS
- 2 TEASPOONS LIQUID SUGAR SUBSTITUTE
- 1 TEASPOON VANILLA
- ½ CUP CHOPPED PECANS

Method

1. Combine dates, prunes, raisins, and water in saucepan. Simmer for 5 minutes, stirring occasionally. Stir in margarine. Cool.
2. Mix flour, soda, salt, and spices until blended.
3. Add fruit mixture, eggs, sugar substitute, and vanilla. Stir until blended. Stir in pecans.
4. Spread in lightly greased 9- by 13-inch pan. Bake in 350° F oven for 15 to 20 minutes. Cool and cut into bars.

Fresh-Fruit Parfait

Yield: 6 or 2 servings
Serving Size: ¾ cup
Exchange List Approximation:
    Meat, medium-fat ½
    Fruit 1½

Nutrient Content Per Serving:
CAL: 131   PRO: 5.7 (gm)
FAT: 3.7 (gm)   CHO: 20.7 (gm)
Na: 54.5 (mg)   K: 332.7 (mg)
Fiber: 2.3 (gm)   Chol: 13 (mg)

Ingredients

Six Servings		*Two Servings*
1	CUP PART SKIM-MILK RICOTTA CHEESE	⅓ CUP
2	PACKETS SUGAR SUBSTITUTE	2 TEASPOONS
½	TEASPOON ALMOND EXTRACT	2 DROPS
1	TABLESPOON MILK	1 TEASPOON
1	CUP SLICED ORANGES	⅓ CUP
1	CUP SLICED STRAWBERRIES	⅓ CUP
1	CUP DICED APPLES	⅓ CUP
1½	CUPS SLICED BANANAS	⅔ CUP

Method

1. Place cheese in mixing bowl. Whip cheese, sugar substitute, and almond extract together. Gradually whip in milk. Chill.
2. Prepare fruits to make 4½ cups.
3. Prepare in parfait glass. Place 2 teaspoons cheese in glass, layer of fruit, 1 tablespoon cheese, layer of fruit, 1 tablespoon cheese, layer of fruit.

Variation: Use other available fruits such as blueberries, seedless grapes, sliced peaches, or melon balls.

Seasonal Fruit Salad with Cardamom

Yield: 6 servings
Serving Size: $\frac{1}{6}$ recipe
Exchange List Approximation:
    Fruit 2

Nutrient Content Per Serving:
CAL: 117   PRO: 1.1 (gm)
FAT: 0.6 (gm)   CHO: 30.1 (gm)
Na: 2.6 (mg)   K: 372.8 (mg)
Fiber: 3.1 (gm)   Chol: 0

Ingredients

1⅓ CUPS SLICED ORANGES
2½ CUPS SLICED, UNPEELED APPLES
  2 CUPS SLICED BANANAS
  6 MARASCHINO CHERRIES, QUARTERED
  1 TABLESPOON CHERRY JUICE
  2 TABLESPOONS LEMON JUICE
  2 TABLESPOONS WATER
1⁄16 TEASPOON CARDAMOM, GROUND (OR 1 POD, CRUSHED)

Method

1. Place fruits in salad bowl.
2. Combine lemon juice, cherry juice, and water. Pour over fruit.
3. Sprinkle with cardamom and mix lightly.
4. Cover, chill about an hour before serving.

Variation: When available, substitute 1 cup of following fruits for 1 cup bananas: red grapes, sliced strawberries, green grapes, or melon balls.

Note: One packet of sugar substitute may be added to marinade.

Marinated Fruit Bowl

Yield: 12 or 4 servings
Serving Size: ½ cup
Exchange List Approximation:
    Fruit 1

Nutrient Content Per Serving:
CAL: 61   PRO: 0.6 (gm)
FAT: 0.3 (gm)   CHO: 15.4 (gm)
Na: 4.5 (mg)   K: 194.5 (mg)
Fiber: 1.4 (gm)   Chol: 0

Ingredients

Twelve Servings		*Four Servings*	
1	CUP UNPEELED, SLICED APPLE (ABOUT 1 MEDIUM)	⅓	CUP
¾	CUP SEEDLESS GREEN GRAPES (ABOUT ¼ POUND)	¼	CUP
1	CUP SLICED ORANGE (ABOUT 1 LARGE)	⅓	CUP
¾	CUP HONEYDEW-MELON BALLS	¼	CUP
1	CUP SLICED BANANA (ABOUT 1 LARGE)	⅓	CUP
1	CUP SLICED STRAWBERRIES (ABOUT ½ PINT)	⅓	CUP
½	CUP SLICED KIWI (ABOUT 1 LARGE)	⅓	KIWI
6	MARASCHINO CHERRIES	3	
3	TABLESPOONS CHERRY JUICE	1½	TABLESPOONS
2	TABLESPOONS WATER	2	TEASPOONS
1	TABLESPOON LIME JUICE	1	TEASPOON
	FRESH MINT LEAVES		

Method

1. Mix fruits, except bananas, in large bowl.

2. Mix cherry juice, water, and lime juice. Add bananas and stir carefully to coat slices.
3. Add to fruit, stir lightly; cover and chill about 2 hours.
4. Garnish each serving with mint leaves.

Orangesicles

Yield: 8 or 2 popsicles
Serving Size: 1 popsicle
Exchange List Approximation:
   Milk, low-fat ½

Nutrient Content Per Serving:

CAL: 60	PRO: 3.5 (gm)
FAT: 1 (gm)	CHO: 9.4 (gm)
Na: 43.4 (mg)	K: 233.1 (mg)
Fiber: 0	Chol: 4 (mg)

Ingredients

Eight Popsicles
- 1 PINT PLAIN LOW-FAT YOGURT
- 6 TABLESPOONS FROZEN ORANGE JUICE CONCENTRATE
- 1 TEASPOON VANILLA
- 30 DROPS LOW CALORIE SWEETENER (1 TABLESPOON SUGAR EQUIVALENT)

Two Popsicles
- ½ CUP
- 1½ TABLESPOONS
- ¼ TEASPOON
- 8 DROPS (¾ TEASPOON)

Method

1. Stir together all ingredients and freeze in popsicle molds or paper cups. Insert sticks when partially frozen.

Light and Luscious Orange Bars

Yield: 12 sandwiches
Serving Size: 1 sandwich
Exchange List Approximation:
    Starch/Bread 1

Nutrient Content Per Serving:
CAL: 84   PRO: 2.7 (gm)
FAT: 1.3 (gm)   CHO: 16.1 (gm)
Na: 110.4 (mg) K: 159.2 (mg)
Fiber: 1.4 (gm) Chol: 1 (mg)

Ingredients

- 1 TEASPOON UNFLAVORED GELATIN
- ¼ CUP FROZEN CONCENTRATED ORANGE JUICE, THAWED
- 2 TABLESPOONS SUGAR
- ½ TEASPOON VANILLA EXTRACT
- ½ CUP INSTANT NONFAT DRY-MILK POWDER
- ½ CUP COLD WATER
- 1 TABLESPOON LEMON JUICE
- 24 GRAHAM CRACKERS

Method

1. Chill small mixing bowl and beaters.
2. In the top section of a double boiler, soften the gelatin in the concentrated orange juice. Place over hot water and stir until the gelatin is completely dissolved.
3. Remove from heat; stir in the sugar and vanilla extract.
4. Using cold bowl and beaters, beat dry milk and water until soft peaks form. Add lemon juice and beat until stiff. Fold in orange juice mixture.
5. Spread on 12 graham crackers. Top with remaining crackers.
6. Wrap individually in aluminum foil; freeze until firm (about 2 hours).

Note: Approximately ½ teaspoon sugar (8 calories) per serving.

Cocoa Ice Milk

Yield: 8 servings (4 cups)
Serving Size: $\frac{1}{2}$ cup
Exchange List Approximation:
    Milk, skim 1

Nutrient Content Per Serving:
CAL: 64   PRO: 6.1 (gm)
FAT: 0.4 (gm)   CHO: 9.8 (gm)
Na: 160.1 (mg)   K: 437.9 (mg)
Fiber: 0   Chol: 1 (mg)

Ingredients

2½ CUPS SKIM MILK
1 ENVELOPE PLAIN GELATIN
3 OUNCES SUGAR-FREE HOT COCOA MIX (SUCH AS 4½ PACKAGES ALBA HOT COCOA OR 6 PACKAGES SWISS MISS)
1 TEASPOON VANILLA

Method

1. Add gelatin to 1 cup milk, stir, heat until gelatin is dissolved.
2. Add cocoa mix, stir until dissolved. Add remaining milk and vanilla.
3. Pour into shallow pan. Place in freezer until firm, about 4 hours.
4. Break into pieces and place in electric mixer or food processor. Whip until smooth.
5. Spoon into 8 individual containers. Serve immediately as soft ice milk or place in freezer to harden.

Peach Cobbler

Yield: 6 servings
Serving Size: $\frac{2}{3}$ cup
Exchange List Approximation:
    Starch/Bread 1
    Fruit $\frac{1}{2}$

Nutrient Content Per Serving:
CAL: 126   PRO: 2.1 (gm)
FAT: 3.9 (gm)   CHO: 21.6 (gm)
Na: 222.2 (mg)   K: 197.2 (mg)
Fiber: 2.1 (gm)   Chol: 1 (mg)

Ingredients

3 CUPS FRESH PEACHES (PEELED AND SLICED)
½ CUP WATER
¼ TEASPOON NUTMEG
¾ CUP BAKING MIX (BISQUICK TYPE)
2 TEASPOONS SUGAR
¼ CUP SKIM MILK
1 TABLESPOON MARGARINE
3 PACKETS SUGAR SUBSTITUTE

Method

1. Bring peaches, water, and nutmeg to a boil. Pour one third into 2-quart casserole.
2. Combine baking mix, sugar, and milk. Stir to form a dough, turn out on floured board, roll out in rectangle ⅛-inch thick and cut into 6 strips.
3. Place 3 strips evenly over peaches. Add remaining peaches. Cover with 3 strips of dough.
4. Pour juice over dough and dot with margarine.
5. Bake in 400° F oven for 30 minutes until brown and bubbly.
6. Remove from oven and sprinkle with 3 packets of sugar substitute.

Pear Crisp

Yield: 6 servings (3 cups)
Serving Size: ½ cup
Exchange List Approximation:
    Starch/Bread 1
    Fruit 1
    Fat 1

Nutrient Content Per Serving:
CAL: 191   PRO: 1.7 (gm)
FAT: 6.2 (gm)   CHO: 33.6 (gm)
Na: 239 (mg)   K: 189.4 (mg)
Fiber: 4.9 (gm)   Chol: 1 (mg)

Ingredients

3 CUPS PEAR SAUCE (SEE FOLLOWING RECIPE)
¾ CUP BAKING MIX (BISQUICK TYPE)
1 TABLESPOON BROWN SUGAR SUBSTITUTE
½ TEASPOON CINNAMON
2 TABLESPOONS MARGARINE
2 PACKETS SUGAR SUBSTITUTE

Method

1. Pour pear sauce into shallow 2-quart casserole or 8- by 8- by 2-inch pan.
2. Mix baking mix, brown sugar substitute, and cinnamon together. Add softened margarine and mix until crumbly.
3. Sprinkle mixture evenly over sauce.
4. Bake in 400° F oven about 30 minutes until top is brown.
5. Remove from oven and sprinkle with sugar substitute.

Variation: Three cups of cooked chopped apples may be used.

Pear Sauce

Yield: 6 servings (3 cups)
Serving Size: $\frac{1}{2}$ cup
Exchange List Approximation:
    Fruit $1\frac{1}{2}$

Nutrient Content Per Serving:
CAL: 83   PRO: 0.5 (gm)
FAT: 0.5 (gm)   CHO: 21.1 (gm)
Na: 0   K: 175.4 (mg)
Fiber: 4.2 (gm)   Chol: 0

Ingredients

  2 POUNDS UNPEELED, CHOPPED PEARS
  ⅓ CUP WATER
1½ TEASPOONS GROUND CINNAMON
  ½ TEASPOON GROUND NUTMEG
  1 TABLESPOON VANILLA EXTRACT

Method

1. Mix ingredients together in saucepan. Cover and cook until pears are tender. Then mash.
2. Serve by itself, or take 2 Tablespoons and serve hot over banana bread. (Two Tablespoons count as a free food.)

Variation: Omit cinnamon, nutmeg, and vanilla; use 1 teaspoon fresh, chopped ginger root and then add 2 packets sugar substitute after cooking.

Date Drops

Yield: 42 cookies	Nutrient Content Per Serving:
Serving Size: 2 cookies	CAL: 78 — PRO: 1.1 (gm)
Exchange List Approximation:	FAT: 4.6 (gm) — CHO: 9 (gm)
Fruit $\frac{1}{2}$	Na: 56.8 (mg) — K: 83.1 (mg)
Fat 1	Fiber: 1 (gm) — Chol: 23 (mg)

Ingredients

2	EGGS, BEATEN
⅓	CUP MARGARINE
½	POUND DATES, FINELY CUT
1½	CUPS CRISP RICE CEREAL
½	CUP NUTS, CHOPPED
1	TEASPOON VANILLA

Method

1. Combine eggs, margarine, and dates. Cook over low heat, stirring constantly.
2. Boil 2 minutes. Remove from heat and add cereal, nuts, and vanilla.
3. Cool; shape into little balls.

Oatmeal Cake

Yield: 9 servings
Serving Size: $\frac{1}{9}$ recipe
Exchange List Approximation:
    Starch/Bread 1
    Fruit 1
    Fat 1

Nutrient Content Per Serving:
CAL: 173   PRO: 4.6 (gm)
FAT: 5.5 (gm)   CHO: 26.4 (gm)
Na: 104.9 (mg)   K: 159.8 (mg)
Fiber: 1.9 (gm)   Chol: 61 (mg)

Ingredients

1½ CUPS OATMEAL
3 TABLESPOONS BROWN SUGAR SUBSTITUTE
3 TABLESPOONS NONFAT DRY MILK
4 TABLESPOONS FLOUR
2 TEASPOONS BAKING POWDER
⅛ TEASPOON BAKING SODA
1 TEASPOON CINNAMON
2 CUPS CRUSHED PINEAPPLE, IN OWN JUICE
2 EGGS
2 TABLESPOONS CORN OIL

Method

1. Combine all ingredients in a large bowl. Mix well.
2. Place in 8- by 8-inch baking pan sprayed with vegetable pan spray.
3. Bake in 375° F oven for 25 minutes.

Low-Calorie Pumpkin Pie

Yield: 8 servings
Serving Size: $\frac{1}{8}$ recipe
Exchange List Approximation:
    Starch/Bread $1\frac{1}{2}$

Nutrient Content Per Serving:
CAL: 114   PRO: 6.3 (gm)
FAT: 1.9 (gm)   CHO: 18.5 (gm)
Na: 174.9 (mg)   K: 304.2 (mg)
Fiber: 1.4 (gm)   Chol: 37 (mg)
Key Source Nutrients:
    Vitamin A: 13668 (IU)

Ingredients

- 1 16-OUNCE CAN SOLID-PACK PUMPKIN
- 1 13-OUNCE CAN EVAPORATED SKIM MILK
- 1 EGG
- 2 EGG WHITES
- ½ CUP BISCUIT MIX (BISQUICK TYPE)
- 2 TABLESPOONS SUGAR
- 8 PACKETS SUGAR SUBSTITUTE
- 2 TEASPOONS PUMPKIN PIE SPICE
- 2 TEASPOONS VANILLA

Method

1. Heat oven to 350° F. Lightly grease or spray 9-inch pie pan with vegetable pan spray.
2. Place all ingredients in blender, food processor, or mixing bowl. Blend 1 minute or beat 2 minutes with mixer.
3. Pour into pie pan and bake for 50 minutes or until center is puffed up.

Peachy Pie

Yield: 6 servings

Serving Size: 5 ounces

Exchange List Approximation:

    Starch/Bread 1

    Fruit $\frac{1}{2}$

    Fat $1\frac{1}{2}$

Nutrient Content Per Serving:

CAL: 179   PRO: 3.3 (gm)

FAT: 10 (gm)   CHO: 19.6 (gm)

Na: 189.3 (mg)   K: 156.5 (mg)

Fiber: 1.6 (gm)   Chol: 0

Ingredients

1 ENVELOPE UNFLAVORED GELATIN

¼ CUP WATER

1 12-OUNCE CAN DIET GINGER ALE

2 CUPS SLICED, FRESH, RIPE PEACHES OR
UNSWEETENED FROZEN PEACHES

1 READY-TO-FILL GRAHAM-CRACKER CRUST OR
PREBAKED 9-INCH PIE SHELL

Method

1. Sprinkle gelatin over water in small mixing bowl. Place in pan of hot water, heat until dissolved.
2. Add diet ginger ale, stir. Add peaches and juice. Chill until thickened.
3. Spoon into prepared crust and chill until firm.
4. May be served with Low-Calorie Whipped Topping (refer to page 329).

Variation: 2 packets of sugar substitute may be added to peaches. 1 package of orange or raspberry flavored low-calorie gelatin dessert and 1¾ cups water may be used with peaches.

Fruit Yogurt Freeze

Yield: 8 servings (4 cups)
Serving Size: $\frac{1}{2}$ cup
Exchange List Approximation:
    Milk, low-fat $\frac{1}{2}$

Nutrient Content Per Serving:
CAL: 60   PRO: 4.3 (gm)
FAT: 1 (gm)   CHO: 9.1 (gm)
Na: 43.9 (mg) K: 249.7 (mg)
Fiber: 0.7 (gm) Chol: 4 (mg)

Ingredients

  2 CUPS UNSWEETENED PEACHES
  2 CUPS PLAIN LOW-FAT YOGURT
  1 PACKAGE UNFLAVORED GELATIN
  6 PACKETS SUGAR SUBSTITUTE
¼ CUP HOT WATER

Method

1. Place peaches and yogurt in blender or food processor. Blend until smooth.
2. Mix gelatin and sweetener, add hot water, stir until dissolved. Add to peach mixture. Blend about 1 minute.
3. Pour into metal container, place in freezer for 1 hour until partially frozen.
4. Put back in blender or processor. Blend until smooth.
5. Immediately pour into 8 individual serving containers or pan. Cover and place in freezer until ready to serve. If frozen hard, let sit in refrigerator about an hour before serving.

Whipped Chocolate Cream

Yield: 6 servings (3 cups)
Serving Size: $\frac{1}{2}$ cup
Exchange List Approximation:
    Milk, skim $\frac{1}{2}$
    Fat 2

Nutrient Content Per Serving:
CAL: 134   PRO: 5 (gm)
FAT: 11.9 (gm)   CHO: 3.5 (gm)
Na: 44.6 (mg)   K: 154.6 (mg)
Fiber: 0   Chol: 119 (mg)

Ingredients

  1 OUNCE UNSWEETENED CHOCOLATE (ABOUT 1 SQUARE)
 ¾ CUP SKIM MILK
  1 ENVELOPE UNFLAVORED GELATIN
 ½ CUP WATER
  2 EGG YOLKS
 ½ CUP WHIPPING CREAM
  2 TEASPOONS VANILLA
  2 EGG WHITES
  3 PACKETS SUGAR SUBSTITUTE

Method

1. Melt chocolate with milk in top of double boiler over simmering water; stir occasionally.
2. Sprinkle gelatin over water and let stand about 1 minute. Add to chocolate mixture and stir until completely dissolved.
3. Beat egg yolks until lemon colored. Stir part of hot mixture into egg yolks, then add back to hot mixture. Cook over low heat until mixture begins to thicken.
4. Remove from heat. Add vanilla and chill until mixture begins to thicken.

5. Whip cream and fold into chocolate mixture.
6. Beat egg whites until peaks begin to form, add sugar substitute, and beat until stiff. Gently fold into chocolate.
7. Spoon into dessert dishes. Chill until set.

Note: Cream may be used as a cake frosting. Also, you can break a sponge cake (see Volume I for recipe) into pieces, pour the cream over it, and chill for a surprising dessert.

Party-Time
Special Effects

Eggplant Appetizers

Yield: 6 servings (24 slices)
Serving Size: 4 slices
Exchange List Approximation:
    Vegetable 1
    Fat $\frac{1}{2}$

Nutrient Content Per Serving:

CAL: 53	PRO: 1.3 (gm)
FAT: 3.6 (gm)	CHO: 4.9 (gm)
Na: 64 (mg)	K: 181.2 (mg)
Fiber: 1.5 (gm)	Chol: 2 (mg)

Ingredients

- 1 POUND EGGPLANT (ABOUT 2 SMALL OR 2 JAPANESE)
- 2 TEASPOONS VEGETABLE OIL
- 2 TEASPOONS MAYONNAISE
- ⅛ TEASPOON EACH: GARLIC SALT, PAPRIKA, BASIL, PEPPER
- ¼ TEASPOON OREGANO
- 2 TABLESPOONS GRATED PARMESAN CHEESE

Method

1. Trim ends from eggplant and cut in ⅜-inch slices.
2. Place slices on oiled sheet pan and brush with oil.
3. Spread top with small amount of mayonnaise.
4. Sprinkle evenly with garlic salt, paprika, basil, pepper, oregano, and cheese.
5. Bake in 425° F oven until lightly browned, about 10 minutes. May be browned under broiler. Do not burn.
6. Serve as appetizer or vegetable.

Guacamole (Avocado Dip)

Yield: 6 servings ($\frac{3}{4}$ cup)
Serving Size: 2 tablespoons
Exchange List Approximation:
    Fat 1

Nutrient Content Per Serving:
CAL: 35   PRO: 0.5 (gm)
FAT: 3.2 (gm)   CHO: 2 (gm)
Na: 24.7 (mg)   K: 138.5 (mg)
Fiber: 0.5 (gm)   Chol: 0

Ingredients

1 LARGE RIPE AVOCADO (ABOUT 6 OUNCES)
1 TABLESPOON LEMON JUICE
1 TABLESPOON FINELY CHOPPED GREEN ONION
2 TABLESPONS DICED TOMATO PIECES, FRESH OR CANNED
DASH SALT

Method

1. Peel avocado, cut in half, and remove pit.
2. Place avocado halves in bowl, add lemon juice, and mash with fork.
3. Add onion, tomato, and salt. Mix lightly. Cover tightly and use as soon as possible as it will darken.

Note: The above is a basic guacamole to be served with lettuce and highly seasoned Mexican dishes. To make dip, add hot sauce, picante sauce, chili powder, or chopped green chilies to taste.

Soy Nuts

Yield: 12 servings (1½ cups)
Serving Size: $\frac{1}{12}$ recipe
Exchange List Approximation:
    Starch/Bread $\frac{1}{2}$
    Meat, lean 1

Nutrient Content Per Serving:
CAL: 88   PRO: 7.5 (gm)
FAT: 3.9 (gm)   CHO: 7.3 (gm)
Na: 1.1 (mg)   K: 366.9 (mg)
Fiber: 3.1 (gm)   Chol: 0

Ingredients

1¼ CUPS SOYBEANS (ABOUT ½ POUND)
4 CUPS WATER

Method

1. Soak soybeans for 12 hours. Remove excess moisture on paper towel.
2. Place on baking sheet and toast in oven for 2 or more hours at 250° F until crisp all the way through.

Note: May be used whole or ground in salads, sandwiches, snacks, dessert toppings, breads, quick breads, etc.

Build-a-Burrito

Select one or more items from each category to match your meal pattern.

Yield: Varies
Exchanges and estimated nutrients per one serving in each category. Nutritional analyses are *averages* of the alternative items listed in each category.

Category	CAL	FAT (gm)	Na (mg)	Fiber (gm)	PRO (gm)	CHO (gm)	K (mg)	Chol (mg)
Bread	74	1.0	73.3	0.9	2.7	13.9	28.7	0
Bean	82	1.0	4.2*	3.6	5.6	13.3	235.5	0
Meat/Cheese	76	4.8	130.2	0	7.2	0.5	67.4	24
Vegetable	28	0.1	314.7	0.9	1.3	5.9	258.9	0
Fat	45	4.5	98.3	0.7	.06	1.2	63.3	3

Exchanges
Bread	1 Starch/Bread
Bean	1 Starch/Bread
Meat/Cheese	1 Meat, medium-fat
Vegetable	1 Vegetable
Fat	1 Fat

Ingredients

Bread Category
1 6-INCH DIAMETER FLOUR TORTILLA (MADE WITH OIL OR SHORTENING—NOT LARD)
1 6-INCH DIAMETER CORN TORTILLA
1 6-INCH DIAMETER WHOLE-WHEAT FLOUR TORTILLA
½ SMALL (6-INCH-DIAMETER) POCKET BREAD (WHOLE-WHEAT, RYE, OR WHITE)

Bean Category
  ¼ CUP COOKED, FORK-MASHED BEANS: PINTO, OR
     GARBANZO, OR RED, OR WHITE, OR NAVY, OR
     LENTILS, OR SPLIT PEAS, OR SOY, OR REFRIED
     (RECIPE, PAGE 254)

Meat/Cheese Category
  1 OUNCE COOKED, DRAINED GROUND ROUND
  1 OUNCE COOKED, SHREDDED CHICKEN BREAST
     (WITHOUT SKIN)
  1 OUNCE COOKED, LEAN SHREDDED PORK (OMIT ½
     FAT EXCHANGE)
  1 OUNCE GRATED, SHARP CHEDDAR CHEESE (OMIT 1
     FAT EXCHANGE)**
  1 OUNCE GRATED, LOW-FAT CHEESE

Vegetable Category (Optional)
  ½ CUP CHOPPED TOMATO
  ½ CUP CHOPPED GREEN PEPPER
  ½ CUP ENCHILADA SAUCE (OMIT 1 FAT EXCHANGE)
  ½ CUP TOMATO SAUCE

Fat Category
  ⅛ RIPE AVOCADO, MASHED
  2 TABLESPOONS SOUR CREAM**
  5 SMALL, BLACK, RIPE OLIVES, SLICED OR CHOPPED

Free Exchange Category
  1 TABLESPOON† CHOPPED TOMATO, OR CHOPPED
     GREEN PEPPER, OR CHOPPED ONION, OR CHOPPED
     JALAPENO PEPPER, OR SALSA, OR PLAIN LOW-FAT
     YOGURT
     CILANTRO TO TASTE
     CUMIN TO TASTE
     CHILI POWDER TO TASTE
     TABASCO SAUCE TO TASTE

Method

1. Select one or more items from each category to match your meal pattern.
2. Fill the item(s) from the Bread Category with items from the other categories to match your meal pattern. Best if served warm.

Example: One 6-inch flour tortilla (1 Starch/Bread exchange) filled with ¼ cup pinto beans (1 Starch/Bread); 1 ounce shredded chicken breast (1 Medium-Fat Meat); ⅛ ripe avocado, mashed (1 Fat exchange); 1 Tablespoon salsa (Free exchange); 1 Tablespoon chopped onion (Free exchange); cilantro and cumin to taste (Free exchanges). Total exchanges per meal used from this recipe:

1 Medium-Fat Meat
2 Starch/Bread
1 Fat

*Beans are cooked or canned without salt.
**Limit to 1 serving per meal; high in cholesterol and saturated fat.
†Limit to 2 servings per meal.

Tofu Pizza

Yield: 6 or 2 servings
Serving Size: ½ muffin
Exchange List Approximation:
    Starch/Bread 1
    Meat, medium-fat 1
    Vegetable 1

Nutrient Content Per Serving:
CAL: 183   PRO: 9.9 (gm)
FAT: 6.8 (gm)   CHO: 21 (gm)
Na: 478 (mg)   K: 348 (mg)
Fiber: 0.8 (gm)   Chol: 11 (mg)

Ingredients

Six Servings		*Two Servings*	
3	ENGLISH MUFFINS	1	
1	CUP PIZZA SAUCE	⅓	CUP
6	OUNCES TOFU	2	OUNCES
⅜	TEASPOON OREGANO	⅛	TEASPOON
⅜	TEASPOON GARLIC POWDER	⅛	TEASPOON
4	OUNCES SHREDDED PART-SKIM MOZZARELLA CHEESE	1⅓	OUNCES

Method

1. Cut English muffins in half.
2. Spread each half with 2½ Tablespoons sauce.
3. Crumble tofu and mix with oregano and garlic powder. Spread evenly over sauce.
4. Cover with shredded cheese, about 3 Tablespoons per pizza.
5. Bake in 350° F oven until cheese melts and starts to brown, about 15 minutes.

Fruit Pizzas
with Apple Juice Glaze

Yield: 6 servings (3- by 4-inch pieces)
Exchanges and estimated nutrients per 1 serving:

	OATMEAL CRUST		CHEESE CRUST	
	Apple-Raisin	-Blueberry	Apple-Raisin	-Blueberry
CAL	185	164	245	224
FAT (gm)	3.3	3.3	6.0	6.0
Na (mg)	206.4	207.8	82.4	83.8
Fiber (gm)	3.1	3.2	3.0	3.2
PRO (gm)	3.7	3.5	6.3	6.2
CHO (gm)	36.7	31.1	42.8	37.1
K (mg)	191.4	128.8	194.7	132.1
Chol (mg)	0	0	9	9
Exchanges	Starch/	Starch/	Starch/	Starch/
	Bread 1	Bread 1	Bread 1½	Bread 1½
	Fruit 1½	Fruit 1	Fruit 1½	Fruit 1
	Fat ½	Fat ½	Fat 1	Fat 1

Ingredients

Oatmeal Crust
- 1 CUP LESS 1 TABLESPOON ALL-PURPOSE FLOUR
- ¾ CUP QUICK OATMEAL
- 1 TABLESPOON OIL
- ½ CUP WARM WATER
- ½ PACKAGE DRY YEAST
- ½ TEASPOON SALT
- ½ TEASPOON BAKING POWDER

Cheese Crust
- 1⅓ CUPS PLUS 2 TABLESPOONS ALL-PURPOSE FLOUR
- 1 TABLESPOON OIL
- ½ CUP WARM WATER
- ½ PACKAGE DRY YEAST

½ TEASPOON BAKING POWDER
⅓ CUP PLUS 2 TABLESPOONS GRATED, SHARP
   CHEDDAR CHEESE

Apple-Raisin Topping
3½ CUPS PARED AND SLICED APPLES
 1 PACKET SUGAR SUBSTITUTE
¾ TEASPOON CINNAMON
⅓ CUP PLUS 1 TABLESPOON SEEDLESS RAISINS

Apple-Blueberry Topping
2¼ CUPS PARED AND SLICED APPLES
1½ CUPS BLUEBERRIES, UNSWEETENED
1¼ PACKETS SUGAR SUBSTITUTE
¾ TEASPOON CINNAMON
 2 TEASPOONS LEMON JUICE

Method

1. Gather together ingredients to make the fruit pizza crust
   and topping desired.
2. Make the crust. Combine flour, oatmeal, salt, and baking
   powder together in a bowl. (Add cheese if making cheese
   crust and omit oatmeal and salt.) Blend oil in with a fork.
3. Dissolve yeast in water and add to the flour mixture. Stir
   with a wooden spoon until all ingredients are combined.
   Cover and let rise 1 hour.
4. Stir down dough and pat into 9- by 8-inch rectangle.
   Combine topping ingredients and arrange over crust.
5. Bake 30 to 40 minutes at 375° F.
6. *Glaze:* Make apple juice glaze. Combine ⅔ cup
   unsweetened apple juice and 1½ teaspoons cornstarch in
   small saucepan. Cook over medium heat until thickened.
   Remove from heat. Spread over fruit pizzas during last 15
   minutes of baking. Cut 2 by 3 into 6 pieces.

Basic Chocolate Milkshake

Yield: 1 serving
Serving Size: $1\frac{3}{4}$ cup
Exchange List Approximation:
    Meat, lean 2
    Milk, skim 2

Nutrient Content Per Serving:
CAL: 298   PRO: 40.2 (gm)
FAT: 5.5 (gm)   CHO: 22.8 (gm)
Na: 1046 (mg)   K: 704 (mg)
Fiber: 0.3 (gm)   Chol: 24 (mg)

Ingredients

1 TABLESPOON COCOA
1 TABLESPOON WATER
1 CUP FROZEN SKIM MILK
1 CUP FROZEN LOW-FAT COTTAGE CHEESE
2 PACKETS SUGAR SUBSTITUTE

Method

1. Boil cocoa and water together for ½ minute.
2. Put cocoa mixture, milk, cottage cheese, and sweetener in blender and blend until well blended, about 3 minutes.

Variations: Chocomint Shake uses recipe as above with a drop of peppermint extract. Cocoa-Coconut Shake uses recipe as above with ¼ teaspoon coconut extract.

Milkshake with Variations

Yield: 1 serving (1¾ cups for plain; 2 cups for variation)
Exchanges and Estimated nutrients are per ½-recipe serving.

Variation	CAL	FAT (gm)	Na (mg)	Fiber (gm)	PRO (gm)	CHO (gm)	K (mg)	Chol (mg)
Plain	188	2.6	586.0	0	24.0	15.9	514.0	14
Banana	240	2.9	587.0	1.1	24.6	29.3	740.0	14
Banana and peanut butter	430	19.3	737.0	3.5	33.8	34.3	960.0	14
Peanut butter	378	19.0	736.0	2.4	33.2	20.9	734.0	14
Unsweetened peach	245	2.7	586.0	2.1	24.9	30.6	774.0	14
Pineapple	238	2.7	587.0	0.7	24.3	29.0	615.0	14
Strawberry	244	3.3	588.0	4.1	25.1	29.0	823.0	14

Exchanges

Plain	2 Meat, lean + 1 Milk, skim
Banana	2 Meat, lean + 1 Fruit + 1 Milk, skim
Banana and peanut butter	4 Meat, medium-fat + 1 Fruit + 1 Milk, skim
Peanut butter	4 Meat, medium-fat + 1 Milk, skim
Peach	2 Meat, lean + 1 Fruit + 1 Milk, skim
Pineapple	2 Meat, lean + 1 Fruit + 1 Milk, skim
Strawberry	2 Meat, lean + 1 Fruit + 1 Milk, skim

Ingredients

Plain
- 1 CUP SKIM MILK
- ½ CUP LOW-FAT COTTAGE CHEESE
- ¼ TEASPOON VANILLA
- 2-3 PACKETS SUGAR SUBSTITUTE

Variation
- ½ BANANA, OR
- ½ BANANA AND 2 TABLESPOONS PEANUT BUTTER, OR
- 2 TABLESPOONS PEANUT BUTTER, OR
- ½ CUP UNSWEETENED PEACHES, OR
- ⅓ CUP CRUSHED PINEAPPLE IN OWN JUICE, OR
- ¾ CUP FRESH STRAWBERRIES OR FROZEN UNSWEETENED STRAWBERRIES

Method

1. Combine ingredients to make Plain Milkshake, place in metal pan, and freeze.
2. Break up mixture and blend or process until smooth.
3. To make a variation, add one of the variations and blend until smooth.

Wine Spritzer

Yield: 8 servings
Serving Size: 8 ounces
Exchange List Approximation:
    Fat 2

Nutrient Content Per Serving:
CAL: 84   PRO: 0.4 (gm)
FAT: 0   CHO: 2 (gm)
Na: 33 (mg)   K: 134 (mg)
Fiber: 0   Chol: 0

Ingredients

1 QUART CLUB SODA
1 QUART DRY WHITE OR RED WINE
   ICE CUBES
   LIME OR LEMON WEDGES

Method

1. Mix soda and wine.
2. Add ice and garnish with lime or lemon wedges.

Note: May be served in pitcher or punch bowl, as well as 8-ounce glass.

12 □ FAST FOOD (HOW TO BYPASS THE BOOBY TRAPS)

Move over, Mom's apple pie. Hamburgers and french fries are giving the old favorite mean competition for first place in Americans' stomachs, if not their hearts. If you're like most Americans, you probably find yourself in line at fast food restaurants 9 to 10 times a month and spend close to a third of your total food budget on meals away from home.

Having diabetes doesn't make you immune to the attractions of quick service and reasonable prices. Fortunately, if you follow a few guidelines, you can usually eat wherever you want without seriously compromising on nutrition.

KNOW YOUR MEAL PLAN and choose foods that fit it as closely as possible. For example, if you're on an exchange diet and are allowed 2 Starch/Bread exchanges and 2 Medium-Fat Meat exchanges during lunch, you would steer clear of the double cheeseburger (which is 2 Starch/Bread exchanges, 3 Medium-Fat Meat exchanges, and 3 Fat exchanges) and instead order a single hamburger.

AVOID SUGAR, FAT, AND SALT. You already know to avoid such obvious "no-nos" as milkshakes, apple pie, and gooey sundaes. But spotting other diet disasters can be tricky. Many fast foods contain "hidden" salt as well as saturated fat, cholesterol, and calories. Salt can be harmful to people who have high blood pressure, and cholesterol is believed to contribute to coronary artery disease. To avoid unhealthy foods, you need to be armed with information about the makeup of fast foods. The accompanying chart will give you specifics about the fat, calorie, and salt content of many popular fast foods, but here are some general tips.

Items that tend to be high in fat and cholesterol are dairy products, meats, and fried foods (which are almost always cooked in saturated fat). Of course, these are the mainstays of many fast food places, so if you must have fast foods, sometimes the best you can do is to get rid of some excess fat (and calories!) by choosing small portions, scraping away greasy breadings, and draining excess oils. Also, be wary of sauces containing mayonnaise. They're high in fat.

Avoiding high-salt foods can be difficult because you can't always taste the salt. For example, who would suspect that a Whopper with Cheese has 1,435 milligrams of sodium, or that a 12-inch pizza may contain 2,700 milligrams of sodium? (The suggested maximum sodium allowance for an entire day is 3,000 milligrams.) Catsup, pickles, mustard, tartar sauce, and salad dressing all have added salt, too, so tell the counter-person to cancel the condiments.

KNOW THE NUTRITIVE VALUES OF FAST FOODS. The nutritional worth of your meal depends on how good your choices are. Fast foods are often low in vitamins A, C, and D, as well as folic acid, fiber, and certain minerals. However, if properly selected, fast food meals *can* give you adequate amounts of protein, thiamine, riboflavin, and calcium. Reasonable choices, in addition to hamburgers (without condiments), are plain roast beef sandwiches, chili, and fresh salads. Fortunately, many fast food restaurants provide salad bars these days. If you miss out on some essential nutrients, vitamins, and minerals in your fast food meal, eat a variety of vegetables, fruits, milk, and whole-grain foods in your other meals and snacks during the day to make up for the lack.

PORTION PREDICAMENTS. Portion sizes are usually standard in fast food restaurant chains across the country, which makes estimating fairly easy once you familiarize yourself with a given chain's menu. But among independent establishments, such as delicatessens and sandwich shops, contents and portions can differ dramatically. When selecting from these menus, you'll need to do some quick calculating on your own.

Begin by breaking down the selection you want into its separate ingredients, noting the *kinds* and *amounts* of ingredients used. Then, see if it fits into your meal plan. If you follow an "exchange" meal plan, try to estimate the proper exchange for each ingredient, taking care not to *underestimate*. For example, a deli-bought turkey sandwich might calculate like this:

Turkey (approx. 3 oz. meat) = 3 Lean-Meat exchanges; tomatoes and lettuce = 1 Vegetable exchange; 1 teaspoon mayonnaise = 1 Fat exchange; 2 slices French bread = 2 Starch/Bread exchanges. (The sandwich would give you 395 calories, with 35 grams carbohydrate, 29 grams protein, and 14 grams fat.)

If you have trouble "guesstimating," train yourself to judge portions by eye. Practice measuring foods at home with your food scale, measuring cups, and spoons. Remind yourself what half a cup of milk looks like; see how many slices of cheese are in one ounce.

CHECK OUT THE CHART. The following chart is included to show you the nutritive values of selected fast foods, so you can make informed choices. It is not meant as an endorsement of fast foods, or any restaurant in particular. Remember, some of the foods listed here may not be appropriate for your meal plan.

If your favorite food isn't here, compare it to a similar food. Be sure to gauge portions accurately. Your diet counselor should be able to help calculate exchanges and determine whether or not the food has a place in your diet.

FAST FOOD EXCHANGES*

	SERVING SIZE	CALORIES (1 SERVING)	CARB. (GM.)	PRO. (GM.)	FAT (GM.)	SODIUM (MG.)	EXCHANGES (1 SERVING)
ARBY'S							
Roast Beef Sandwich	5 oz.	350	32	22	15	880	2 Bread, 2 Med.-Fat Meat, 1 Fat
Junior Roast Beef Sandwich	3 oz.	220	21	12	9	530	1½ Bread, 1 Med.-Fat Meat, 1 Fat
Turkey Sandwich	6 oz.	410	36	24	19	1,060	2½ Bread, 2 Med.-Fat Meat, 2 Fat
ARTHUR TREACHER'S							
Fish	2 pieces	355	25	19	20	450	2 Bread, 2 Med.-Fat Meat, 2 Fat
Fish	3 pieces	533	38	29	30	675	2 Bread, 3 Med.-Fat Meat, 3 Fat
Fish Sandwich	1	440	39	16	24	836	3 Bread, 1 Med.-Fat Meat, 4 Fat
Chips	4 oz.	276	35	4	13	393	2 Bread, 3 Fat
Cole Slaw	3 oz.	123	11	1	8	266	1 Bread, 1 Fat
Chowder	1 bowl	112	11	5	5	835	1 Bread, 1 Fat
BURGER KING							
Hamburger	3.9 oz.	290	29	15	13	525	2 Bread, 1 Med.-Fat Meat, 2 Fat
Cheeseburger	4.4 oz.	350	30	18	17	730	2 Bread, 2 Med.-Fat Meat, 1 Fat
Whopper	9.2 oz.	630	50	26	36	990	3½ Bread, 2 Med.-Fat Meat, 5 Fat
Whopper Jr.	5.1 oz.	370	31	15	20	560	2 Bread, 1 Med.-Fat Meat, 3 Fat

	Serving Size	Calories	Carbohydrate (g)	Protein (g)	Fat (g)	Sodium (mg)	Exchanges
French Fries	2.4 oz.	210	25	3	11	230	1½ Bread, 2 Fat
Onion Rings	2.7 oz.	270	29	3	16	450	2 Bread, 3 Fat

DAIRY QUEEN

	Serving Size	Calories	Carbohydrate (g)	Protein (g)	Fat (g)	Sodium (mg)	Exchanges
Single Hamburger	5 oz.	360	33	21	16	630	2 Bread, 2 Med.-Fat Meat, 1 Fat
Hot Dog	3.5 oz.	280	21	11	16	830	1½ Bread, 1 Med.-Fat Meat, 2 Fat
French Fries (Regular)	2.5 oz.	200	25	2	10	115	1½ Bread, 2 Fat
Cone (Small)**	3 oz.	140	22	3	4	45	1 Bread, 1 Fat
Chocolate Sundae (Small)**	3.7 oz.	190	33	3	4	75	2 Bread, 1 Fat
"Dilly" Bar**	3 oz.	210	21	3	13	50	1½ Bread, 3 Fat
"DQ" Sandwich**	2 oz.	140	24	3	4	40	1½ Bread, 1 Fat

KENTUCKY FRIED CHICKEN

Original Recipe Chicken (Edible Portion)

	Serving Size	Calories	Carbohydrate (g)	Protein (g)	Fat (g)	Sodium (mg)	Exchanges
Wing (one piece)	1.5 oz.	136	4	10	9	302	1½ Med.-Fat Meat
Drumstick	1.6 oz.	117	3	12	7	207	1½ Lean Meat
Side Breast	2.4 oz.	199	7	16	12	558	½ Bread, 2 Med.-Fat Meat
Thigh	3 oz.	257	7	18	18	556	½ Bread, 2½ Med.-Fat Meat, 1 Fat
Keel	3.3 oz.	236	7	24	12	631	½ Bread, 3 Med.-Fat Meat
(Extra crispy has more fat and approx. 50 cal. extra per piece.)							
Chicken Breast Sandwich	5.5 oz.	436	34	25	23	1,093	2 Bread, 3 Med.-Fat Meat, 2 Fat
Mashed Potatoes	3 oz.	64	12	2	1	268	1 Bread
Gravy	2 Tbsp.	46	2	–	4	57	1 Fat
Roll	0.7 oz.	61	11	2	1	118	1 Bread
Cole Slaw	¾ Cup	121	13	1	7	225	1 Bread, 1 Fat
Kentucky Fries	3.4 oz.	184	28	3	7	174	2 Bread, 1 Fat

FAST FOOD EXCHANGES*

	SERVING SIZE	CALORIES (1 SERVING)	CARB. (GM.)	PRO (GM.)	FAT (GM.)	SODIUM (MG.)	EXCHANGES (1 SERVING)
LONG JOHN SILVER'S							
Chicken Planks	4	457	35	27	23	NA	2 Bread, 3 Med.-Fat Meat, 2 Fat
Seafood Platter							
Fish	1	183	11	11	11	NA	1 Bread, 1 Med.-Fat Meat, 1 Fat
Scallops	2	94	10	4	5	NA	½ Bread, 1 Fat
Shrimp	2	89	10	3	4	NA	½ Bread, 1 Fat
Hush Puppies	2	102	13	2	4	NA	1 Bread, 1 Fat
Fryes	3 oz.	288	33	4	16	NA	2 Bread, 3 Fat
Cole Slaw	4 oz.	138	16	1	8	NA	1 Bread (or 3 Vegetable,) 2 Fat
Total		894	93	25	48	NA	6 Bread, 1 Vegetable, 1 Med.-Fat Meat, 8 Fat
Clams on Clam Dinner	5 oz.	465	46	13	25	NA	3 Bread, 1 Med.-Fat Meat, 4 Fat
Clam Chowder	8 oz.	107	15	5	3	NA	1 Bread, 1 Fat
McDONALD'S							
Hamburger	3.5 oz.	255	30	12	10	520	2 Bread, 1 Med.-Fat Meat, 1 Fat
Cheeseburger	4 oz.	307	30	15	14	767	2 Bread, 1 Med.-Fat Meat, 2 Fat
Big Mac	7 oz.	563	41	26	33	1,010	3 Bread, 3 Med.-Fat Meat, 3 Fat
Quarter Pounder	5.8 oz.	424	33	24	22	735	2 Bread, 3 Med.-Fat Meat, 1 Fat

Item	Serving	Calories				Sodium	Exchanges
Filet-O-Fish	4.8 oz.	432	37	14	25	781	2½ Bread, 1 Med.-Fat Meat, 4 Fat
French Fries (Regular)	2.4 oz.	220	26	3	12	109	2 Bread, 2 Fat
Egg McMuffin	4.8 oz.	327	31	19	15	885	2 Bread, 2 Med.-Fat Meat, 1 Fat
Scrambled Eggs (1 Order)	3.4 oz.	180	2	13	13	205	2 Med.-Fat Meat, 1 Fat
Hash Brown Potatoes (1 Order)	2 oz.	125	14	2	7	325	1 Bread, 1 Fat

PIZZA HUT

Thin 'N Crispy Pizza

Item	Serving	Calories				Sodium	Exchanges
Beef	½ 10" Pizza (3 Slices)	490	51	29	19	NA	3 Bread, 3 Med.-Fat Meat, 1 Fat
Pork	"	520	51	27	23	NA	3 Bread, 3 Med.-Fat Meat, 2 Fat
Cheese	"	450	54	25	15	NA	3½ Bread, 2 Med.-Fat Meat, 1 Fat
Pepperoni	"	430	45	23	17	NA	3 Bread, 2 Med.-Fat Meat, 1 Fat
Supreme	"	510	51	27	21	NA	3½ Bread, 2 Med.-Fat Meat, 2 Fat

Thick 'N Chewy Pizza

Item	Serving	Calories				Sodium	Exchanges
Beef	½ 10" Pizza (3 Slices)	620	73	38	20	NA	5 Bread, 3 Med.-Fat Meat, 1 Fat
Pork	"	640	71	36	23	NA	5 Bread, 3 Med.-Fat Meat, 1 Fat
Cheese	"	560	71	34	14	NA	5 Bread, 3 Med.-Fat Meat
Pepperoni	"	560	68	31	18	NA	4½ Bread, 3 Med.-Fat Meat, 1 Fat
Supreme	"	640	74	36	22	NA	5 Bread, 3 Med.-Fat Meat, 1 Fat

FAST FOOD EXCHANGES*

	SERVING SIZE	CALORIES (1 SERVING)	CARB. (GM.)	PRO (GM.)	FAT (GM.)	SODIUM (MG.)	EXCHANGES (1 SERVING)
TACO BELL							
Beef Burrito	6.5 oz.	466	37	30	21	327	2½ Bread, 3 Med.-Fat Meat, 1 Fat
Beefy Tostada	6.5 oz.	291	21	19	15	138	1½ Bread, 2 Med.-Fat Meat, 1 Fat
Enchirito	7 oz.	454	42	25	21	1,175	3 Bread, 3 Med.-Fat Meat, 2 Fat
Taco	3 oz.	186	14	15	8	79	1 Bread, 2 Med.-Fat Meat
WENDY'S							
Hamburger	7 oz.	470	34	26	26	774	2 Bread, 3 Med.-Fat Meat, 2 Fat
Cheeseburger	8.5 oz.	580	34	33	34	1,085	2 Bread, 4 Med.-Fat Meat, 3 Fat
French Fries	4.2 oz.	330	41	5	16	112	2½ Bread, 3 Fat
Chili	8.8 oz.	230	21	19	8	1,065	1½ Bread, 1½ Med.-Fat

Adapted from *Fast Food Facts*, a 1983 publication of the International Diabetes Center, 4959 Excelsior Blvd., Minneapolis, MN 55436.

*Nutritive values are supplied by companies. Some foods here also appear in *Family Cookbook* Volume I. Where there is a discrepancy, use the figures in this, the more current, chart.

**For occasional use *only*, preferably before exercise.

NA = not available.

13 □ INTRODUCING TOFU

You're tired of chicken but you want to cook with a food that's equally versatile, is high in protein, has no saturated fat, and is low in calories? Consider tofu, otherwise known as bean curd— a staple of Oriental cooking that is gaining increasing popularity in America's health-conscious homes.

Tofu is derived from pureed soybeans and is pressed into white cakes with a custardlike texture. This inexpensive protein source can be served raw (uncooked) or used in many other ways: boiled, steamed, stir-fried, baked, marinated, or deep-fried. Its natural taste is subtle, but when prepared with other ingredients it absorbs and complements the stronger flavors around it, mixing well with most foods.

Tofu can be "counted" in a few different ways, each of them equally acceptable.

3 oz. = 1 Lean Meat

Estimated nutrients per serving =   CAL 61
                                                      PRO 7 gm.
                                                      FAT 4 gm.
                                                      CHO 2 gm.

4 oz. = 1½ Lean Meat or 1 Medium-Fat Meat

Estimated nutrients per serving =   CAL 82
                                                      PRO 9 gm.
                                                      FAT 5 gm.
                                                      CHO 3 gm.

For anyone new to the delights of tofu, here is some advice for buying, storing, and preparing it.

BUYING TOFU

1. Buy only fresh tofu, which has by far the best flavor.
2. Check the date stamped on the package. For best results, serve before that date, which is usually seven days after the tofu was made.
3. If the store sells tofu in a large container filled with water, make sure the container has a lid on top. Tofu must be kept in clean water, and an open lid is an invitation for contaminants to drop in.
4. When the water in the container looks somewhat yellow, yet the date shows that the tofu is not out of date, you can generally assume that the color is from the soybean protein and that you do not necessarily need to worry about the tofu's freshness. However, put tofu in fresh water if storing it.
5. Read the label on the container to make sure the tofu is made without any preservatives or chemical additives.

STORING TOFU

1. Tofu should be kept in a sealed container in a refrigerator at all times; do not let it freeze.
2. Change the water daily until the tofu is used. In summer, tofu will last three to four days beyond the date stamped on the package. In winter, however, it will last up to seven days. Keep in mind, though, that tofu loses its flavor as the days go by.
3. Particularly in hot weather when you plan to serve tofu raw (uncooked), place it in a strainer and rinse with boiling water before using. This eliminates bacteria that may be present. Then put the tofu in cold water, cover, and refrigerate until used.
4. You may refresh old or leftover tofu by rinsing with boiling

water as described above; however, such tofu should be used within a day.

DRAINING TOFU

It is very important to drain tofu very well before cooking, otherwise it becomes somewhat watery and loses flavor. The following two methods of draining are most popular.

1. At least an hour before cooking, wrap the tofu with a clean dish towel. Place the tofu on something flat, such as a large plate or a chopping board, next to the sink. Raise one end of the board or plate several inches so that any liquid will go into the sink. Put another board or something flat on top of the tofu to act as a press. You can also put another weight, such as a plate on top of this, if necessary.
2. You may drain the tofu gradually in the refrigerator overnight. In this case, wrap the tofu with a clean dish towel in several layers; place on a large, flat plate. Just before using, dry the tofu well with either a paper towel or another clean dish towel.

Tofu
Recipes

Sprouts Salad with Low-Calorie Tofu Dressing

Yield: 4 servings
Serving Size: $\frac{1}{4}$ recipe
Exchange List Approximation:
    Meat, medium-fat $1\frac{1}{2}$
    Vegetable 2

Nutrient Content Per Serving:
CAL: 158   PRO: 13.6 (gm)
FAT: 6.8 (gm)   CHO: 14.4 (gm)
Na: 182 (mg)   K: 456.5 (mg)
Fiber: 2.6 (gm)   Chol: 68 (mg)

Ingredients

  1 POUND TOFU, TOWEL-DRIED
  ½ MEDIUM ONION, CHOPPED
  3 TABLESPOONS TOMATO PASTE
  1 TABLESPOON APPLE-CIDER VINEGAR OR LEMON JUICE
  ¼ TEASPOON DRY MUSTARD
  2 TABLESPOONS TOMATO JUICE
  1 HARD-BOILED EGG, CHOPPED FINE
  3 TEASPOONS SWEET RELISH
  1 CUP SHREDDED CABBAGE
  ½ CUCUMBER, THINLY SLICED
  1 LARGE (OR 2 SMALL) TOMATOES, CUT INTO 8 WEDGES
  1 CUP BEAN SPROUTS
  1 CUP ALFALFA SPROUTS
    LETTUCE LEAVES

Method

1. Combine tofu, onion, tomato paste, vinegar, mustard, and tomato juice; blend thoroughly.
2. Add chopped egg and relish; mix well.
3. Arrange vegetables and sprouts on lettuce in a salad bowl. Serve the dressing separately.

Fruit Salad with Tofu Dressing

Yield: 4 servings
Serving Size: $\frac{1}{4}$ recipe
Exchange List Approximation:
    Meat, medium-fat 1
    Fruit 1
    Fat 2

Nutrient Content Per Serving:
CAL: 223   PRO: 6.5 (gm)
FAT: 16.3 (gm)   CHO: 16.2 (gm)
Na: 66.2 (mg)   K: 308.7 (mg)
Fiber: 2.6 (gm)   Chol: 1 (mg)
Key Source Nutrients:
    Ascorbic acid: 54 (mg)

Ingredients

  3 CUPS MIXED FRESH FRUIT (SUCH AS ORANGES, GRAPEFRUIT, APPLES, BANANAS, STRAWBERRIES, PINEAPPLE, AND GRAPES)
  ½ STALK CELERY, THINLY SLICED CROSSWISE
  ½ CAKE (8 OUNCES) TOFU, TOWEL-DRIED
  1 TABLESPOON APPLE-CIDER VINEGAR OR LEMON JUICE
3½ TABLESPOONS VEGETABLE OIL
  ½ TEASPOON SOY SAUCE
3½ TABLESPOONS PLAIN YOGURT
     LETTUCE
     WATERCRESS

Method

1. Soak celery in cold water for 1 to 2 minutes. Drain well.
2. Combine tofu, vinegar, oil, soy sauce, and yogurt in blender. Blend thoroughly for about 2 minutes.
3. Mix together fruit and celery. Arrange on lettuce leaf. Garnish with watercress.
4. Serve the dressing separately. If it separates, stir before serving.

Eggplant-and-Tofu Casserole

Yield: 4 servings
Serving Size: $\frac{1}{4}$ recipe
Exchange List Approximation:
    Starch/Bread 1
    Meat, medium-fat $1\frac{1}{2}$
    Vegetable 2
    Fat $1\frac{1}{2}$

Nutrient Content Per Serving:
CAL: 300   PRO: 17.3 (gm)
FAT: 16.2 (gm)   CHO: 28 (gm)
Na: 925.2 (mg)   K: 1141.2 (mg)
Fiber: 5.2 (gm)   Chol: 137 (mg)
Key Source Nutrients:
    Ascorbic acid: 59 (mg)
    Folacin: 463 (mcg)

Ingredients

- 1 POUND TOFU, TOWEL-DRIED
- 2 TEASPOONS MINCED PARSLEY
- 2 EGGS, BEATEN
- 2 TEASPOONS UNBLEACHED FLOUR
- 2 SMALL EGGPLANTS, SLICED ½″ THICK
- 1 MEDIUM ONION, THINLY SLICED
- 1 MEDIUM-SIZED, RIPE TOMATO, QUARTERED, THINLY SLICED
- ½ MEDIUM-SIZED GREEN PEPPER, HALVED, THINLY SLICED
- 8 PIECES FRESH MUSHROOM, THINLY SLICED
- 1 CLOVE GARLIC, MINCED OR CRUSHED
- 1 TEASPOON OREGANO
- 2 TABLESPOONS VEGETABLE OIL
- 4 TABLESPOONS TOMATO PASTE
- 2 CUPS TOMATO JUICE
- 3-4 TEASPOONS SOY SAUCE
-    GRATED CHEESE (OPTIONAL)
-    MINCED PARSLEY

Method

1. Combine tofu, minced parsley, eggs, and flour in a bowl. Mix until well blended.
2. Boil eggplant slices for 7 to 8 minutes until tender.
3. Heat oil in large frying pan, saute garlic briefly, then add remaining vegetables. Cook for 2 minutes over medium-high heat, stirring constantly.
4. Add tomato paste, tomato juice, soy sauce, and oregano and bring to boil. Reduce heat and add eggplant slices. Simmer for another 2 to 3 minutes.
5. Spread tofu mixture evenly over the vegetables. Cover and cook over low heat for another 5 minutes.
6. Sprinkle the top with grated cheese. Remove from heat. Leave covered another 5 minutes or until cheese melts. Garnish with minced parsley.
7. If a crispy top is preferred, bake in a preheated hot oven for 5 minutes.

Tofu-Stuffed Rolled Cabbage

Yield: 4 servings
Serving Size: $\frac{1}{4}$ recipe
Exchange List Approximation:
    Meat, lean 2
    Vegetable 2
    Fat 1

Nutrient Content Per Serving:
CAL: 192   PRO: 17 (gm)
FAT: 11 (gm)   CHO: 8.3 (gm)
Na: 608.9 (mg) K: 281.4 (mg)
Fiber: 1.5 (gm)   Chol: 92 (mg)

Ingredients

  4 LARGE OR 8 SMALL CABBAGE LEAVES
  ½ CAN (6½-OUNCE SIZE) WATER-PACKED TUNA FISH OR
      CRAB MEAT, DRAINED
  ½ MEDIUM ONION, MINCED
  1 POUND TOFU, WELL DRAINED
  2 TEASPOONS MINCED PARSLEY
  ¼ MEDIUM-SIZED GREEN PEPPER, MINCED
  ¼ STALK CELERY, MINCED
  1 TABLESPOON UNBLEACHED FLOUR
  1 EGG, BEATEN
1½-2 CUPS SOUP STOCK: 2 HEAPING TEASPOONS
      SOUP MIX TO 1½-2 CUPS WATER
  1 TABLESPOON VEGETABLE OIL

Method

1. Steam cabbage leaves in boiling water for 1 minute. Drain.
2. Preheat oven to 350° F.
3. Heat oil in frying pan, saute onion, green pepper, and
    celery over medium-high heat for 1 minute.
4. In a mixing bowl, crumble tofu; add parsley, tuna fish,
    flour, and beaten egg. Mix well.
5. Add the vegetables and mix thoroughly.

6. Spread equal amounts of the mixture on top of each cabbage leaf. Roll tightly.
7. Put the cabbage rolls in a single layer in a large casserole. Add soup stock and cover the casserole with foil.
8. Bake for 25 minutes.
9. Cooking may be finished on top of stove by covering pan and simmering over low heat for 25 minutes.

Tofu Salad with Garlic Dressing

Yield: 4 servings
Serving Size: $\frac{1}{4}$ recipe
Exchange List Approximation:
    Meat, medium-fat 1
    Vegetable 2
    Fat* 5

Nutrient Content Per Serving:
CAL: 345   PRO: 11.5 (gm)
FAT: 30.2 (gm)*   CHO: 12.1 (gm)
Na: 107 (mg)   K: 325.1 (mg)
Fiber: 1.7 (gm)   Chol: 0

Ingredients

1 POUND TOFU, WELL DRAINED
1 MEDIUM-SIZED TOMATO, QUARTERED
½ CUCUMBER, PEELED, QUARTERED LENGTHWISE
½ STALK CELERY, CUT LENGTHWISE, SLICED INTO ½-INCH PIECES
¼ CUP WALNUTS, CHOPPED
2 TABLESPOONS RAISINS
2 TABLESPOONS APPLE-CIDER VINEGAR OR LEMON JUICE
5½ TABLESPOONS VEGETABLE OIL

1 TEASPOON SOY SAUCE
1 CLOVE GARLIC, MINCED OR CRUSHED
   LETTUCE LEAVES

Method

1. Cut the well-drained tofu into ½-inch cubes.
2. Soften the raisins in warm water for 5 minutes; drain and towel-dry.
3. Quarter the tomato; slice into ½-inch thickness.
4. Peel and quarter cucumber lengthwise; then slice into ½-inch thickness.
5. Halve the celery lengthwise; then slice into ½-inch thickness.
6. Mix together vinegar, oil, soy sauce, and garlic.
7. Arrange all the vegetables on lettuce in a salad bowl. Sprinkle with walnuts and raisins. Serve dressing separately.

*Note recipe is high in fat and may be more acceptable if divided into eight servings.

Marinated Tofu Salad

Yield: 4 servings
Serving Size: ¼ recipe
Exchange List Approximation:
    Meat, medium-fat 1
    Vegetable 1
    Fat 3

Nutrient Content Per Serving:
CAL: 236   PRO: 10.2 (gm)
FAT: 20.3 (gm)   CHO: 6.9 (gm)
Na: 99.7 (mg)   K: 209.5 (mg)
Fiber:.1.6 (gm)   Chol: 0

Ingredients

1 POUND TOFU, WELL-DRAINED
4 LARGE RED RADISHES, MINCED
1 MEDIUM GREEN PEPPER, MINCED
½ MEDIUM ONION, MINCED

Marinade
2 TABLESPOONS APPLE-CIDER VINEGAR OR LEMON
    JUICE
4 TABLESPOONS VEGETABLE OIL
1 TEASPOON SOY SAUCE
    LETTUCE LEAVES
    MINCED PARSLEY

Method

1. Cut tofu into 1-inch cubes.
2. Mix vinegar, oil, and soy sauce. Add the vegetables and mix well.
3. Pour mixture over tofu cubes in covered container and chill for at least 1 hour before serving.
4. Arrange on lettuce leaves and garnish with minced parsley.

*Fat is reduced if marinade is drained off before serving. Measure the amount drained.

14 □ HEALTHFUL HINTS

The practical aspects of preparing and choosing healthful foods are sometimes the most challenging part of meal planning. But there's a lot you can do fairly easily to enhance the value and variety of your meals, reduce kitchen costs, increase your food sense, and prepare for special events (such as that camping or canoeing vacation you've always wanted to take). And if these tips don't tell you all you need to know, the chapter also includes advice on how to find a Registered Dietitian (R.D.) who should be able to help you with just about anything else you need to know about food!

SUBSTITUTE WITH SPICE

Most of us relish a touch of the exotic in our lives. By rediscovering herbs and spices used by creative cooks for thousands of years, you can add a dash of the exotic to otherwise ordinary meals. Try rubbing rosemary on chicken before baking to transport yourself to the sea-sprayed cliffs of the Mediterranean, where rosemary, which means, "dew of the sea," was given its name. Use basil in a cucumber salad to conjure up visions of Italy and of glowing girls wearing sprigs of basil to show they are in love. Or, add a pinch of saffron to bread to feel as if you are sprinkling gold on dough. The thread-like stigmas of 70,000 crocus blooms are collected in southern Europe and western Asia to make just one pound of saffron powder!

But the best news is that sweet-tasting (but sugar-free) spices and some flavoring extracts can be used to sweeten foods without sugar. (See the heading "Ways to Cut Back on Sugar" for a list of spices.)

If you're concerned about high blood pressure, you will find using herbs and spices useful here too. They do such a wonderful job of flavoring food that you may be able to skip the salt, which can aggravate high blood pressure. And, a dash of the right spice can add zest to a dish without adding a single calorie!

Be sure your herbs and spices are as fresh as possible. It's best to buy in small quantities to keep infrequently-used spices, such as cardamom, at the peak of potency. Buy just a few tablespoons at a time and check freshness by looking for rich color and a full aroma. Or grow your own and dry them yourself.

Store your dried herbs and spices in airtight glass or tin containers in a cool, dry, dark location. (Paper is not airtight, and cardboard and plastic can absorb flavors.) Never keep your spices over the stove. Also, be sure to date each container; ground spices and dried herbs lose much of their flavor after six months.

Some herbs are better frozen than dried. These include chives, fennel leaves, parsley, winter savory, and tarragon. To prepare for storing, wash the fresh herbs and pat dry. Mince with kitchen shears or a knife, spread on a cookie sheet and freeze, then transfer to a plastic bag. This way, the minced herbs and spices will stay in separate easy-to-measure pieces.

When you are ready to use any herb or spice, give it the sniff test. If it doesn't have a strong aroma, it's best to discard it. Heat brings out the flavor of fresh herbs and spices. Rubbing them between warm fingers before adding to a recipe draws out the best flavor. For long-cooking dishes, most cooks recommend waiting until the last 30 to 45 minutes before adding the herbs. This prevents the flavoring oils from evaporating.

When doubling a recipe, add only 1½ times the amount of herbs and spices. If tripling a recipe, add twice the amount. When substituting use the following guide:

1 Tablespoon fresh herb =
1 teaspoon dried = ⅓ teaspoon ground

Use a light hand when trying out a new herb or spice. Start out with about ¼ teaspoon for four servings, adding more later if needed. To get started in the exotic world of spices, experiment with these suggestions:

DILL WEED: Sprinkle on fish, potatoes, or cucumbers.

CUMIN: Sprinkle on cheese when grilling a sandwich. Add 1 teaspoon to cornbread batter.

MARJORAM: Add to egg or tomato dishes, using ½ teaspon for four servings.

FENNEL SEED: Crush one teaspoon and add to a pound of hamburger when browning to give a taste similar to Italian sausage.

CILANTRO: Its leaves are known as Chinese parsley. Its seeds are called coriander. Try this herb in tomato sauce to give it a truly Mexican flavor. Also good in curries.

To avoid the salt found in many prepackaged herb mixtures, combine herbs and spices to make your own tasty blends. Try the following instead of salt on vegetables, meats, eggs, and in soups (calories and sodium content are negligible):

HERB BLEND 1 (RED)

Ingredients

- ½ TEASPOON EACH DRIED THYME LEAVES, DRIED MARJORAM LEAVES, CELERY SEED, GARLIC POWDER
- ¼ TEASPOON EACH ONION POWDER, CURRY POWDER, AND DRIED DILL WEED
- 3 TEASPOON PAPRIKA

HERB BLEND 2 (GREEN)

Ingredients

- 1 TEASPOON THYME
- 1½ TEASPOON SAVORY

1   TEASPOON SAGE
1½ TEASPOON MARJORAM
1   TEASPOON ROSEMARY
1   TEASPOON TARRAGON

WAYS TO CUT BACK ON SUGAR

You have many options for cutting back on sugar:

INSTEAD OF:	USE MORE:
Soft drinks/fruit drinks	Diet soft drinks
	Seltzer
	Juices mixed with seltzer/carbonated water
	Herb teas
	Water
Super-sweet desserts	Desserts that use fruit
	Desserts that use sweet spices (see section following)
Sugar or honey in coffee or tea	Dash of vanilla or cinnamon in coffee
	Lemon in tea
	Herb teas
Sugar-coated cereals	Low-sugar cereals
Candy	Nuts
	Seeds
	Popcorn
Canned fruit in heavy syrup	Canned fruit in its own juice or fruit juice
Sweet rolls	Fruited muffins
	Bagels
	English muffins

SWEET SPICES*

CINNAMON: Bark of true cinnamon tree that grows in Ceylon. Mild in flavor. Used to flavor pickles, preserves, fruits, hot drinks, and as "spoons" for after-dinner coffee. When ground, used in baked goods, puddings, cake, mincemeat.

CLOVES: Nail-shaped dried flower bud of the clove tree. Rich and pungent in flavor. Used whole in baked ham, pickling, and drinks. Used ground in cakes, cookies, conserves, desserts.

NUTMEG: Kernel of fruit of the nutmeg tree. One of the oldest known spices. Used as traditional flavoring for baked custard and other desserts. Also used in cream soups, sauces, stews, and vegetables such as spinach.

ALLSPICE: Dried berry with a flavor resembling a blend of cinnamon, nutmeg, and cloves. Used whole in stews, soups, gravy, preserved fruit, boiled fish, and for spicing meat. The ground form is used to season pot roast, baked goods, catsup, mincemeat.

ANISE: Seed of herbaceous plant of Mediterranean regions, has subtle licorice overtones. Used in cookies. Oil used in spongecake. Chinese star anise used in watermelon-rind pickle.

CARDAMOM: The aromatic seed capsule of a plant native to tropical Asia. Used in cakes, cookies, and bread. Delicious in coffee. Smaller type is used whole in barbecue and basting sauces, and pickles.

CORIANDER: Seed or seedlike fruit of the coriander plant. Used in gingerbread, apple pie, or as an ingredient of curry. Fresh leaves of plant is Chinese parsley. Use leaves only, no stems, and do not chop. Float leaves in pea or chicken soup and in stews.

GINGER: Dried root of a subtropical plant. Warm in flavor. Cracked root used in pickles, preserves, chutney. Ground root used in cake, gingerbread, cookies, puddings, soups, pot roasts.

*Adapted from *Nutritious and Delicious,* by the Greater Cincinnati Dietetic Association and the Greater Cincinnati Nutrition Council, Joerger-Vetter Printing, Cincinnati, OH, 1982.

MACE: Lace covering on inner shell holding nutmeg. Flavor more delicate than nutmeg. Used in pound and yellow cake, oyster stew, spinach. Used whole in pickling, preserving, and fish sauces.

PUMPKIN PIE SPICE: Blend of cinnamon, nutmeg, ginger, and cloves. Used in pumpkin pie, on fruit desserts, apple pie, and on sweet yellow vegetables such as squash, sweet potatoes, and carrots. Also used in cookies, gingerbread, and breakfast buns.

Note: Even without using spices, you can usually cut back ¼ to ⅓ on the sweetener (and oil) called for in many recipes.

USING EGG WHITES
FOR WHOLE EGGS

The American Diabetes Association recommends a moderate intake of dietary cholesterol, which would be less than 300 milligrams per day. Since one egg yolk contains more than 250 milligrams, egg yolks should be limited to three a week. This prudent recommendation for cholesterol intake is consistent with the recommendations of the American Heart Association and other health groups.

What can you do if a recipe calls for eggs and you've already eaten your allotment of eggs for the week? Egg white can be substituted for whole eggs in most recipes. Most recipes listing eggs as an ingredient assume you will use a large egg, which is a 2-ounce egg (this weight includes the weight of the shell). You can use 2 egg whites (1½ fluid ounces) for each egg listed in a recipe. If you prefer to measure in tablespoons and teaspoons, you can use 3 Tablespoons + 1 teaspoon of egg white for one whole egg. If the recipe calls for 2 whole eggs you can use 3 egg whites.

Remember that egg yolks are not only high in cholesterol but also contain most of the calories in an egg. The yolk of one large egg contains about 64 calories, and the white contains only about 16 calories, so you not only decrease cholesterol consumption but save calories as well. The commercially available egg substitutes use 2 Tablespoons of egg white and 1 teaspoon of vegetable oil for each whole egg. If you are preparing an omelet or scrambled eggs, you may want to add similar amounts of vegetable oil for flavoring and yellow coloring to egg white. To achieve the yellow color of the egg yolk, you can also use ⅛ teaspoon saffron with your egg white mixture.

DECREASING CALORIES IN FAMILY MEAL PLANNING AND PREPARATION

To save calories, the most important food item to trim or delete from the family's meals is fat. Remember that fat is 2¼ times higher in calories than carbohydrate or protein foods. Simply pouring oil into a skillet unmeasured can increase the calories of the completed dish by several hundred. By making some permanent changes in your cooking techniques and learning to modify recipes, you can save thousands of calories per year.

Learn to "saute" or "brown" food using nonstick skillets or pans sprayed with a nonstick spray. Or try using a measured amount of oil or margarine, while cooking at a bit lower temperature than usual. You'll be surprised at how little fat you need.

You can easily get by without using any fat at all—instead use beef, chicken, or vegetable broth, lime juice, wine, or water. Add a couple of tablespoons of the liquid to the heated pan and allow it to reduce somewhat. Then add your items to be sauteed or browned and add more broth or water as needed. Mushrooms are a very low-calorie food—½ cup cooked contains fewer than 25 calories. They are often served as a side dish and are usually laden with butter, margarine, or oil used for cooking. This makes a low-calorie, nutritious dish very high in calories. Cooking them in a few tablespoons of chicken broth (or even wine), however, adds negligible calories. Otherwise, every teaspoon of fat in a serving raises the calories by 45. (Alcohol is safe in cooking because most of the calories burn off, leaving primarily good flavor behind.)

If you normally put a chunk of butter or margarine on all of your cooked vegetables, begin experimenting with spices and herbs instead. In fact, once your palate has become used to much less fat you will be surprised how good the vegetables taste all by themselves—especially if fresh or fresh-frozen and steamed until just crisp-tender.

When using milk in cooking, always use nonfat or low-fat, never whole milk. You will get the same nutritional value minus the fat calories (low-fat milk—2%—contains about the equivalent of one teaspoon of fat per 8-ounce glass, and nonfat milk contains a negligible amount). You may find it convenient to use powdered low-fat or non-fat milk, and don't forget to keep a few cans of evaporated skim milk on hand. It has many uses including as a luscious low-calorie topping when chilled and whipped.

Be sure to switch to low-calorie salad dressing whether homemade or store-bought, and not just for salads. For example, use a low-calorie Italian dressing as a marinade for chicken or fish. Brush it on while broiling or barbecueing instead of using heavy, calorie-laden sauces. Marinate crisp-cooked and cooled vegetables for a different type of salad or side dish.

Sour cream has fewer calories than butter, margarine, mayonnaise, or oil per tablespoon, and plain nonfat or low-fat yogurts have even less than sour cream. Try yogurt instead of mayonnaise as a base for salad dressings or for use in sauces and baking. Mix yogurt with chives and a touch of garlic powder for a delicious topping on baked potatoes.

Be sure to "de-fat" all of your soups, stocks, and stews. Let the dish chill and lift the chilled fat off the top. Remember that each teaspoon you skim off is 45 calories less. Make tasty gravies or sauces by using de-fatted drippings thickened with flour, cornstarch, or arrowroot. Remember that the majority of the calories in sauces and gravies are not in the thickener used but, rather, in the fat. Keep canned broth and soups (except creamed) in the refrigerator for easy use.

Just using some of these simple techniques will help you and your family save a significant number of fat calories.

FREEZING IN INDIVIDUAL PORTIONS

Fruits can be frozen in individual portion sizes to allow you to enjoy the taste of products from gardens and orchards year-round. Choose fruits that are in their prime—ripe, and firm. Prepare fruits for the way you plan to use them, such as peeled or diced. For fruits that tend to discolor you can add lemon juice, ascorbic acid, or a compound containing ascorbic acid, such as Fruit Fresh.

Fruits are sometimes packed with sugar or syrups when frozen to add texture and flavor. This is not necessary to prevent spoilage. Fruits can be packed unsweetened. Some fruits can also be packed dry without adding liquid. A syrup for freezing may be made from an artificial sweetener and water. The syrup should completely cover the fruit when used. Freeze in individual portions.

Fruits and vegetables stored at 0° F or below will maintain high quality for 8 to 12 months. However, unsweetened fruit may lose quality more rapidly.

CUTTING KITCHEN COSTS

With the rising costs of food, utilities, and medication, making ends meet is becoming more and more difficult. You may be tempted to try to save money by scrimping on food, but eating a well-balanced diet is an important part of controlling diabetes. Here are some ways to keep down food and energy costs and stay within your diet.

Efficiency can save you money. When cooking small amounts of food, save energy by using a small appliance such as a grill, toaster oven, slow-cooking pot, or frying pan instead of the oven.

When using the oven, make the most of its heat by planning complete oven meals so that all foods are baked at once (for instance, chicken, potato, squash, and custard), or by making many casseroles at once and freezing them for future use. To save oven time, be sure to thaw all frozen foods. Also, try not to open the door often, since every time you do, the temperature drops 25 degrees. Cooking temperature also drops when lids are lifted off pots. Check the heat in your oven with a thermometer to be sure you're not losing heat because of a faulty temperature gauge.

Preheating is necessary only for cakes and pastries, not roasts and casseroles. Overcooking shrinks foods and destroys many vitamins. Set a timer so you don't forget to turn off the oven on time.

Use pans with flat bottoms, straight sides, and tight-fitting covers for range-top cooking; they cook food more quickly and uniformly. Bring food to cooking temperature on high heat, then reduce to complete cooking.

If you use electric appliances, check with the electric company to find out which hours are off-peak in your area. Try to plan cooking times around these hours because the rate charged for electricity is lower.

Because electrical cooking units retain heat, you can turn off an electric "burner" or the oven 2 to 5 minutes before you expect the item cooking to be done.

Smart shopping and storage can also stretch your food dollars:

☐ Plan your menus for a week at a time to make the most of leftovers and save trips to the store.
☐ Do use a list and stick to it.
☐ Don't go shopping hungry.
☐ Don't let attractive displays entice you into buying on impulse.
☐ Take a calculator with you. That way you can figure costs per serving or keep a running total of your bill.
☐ When buying inexpensive cuts of meat, avoid those with

a lot of fat, gristle, or bone. Pressure cookers or slow-cooking pots are best for cooking "thrifty" cuts of meat, since such meats should be cooked at a low temperature for a long time (to avoid shrinkage and to lock in vitamins). Don't be deceived by low prices. Though some cuts of meat are a few cents more a pound, they are better buys because they include more meat.

□ Make full use of bones (beef, chicken, and ham) by making broth, soups, or stews from them.

□ Use all your leftovers! Try putting them into soup (if necessary freeze leftovers until you have enough), spaghetti sauce, pita (pocket) bread sandwiches, tortillas with a touch of cheese melted on top, or casseroles.

□ Chicken is still one of the best buys around. Save money by cutting up whole chickens instead of buying parts. Sometimes there are good sales on fowl (mature female birds). Fowl may be tough, so use it for boiling, roasting, and making soups.

□ Use dry beans and peas as protein source (see chart).

□ When buying cheese, remember that domestic is less expensive than imported, and mild is less expensive than sharp.

□ Powdered nonfat or low-fat milk is as nutritious as nonfat or low-fat liquid milk, and less expensive. Use powdered skim milk in cooking.

□ "Day-old" bread is not necessarily stale. Enriched or whole wheat is best and can be used for toast or stuffing.

□ Freeze breads and other baked goods that you will not eat within a day or two. Bread becomes moldy easily at room temperature (especially during hot weather) and becomes stale when refrigerated. These foods are easily defrosted.

□ In addition to meat and bread, save room in your freezer for a large bag of frozen vegetables. They have less salt than canned vegetables and usually taste better. You can also freeze most fresh vegetables if you submerge them first in boiling water for a few seconds. This is called "blanching" and will keep the vegetables from turning tough later on.

□ When storing fresh produce in the refrigerator, keep it unwashed in plastic bags until you use it.

□ If your orange juice often becomes sour in the refrigerator, buy frozen concentrate in cans. To save money, cut cans into halves and store the parts in aluminum foil in your freezer. Defrost one at a time. Or prepare the full container and then freeze small portions of the reconstituted juice.

□ Hot cereals cost less per serving than ready-to-eat cereals. Small boxes may cost as much as three times more per serving than large "economy" boxes.

□ Remember that in most cases plain is cheaper. For example, saltines and graham crackers cost less than fancy, filled, or flavored cookies and crackers. Long-cooking white rice or brown rice is cheaper than precooked or seasoned rice mixes. Precooked, convenience, and snack foods are always more expensive. Read the labels and avoid expensive, nutrition-poor foods whenever possible.

□ Check unit prices.

□ Generic labels may be a good buy depending on use. For instance, "generic" canned tomatoes can be cheaper for use in casseroles or spaghetti sauce than national brands.

WAYS TO MAKE COMPLETE PROTEINS FROM VEGETABLE COMBINATIONS

COMBINE THIS:	WITH THIS:
Rice	Legumes
	Cheese
	Sesame seeds
Wheat	Legumes
	Peanuts and milk
	Sesame seeds and soybeans

Corn	Legumes
Beans	Wheat or corn
Soybeans	Rice and wheat
	Corn and milk
	Wheat and sesame seeds
	Peanuts and sesame seeds
	Peanuts and wheat and rice
Sesame seeds	Beans or peanuts, and soybeans
	Soybeans and wheat
Peanuts	Sunflower seeds

MAKING SENSE OF FOOD CLAIM NONSENSE

Looking for straightforward nutrition advice? Good luck! Now that health has become a national obsession, con artists eager to make big money are competing with truly knowledgeable diet counselors for your attention. And you are left trying to sift the sound advice from the abounding fads and fallacies! Don't despair; here are some pointers:

MAKE SURE THE SOURCE IS UP-TO-DATE. New nutrition discoveries are being made all the time. If an article is more than a year old, be suspicious. It may be outdated.

SEEK RELIABLE SOURCES. This may be difficult because so many authors claim to be nutrition experts. Generally, however, you can trust nutrition textbooks or publications put out by reputable organizations, such as the American Diabetes Association, The American Dietetic Association, government agencies, and some popular sports, fitness, and women's magazines. Recognized nutrition experts include registered dietitians (R.D.s). A number of doctors (M.D.s and Ph.D.s), although not all, are also experts. If an author has a degree or claims to be a nutritionist, note whether he or she is affiliated with a hospital, a university medical or nutrition program, or some other accredited health institution.

GET ALL SIDES OF THE STORY. When reading about

controversial nutrition topics, such as the role of vitamin E, look for fair treatment of all sides of the issue. Try to differentiate between opinion and fact. Does the author back up his or her theories with confirmation by respected doctors and other officials? Is the information supported by research data? Also, who did the research? For example, a study that said cholesterol was great for you sponsored by someone interested in selling eggs may well be biased. (Eggs are high in cholesterol.)

DON'T BE DUPED BY UNSUPPORTED CLAIMS. One favorite selling tactic in advertising is to have celebrities endorse a product. But, what's good for a star might not shine for you. Another promotion technique is to call a product the "Newest Vitamin." In truth, no new vitamins have been uncovered since vitamin B_{12} was discovered in 1948. In addition, steer clear of products that promise overnight success or miracle cures. Just because a product is marketed doesn't mean it works.

DIETERS, BEWARE! People who are trying to lose weight are particularly vulnerable to sensational advertising. Watch out for illogical claims, such as "Lose 15 pounds a week eating all you want." They sound tempting, but the safest rate of weight loss for most people is 1 to 1½ pounds a week (unless you are on an unusually strict diet that is closely monitored by a doctor familiar with your health history). Also, approach with caution any diet that focuses on one particular food or nutrition. These diets are unbalanced and unhealthy and can have harmful side effects.

For more sound nutrition know-how, contact your local American Diabetes Association; local registered dietitian; city, county, or state health department; local or county Agriculture Extension Service; local community college or university.

FOR OUTDOOR ENTHUSIASTS

Camping, backpacking, canoeing. There's nothing like them— but to enjoy them safely, you will want to take some precautions.

These sports are so physically demanding that most people

need to take in many more calories than usual. On strenuous days of backpacking or canoeing, you may need as many as 1,000 extra calories a day. Enjoy the extra food, being sure that you eat enough to cover any insulin you take. (Also see Chapter 9, on exercise.) Snacks are always important for insulin users, but even more so with increased activity.

If you do any type of camping, pack enough food for the duration of the trip. It's helpful to plan daily menus in advance and then to pack foods for each meal together. Label each packet accordingly. Include extra food, too, in case a pack is lost or damaged. Remember to include plenty of food for snacks as well.

For canoeing and backpacking, choose compact, light-weight, nonperishable foods that are filling yet provide a concentrated source of nutrients. You'll be glad you packed compactly when that pack starts to feel heavier as the hiking goes on.

For people who take insulin, lunch should be an all-day meal during days of hard hiking or canoeing, and should be consumed in small and frequent feedings to provide a steady flow of fuel without overloading the stomach. Weariness tends to kill the appetite, but keep your food needs in mind.

You may use freeze-dried and other dried (dehydrated) foods. Freeze-dried foods are usually the best choice because their flavor is more like fresh foods, and freeze-dried items are virtually foolproof to prepare. Just add water and serve. (They also last indefinitely when kept dry.)

Be sure to take more than enough insulin and other medical supplies to last the duration of the trip. Divide your supplies between packs in case one pack gets lost or damaged and keep insulin well-cushioned and out of direct sunlight, although it does not need to be refrigerated unless you are on the trail for three months or more. To be sure that diabetes is kept in good control, test blood glucose regularly. This is not the time for a vacation from testing! Also be sure to wear your medical identification at all times.

MENU IDEAS FOR HIKERS AND CAMPERS

Be sure to include foods from all four major food groups: milk, fruit, bread, and meat. Also, drink enough liquid to avoid dehydration. Exchanges for common portion sizes accompany the suggested menu items here, but work out other menu ideas and the amounts you are likely to need with your diet counselor.

Note 1: Instant cocoa, instant oatmeal, peanut butter, granola, and Cheddar, Edam, Gouda, and provolone cheeses all keep well if wrapped in cellophane and kept out of the sun. See recipe section, Chapter 11, for granola recipes.

Note 2: Single serving packets of a sugar substitute can be carried for sweetening cocoa, cereal, beverages, and such.

BREAKFAST:

Fruit	Fruit juices (½ cup = 1 Fruit) or
	Dried fruit (see Fruit Exchange list in Appendix I)
Meat	Eggs (2 Tbsp. dried = 1 Med.-Fat Meat) or
	Canned meats (1 oz. = 1 High-Fat Meat)
Bread	Cooked cereal (½ cup = 1 Starch/Bread), or
	Biscuits (2-inch square = 1 Starch/Bread, 1 Fat) or
	Pancakes (3–4-inch = 2 Starch/Bread, 1 Fat), or
	French toast (1 = 1 Starch/Bread, 1 Med.-Fat Meat)
Milk	Cocoa (cocoa, artificially sweetened; instant dried skim milk) (1 cup = 1 Skim Milk)

A.M. SNACK

Bread	Granola (¼ c. = 1 Starch/Bread, 1 Fat)

TRAIL LUNCH

Fruit	Raisins (2 Tablespoons = 1 Fruit)
Bread	Ry Krisp (4 triple crackers = 1 Starch/Bread)
Meat	Hard salami (1 slice, ¼-inch thick = 1 High-Fat Meat), or
	Cheese (1 oz. = 1 High-Fat Meat), or

| | Peanut butter (1 Tablespoon = 1 High-Fat Meat) |
| Beverage | Artificially sweetened Kool-Aid |

AFTERNOON SNACK

Bread	Graham crackers (3 squares = 1 Starch/Bread), or
	Trail mix (without chocolate candy) (⅓ cup = 1 Starch/Bread, 1 Fat), or
	Granola bar (1 small bar = 1 Starch/Bread, 1 Fat)
Fruit	Fruit jerkey (1 strip = 1 Fruit) or
	Dried fruit (¼ cup = 1 Fruit)
Beverage	Artificially sweetened Kool-Aid

DINNER

| Bread and Meat | Casserole (1 cup = 2 Starch/Bread, 2 Med.-Fat Meat, 1 Fat) |

Examples:
Macaroni and cheese
Spaghetti and meat sauce
Chicken and dumplings
Tuna and noodle
Spam and potatoes

Bread	Biscuits or cornbread (2-inch square = 1 Starch/Bread, 1 Fat)
Vegetable	Dried vegetables (1 ounce dried weight = 1 Vegetable)
Fruit	Dried fruit (¼ cup = 1 Fruit)

EVENING SNACK

Bread	Soda crackers (4–5) = 1 Starch/Bread, 1 Fat) or
	Popcorn (3 cups = 1 Starch/Bread)
Meat	Sunflower or pumpkin seeds (¼ Tablespoon = 1 Med.-Fat Meat) or
	Peanut butter (1 Tablespoon = 1 High-Fat Meat, 2 Fat)
Fruit	Marshmallows (2 large = 1 Fruit)
Milk	Cocoa (as above, 1 cup = 1 Skim Milk)

Recipes

Meat

Meat □ 151

Beef Burgundy

Yield: 4 servings
Exchanges per
1-cup serving:
  2 Lean Meat
  2 Vegetable
  1 Bread

Estimated nutrients
per serving:
CAL 211   Na 346
CHO 19   K 695
PRO 21   Fiber 3
FAT 4

Ingredients

3/4 POUND BEEF ROUND, WELL-TRIMMED
1/2 TEASPOON SALT
1/8 TEASPOON PEPPER
1 BAY LEAF
1/8 TEASPOON THYME LEAVES
1 1/2 CUPS WATER
1 1/2 CUPS DICED POTATOES
1 CUP SLICED CARROTS
1/2 CUP DICED CELERY
1/3 CUP CHO
1 CUP SL
3 TABLE
1/4 CUPS
1/2 CUP
PARSLEY

Summersausage

Yield: 80 slices (¼-inch thick)
Serving Size: 3 slices
Exchange List Approximation:
    Meat, medium-fat 1

Nutrient Content per Serving:
CAL: 65   PRO: 5.4 (gm)
FAT: 4.7 (gm)   CHO: 0
Na: 255.8 (mg) K: 65.5 (mg)
Fiber: 0   Chol: 21 (mg)

Ingredients

2 POUNDS HAMBURGER
2 TABLESPOONS TENDERIZER
1 TEASPOON ONION POWDER
½ TEASPOON GARLIC POWDER
1 CUP WATER

Method

1. Hickory smoke if desired.
2. Roll into two rolls, each about 12 inches long.
3. Refrigerate 24 hours.
4. Bake on rack, after piercing with fork, at 150° F for at least 8 hours.

Beef Jerky

Yield: 8 servings
Serving Size: 1 ounce
Exchange List Approximation:
Meat, lean 2

Nutrient Content per Serving:
CAL: 119   PRO: 10 (gm)
FAT: 8.6 (gm)   CHO: 0.1 (gm)
Na: 40.6 (mg)   K: 118.7 (mg)
Fiber: 0   Chol: 69 (mg)

Ingredients

1   POUND HAMBURGER, BEEF, OR CHICKEN
1   EGG
    SPICES, SEASON TO TASTE

Method

1. Roll out as thinly as possible.
2. Place on cookie sheet and bake at 150° F for at least 8 hours.
3. Cut or break into 8 equal pieces.

Biscuits

Yield: 4 biscuits
Serving Size: 1 biscuit
Exchange List Approximation:
    Starch/Bread 1

Nutrient Content per Serving:
CAL: 92   PRO: 2.4 (gm)
FAT: 1.2 (gm) CHO: 17.5 (gm)
Na: 95 (mg)   K: 22.6 (mg)
Fiber: 0.8 (gm) Chol: 0

Ingredients

2 PINCHES SALT
2 FISTFULS FLOUR
3 PINCHES BAKING POWDER
1 TEASPOON FAT

Method

1. Add water until dough is formed.
2. Place in aluminum foil and roll edges of foil tightly.
3. Bake on hot coals for 15 to 20 minutes, turning once after 7 to 10 minutes.

Gorp

Yield: 20 servings
Serving Size: ⅓ cup
Exchange List Approximation:
    Starch/Bread 1
    Fat 1½

Nutrient Content per Serving:
CAL: 135   PRO: 3.7 (gm)
FAT: 8 (gm)   CHO: 14.6 (gm)
Na: 151 (mg)   K: 188.5 (mg)
Fiber: 2.6 (gm)   Chol: 0

Ingredients

1 CUP SALTED PEANUTS
1 CUP RAISINS
1 CUP COCONUT
1 CUP SALTED SUNFLOWER SEEDS
1 CUP OF EACH CEREAL: BRAN, WHEAT, CORN CHEX

Method

1. Mix all ingredients together.

HOW TO CHOOSE
A DIET COUNSELOR

The cornerstone of good diabetes management is good nutrition. And to meet your particular lifestyle and medical needs you should have individual counseling. Good counseling includes more than a preprinted meal plan with a list of foods to eat or avoid. It includes personal talks even after you leave the hospital to insure that the meal plan you receive is one you can live with.

THE COUNSELING PROCESS

What can you expect when you go to a dietitian or other diet counselor? Often, good counseling consists of three phases. During the first phase, the dietitian gets to know you by asking questions about your lifestyle and your diabetes treatment program. Do you take insulin and, if so, how much? Are you trying to lose or gain weight? Do you have any food allergies? What foods do you like or dislike? Who prepares your meals, and where do you usually eat them? If you eat in a restaurant every day, you probably have less control over calories than if you prepare your meals at home. And if you frequently eat with a lot of people, you might be overinfluenced by what others are eating.

Once these questions are answered, your counseling moves into the second phase. You and your diet counselor prepare a meal plan listing foods you can eat and foods you usually cannot. You will probably be advised to try your new meal plan for a week to a month, depending on your condition and the diet counselor's judgment. After the trial period, you will visit the dietitian again (phase three) to review the plan's success and make any needed adjustments.

FINDING A DIET COUNSELOR

Now that you know what good counseling involves, where do you find a good dietitian? Almost anyone can hang a shingle in front of his or her home proclaiming, "Nutritionist." But the most qualified ones are registered dietitians (R.D.). To become an R.D., a person must have a bachelor's degree with an emphasis in nutrition, plus qualifying experience in an American Dietetic Association accredited or approved program. In addition, the candidate must pass an examination given by the Commission on Dietetic Registration. Once someone becomes a registered dietitian, he or she may work in a hospital or go into private practice as a consulting dietitian. To keep "registered" status, the dietitian must have continuing education, which assures the public of the person's continuing competence to practice.

You can find a consulting or registered dietitian in several ways. One, ask your doctor for recommendations. Two, check your local American Diabetes Association affiliate or American Heart Association chapter. They may have a referral service or offer some counseling themselves. Three, see if any hospital outpatient clinics in your area offer nutrition counseling for diabetics. Four, write to The American Dietetic Association. Five, telephone or write to government health agencies, such as your county or state health department or the nutrition division of the Agriculture Extension Service. Their numbers can be found in the telephone white pages under "Government."

WHAT TO LOOK FOR

Once you find the name of a registered dietitian who counsels diabetics, how do you know you'll receive the best care possible? Call several dietitians and ask questions to find out which are most thorough and compatible with you. For example:

- □ Will he or she ask questions about your diabetes history?
- □ Will the diet be tailored specifically to you, or will it be a general meal plan? Of course, you'll want an individual diet.
- □ Will you be asked to keep a diary of what you eat? Dietitians usually like to see a record of what you've eaten.
- □ Will you have to go back for follow-up visits? At least one should be recommended to check the progress of the diet.

□ Does the dietitian require a medical examination? Many dietitians want you to have a physical no more than two months prior to your visit because such disorders as high blood pressure or high cholesterol levels can affect diet. If no medical examination is required, you might be better off with someone else.

Dietitians can be thorough but still work in different styles. Some like to conduct a long first visit, lasting up to an hour. Others may prefer to have a longer second visit to check on your progress. Either way is all right as long as you receive complete, personal attention.

Dietitians also differ in their fees, usually charging from $25 to $60 per hour. Sometimes a less expensive fee means inferior service, but it can also mean that the dietitian has fewer overhead expenses to meet. Don't judge a dietitian solely by price. Remember, too, that these fees are sometimes covered by medical insurance, depending on the state where you live and the type of insurance you have.

Once you've found a suitable dietitian, don't go to him or her expecting miracles. Good nutrition counseling will help you control your diabetes, but only if you stay on your prescribed diet. By taking the responsibility for following your meal plan, you'll be helping yourself live a comfortable, healthy life.

APPENDIX I: MEAL PLANNING USING EXCHANGE LISTS*

A widely used guide to meal planning for people with diabetes and for others who want a healthful diet is the *Exchange Lists for Meal Planning. The Exchange Lists* enable people to include a wide variety of foods in what they eat each day, without having to calculate calories and balance nutrients. There are six Exchange Lists, or food classes:

1. Starch/Bread
2. Meat (Lean, Medium-Fat, High-Fat)

*The Exchange Lists are the basis of a meal-planning system designed by a committee of the American Diabetes Association and The American Dietetic Association. While designed primarily for people with diabetes and others who must follow special diets, the Exchange Lists are based on principles of good nutrition that apply to everyone. Copyright © 1986 American Diabetes Association, Inc., The American Dietetic Association.

This appendix is adapted from the book *The American Diabetes Association/The American Dietetic Association Family Cookbook* by the American Diabetes Association/The American Dietetic Association, copyright © 1980 by The American Diabetes Association/The American Dietetic Association. Published by Prentice Hall Press, New York, NY 10023.

3. Vegetable
4. Fruit
5. Milk (Skim, Low-Fat, Whole)
6. Fat

Think of exchanges as trades or options. A food within a particular Exchange List can be substituted, traded, or exchanged for another food within the same list. Specific serving sizes are indicated for each food and must be substituted in the amounts specified. Trading one food for another within one Exchange List does not significantly alter the calorie, protein, fat, and carbohydrate content of your meal plan, although foods do vary slightly. To ensure that all your nutrient needs are met, choose a variety of foods even *within* lists.

When prescribing a meal plan for treatment of diabetes, a diet counselor considers an individual's nutritional status, weight, age, sex, daily activity, and whether or not medication is needed to help control diabetes. If insulin is taken, the counselor will also take into account the type and the number and timing of injections daily. (See Chapter 15 for advice on how to choose a dietitian.)

The diet is prescribed in terms of the number of calories and amounts of carbohydrate, protein, and fat for each day. These can be translated into a variety of meals and snacks. A daily meal plan can be tailored to suit the individual's lifestyle, tastes, and budget. It can be altered from time to time even if the basic diet prescription remains the same.

A SAMPLE MEAL PLAN

A sample meal-planning pattern similar to one a registered dietitian might help you develop is shown in the following table. *Note: Do not use this for your meal plan.* Each person who has diabetes should have an individual plan that he or she works out with a diet counselor.

YOUR MEAL PLAN IN EXCHANGES

Must be planned with the assistance of your diet counselor

Meal plan for _____ John Doe _____
(name)

Carbohydrate __274__ Protein __88__ Fat __57__ Calories __1961__
grams   grams   grams

	1 Starch/ Bread	2 Med.- Fat Meat	3 Veg.	4 Fruit	5 Milk	6 Fat
Breakfast Time 8:00 AM	3	—	—	2	1 skim	2
Snack Time none	—	—	—	—	—	—
Lunch or Dinner Time 12:30 PM	4	2	1	1	—	2
Snack Time none	—	—	—	—	—	—
Dinner or Supper Time 6:00 PM	3	3	1	1	—	2
Bedtime Snack Time 9:30 PM	1	—	—	1	1 skim	1

The numbers 1 to 6 across the top of the table above refer to specific numbered Exchange Lists at the end of this chapter. Meals and snacks are identified in the left margin. The number in the box indicates how many choices to make from the specified Exchange List.

For example, follow across the middle of the chart and see what's for lunch: One Vegetable (list 3) and a serving of fruit or juice (list 4). The four choices from the Starch/Bread list (1) will permit two sandwiches, each made with two slices of whole-grain bread, 1 ounce of meat (list 2), and 1 teaspoon of mayonnaise-type dressing (list 6). A noncaloric beverage of choice can be added. This is just one possible menu; your imagination is the limit.

The reason for dividing food into six different groups is that foods vary in their carbohydrate, protein, fat, and calorie content. Each Exchange List contains foods that are alike — each choice contains about the same amount of carbohydrate, protein, fat, and calories.

The following chart shows the amount of these nutrients in one serving from each Exchange List.

EXCHANGE LIST	CHO (grams)	PRO (grams)	FAT (grams)	CALORIES
Starch/Bread	15	3	trace	80
Meat				
Lean	–	7	3	55
Medium-Fat	–	7	5	75
High-Fat	–	7	8	100
Vegetable	5	2	–	25
Fruit	15	–	–	60
Milk				
Skim	12	8	trace	90
Low-Fat	12	8	5	120
Whole	12	8	8	150
Fat	–	–	5	45

As you read the Exchange Lists, you will notice that one choice often is a larger amount of food than another choice from the same list. Because foods are so different, each food is measured or weighed so the amount of carbohydrate, protein, fat, and calories is the same in each choice.

You will notice footnotes on some foods in the exchange groups. For example, foods that are high in fiber (3 grams or more per normal serving). High-fiber foods are good for you. It is important to eat more of these foods.

Foods that are high in sodium (400 milligrams or more of sodium per normal serving) are also footnoted. It's a good idea to limit your intake of high-salt foods, especially if you have high blood pressure.

If you have a favorite food that is not included in any of these groups, ask your dietitian about it. That food can probably be worked into your meal plan, at least now and then.

LIST 1   STARCH/BREAD EXCHANGES

Each item in this list contains about 15 grams of carbohydrate, 3 grams of protein, a trace of fat, and 80 calories.

Whole grain products average about 2 grams of fiber per serving. Some foods are higher in fiber.

You can choose your starch servings from any of the items on this list. If you want to eat a starch food that is not on this list, the general list is:

- ½ cup of cereal, grain, or pasta is one serving
- 1 ounce of a bread product is one serving

Your dietitian can help you be more exact.

CEREALS/GRAINS/PASTA

Bran cereals*, concentrated (such as
  Bran Buds®, All Bran®)

*3 grams or more of fiber per serving.

Bran cereals, flaked	½ cup
Bulgur (cooked)	½ cup
Cooked cereals	½ cup
Cornmeal (dry)	2½ tablespoons
Grape nuts®	3 tablespoons
Grits (cooked)	½ cup
Other ready-to-eat unsweetened cereals	¾ cup
Pasta (cooked)	½ cup
Puffed cereal	1½ cups
Rice, white or brown (cooked)	⅓ cup
Shredded wheat	½ cup
Wheat germ*	3 tablespoons

DRIED BEANS, PEAS/LENTILS

Beans* and peas* (cooked), such as kidney, white, split, blackeye	⅓ cup
Baked beans*	¼ cup
Lentils* (cooked)	⅓ cup

STARCHY VEGETABLES

Corn*	½ cup
Corn on cob, 6 inches long	1
Lima beans*	½ cup
Peas, green* (canned or frozen)	½ cup
Plantain*	½ cup
Potato, baked	1 small (3 ounces)
Potato, mashed	½ cup
Squash, winter* (acorn, butternut)	¾ cup
Yam, sweet potato, plain	⅓ cup

BREAD

Bagel	½ (1 ounce)

*3 grams or more of fiber per serving.

Bread sticks, crisp, 4 inches long x ½ inch wide	2 (⅔ ounce)
Croutons, low-fat	1 cup
English muffin	½
Frankfurter or hamburger bun	½ (1 ounce)
Pita, 6 inches across	½
Plain roll, small	1 (1 ounce)
Raisin, unfrosted	1 slice (1 ounce)
Rye*, pumpernickel*	1 slice (1 ounce)
Tortilla, 6 inches across	1
White (including French, Italian)	1 slice (1 ounce)
Whole wheat	1 slice (1 ounce)

CRACKERS/SNACKS

Animal crackers	8
Graham crackers, 2½-inch square	3
Matzo	¾ ounce
Melba toast	5 slices
Oyster crackers	24
Popcorn (popped, no fat added)	3 cups
Pretzels	¾ ounce
Rye crisp, 2 inches x 3½ inches	4
Saltine-type crackers	6
Whole wheat crackers, no fat added (crisp breads, such as Finn®, Kavli®, Wasa®)	2-4 slices (¾ ounce)

STARCH FOODS PREPARED WITH FAT
(Count as 1 Starch/Bread serving, plus 1 Fat serving)

Biscuit, 2½ inches across	1
Chow mein noodles	½ cup
Corn bread, 2-inch cube	1 (2 ounces)
Cracker, round butter type	6

*3 grams or more of fiber per serving.

French fried potatoes, 2 to 3½ inches long	10 (1½ ounces)
Muffin, plain, small	1
Pancake, 4 inches across	2
Stuffing, bread (prepared)	¼ cup
Taco shell, 6 inches across	2
Waffle, 4½-inch square	1
Whole wheat crackers, fat added (such as Triscuits®)	4-6 (1 ounce)

LIST 2   MEAT EXCHANGES

Each serving of meat and substitutes on this list contains varying amounts of fat and calories. The list is divided into three parts based on the amount of fat and calories: Lean Meat, Medium-Fat Meat, and High-Fat Meat. One ounce (1 Meat Exchange) of each of these includes:

	Carbohydrate (grams)	Protein (grams)	Fat (grams)	Calories
Lean	0	7	3	55
Medium-Fat	0	7	5	75
High-Fat	0	7	8	100

You are encouraged to use more lean and medium-fat meat, poultry, and fish in your meal plan. This will help decrease your fat intake, which may help decrease your risk for heart disease. The items from the high-fat group are high in saturated fat, cholesterol, and calories. You should limit your choices from the high-fat group to three times per week. Meat and substitutes do not contribute any fiber to your meal plan.

Tips:

• Bake, roast, broil, grill, or boil these foods rather than frying them with added fat.

- Use a nonstick pan spray or a nonstick pan to brown or fry these foods.
- Trim off visible fat before and after cooking.
- Do not add flour, bread crumbs, coating mixes, or fat to these foods when preparing them.
- Weigh meat after removing bones and fat, and after cooking. Three ounces of cooked meat is about equal to 4 ounces of raw meat. Some examples of meat portions are:

> 2 ounces meat (2 Meat = 1 small chicken leg or thigh
> Exchanges ½ cup cottage cheese or tuna

> 3 ounces meat (3 Meat = 1 medium pork chop
> Exchanges 1 small hamburger
> ½ chicken breast (1 side)
> 1 unbreaded fish fillet
> cooked meat, about the size of a
> deck of cards

- Restaurants usually serve prime cuts of meat, which are high in fat and calories.

LEAN MEAT AND SUBSTITUTES
(One Exchange is equal to any one of the following items.)

Beef:	USDA good or choice grades of lean beef, such as round, sirloin, flank steak, tenderloin, chipped beef*.	1 ounce
Pork:	Lean pork, such as fresh ham; canned, cured or boiled ham*; Canadian bacon*; tenderloin.	1 ounce
Veal:	All cuts are lean except for veal cutlets (ground or cubed). Examples of lean veal are chops and roasts.	1 ounce

*400 milligrams or more of sodium per serving.

Poultry:	Chicken, turkey, Cornish hen (without skin)	1 ounce
Fish:	All fresh and frozen fish	1 ounce
	Crab, lobster, scallops, shrimp, clams* (fresh, or canned in water)	1 ounce (¼ cup)
	Oysters	3 ounces (5 to 7 medium)
	Tuna* (canned in water)	¼ cup
	Herring (uncreamed or smoked)	1 ounce
	Sardines (canned)	2 medium
Wild Game:	Venison, rabbit, squirrel	1 ounce
	Pheasant, duck, goose (without skin)	1 ounce
Cheese:	Any cottage cheese	¼ cup
	Grated parmesan	2 tablespoons
	Diet cheeses* with less than 55 calories per ounce	1 ounce
Other:	95 percent fat-free luncheon meat*	1 ounce
	Egg whites	3 whites
	Egg substitutes with less than 55 calories per ¼ cup	¼ cup

MEDIUM-FAT MEAT AND SUBSTITUTES
(One exchange is equal to any one of the following items.)

Beef:	Most beef products fall into this category. Examples are: all ground beef, roast (rib, chuck, rump), steak (cubed, Porterhouse, T-bone), and meatloaf	1 ounce
Pork:	Most pork products fall into this category. Examples are: chops, loin roast, Boston butt, cutlets	1 ounce

*400 milligrams or more of sodium per serving.

Lamb:	Most lamb products fall into this category. Examples are: chops, leg, and roast.	1 ounce
Veal:	Cutlet (ground or cubed, un-breaded)	1 ounce
Poultry:	Chicken (with skin), domestic duck or goose (well-drained of fat), ground turkey	1 ounce
Fish:	Tuna* (canned in oil and drained), salmon* (canned)	¼ cup
Cheese:	Skim or part-skim milk cheeses, such as:	
	Ricotta	¼ cup
	Mozzarella	1 ounce
	Diet cheeses* with 56–80 calories per ounce	1 ounce
Other:	86 percent fat-free luncheon meat*	1 ounce
	Egg (high in cholesterol, limit to 3 per week)	1
	Egg substitutes with 56–80 calories per ¼ cup	¼ cup
	Tofu (2½ x 2¾ x 1 inches)	4 ounces
	Liver, heart, kidney, sweetbreads (high in cholesterol)	1 ounce

HIGH-FAT MEAT AND SUBSTITUTES

Remember, these items are high in saturated fat, cholesterol, and calories, and should be used only three times per week. One exchange is equal to any one of the following items.

Beef:	Most USDA prime cuts of beef, such as ribs, corned beef*	1 ounce

*400 milligrams or more of sodium per serving.

Pork:	Spareribs, ground pork, pork sausage* (patty or link)	1 ounce
Lamb:	Patties (ground lamb)	1 ounce
Fish:	Any fried fish product	1 ounce
Cheese:	All regular cheeses*, such as American, Blue, Cheddar, Monterey, Swiss	1 ounce
Other:	Luncheon meat*, such as bologna, salami, pimento loaf	1 ounce
	Sausage*, such as Polish, Italian, knockwurst, smoked	1 ounce
	Bratwurst*	1 ounce
	Frankfurter* (turkey or chicken)	1 frank (10 per pound)
	Peanut Butter (contains unsaturated fat)	1 tablespoon

Count as one High-Fat Meat plus one Fat Exchange:

	Frankfurter* (beef, pork, or combination)	1 frank (10 per pound)

LIST 3   VEGETABLE EXCHANGES

Each vegetable serving on this list contains about 5 grams of carbohydrate, 2 grams of protein, and 25 calories. Vegetables contain 2 to 3 grams of dietary fiber.

Vegetables are a good source of vitamins and minerals. Fresh and frozen vegetables have more vitamins and less added salt. Rinsing canned vegetables will remove much of the salt.

Unless otherwise noted, the serving size for vegetables is:

*400 milligrams or more of sodium per serving.

- ½ cup of cooked vegetables or vegetable juice
- 1 cup of raw vegetables

Artichoke	Cauliflower	Rutabaga
(½ medium)	Eggplant	Sauerkraut*
Asparagus	Greens (collard,	Spinach, cooked
Beans (green,	mustard, turnip)	Summer squash
wax, Italian)	Kohlrabi	(crookneck)
Bean sprouts	Leeks	Tomato (one large)
Beets	Mushrooms, cooked	Tomato/vegetable
Broccoli	Okra	juice*
Brussels sprouts	Onions	Turnips
Cabbage, cooked	Pea pods	Water chestnuts
Carrots	Peppers (green)	Zucchini, cooked

Starchy vegetables such as corn, peas, and potatoes are found on the Starch/Bread List.

For free vegetables, see Free Food List on pages 429–432.

LIST 4   FRUIT EXCHANGES

Each item on this list contains about 15 grams of carbohydrate, and 60 calories. Fresh, frozen, and dry fruits have about 2 grams of fiber per serving. Fruit juices contain very little dietary fiber.

The carbohydrate and calorie content for a fruit serving are based on the usual serving of the most commonly eaten fruits. Use fresh fruits, or fruits frozen or canned without sugar added. Whole fruit is more filling than fruit juice, and may be a better choice for those who are trying to lose weight. Unless otherwise noted, the serving size for fruit is:

- ½ cup of fresh fruit or fruit juice
- ¼ cup of dried fruit

*400 milligrams or more of sodium per serving.

FRESH, FROZEN, AND UNSWEETENED CANNED FRUIT

Apple (raw, 2 inches across)	1 apple
Applesauce (unsweetened)	½ cup
Apricots (medium, raw)	4 apricots
Apricots (canned)	½ cup, or 4 halves
Banana (9 inches long)	½ banana
Blackberries* (raw)	¾ cup
Blueberries* (raw)	¾ cup
Cantaloupe (cubed)	1 cup
Cantaloupe (5 inches across)	⅓ melon
Cherries (large, sweet, raw)	12 cherries
Cherries (canned)	½ cup
Figs (raw, 2 inches across)	2 figs
Fruit cocktail (canned)	½ cup
Grapefruit (medium)	½ grapefruit
Grapefruit (segments)	¾ cup
Grapes (small)	15 grapes
Honeydew melon (medium)	⅛ melon
Honeydew melon (cubed)	1 cup
Kiwi (large)	1 kiwi
Mandarin oranges	¾ cup
Mango (small)	½ mango
Nectarine* (1½ inches across)	1 nectarine
Orange (2½ inches across)	1 orange
Papaya	1 cup
Peach (2¾ inches across)	1 peach, or ¾ cup
Peaches (canned)	½ cup, or 2 halves
Pear	½ large, 1 small
Pears (canned)	½ cup, or 2 halves
Persimmon (medium, native)	2 persimmons
Pineapple (raw)	¾ cup
Pineapple (canned)	⅓ cup
Plum (raw, 2 inches across)	2 plums

*3 grams or more of fiber per serving.

Pomegranate*	½ pomegranate
Raspberries* (raw)	1 cup
Strawberries* (raw, whole)	1¼ cup
Tangerine* (2½ inches across)	2 tangerines
Watermelon (cubes)	1¼ cups

DRIED FRUIT

Apples*	4 rings
Apricots*	7 halves
Dates	2½ medium
Figs*	1½
Prunes*	3 medium
Raisins	2 tablespoons

FRUIT JUICE

Apple juice/cider	½ cup
Cranberry juice cocktail	⅓ cup
Grapefruit juice	½ cup
Grape juice	⅓ cup
Orange juice	½ cup
Pineapple juice	½ cup
Prune juice	⅓ cup

LIST 5   MILK EXCHANGES

Each serving of milk or milk products on this list contains about 12 grams of carbohydrate and 8 grams of protein. The amount of fat in milk is measured in percent of butterfat. The calories vary, depending on what kind of milk you choose. The list is divided into three parts based on the amount of fat and calories: skim/very low-fat milk, low-fat milk, and whole milk. One serving (1 Milk Exchange) of each of these includes:

*3 grams or more of fiber per serving.

	Carbohydrate (grams)	Protein (grams)	Fat (grams)	Calories
Skim/Very Low-Fat	12	8	trace	90
Low-Fat	12	8	5	120
Whole	12	8	8	150

Milk is the body's main source of calcium, the mineral needed for growth and repair of bones. Yogurt is also a good source of calcium. Yogurt and many dry or powdered milk products have different amounts of fat. If you have questions about a particular item, read the label to find out the fat and calorie content.

Milk is good to drink, but it can also be added to cereal, and to other foods. Many tasty dishes such as sugar-free pudding are made with milk. Plain yogurt is delicious with one of your fruit servings mixed with it.

SKIM AND VERY LOW-FAT MILK

1 cup skim milk
1 cup ½ percent milk
1 cup 1 percent milk
1 cup low-fat buttermilk
½ cup evaporated skim milk
⅓ cup dry nonfat milk
8-ounce carton plain nonfat yogurt

LOW-FAT MILK

1 cup fluid 2 percent milk
8-ounce carton plain low-fat yogurt (with added nonfat milk solids)

WHOLE MILK

The whole milk group has much more fat per serving than the skim and low-fat groups. Whole milk has more than 3¼ percent butterfat. Try to limit your choices from the whole milk group as much as possible.

1 cup whole milk
½ cup evaporated whole milk
8-ounce carton whole plain yogurt

LIST 6   FAT EXCHANGE

Each serving on the fat list contains about 5 grams of fat and 45 calories.

The foods on the fat list contain mostly fat, although some items may also contain a small amount of protein. All fats are high in calories, and should be carefully measured. Everyone should modify fat intake by eating unsaturated fats instead of saturated fats. The sodium content of these foods varies widely. Check the label for sodium information.

UNSATURATED FATS

Avocado	⅛ medium
Margarine	1 teaspoon
Margarine, diet*	1 tablespoon
Mayonnaise	1 teaspoon
Mayonnaise, reduced-calorie*	1 tablespoon
Nuts and Seeds:	
Almonds, dry roasted	6 whole
Cashews, dry roasted	1 tablespoon
Pecans	2 whole
Peanuts	20 small, 10 large
Walnuts	2 whole
Other nuts	1 tablespoon
Seeds, pine nuts, sunflower (without shells)	1 tablespoon
Pumpkin seeds	2 teaspoons
Oil (corn, cottonseed, safflower, soybean, sunflower, olive, peanut)	1 teaspoon

*If more than one or two servings are consumed, sodium levels will equal or exceed 400 milligrams.

Olives*	10 small, 5 large
Salad dressing, mayonnaise-type	2 teaspoons
Salad dressing, mayonnaise-type, reduced-calorie	1 tablespoon
Salad dressing (all varieties)*	1 tablespoon
Salad dressing, reduced-calorie†	2 tablespoons

(Two tablespoons of low-calorie salad dressing is a Free food.)

SATURATED FATS

Butter	1 teaspoon
Bacon*	1 slice
Chitterlings	½ ounce
Coconut, shredded	2 tablespoons
Coffee whitener, liquid	2 tablespoons
Coffee whitener, powder	4 teaspoons
Cream (light, coffee, table)	2 tablespoons
Cream, sour	2 tablespoons
Cream (heavy, whipping)	1 tablespoon
Cream cheese	1 tablespoon
Salt pork*	¼ ounce

FREE FOODS

A free food is any food or drink that contains 20 calories or less per serving. You can eat as much as you want of those items that have no serving size specified. You may eat two or three servings per day of those items that have a specific serving size. Be sure to spread them out through the day.

Drinks

Bouillon,† or broth without fat
Bouillon, low-sodium

*If more than one or two servings are consumed, sodium levels will equal or exceed 400 milligrams.
†400 milligrams or more of sodium per serving.

Carbonated drinks, sugar-free
Carbonated water
Club soda
Cocoa powder, unsweetened
 (1 tablespoon)
Coffee/Tea
Drink mixes, sugar-free
Mineral water
Tonic water, sugar-free

Nonstick pan spray

Fruit

Cranberries, unsweetened
 (½ cup)
Rhubarb, unsweetened (½ cup)

Vegetables (raw, 1 cup)

Cabbage
Celery
Chinese cabbage*
Cucumber
Green onion
Hot peppers
Mushrooms
Radishes
Zucchini*
Salad greens:
 Endive
 Escarole
 Lettuce
 Romaine
 Spinach

*3 grams or more of fiber per serving.

Sweet Substitutes

Candy, hard, sugar-free
Gelatin, sugar-free
Gum, sugar-free
Jam/jelly, sugar-free
   (2 teaspoons)
Pancake syrup, sugar-free
   (¼ cup)
Sugar substitutes
   (saccharin, Equal)
Whipped topping,
   low-calorie

Condiments

Catsup (1 tablespoon)
Horseradish
Mustard
Pickles*, dill, unsweetened
Salad dressing, low-calorie
   (2 tablespoons)
Taco sauce (1 tablespoon)

Seasonings can be very helpful in making food taste better. Be careful of how much sodium you use. Read the label, and choose seasonings that do not contain sodium or salt.

Basil (fresh)	Flavoring extracts	Herbs
Celery seeds	(vanilla, lemon,	Hot pepper
Cinnamon	almond, walnut,	sauce
Chili powder	peppermint, butter,	Lemon
Chives	and the like)	Lemon juice
Curry	Garlic	Lemon pepper
Dill	Garlic powder	Lime

*400 milligrams or more of sodium per serving.

Lime juice
Mint
Onion powder
Oregano
Paprika
Pepper

Pimento
Spices
Soy sauce*
Soy sauce, low
 sodium

Wine, used in
 cooking (¼ cup)
Worcestershire sauce

COMBINATION FOODS

Much of the food we eat is mixed together in various combinations.
These combination foods do not fit into only one Exchange List. It
can be quite hard to tell what is in a certain casserole dish or baked
food item. This is a list of average values for some typical
combination foods. This list will help you fit these foods into your
meal plan. Ask your dietitian for information about any other foods
you'd like to eat.

FOOD	AMOUNT	EXCHANGES
Casseroles, homemade	1 cup (8 ounces)	2 Starch, 2 Medium-Fat Meat, 1 Fat
Cheese pizza*, thin crust	¼ of 15 ounces or ¼ of 10 inches	2 Starch, 1 Medium-Fat Meat, 1 Fat
Chili with beans*†, (commercial)	1 cup (8 ounces)	2 Starch, 2 Medium-Fat Meat, 2 Fat
Chow mein*†, (without noodles or rice)	2 cups (16 ounces)	1 Starch, 2 Vegetable, 2 Lean Meat
Macaroni and cheese*	1 cup (8 ounces)	2 Starch, 1 Medium-Fat Meat, 2 Fat

*400 milligrams or more of sodium per serving.
†3 grams or more of fiber per serving.

FOOD	AMOUNT	EXCHANGES
Soup:		
Bean*†	1 cup (8 ounces)	1 Starch, 1 Vegetable, 1 Lean Meat
Chunky, all varieties*	10¾-ounce can	1 Starch, 1 Vegetable, 1 Medium-Fat Meat
Cream* (made with water)	1 cup (8 ounces)	1 Starch, 1 Fat
Vegetable* or broth-type*	1 cup (8 ounces)	1 Starch
Spaghetti and meatballs* (canned)	1 cup (8 ounces)	2 Starch, 1 Medium-Fat Meat, 1 Fat
Sugar-free pudding (made with skim milk)	½ cup	1 Starch
If beans are used as a meat substitute:		
Dried beans†, peas†, lentils†	1 cup (cooked)	2 Starch, 1 Lean Meat

FOODS FOR OCCASIONAL USE

Moderate amounts of some foods can be used in your meal plan, in spite of their sugar or fat content, as long as you can maintain blood-glucose control. The following list includes average exchange values for some of these foods. Because they are concentrated sources of carbohydrate, you will notice that the portion sizes are very small. Check with your dietitian for advice on how often and when you can eat them.

*400 milligrams or more of sodium per serving.
†3 grams or more of fiber per serving.

FOOD	AMOUNT	EXCHANGES
Angel food cake	¹⁄₁₂ cake	2 Starch
Cake, no icing	¹⁄₁₂ cake, or a 3-inch square	2 Starch, 2 Fat
Cookies	2 small (1¾ inches across)	1 Starch, 1 Fat
Frozen fruit yogurt	⅓ cup	1 Starch
Gingersnaps	3	1 Starch
Granola	¼ cup	1 Starch, 1 Fat
Granola bars	1 small	1 Starch, 1 Fat
Ice cream, any flavor	½ cup	1 Starch, 2 Fat
Ice milk, any flavor	½ cup	1 Starch, 1 Fat
Sherbet, any flavor	¼ cup	1 Starch
Snack chips*, all varieties	1 ounce	1 Starch, 2 Fat
Vanilla wafers	6 small	1 Starch, 1 Fat

*If more than one serving is consumed, sodium levels will equal or exceed 400 milligrams.

APPENDIX II: ETHNIC EXCHANGES FOR EXTRA FREEDOM IN MEAL PLANNING

Do you love ethnic foods but have no idea how to fit your favorite dishes into your meal plan? For those of you who use the *Exchange Lists for Meal Planning*, here are additional exchanges for Black American, Indian, Jewish, Mexican, and Oriental cuisines.*
Because some foods here are high in salt and fat, check with your diet counselor before including them in your meal plan.

Note: This book contains several ethnic recipes. Each one of the recipes includes exchanges for one serving.

FOOD ITEM	SIZE OF SERVING	EXCHANGE VALUES
BLACK AMERICAN		
Chicken and dumplings	3 oz. chicken and 1 large or 2 small dumplings	3 Lean Meat, 1 Vegetable, 1 Starch/ Bread, 1 Fat

*The Indian, Jewish, Oriental, and many of the Black American food exchanges appear courtesy of the American Diabetes Association, Washington, D.C. Area Affiliate, Inc., and the Mexican food exchanges are from Loma Linda University Medical Center, in California.

435

Chitterlings	¼ cup	2 Fat
	2 ounces	1 Fat
Coo coo (cornmeal, ochra, butter, salt, water)	¾ cup	1 Starch/Bread, 1 Vegetable, ½ Fat
Fatback	1 slice	1 Fat
Hog mow	¾ cup	2 Lean Meat
Pig's ear	3 ounces	2 Lean Meat
Pig's feet	4 ounces (1 inch × 1 inch × ¼ inch)	1 High-Fat Meat
Smothered chicken (chicken, flour, milk)	¼ broiler	4 Lean Meat, ½ Starch/Bread
Steamed fish (cooked with a dab of butter)	4 ounces	4 Lean Meat, ½ Fat
Turnip greens (cooked with fat back)	½ cup	1 Vegetable, 2 Fat

INDIAN

Alu mattar (curried potatoes and peas)	1 cup	1½ Starch/Bread, 1 Vegetable, 3 Fat
Alu paratha (flat whole wheat bread with spiced potato filling)	1 6-inch bread	½ Starch/Bread, 6 Fat
Chana dal (curried chick peas)	½ cup	2 Lean Meat, 2 Fat
Kheema do pyaza (curried ground lamb with onions)	1 cup	3 Lean Meat, 2 Vegetable, 3 Fat

Kofta
  (ground lamb
  meatballs stuffed
  with almonds in
  curry sauce)
	3 balls
	(approx.1½
	inches)
		3 Lean Meat, 7 Fat

Machli aur tamatar
  (curried halibut)
	3 ounces fish	3 Meat, ½ Vegetable,
		  1½ Fat

Masala dosa*
  (crepelike pancake
  with spiced potato
  filling)
	1	2 Starch/Bread, 4 Fat

Mattar pannir	½ cup	1 High-Fat Meat,
		  1 Starch/Bread,
		  1 Vegetable, 3 Fat

Murg kari
  (chicken curry)
	3 ounces
	chicken
		3 Lean Meat,
		  ½ Vegetable, 2 Fat

Pakoras
  (deep-fried potato
  and chick-pea
  flour balls)
	2 1-inch balls	1 Lean Meat, 5 Fat

Samosas
  (deep-fried filled
  pastries)		

with potato filling	1 large or 3 small	1 Starch/Bread, 2 Fat
with lamb filling	1 large or 3 small	1 Starch/Bread, ½ Lean Meat, 2½ Fat
JEWISH		
Bialy	½ of 1	1 Starch/Bread
Borscht, no sugar	½ cup	1 Vegetable
Challah	1 slice	1 Starch/Bread
Chopped liver, (homemade)	1 ounce	1 High-Fat Meat
Flanken	1 ounce	1 High-Fat Meat, 1 Fat

Gefilte fish	1 ounce	1 Lean Meat
Kippered herring	1 ounce	1 Lean Meat
Lox (smoked salmon)	1 ounce	1 Lean Meat
Matzoh meal	2½ Tablespoons	1 Starch/Bread
Pastrami	1 ounce	1 High-Fat Meat
Pickled Herring*	1 ounce	1 Lean Meat
Pot cheese	½ cup	1 Lean Meat
Potato knish	3-inch round (2)	1 Starch/Bread, 2 Fat
Sablefish	2 ounce	1 High-Fat Meat
Sorrel (Schav)	½ cup	1 Vegetable

*If in sour cream, omit 1 Fat from meal plan.

ORIENTAL

These figures do not include the rice usually served with these dishes.

Chicken with nuts	1 cup	2 Medium-Fat Meat, 1 Starch/Bread 3 Fat
Beef chow mein with	1½ cups	3 Medium-Fat Meat, 1 Starch/Bread, 2 Fat
chow mein noodles	½ cup	1 Starch/Bread, 1 Fat
Chicken chow mein with	1½ cups	3 Medium-Fat Meat, 1 Starch/Bread, 4 Vegetable, 2 Fat
chow mein noodles	½ cup	1 Starch/Bread, 1 Fat
Pork chow mein with	1½ cups	3 Medium-Fat Meat, 1 Starch/Bread, 4 Vegetable, 4 Fat
chow mein noodles	½ cup	1 Starch/Bread, 1 Fat

Eggdrop soup	1 cup	Negligible
Egg foo yung (shrimp)	2 patties with sauce	3 Medium-Fat Meat, 3 Fat
Egg roll	1	1 Medium-Fat Meat 1 Vegetable, 1 Fat
Ham-and-egg fried rice	1 cup	1 Medium-Fat Meat, 2 Fat
Moo goo gai pan	1½ cups	3 Medium-Fat Meat, 1 Vegetable, 2 Fat
Pepper steak	¾ cup	3 Medium-Fat Meat, 1 Vegetable, 1 Fat
Sweet-and-sour pork*	1 cup	2 Medium-Fat Meat, 2 Vegetable, 2 Fruit, 3 Fat
Wonton soup	2 wontons and 1 cup broth	1 Starch/Bread

*Part of the carbohydrate in this recipe, although called fruit exchanges, is derived from sugar (approximately 12 grams and 50 calories of sugar per serving).

MEXICAN

Guacamole	2 Tablespoons	1 Fat
Taco (meat, cheese, lettuce, tomato)	1	2 Medium-Fat Meat, 1 Starch/Bread
Tostada with refried beans	1 small	2 Starch/Bread
with meat	1 small	1 Medium-Fat Meat, 1 Starch/Bread
Tostada, beef	1 large	2 Medium-Fat Meat, 1½ Starch/Bread, 1 Fat
Burrito, bean	1 small	2 Starch/Bread
	1 large	1 Medium-Fat Meat, 3 Starch/Bread, 2 Fat

beef	1 small	1 Medium-Fat Meat, 2½ Starch/Bread, 1 Fat
Chili	1 cup	2 Medium-Fat Meat, 2 Starch/Bread, 1 Fat
Chili sauce	2 teaspoons	1 Fruit
Corn chips	1 cup (1 ounce)	1 Starch/Bread, 2 Fat
Enchilada	1 small	1 Medium-Fat Meat, 1 Starch/Bread
Meat or cheese	(6-inch tortilla)	
Refried beans	½ cup	1 Starch/Bread, 1 Fat
Spanish rice	1 cup	2 Starch/Bread, 1 Fat
Spanish sauce	½ cups	1 Fruit, 1 Fat
Tamale with sauce	1	1 Medium-Fat Meat, 1 Starch/Bread

APPENDIX III: METRIC CONVERSION MADE EASY

	To Change	to	Multiply by
W			
E	Ounces	Grams	30*
I	Pounds	Kilograms	0.45
G	Grams	Ounces	0.035
H			
T	Kilograms	Pounds	2.2
	Teaspoons	Milliliters	5
	Tablespoons	Milliliters	15
	Fluid ounces	Milliliters	30
V	Cups	Liters	0.24
O			
L	Pints	Liters	0.47
U	Quarts	Liters	0.95
M	Gallons	Liters	3.8
E	Milliliters	Fluid ounces	0.03
	Liters	Pints	2.1
	Liters	Quarts	1.06
	Liters	Gallons	0.26
L	Inches	Centimeters	2.5
E	Feet	Centimeters	30
N			
G	Yards	Meters	0.9
T	Millimeters	Inches	0.04
H	Centimeters	Inches	0.4

441

Meters	Feet	3.3
Meters	Yards	1.1

*The precise figure is 28.25. However, some dietitians find it more convenient to use 30.

□ INDEX

LIBRARY
ST. LOUIS COMMUNITY COLLEGE
AT FLORISSANT VALLEY